studies in jazz

Institute of Jazz Studies
Rutgers—The State University of New Jersey
General Editors: Dan Morgenstern and Edward Berger

1. BENNY CARTER: A Life in American Music, *by Morroe Berger, Edward Berger, and James Patrick, 2 vols., 1982*
2. ART TATUM: A Guide to His Recorded Music, *by Arnold Laubich and Ray Spencer, 1982*
3. ERROLL GARNER: The Most Happy Piano, *by James M. Doran, 1995*
4. JAMES P. JOHNSON: A Case of Mistaken Identity, *by Scott E. Brown;* Discography 1917–1950, *by Robert Hilbert, 1986*
5. PEE WEE ERWIN: This Horn for Hire, *as told to Warren W. Vaché Sr., 1987*
6. BENNY GOODMAN: Listen to His Legacy, *by D. Russell Connor, 1988*
7. ELLINGTONIA: The Recorded Music of Duke Ellington and His Sidemen, *by W. E. Timner, 1988; 4th ed., 1996*
8. THE GLENN MILLER ARMY AIR FORCE BAND: Sustineo Alas / I Sustain the Wings, *by Edward F. Polic;* Foreword *by George T. Simon, 1989*
9. SWING LEGACY, *by Chip Deffaa, 1989*
10. REMINISCING IN TEMPO: The Life and Times of a Jazz Hustler, *by Teddy Reig, with Edward Berger, 1990*
11. IN THE MAINSTREAM: 18 Portraits in Jazz, *by Chip Deffaa, 1992*
12. BUDDY DeFRANCO: A Biographical Portrait and Discography, *by John Kuehn and Arne Astrup, 1993*
13. PEE WEE SPEAKS: A Discography of Pee Wee Russell, *by Robert Hilbert, with David Niven, 1992*
14. SYLVESTER AHOLA: The Gloucester Gabriel, *by Dick Hill, 1993*
15. THE POLICE CARD DISCORD, *by Maxwell T. Cohen, 1993*
16. TRADITIONALISTS AND REVIVALISTS IN JAZZ, *by Chip Deffaa, 1993*
17. BASSICALLY SPEAKING: An Oral History of George Duvivier, *by Edward Berger;* Musical Analysis *by David Chevan, 1993*
18. TRAM: The Frank Trumbauer Story, *by Philip R. Evans and Larry F. Kiner, with William Trumbauer, 1994*
19. TOMMY DORSEY: On the Side, *by Robert L. Stockdale, 1995*
20. JOHN COLTRANE: A Discography and Musical Biography, *by Yasuhiro Fujioka, with Lewis Porter and Yoh-ichi Hamada, 1995*
21. RED HEAD: A Chronological Survey of "Red" Nichols and His Five Pennies, *by Stephen M. Stroff, 1996*
22. THE RED NICHOLS STORY: After Intermission 1942–1965, *by Philip R. Evans, Stanley Hester, Stephen Hester, and Linda Evans, 1997*
23. BENNY GOODMAN: Wrappin' It Up, *by D. Russell Connor, 1996*

An Unsung Cat

The Life and Music of Warne Marsh

Safford Chamberlain

Studies in Jazz, No. 37

The Scarecrow Press, Inc.
Lanham, Maryland, and London
and
Institute of Jazz Studies
Rutgers—The State University of New Jersey
2000

SCARECROW PRESS, INC.

Published in the United States of America
by Scarecrow Press, Inc.
4720 Boston Way
Lanham, Maryland 20706

4 Pleydell Gardens, Folkestone
Kent CT20 2DN, England

British Library Cataloguing in Publication Information Available

Library of Congress Cataloging-in-Publication Data

Chamberlain, Safford, 1926–
    An unsung cat : the life and music of Warne Marsh / Safford Chamberlain.
        p.   cm.   —(Studies in jazz; no. 37)
    Includes bibliographical references and index.
    ISBN 0-8108-3718-8 (cloth : alk. paper)
    1. Marsh, Warne.   2. Jazz musicians—United States—
Biography.   I. Title. II. Series.

ML419.M313 C5   2000
788.7′165′092—dc21   99-054368

⊗™ The paper used in this publication meets the minimum requirements of
American National Standard for Information Sciences—Permanence of
Paper for Printed Library Materials, ANSI/NISO Z39.48-1992.
Manufactured in the United States of America

For my brother,

Thornton Chase Chamberlain, 1921–1945,

flutist, conductor,

killed in World War II at Bastogne, Belgium,

January 14, 1945

Contents

Foreword

In 1985, Whitney Balliett profiled Warne Marsh in the *New Yorker* magazine. The title of Mr. Balliett's penetrating piece was "A True Improviser." Warne, though he would never have thought it out loud, probably approved of that designation. A true improviser is what Warne most aspired to be.

Nearly always a man of few words, Warne's terse advice to his students and colleagues was always something like, "Think when you practice, don't think when you play." Amplified a bit, that remark was meant to suggest that great thought is required, during practice, to acquire the sophisticated harmonic and rhythmic language of the jazz improviser. As the technical becomes ingrained, intuition can then follow knowledge.

During a period in the 1960s when we both taught at a music studio in Pasadena, California, I often heard Warne practice. He would play a complex melodic motif in every key and at every possible rhythmic displacement within 4/4 time. This was an extension of Lennie Tristano's rigorous teaching and a technique mastered by very few. The idea that prelearned patterns, or "licks," might be used to organize an improvised solo was completely foreign to Warne's beliefs. For Warne, spontaneity was everything.

Warne was easily identifiable by his unique sound and unusual approach. His improvised line over the years contained one surprise after another and was virtually free from repetition. This made Warne one of the only improvisers who did not become a captive of his own "isms." Most of us warm up on our instruments by playing, usually without thinking, the same long-established finger patterns. Warne's warm-up was unpredictable and worth paying attention to. He simply seemed to resume where he had left off when he last returned the instrument to its case.

One memorable example of Warne's rhythmic prowess occurred in the late 1970s just before he returned to New York City for the last time. At Donte's, then a jazz club in North Hollywood, and on the same bandstand where Warne died in 1987, we performed as a quintet with Alan Broadbent, Fred Atwood, and Nick Ceroli. A standard piece in the repertoire was "Two Not One," an original line by Lennie Tristano composed to the chord changes of the standard "I Can't Believe That You're in Love with Me." Hearing that line as recorded by Warne and Lee Konitz in 1955, one might have assumed that the title alluded to the two-saxophone unison that was so cleanly played. Two saxophones, not one, as it seemed to the ear. The truth is more subtle. Lennie's line begins each eight-measure phrase on an accented second beat of the bar, thereby creating a lovely rhythmic tension. Warne played the first solo after the line and continued to displace almost his entire solo by one beat. The rhythm section, accustomed to Warne's ways, held on to the form beautifully. During other solos, the improvising returned to straight-ahead time with the rhythmic tension removed.

Building up to the out-chorus, Warne and I improvised together so that when the line returned, it would seem to grow out of the collective improvisation. While the saxophones were improvising together, Warne again began to displace the rhythm so that second beats of each bar felt like first beats. When the last chorus finally emerged out of the improvising, it landed correctly, and we were on our way to a smooth ending. As the last notes faded, Nick Ceroli, our drummer, stood up and remarked, "My God Warne, you sure can keep *one* a secret!"

With great care and dedication, Safford Chamberlain has spent nearly ten years acquiring the often quite surprising truths of Warne's life, and he has chronicled it with respect and love. To me, Warne Marsh was the kind of individual and artist one is forever grateful for having encountered in life. A true improviser.

Gary Foster

Editor's Foreword

Safford Chamberlain has had a long career teaching English and is an accomplished writer of short fiction, news reports, and political op-ed pieces. But he also wrote about jazz for all those years and studied saxophone with Warne Marsh, a spectacularly brilliant improviser who has not had much recognition outside of a small, almost cultish following. The popular young tenor saxophonist Mark Turner currently sings Marsh's praises, which may help to bring him some belated attention.

Chamberlain addresses the many possible reasons that Marsh is not better known, among them that Marsh was in some ways his own worst enemy. I think it helped if you saw Marsh live. There was something about his unique tone that didn't transfer well to most recording situations, but when I first saw him at the Village Vanguard in 1980, his sound filled the room with electricity. I saw him on several occasions after that, each time confirming the uselessness of labels like *cool* and *reserved*. Maybe those labels worked for certain groups, but they sure didn't fit Marsh, nor most of his colleagues in the circle that formed around Lennie Tristano.

I personally like Marsh's live recordings best, especially those from the '70s. Chamberlain has his own preferences, which he supports with solid musicianship, carefully transcribed solos, and persuasive aesthetics. During the ten or so years that I have looked over his drafts and helped with a question here and there, I have found myself constantly impressed by how little he really needed me. His biographical research skills are superb, and he has done a thorough and revealing history of Marsh's family background. He has combed through archives and old newspapers and periodicals and has compiled a thorough listing of every known Marsh recording. Best of all, as a onetime student of Marsh's, he has been welcomed by all of the key figures in the drama, who have given him interviews and offered assistance. Chamberlain's fine work is a stellar addition to the studies in Jazz series.

Lewis Porter
Professor of Music
Rutgers University, Newark, NJ

Preface

Neither Warne Marsh nor his immediate family were given to keeping records of his life. Hence this book could not exist without the oral contributions of his family, friends, and associates. Particular thanks must go to Warne's late mother, Elizabeth Marion Marsh; his very gracious sister, Gloria Oxford, who also, sadly, passed away during the writing of this book; his brother, Owen Marsh; and his wife, Geraldyne Marsh. The book would have been impossible without their trust and cooperation.

The spiritual godfather of the book is Gary Foster. Besides the factual information he was able to provide from his twenty-year friendship with Marsh, his support and encouragement were invaluable, as they were to Marsh himself. Special thanks go to bassist and friend Putter Smith; my saxophone teacher, Lee Callet; jazz biographer, Gary Carner; my friend Bill Fick; and my wife, Sharyn Crane, for their willingness to read various stages of the manuscript. And to Jim Seeley and my son, Thornton, for all their help with computer problems.

Among my informants, Ted Brown, whose life was intermittently intertwined with Marsh's over a period of forty years, was remarkable for the clarity and reach of his memory. He is also one of the nicest people in jazz. The late Billy Byers, Ronnie Lang, Betty Churchill Nearhoff, Don Walter, and Beverly Carpenter McComb were prime informants on Marsh's teenage career. The input of Lee Konitz, Judy Tristano Gilbert, Sal Mosca, Arnold Fishkin, Peter Ind, the late Alan Levitt, John LaPorta, Steve Silverman, and Sonny Dallas was crucial to my sense of the years with Lennie Tristano, while Pete Christlieb, Lou Ciotti, Jim Hughart, Med Flory, Joe Lopes, Carol Waters, Rhonda Dameron Gianelli, John Klopotowski,

George Khoury, Larry Koonse, Jon Whinnery, Jim Amaresco, and Lou Levy contributed significantly to my knowledge of Marsh in Los Angeles in the later years. The chapter on the Norwegian connection could not have been written without the generous input, by phone and e-mail, of trumpeter Torgrim Sollid. Insight into Marsh's teaching was provided by Judy Niemack, Janet Lawson, and Jon Whinnery. Jazz film specialist Mark Cantor provided facts about the films Marsh was involved in as a teenager.

John Breckow, for twenty-three years the host of *Smoke Rings*, the excellent but now defunct all-Sunday-night jazz program on KPFK-FM, was one of the first of Marsh's acquaintances I contacted. He and several friends made extensive tape recordings of Marsh in Los Angeles in 1974–75, copies of which he provided me. Also his general discographical knowledge proved helpful on several occasions. Another early contact was Marcus Cornelius of Australia, author of a novel based on Marsh's life, who allowed me to see his list of contacts, his list of known performances, and an early version of his discography. He tells me that his novel, *Out of Nowhere*, which he completed in 1991, will be published in the near future. Important tapes and discographical information were provided by Claude Alexander, Jeremy Kellock, George Ziskind, Bill Miner, Tom Everett, Pete Christlieb, John William Hardy, Harold Sewing, John Burton, Ronnie Lang, Steve Lang, Karl Kiffe, Johan Helo, Eunmi Shim, Jack Goodwin, and Gary Foster.

Several jazz writers have contributed time and information. Barry Ulanov, editor of *Metronome* from 1943 to 1955 and then, successively, professor of English at Barnard College, professor of religion at Columbia, and in his most recent avatar, lecturer in psychiatry and religion at Union Theological Seminary, graciously agreed to interviews and read early portions of the manuscript. The British critic Alun Morgan provided me not only with information and commentary but also with tapes from Marsh's visits to England and Denmark in 1975. Thomas Owens, whose book, *Bebop,* is by now required reading for jazz scholars, helped by allowing me to audit his class at UCLA in "Charlie Parker and His Followers." Chicagoans John Litweiler and Terry Martin kindly gave me a transcript of their important unpublished interview with Marsh in 1975, which contained a wealth of material, and also introduced me to fellow Warne Marsh aficionados and jazz critics Harriet Choice and Lawrence Kart. I am also indebted to Stanley Crouch for several long-distance phone conversations, and to Los Angeles jazz writer Kirk Silsbee for certain documents and for his continuing interest.

The title of the book was unwittingly given me by the saxophonist Branford Marsalis. Although I was never able to conduct an extended interview with him, when I spoke to him briefly about Marsh at the Jazz Bakery in Los Angeles, he said, "Oh man, he was a really unsung cat."

Ed Berger of the Institute of Jazz Studies has my gratitude not only for his assistance at the Institute but also for securing for me a Rutgers University grant as a jazz scholar. Finally, I must thank my editor, Lewis Porter. For reasons known only to him, he seemed to have faith in me from the moment we met at the Institute; he has been unfailingly helpful and supportive ever since.

About the text: All use of printed materials other than general reference works has been footnoted. Wherever a quotation is not footnoted, the source is one of the over two hundred interviewees listed in the List of Persons Interviewed and is clearly indicated in the text. In all instances, I was the interviewer.

Inevitably there will be information that I have either failed to obtain or have reported incorrectly, and I welcome contacts from those in possession of such material. My e-mail address is SaffordC@aol.com. The discography especially should be regarded as a work in progress, particularly with regard to private tapes, and it is to be hoped that Warne Marsh devotees the world over will take up the burden of completing in their own discographies what is offered here.

Introduction

Warne Marion Marsh elicits wildly divergent evaluations, if he is mentioned at all. The dean of jazz critics in this country, Leonard Feather, largely ignored Marsh throughout his career. The essayist and critic Stanley Crouch, though acknowledging Marsh as "one of the most impressive" followers of Lennie Tristano, expressed a common attitude when he declared to me that Marsh "couldn't have stood up on the bandstand with [John] Coltrane or [Sonny] Rollins. They were in another dimension."[1] Marsh, according to Crouch, was a gifted second-level player who should be ranked with good but not great tenor saxophonists like Paul Gonsalves, Charlie Rouse, Eddie "Lockjaw" Davis, or Johnny Griffin.

But to Barry Ulanov, coeditor of *Metronome* during the 1940s and 50s, Marsh is "a major figure in jazz, one of the ten greatest on his instrument," and as early as 1961 the English critic Alun Morgan wrote that he considered Marsh "one of the greatest of jazz improvisers since Charlie Parker."[2] Some twenty years later, when it could be argued that Marsh's greatest playing was behind him, Francis Davis wrote that the Warne Marsh of the 1980s was "one of the most stimulating improvisers in all of jazz."[3] *New Yorker* jazz critic Whitney Balliett echoed this opinion in 1985: "[Marsh] is one of the most original and daring jazz improvisers alive. . . ."[4]

Among musicians, the admiring views of second generation students of Tristano like pianist Connie Crothers and saxophonist Lenny Popkin, who see Marsh as an improviser superior to Coltrane and Rollins and the equal and natural heir of Lester Young and Charlie Parker, must be considered with some caution because of their strong allegiance to Tristano.

But the judgment of Lee Konitz, who long ago established his independence from Tristano, his early mentor, is subject to no such reservation. Marsh's music, he has said, "of any music that I can think of, was the most difficult to anticipate. . . . It was always so rich with surprise. That was a very special experience that I've never gotten from anybody else."

Other respected saxophonists of varying backgrounds and styles, from mainstreamers like Lanny Morgan, Bill Perkins, and Joe Henderson to the avant-gardist Anthony Braxton, have expressed similar admiration, and Wayne Shorter has said that Marsh was one of his favorite saxophonists.

Of special interest is the experience of the young pianist and organist Larry Goldings, both because he belongs to a new generation of jazz players and because his formative influences included not only Coltrane but hard-swinging, blues-oriented players like Oscar Peterson. Goldings was unaware of Marsh until he heard him on a recording from 1975 of a live performance at Ronnie Scott's club in London.[5] He fell in love with the record and with Marsh: "He was brilliant, the way he put lines together, absolutely genius. And he swung so hard!" Asked if he considered Marsh in the same class as Coltrane, Goldings replied, "Oh, totally, even on the basis of that one record!" Sadly, he finds that most of his younger colleagues know nothing of Marsh, and that the few who do know and appreciate him are usually white.

It is highly probable that race is one factor in the neglect of Marsh. "Quiet as it's kept," wrote critic and lyricist Gene Lees a few years ago, "anti-white bias has existed in jazz for a long time."[6] Lees cites Sonny Rollins and Oscar Peterson as having endured disapproval from other blacks for hiring white guitarists Jim Hall and Herb Ellis.[7] The black trumpeter Art Farmer describes how, growing up in Arizona and California, "You just wouldn't listen to some white person playing jazz, just wouldn't give a damn. . . . White people playing jazz, it didn't make any sense to me at all. . . . After I got away from that, and was able to be more objective about it, then I could hear what people were doing. And then it seemed to me the most stupid thing on earth to think that just because somebody is white they can't play, and vice versa—that just because somebody is black, they can play."[8] Fellow trumpeter Clark Terry summed up his rejection of anti-white bias this way: "My theory is that a note doesn't give a fuck who plays it, as long as he plays it well."[9]

The term "Crow Jim" began to be used to indicate anti-white bias in jazz as early as the late 1940s, when Barry Ulanov commented on the practice by European jazz festival producers of hiring only black musicians: "To Europeans and to some Americans, jazz is a Negro product. It can't really be played by white men, they think. . . . Some even go so far as to make the distinction genetic. . . ." Arguing that differences in the styles of different players are individual, not racial, he concluded, "No, Crow Jim is no more correct and no more appetizing than Jim Crow."[10]

Lennie Tristano believed that Marsh was the victim of anti-white bias. Recounting, in 1958, that Charlie Parker had once said to him about Marsh, "You watch that kid; he's got it," Tristano continued: "Of course, he's right. Not too many people know it, though. Warne is the only sax man today. One of the reasons no one knows it is that it's believed the great contributions are made to jazz by Negroes. And that's true. But the white man is considered not really able to play. The color line is sharper than it ever was, and it's getting worse."[11]

Whatever the role of anti-white bias, the jazz press in America has never given Marsh the attention he deserves. Neither *Metronome,* which under Ulanov's editorship championed Tristano and his school, nor *Down Beat* ever ran a profile or extended article about him until 1983, when Francis Davis's article, "Warne Marsh's Inner Melody," appeared in the latter magazine.

European critics have been much more appreciative. Alun Morgan reaffirmed his high opinion of Marsh in 1976, after hearing him in person for the first time: "My admiration for his skill and my overt enthusiasm for his total musical concept have increased."[12] Similar evaluations have been expressed more or less routinely by critics in England, France, and the Scandinavian countries. Unfortunately, the opinions of European critics didn't help Marsh win over musicians, critics, record companies, or club owners in this country.

But one cannot simply blame anti-white bias or the American jazz press for the relative failure, in terms of recognition, of Marsh's career. The truth is that deep-seated elements of Marsh's own character and background led him to mismanage his affairs and in effect to court his own obscurity. Temperamentally he was always an outsider, and his relations with the two most influential persons in his life, his mother and his mentor, Lennie Tristano, reflected, in different ways, his alienation.

Family members have said that as a child Marsh did not talk until very late, perhaps as late as three and a half or even four. He understood perfectly well, would follow directions such as "Go get Aunt Minnie's straw hat," but he did not speak. When pianist Susan Chen, his student, colleague, and lover in the early 1980s, asked him about it, he replied in characteristically laconic fashion, "There wasn't much to say."

The story is suggestive. By all accounts, Marsh was extremely intelligent. According to his mother, he was an A-student all through school, despite the fact that from age twelve his mind and leisure time were primarily devoted to music. He had the kind of analytical mind that made him an advanced chess player and that in music led him to exploit unusual time divisions and manipulations of meter. One of his girlfriends, wondering at his choice of jazz as a profession, expressed a common attitude when she said, "He could have been a nuclear physicist."[13]

So one may imagine the infant Marsh, with his keen analytical intelligence at work, observing the adult world from behind a mask of silence for three-plus years. Presumably he was able to speak long before he actually did. The adult Marsh who quipped that there wasn't much to say clearly preferred to present it as a matter of will, and one must admit that toddlers can be willful, but surely fear was primary. Marsh once said that he did not get over his fear of expressing himself until 1963 or 1964.[14]

However that may be, Marsh was an intensely private person who seemed determined to keep his inner life inviolate at all costs. This guardedness could be, and was, variously interpreted. Many people found him aloof, unapproachable. Francis Davis, interviewing the fifty-five-year-old Marsh in 1982, perceived him at first as "guarded and rather distant," but soon concluded that he was "painfully shy, almost jittery."[15] A similar view was suggested by Barry Ulanov, who felt that Marsh, twenty-one years old when Ulanov heard him with Tristano in late 1948 or early 1949, "wanted to disappear into the woodwork" when not playing. His sister Gloria, two years younger, perceived him as "an outsider" almost from the time she was aware of him, and a few years after Marsh's death she said she knew her next-door neighbor better than she had ever known her brother Warne. A cousin, Frances Mayer, observed that even in family baby pictures, he was usually by himself, or if with others, "his face was scrunched up and he really couldn't wait to get away." His younger brother, Owen, speaking of Marsh's performance as a member of a teenage band in a Jane Powell movie, remarked that "he had a way of looking like he didn't want to be there, a look that would say, 'I'm disappearing, I'm not here.'"

But there was about Marsh a steely, self-willed quality that makes the word "shy" at least superficially inappropriate. Lee Konitz, whose recordings with Marsh suggest, in passages of joint improvisation, an almost magical rapport, stated in 1990 that he was "never really close" to Marsh in a personal sense. Especially in the early days when both were students of Tristano, he said, Marsh was so involved in his private world, often going about singing to himself, that Konitz felt he would be intruding by talking to him. The emotional distance that Konitz observed seems to have involved an intense self-absorption, a deep preoccupation with his own thoughts, especially musical thoughts.

Moreover, he was not a loner in the sense of being antisocial or misanthropic. It is true, as the critic Whitney Balliett noted, that he had "no small talk,"[16] no purely social conversational gambits. Yet he had many friends, liked to "hang out" and play games like chess, bridge, or scrabble, and apparently had little difficulty establishing relationships with women. There seems, in fact, to have been a certain independent, even aggressive quality about his inwardness that women found attractive.

That being said, with allowances made for the tough-minded, gruff austerity with which he guarded his inner life, his lifelong use of a variety of drugs suggests that at the bottom of it all, at the deepest level, was indeed fear. He was a daily user of marijuana from at least the age of fifteen, more probably as early as thirteen. His habit began in 1940–42, long before marijuana became a part of the counterculture of the 1950s and 1960s, though it had long been common among musicians. He was also fond of methamphetamine and, in the last twenty years of his life, cocaine. Never addicted to heroin, he was not averse to an occasional snort if available, though he always disliked needles. Nor was he averse to alcohol. He tried LSD, probably only once. Characteristically, his objection to it was not physiological but musical: asked how he liked it, he said, "It makes the notes too far apart."[17]

Scientific technicalities aside, whatever else drugs like marijuana, methamphetamine, cocaine, and alcohol do, they hang an insulating veil between the user and both the outside world and certain aspects of the user's inner self. The reaction of the user to the veil, how he or she chooses to use it, can vary greatly from individual to individual, and even from time to time for the same user. But when the use is habitual, as distinct from occasional or recreational, the veil is always there, the user is always behind it, and it is likely that the need for the veil, and the drug, is based on fear.

This would seem especially true of a sensitive, intelligent, inward-looking thirteen or fifteen year old like Marsh, who appears to have hidden behind a wall of silence for the first few years of his life. Whatever the ultimate motivation, drugs were a regular part of Marsh's daily life that entered into his intense self-involvement and into the distance he kept between himself and the outside world. At the same time it must be emphasized that, unlike so many of his generation, including once-close associates such as saxophonists Art Pepper and Joe Maini, he never allowed drugs to dominate his life or enmesh him in police problems.

What gave a special quality to Marsh's character was the combination of a fierce inwardness and a powerfully analytical mind. His penchant for analysis was reflected in his passion for chess. Altoist Gary Foster, a close friend from 1966 on, told of buying books on chess in order to play with him, only to realize that to play on Marsh's level would require more time and attention than he was willing to give. Don Specht, a pianist and arranger who jammed with Marsh and formed a close friendship with him in the late 1950s and early 1960s, described Marsh as "close to a master" in chess and felt that the kind of analysis and problem solving involved in chess was "a major key" to his character, whether in music, games, or such other of Marsh's activities as working as a TV repairman for a time. By way of illustration, Specht cited an incident during one of their duo jam sessions in Specht's Los Angeles apartment. Marsh had just opened a champagne bottle, and the flying cork had blown out a window. "With his analytical mind," said Specht, "he calculated the odds of hitting that exact trajectory again."

Undoubtedly a shared predilection for intellectual analysis was an important reason for Marsh's attraction to Tristano, the blind pianist who was the single greatest influence on his music as well as a profound influence on his life. Tristano was the first major jazz musician to set himself up as a teacher not merely of instrumental technique but of jazz improvisation. Classically trained, thoroughly familiar with the European tradition from Bach to Bartok, Tristano felt that the jazz improviser had to be not only as proficient on his instrument as a classical musician but also had to know much more. His analysis of improvisation resulted in a comprehensive methodology that ranged from an intensive study of scales, harmony, and rhythm, to learning and analyzing solos by a select group of jazz masters, to regular jam sessions with on-the-spot critiques of individual performances.

Tristano's rigorous, systematic approach had an immediate appeal for Marsh, and his allegiance to his mentor, though not without signs of ambivalence, continued from their first encounter in 1947 to Tristano's death in 1978. Indeed, his acceptance of Tristano as a father figure was so pronounced and long-lasting as to give rise to speculation concerning extramusical, psychological reasons for it.

One such reason may have been the death of Marsh's father in 1941, when Marsh was thirteen and a half. Even more significant than his father's death may have been his alcoholism and what Marsh later described as his total lack of interest in music. There seems to have occurred a kind of mutual abandonment, the father retreating into his alcoholism and the son into his resentment and his music. It is not surprising, then, that the half-orphaned, nineteen-year-old Marsh was psychologically receptive to a powerful personality like Tristano, who liked to set himself up as a father figure and who possessed in addition a penetrating intelligence.

Although throughout his life Marsh credited Tristano as his inspiration and saw himself as the bearer of Tristano's musical message to the world, it may be questioned whether Tristano's influence was entirely positive. Certainly his purist, art-for-art's-sake attitude, his disdain for the slightest tinge of what he saw as commercialism, reinforced Marsh's own tendency to withdraw from the world of affairs, and it can be argued that the cultishness, and whiteness, of the Tristano school played a part in dissuading Marsh from seeking out major non-Tristanoites to play with, especially black players.

The only person whose influence outweighed that of Tristano was Marsh's mother, Elizabeth Marion Marsh. A classically trained violinist who egocentrically saw Marsh's musical talent as passed from her father to her and through her to Marsh, she made no secret of the fact that Warne was her favorite child. Marsh's deep ambivalence toward her runs like a half-hidden thread through his account of her to Whitney Balliett: "Mother hasn't remarried, and she kept us together after my father's death. She was a generous mother, and she still helps me if I need it. She's had trouble with my career, though—with improvising. What turned her on musically was Gilbert and Sullivan, light opera—that kind of thing. I have to ask myself what jazz means in her mind. Maybe it's the association with New York, which she doesn't like. I don't know."[18]

One thing that jazz meant to Elizabeth Marsh was that her favorite son left her in late summer of 1948 to take up his studies with Tristano in New York, a city which she probably disliked for just that reason.

She seems to have had little understanding or sympathy for jazz. In general, said Warne's sister Gloria, their mother placed jazz in the category of "too noisy," where she also placed Igor Stravinsky and other modernists. Her taste in music actually extended considerably farther than Gilbert and Sullivan, but she was extremely intolerant of what she didn't like. She loved Bach and certain violin music, especially as performed by Jascha Heifetz; Tchaikovsky was fine, Brahms was acceptable; but if one tried to interest her in, say, Stravinsky's *Petrouchka*, her response, said Gloria, would be something like, "Oh no, that's too dissonant, it's too noisy, oh how can you listen to those awful notes, there's no melody, there's no harmony!" According to Gloria, her mother could not abide the great classical guitarist Andrés Segovia's renditions of her beloved Bach. "The guitar," she would say, "sounds so cold, turn it off, the sound of the guitar just bothers me."

Late in his life Marsh took her to a club in North Hollywood, probably Donte's or Alphonse's, where he was playing. Said Gloria, "She talked about that for a week afterwards. But you know what she talked about? 'They treated me like a queen, everybody came over and said, "Oh! You're Warne's mother!"' and she just went on and on about what a wonderful and exciting night it was. I said, 'What did he play?' and she couldn't tell me what he played, because to her the idea of going there was to be put on this pedestal and revered as Warne Marsh's mother."

In 1990, when I visited Mrs. Marsh, only a few of her son's records were in evidence, including two copies of his 1986 duo recording with pianist

Susan Chen, which she indicated she had not listened to—she said she might "break down" if she did—and the original 78-rpm pressing of "Wow" and "Marionette," Marsh's first record with Tristano. "Wow" did impress her. It was, she said, "One of the most wonderful things they did." Her reference, however, was undoubtedly to the brilliant doubletime ensemble passages by Marsh and Konitz, the technical virtuosity of which would impress any trained musician. As Marsh told Balliett, she had trouble with the concept of jazz improvisation.

As Marsh also said to Balliett, his mother was generous, but only up to a point. She supported him at need, and she made the down payments and often the mortgage payments on two houses, once in the early 1970s when he was living in Pasadena, California, and again in 1985–86 when he had returned again from New York to Los Angeles. There was, however, a distinct downside to her generosity. Although she gave him a good deal of money over the years, she never gave him enough to make him financially independent of her. She considered him irresponsible with money, with some justification. She had put the first house she bought for him in his name, only to see him sell the house a few years later and use the money to move back to New York. When, after eight years, he again returned to Los Angeles, she did not make the same mistake but kept the second house in her name.

Money was a constant source of conflict, the ultimate bone of contention being the trust fund left by Warne's father, Oliver Marsh, at his death in 1941. Although set up for the three children, the fund was controlled by their mother. "Many, many times," said Gloria, "Warne tried to break that trust," even gaining her and Owen's agreement to act with him, "but it was never possible because it had to be with Mo's [Mrs. Marsh's] approval, and she would never approve."

A related source of conflict was Marsh's persistent fantasy, beginning as early as his late teens and recurring to the end of his life, of owning his own jazz club. Said his sister, "He was always begging her [Mrs. Marsh] for money to open one music bar or another, and she would absolutely refuse, and he would get furious. He wanted the freedom to do just what he wanted to do, and she just wouldn't hand over that kind of money."

Unlike Warne, both Gloria and Owen were markedly independent of their mother. Owen, who became a Hollywood cinematographer like his father, prided himself on never having taken a nickel from her since the age of eleven, and Gloria married at twenty-one and established her own family. Both saw their mother's limited generosity toward Warne as a means of control.

"She had a way of talking about Warne as though he were twelve years old," said Gloria. "A couple times I'd call her on it. I'd say, 'Mo, you really shouldn't talk that way about Warne. You talk like he doesn't have any sense.' And she'd come right back, 'Well, as far as money is concerned he doesn't have any sense.' And I'd say, 'Well, if you'd ever treat him like an adult and stop giving him a goddam allowance—the man is fifty years old! Sit down and make a business contract with him and treat him like a man. If he defaults on it, then take the money. Just stop playing games with him.' But that was a way of control with her."

Owen confirmed that their mother had basically supported Warne "for many, many years," adding that "there isn't a penny that goes out from that lady without a string of some kind attached to it." He summed up the relationship harshly: "She castrated the man." A statement by Gloria suggests more of the complexity of the situation: "She was so proud of Warne. I felt it was really an unhealthy relationship, to tell you the truth. Warne's talent seemed to excuse him from all other phases of life in her eyes. He could have committed murder and she would have said, 'Well, you know, he's so special that it's all right'. . . . She couldn't tolerate that music [of Warne's]. But by the same token, she realized what a remarkable musician he was. And she loved the adoration that other people gave him. . . . If he had been Heifetz, she couldn't have admired him more."

Despite the obviously Freudian, Oedipal nature of Marsh's relations with his mother and with Tristano, their influences neatly dovetailed. Only through her financial support throughout his career was he able to adhere to Tristano's strict artistic standards. Not only was he able generally to avoid studio work, big bands, pit orchestras, strip joints, wedding receptions, and other "casuals," all of which, according to Tristano, were artistically corrupting; he was also effectively relieved of any practical need to advance his reputation or expand his musical world. He could concentrate on the only thing he really cared about, his music—which was improvising on standards as he had learned to do with Tristano—and let the world come to him, in whatever haphazard way it cared to. As his friend Gary Foster remarked to Whitney Balliett, apropos of the jazz world's having passed Marsh by, "He is never aggressive. His nature is to let people seek him out."[19] It is not surprising that the jazz world has been slow to do so.

Another result of this professional passivity is observable in his records. The majority of them were not done under studio conditions but were either culled from private jam sessions or recorded live in a club, often with inferior equipment, resulting in inferior sound quality. Many were not issued until years after they were recorded. Only a few were for major labels. In general there was little concern for "presentation values," such as arrangements or planned introductions and endings. In two instances the producers of the record did not even bother to obtain the master tapes but used copies that were one or more generations removed.

Despite the brilliance of Marsh's playing as thus preserved, the fact that such material constitutes such a significant portion of his recorded output gives the whole corpus something of an esoteric, ingrown, hermetic flavor, as if to question the value of more structured, more audience-friendly recordings.

Something of the same hermetic flavor can be found in Marsh's playing, especially in that most personal aspect of a jazz player's expression, his tone. Most players strive for a more or less conventionally attractive tone. They know that their adherence to generally accepted standards of tone will sustain them when inspiration fails, will please the audience even when the notes they play are ordinary. Warne Marsh refused to rely on a conventionally "pretty" tone as a substitute for ideas. As his frequent colleague Lee Konitz said, tone for Marsh was a function of the depth of his inspiration at any particular moment. He was committed to the process of improvisation, and tone was an aspect of that process. He did not start with what his instrument would let him do and work within that, as one imagines players with consistently pleasing tone like Zoot Sims or Ben Webster or Stan Getz did. Sound, like everything else, came from within, and in the moment. There is, of course, an intensely personal substratum through all the variations that is constant, and that one can acquire a taste for, a sound that is extremely distinctive but somewhat odd. As one listener said, it is as though the sound is not happening in the horn but in Marsh's head. Another characterized him as a kind of ventriloquist, with the sound seeming to come from another part of the room. He could sound, as on the 1983 *A Ballad Album*, as accessible and pretty as Getz, or he could sound harsh and aggressive, as on the records made on his first European tour in 1975–76. Or he could, as in his late duos with bassist Red Mitchell or with his quintet of 1956–57, strike a highly idiosyncratic balance between acerbity and warmth that many find thrilling. But when one enters the circle of Warne Marsh admirers, one must make room for a unique, at times almost perverse tonal conception quite different from that of other great tenor players. Frequently Marsh seems to have deliberately sacrificed tonal appeal in order to force the listener to focus on the energy of his ideas.

By and large it is an intellectual energy. This is not to say that it lacks passion. When he is at his best, the fusion of intellect and emotion is as moving as anything ever done by a jazz musician. If he is not always at his best, one reason is his radical commitment to improvisation. Asked by record producer Michael Cuscuna how he achieved such "an unceasing flow of creativity every time you put the horn into your mouth," Marsh responded, "You have to look at music fresh in the face every day and say, 'I'm going to play something different than I did yesterday' . . . . Somehow or other I have to get through that same song in a new way tomorrow."[20] Searching for that new way at the same time as he searches for some elusive kernel of self-knowledge, he will sometimes find only an abstract skeleton of the tune, and little of himself except the fierce integrity that says, "If I find nothing, I will play nothing." But when one draws aside the veils of Tristano-cult idolatry on the one hand and mainstream neglect on the other, there remains, as Warne Marsh's legacy to jazz, a significant body of undeniably brilliant and powerful music.

NOTES

1. Interview, 1990. Quotations from oral interviews will henceforth not be footnoted as long as the source is clear from the text.

2. Alun Morgan, "Warne Marsh," *Jazz Monthly*, June 1961, 7.

3. Francis Davis, "Warne Marsh's Inner Melody," *Down Beat*, January 1983, 27.

4. Whitney Balliett, "A True Improviser," *New Yorker*, October 14, 1985, 110.

5. *Lee Konitz Meets Warne Marsh Again*, PAUSA PR7019.

6. Gene Lees, *Cats of Any Color: Jazz Black and White* (New York and Oxford: Oxford University Press, 1995), 188.

7. Ibid. 187–188.

8. Ibid. 188.

9. Ibid. 190.

10. Barry Ulanov, "Crow Jim," *Metronome*, May 1949, 42.

11. Anonymous, "Lennie Tristano," *Down Beat*, October 30, 1958, 18.

12. Alun Morgan, "Warne Marsh 1975—All Music," *Jazz Journal,* February 1976, 4.

13. Anita Leonard, interview.

14. Davis, p. 28.

15. Ibid. 27.

16. Balliett, 112.

17. Claude Alexander, interview.

18. Balliett, 113.

19. Ibid., 111.

20. Michael Cuscuna, interview at Sweet Basil, New York, June 5, 1980.

Ancestors

Speaking of his mother, Elizabeth Marion Marsh, Warne Marsh told an interviewer, "Her parents were Russian Jews. Her father, Louis Marionofsky, had played trumpet in the Imperial Army. He deserted and came over in the 1890s, settling in Philadelphia and changing his name to Marion, which is my middle name. He ran five-and-dime stores in Philly, and he moved to Los Angeles when my mother was in her late teens."[1]

According to Elizabeth, her father arrived in Philadelphia around 1900—he was then twenty-six years old—and found work in a factory that made uniforms for the army.[2] He sent to Russia for his fiancée, Fannie Rabinowitz; they were married, and Elizabeth was born in Philadelphia on February 22, 1902.

Her father, said Elizabeth, was "a very strong character" who "just breathed music." As soon as she, her brother Jack, and her sister Minnie were old enough, he began to give them music lessons. "He started with Jack, who was fifteen months younger than I was, started teaching him notes. . . . [But] Jack was a little bit stupid. . . . My dad would say, 'Now what is that?' and Jack would stop and I'd say, 'That's an A! That's a B!' So after a session of that he said, 'Okay, young lady, come on,' and Jack was out and I was in."

When she was six years old her father bought her a violin and hired a teacher. "I remember running and hiding when the teacher would come. I didn't want to play one of those things. But Dad stuck with it. I remember him coming home from work and saying, 'Did you practice?' And if I said no, I actually got a licking, he actually spanked me. . . . So it

13

was my father that started the whole musical thing that Warne got through me."

By the time Elizabeth Marion was in high school she was playing regularly for various social occasions. Every commencement she had to play a solo, a task that she disliked, though she was comfortable in an ensemble.

In January or February of 1920, just two days before Elizabeth was to graduate from high school and shortly before her eighteenth birthday, Louis Marion and his family left Philadelphia for Los Angeles, where he opened a dry goods store on East Florence Avenue, a block and a half from the old "red car" line, the Pacific Electric streetcar tracks running between downtown Los Angeles and Long Beach.[3] The family lived on the second floor above the store.

Louis Marion was "such a good businessman that if a woman came in and wanted a dress and he looked and didn't have one. . . , he went upstairs and got one of my mother's dresses. . . , and he'd sell [the woman] a dress. . . . They never walked out [empty-handed]." Within a few years, Elizabeth recalled, her father was so successful that he bought the property across the street and built a bigger store, and then opened yet another, a furniture store, in the same block.[4]

Sometime in the early 1920s, Elizabeth launched a career of her own. It was the heyday of the silent screen, Hollywood had established itself as the center of the burgeoning film industry, and young Elizabeth Marion quickly found a niche in what came to be known as a "sideline musician."

Her first job, as a member of a piano-and-strings quartet, was on the set of a Mary Pickford movie.[5] "We were her mood music. . . . If she had to act sad, we would play something to put her in the mood." Pickford's favorite sad song, Mrs. Marsh said, was "Roses of Picardy," which invariably made her weep.[6] "We were on the Mary Pickford lot for quite awhile. Then came [Douglas] Fairbanks, she married Doug, and we were on the Fairbanks lot."

One day Elizabeth Marion's quartet received a call to play for a Robert Z. Leonard-Mae Murray film at the Metro-Goldwyn-Mayer (MGM) studios, and on the set she met her future husband, Oliver T. Marsh.

Although Warne Marsh told an interviewer that his father was born in Lawrence, Kansas,[7] Oliver Marsh seems actually to have been born in Kansas City, Missouri, on May 5, 1893.[8] He was the only son of Charles M. Marsh, a traveling auditor or accountant with the Atchison, Topeka, and Santa Fe railroad, and Mary Warne Marsh, born in Illinois and described by her grandson Warne as "a tenth-generation Brewster, of the Pilgrim Brewsters."[9] Photographs reveal that Mary Warne was a stunningly beautiful woman.[10] Regardless of her great physical beauty, family lore has it that Charles Marsh deserted her and their children at some point before the family settled in California. This was the belief not only of Warne Marsh but also of four other surviving grandchildren: Owen and Gloria Marsh and their cousins, Brewster Lee Arms and Meri Arms Swofford. An article on the film star Mae Marsh, one of Charles and Mary Warne Marsh's four daughters, however, states that Charles Marsh died around 1900, when the family was living in Texas.[11]

At any rate, the 1910 census for Los Angeles County lists the woman who must have been Charles Marsh's wife, identified as May Hall, living in Los Angeles with a purported second husband, William Hall, and her five children, four of whom, including seventeen-year-old Oliver, bear the last name "Marsh" and are identified as step-children of Hall. The fifth child, Margaret, was married to a Donald Loveridge, another member of the household, and was listed under her husband's name.[12] Whether May Marsh—her maiden name was Mary Warne, and her gravestone identifies her as Mae Warne Marsh—was actually married to Hall, identified in the census as an "inspector" in the oil fields, is open to question. No records exist either of such a marriage or of a divorce or annulment of her previous marriage. If Charles Marsh deserted her, as family tradition has it, presumably she was still legally married to him.

That Charles Marsh moved around a good deal is indicated by the birthplaces given for the children of the woman known to the census taker as May Hall: Margaret, the oldest, was born in Kansas;[13] Oliver was born in Missouri; May, named after her mother, and Frances were born in New Mexico; and Mildred, the youngest, was born in Texas.

If Charles Marsh did in fact desert his family, one surmises that he may have done so around the time of the birth of this last child. As she was eleven at the time of the 1910 census, the alleged desertion might have occurred around 1899 in Texas, where Mildred was born. Not long afterward Mary Warne Marsh took her children to San Francisco where, in 1906, their home was destroyed by the great San Francisco earthquake and fire. Shortly thereafter Mrs. Marsh and her five children settled in Los Angeles.[14] She may have become attached to William Hall in 1902, as the length of their purported marriage is given in the 1910 census as eight years.

The most celebrated of Mary Warne Marsh's children was not Warne's father, Oliver, who became an Academy Award-winning cinematographer, but his aunt, the movie actress Mae Marsh, who achieved fame in 1915 as Flora Cameron, the "Little Sister" in D. W. Griffith's epic movie *The Birth of a Nation*. Two years later she signed a lucrative contract with Goldwyn pictures and was named the original "Goldwyn Girl." In 1918, she married Louis Lee Arms, a publicity man for Goldwyn, and after their children were born she took a temporary retirement in 1925 to devote time to her family. Returning to films in 1932, after the advent of talkies, she continued her film career as a character actress throughout the 1930s, 1940s, 1950s, and even into the 1960s, appearing in thirty-six John Ford films, among others. In 1955, she received the Eastman Award as one of the five leading actresses of the Silent Era (the others being Mary Pickford, Lillian Gish, Gloria Swanson, and Norma Talmadge). Her older sister, Margaret, or Marguerite, Marsh, also acted in a number of silent films and was supposedly responsible for bringing Mae to the attention of film producer D. W. Griffith in 1912.[15] Even the youngest sister, Mildred, seems to have appeared in at least one film, as a Mildred Marsh is listed as appearing in *The Country Flapper* in 1922.[16]

It was a family tradition that Mae Marsh helped her older brother, Oliver, Warne Marsh's father, gain his foothold in the film industry. Marsh told Whitney Balliett, "Mae Marsh, who was a star in silent films and was one of his sisters and who I'm named after—she was Mary Warne Marsh—got [my father] a job as a second cameraman in Hollywood."[17]

There are two problems with this statement. First, although it is true that Mae Marsh the film star was born Mary Warne Marsh, she was so named after her mother. Whom Oliver and Elizabeth Marsh had more in mind, Warne's grandmother or his famous aunt, is impossible to know. Mae Marsh reportedly had strong affection for her older brother, Oliver, and their families maintained cordial relations until Oliver's death in 1941.[18] The grandmother, the first Mary/Mae Warne Marsh, died September 22, 1928, when Warne was not quite one year old.[19]

The other problem concerns when and where Oliver Marsh began his career in the movies. According to one source, Oliver "entered the industry in 1911, joining ph[otography] staff of Biograph studio, Fort Lee, New Jersey, with D. W. Griffith. Dir. [director] of ph. [photography] since 1918, working with Goldwyn Pictures, First National and (from 1922) Metro."[20] Another source stated that "while with Griffith he worked under that producer's ace cameraman, Billy Bitzer."[21]

Thus the tradition is very strong that Oliver Marsh began as a cameraman with Griffith and Biograph in 1911. Yet if that date is correct, Mae Marsh could not have helped him because she herself did not begin her film career until 1912, when she signed at the age of sixteen with Griffith, and it was not until the release of *The Birth of a Nation* in 1915 that she became famous enough to wield some influence in the studios.[22] An article written in 1958, when Mae Marsh was still alive and active in films, and when the author clearly had access to her, confirms that after *The Birth of a Nation* the actress was indeed "now able to do something for her family, and help her brother Oliver"—but "to train as an electrician," not to become a second cameraman![23]

This seems to suggest that Oliver Marsh was not even in films or at least not a cameraman before 1915, which brings family tradition into direct conflict with recorded biographical data. The possibility arises that Oliver Marsh did not, in fact, join the photography staff of Biograph in Fort Lee, New Jersey, in 1911, at the age of eighteen. In 1910, according to the census, he was a "worker" in "typewriters" in Los Angeles.[24] He could, of course, have been hired in Los Angeles by Biograph, which established a Hollywood branch studio in 1909–10, and then been transported by the company to its home base in New Jersey, dividing his time in the next several years between there and California as the studio dictated. But it is also possible that he entered the industry not in 1911 but sometime after 1915, after his sister Mae Marsh became famous.

What is known for certain is that Mae Marsh's first film for Goldwyn Pictures was made in 1917 at Fort Lee, New Jersey; that in March 1918 Oliver Marsh was chief cameraman for a film called *The Floor Below;* and that between March 1918 and February 1919 he photographed, as chief cameraman, five Goldwyn films starring his sister Mae Marsh.[25] One may speculate that it was while making her first Goldwyn picture in 1917 that she was able to help her brother Oliver become a second cameraman, not for Biograph but for Goldwyn, and that it was shortly afterward that the incident that Warne Marsh related to Whitney Balliett occurred: "He [Oliver Marsh] taught himself how to take a motion picture camera apart and put it back together, and once, on location, when the only camera the company had broke, he fixed it and was promoted to first cameraman."[26] It is also possible that in 1917 Oliver had been working for Biograph, as an understudy to Billy Bitzer, for the last six years, and that the training "as an electrician" that Mae Marsh helped him to get was in connection with that long-standing job.

According to an obituary, Oliver Marsh "attended the University of Missouri," but that university has no record of his attendance.[27]

From 1918 to 1924 Oliver Marsh photographed films for Goldwyn Pictures, First National, Tiffany Productions, and Metro, working frequently with Robert Z. Leonard and Mae Murray.[28] Around October of 1924 he began shooting Leonard and Murray's first film for the recently consolidated MGM Productions, titled *Married Flirts,* and it was probably on this set that he first met Elizabeth Marion.[29]

Oliver Marsh and Elizabeth Marion were married September 28, 1926. On that day Paul Whiteman, billed as the "Monarch of Jazz," and his thirty-two-piece orchestra were ending the first week of a two-week engagement at the Million Dollar theater in downtown Los Angeles, and the trial of evangelist Aimee Semple McPherson for conspiracy to commit perjury, concerning her ten-day tryst with one Kenneth Ormiston in a cottage in Carmel, was all over the *Los Angeles Times.* About a year later, on

October 26, 1927, Oliver and Elizabeth Marsh's first child, Warne Marion Marsh, was born. A second child, Gloria, was born a year and a half later on May 26, 1929, and a third, Owen, on May 29, 1930.

NOTES

1. Whitney Balliett, "A True Improviser," *New Yorker,* October 14, 1985, 112.

2. Elizabeth Marsh was eighty-eight years old when I interviewed her several times in 1990. She died December 20, 1990, having outlived her son Warne by three years.

3. Her eighteenth birthday would have been February 22, 1920. Apparently she was a midterm graduate.

4. On Louis Marion's Los Angeles County death certificate his business is given as "variety store," but Mrs. Marsh mentioned only dry goods and furniture stores.

5. How soon Elizabeth Marion looked for and found work as a musician is not known, but the family no doubt needed money. Mary Pickford made three films in 1921 *(The Love Light, Through the Back Door,* and *Little Lord Fauntleroy),* one in 1922 *(Tess of the Storm Country),* two in 1923 *(Garrison's Finish* and *Rosita),* and one in 1924 *(Dorothy Vernon of Hadden Hall).* Elizabeth could have worked on any or all of these, and she may also have played for later films by Pickford and Douglas Fairbanks Sr. up until sometime in 1927, the year Warne was born. She stated that she abandoned her musical career at that time.

6. A photograph in *Music for Silent Films, 1894–1924,* compiled by Gillian B. Anderson (Washington, D.C.: Library of Congress, 1988, page vi), shows an unidentified young actress sprawled face down at the edge of a cliff, clutching the shoulder of a male actor who is dangling from the edge, about to fall. The "cliff," however, is really just a large overhanging rock, and the man's feet are perhaps an inch off the ground. A few feet downslope, just out of camera range, a violinist in knickers and bow tie and a keyboardist seated at a portable harmonium diligently play what one presumes were appropriately mood enhancing melodies for the actors' benefit.

7. Balliett, 112.

8. "Great Cameramen," *Focus on Film,* No. 13 (January-February 1973): 50. This source does not specify whether Oliver Marsh's birthplace was Kansas City, Kansas, or Kansas City, Missouri, but Missouri is given as the state of his birth in a 1910 census entry listing the Marsh children. See remarks in text concerning Mary, a.k.a. Mae or May, Marsh, Oliver's mother, who seems to have become attached to a William Hall after Charles Marsh deserted her.

9. Balliett, 112.

10. Photographs are in the Mae Marsh file at the Margaret Herrick Library of the Academy of Motion Picture Arts and Sciences, 333 S. La Cienega Blvd., Beverly Hills, California, 90211.

11. Harold Dunham, "Mae Marsh," *Films in Review* (June-July 1958): 306.

12. Department of Commerce and Labor, Bureau of the Census, *Thirteenth*

Census of the United States: 1910 Population, Los Angeles County, California. Other information in the listing conforms to known facts and family traditions about Mary Warne Marsh and her children: for example, that Mrs. Marsh was born in Illinois; that Mae Marsh was born in Madrid, New Mexico; that the family lived for a time in Texas; and that Oliver Marsh, Warne's father, was a "worker" in "typewriters." The only mysteries are the identity of William Hall and his relationship to Mary Warne Marsh and her children. In the column showing marital status, the census-taker entered "M1" for Hall and "M2" for his alleged wife, "May," apparently indicating that this was his first marriage and her second; and in the column titled "number of years of present marriage" he entered an eight. A difficulty here is that neither Gloria nor Owen Marsh, nor their cousins Meri Arms Swofford and Brewster Lee Arms, had ever heard of William Hall, nor had they ever been told that Mary Warne Marsh, their grandmother, married a second time, or was ever divorced from Charles Marsh.

13. The census lists Margaret as Margaret Loveridge, married to Donald Loveridge, and she is identified as a daughter, not stepdaughter, of William Hall. But Charles Marsh must have been her biological father, as the birthplaces of her father and mother are given as Missouri and Illinois, the same as for the other Marsh children. Later she uses the name "Marguerite Marsh" in her career as a film actress.

14. Dunham, 306.

15. According to an account in the *New York Morning Telegraph,* 12 December 1922, page unknown, when Mae was fifteen "she went to the Griffith studio with her older sister [Marguerite] and was busily upturning stones to see the black beetles crawl from under, when Mr. Griffith saw the play of expression that made her features unusual. A year later she was known throughout the world as the little sister of the Cameron family in *The Birth of a Nation.*" This story sounds suspiciously like Hollywood puffery. Other accounts give her age at the time of her discovery by Griffith as fourteen, but by her own account she met Griffith in 1912, at which time she was sixteen or seventeen, having been born November 9, 1895.

16. *American Film Institute Catalog,* 1248.

17. Balliett, 111.

18. Merry Arms Swofford, daughter of Mae Marsh, interview, October 1992.

19. "Funeral of Mrs. Marsh Tomorrow," *Los Angeles Times,* 23 September 1928, 2 (Part 2).

20. "Great Cameramen," 50–51.

21. *Hollywood Citizen-News,* c. 7 May 1941, page unknown.

22. Dunham, 307, 310.

23. Ibid., 310.

24. Department of Commerce and Labor, Bureau of the Census, op. cit.

25. *American Film Institute Catalog, Personal Name Index, Feature Films, 1911–1920,* p. 146. The five Mae Marsh films for which Oliver Marsh was chief cameraman were *All Woman, Hidden Fires, Money Mad, The Racing Strain,* and *The Bondage of Barbara.*

26. Balliett, 112.

27. *Hollywood Citizen-News,* c. 7 May 1941, page unknown.

28. "Great Cameramen," 50–51; also *Hollywood Citizen-News*, c.7 May 1941, page unknown.

29. Elizabeth Marsh said that when she met Oliver, Leonard and Murray had just made "their first trip to make movies out west" and that he "had been their cameraman for years." But all of the earlier Leonard-Murray films with Marsh as cameraman were produced by Tiffany, though distributed by Metro. *Married Flirts* was Leonard's and Marsh's first film produced by MGM as such, and it was also the last film that Leonard made with his then wife, Murray. Also, the beginning date of Oliver Marsh's career with MGM is generally given as 1924.

The Un-Family

Though not among the super-rich, the Marshes in the late 1920s and throughout the 1930s were more than comfortably well off. In addition to their home on Woodrow Wilson Drive in the Hollywood Hills, for the first eight or nine years of marriage they leased a second home on the beach in the film colony at Malibu, where they spent their summers and where their nearby neighbors included film stars Leslie Howard and Norma Shearer.

Although Elizabeth abandoned her career as a studio musician after Warne was born, Oliver Marsh was solidly established as one of Hollywood's most highly regarded cameramen. An index of his success was a breach of contract suit brought against him in 1926, in which Corinne Griffith Productions charged him with refusing to honor a fifty-two-week contract and signing instead with another producer, probably MGM again. The suit alleged that Griffith thereby suffered irreparable loss, as the company could not find another cameraman "with the same degree of skill and ability."[1]

Legal hyperbole aside, the suit, which was dismissed, indicates that Oliver Marsh was able to use his bargaining leverage to obtain a better contract at MGM, for whom he made some eighty more films between 1926 and his sudden death in 1941. These included, in the 1930s, such films as *San Francisco, David Copperfield, A Tale of Two Cities, After the Thin Man,* and such Jeanette MacDonald musicals as *Rosalie* and *The Merry Widow.* Marsh's importance to MGM is suggested in laudatory captions from a picture history of MGM: "Many names that were to become famous on MGM credit titles worked on this film [*Our Modern Maidens,* 1929]: Gowns

by Adrian, photography by Oliver Marsh. . . ." The same source said about
a 1935 film, "This is it: the MGM Look, personified by Joan Crawford in
an Adrian gown and Oliver Marsh lighting. . . ."[2] In 1938 Oliver Marsh
and his co-cinematographer Allen Davey won a special Academy Award
for their color photography on *Sweethearts,* and in 1940 they were nominated for an award for *Bittersweet.*[3]

The stock market crash of 1929 and the Great Depression of the 1930s
seem hardly to have affected the Marsh family fortunes at all. In June 1935,
although they gave up the house in the hills and the leased beach home
at Malibu, they acquired a three-acre estate then known as Rancho Val
Verde. Located in a rustic, farmland area at 5717 Laurel Canyon Road in
North Hollywood, it had been built by a film producer in 1926 for $60,000[4]
and came complete with tennis courts, swimming pool, track, a guest
house that doubled as a recreation room, and a fourteen-room Spanish-
style ranch house "with the red tile roof and the archways."[5] There they
maintained, as the children were growing up, three servants: a governess, a cook, and a gardener.

Although Oliver Marsh was, in Warne's words, "socially retiring," and
although they did not move in the more glamorous Hollywood circles,
the Marshes entertained fairly regularly, and directors, writers, fellow
cameramen, and an occasional star, such as Jeanette MacDonald, were
frequent guests at their parties.[6] Owen's first dog, a puppy, was a gift from
Miss MacDonald. A niece, Frances Mayer, described Elizabeth Marsh, her
Aunt Betty, as "very much a party animal. She loved to dance, smoked,
drank, dressed well, had lots of clothes and jewelry." Although Frances
was born in 1940 and was speaking of her aunt as she knew her during
the 1940s and 1950s, her description undoubtedly applies as well to Elizabeth Marsh in the years before Oliver Marsh's death.

Despite their professional, financial, and social success, however, Oliver
and Elizabeth Marsh failed to provide for their children a close-knit family atmosphere. "As a family," said Owen Marsh, "we weren't much of a
family. . . . We were an un-family." The three children were left largely to
the supervision of the governess or housekeeper. They never ate with their
parents. "Our parents had the dining room," said Owen, "and the children, the three of us, had the little breakfast room. . . . We'd eat when the
nurse or the governess and the cook fed us." One housekeeper, Louella,
who remained with the family all through the children's teenage years,
functioned as a surrogate mother. As Elizabeth Marsh rarely made an
appearance before noon, Louella would fix breakfast, make lunch bags,
and get the children off to school. When Gloria started dating at about
sixteen, it was Louella who set the rules. "I dated boys for months, and
[my mother] never said she wanted to meet them." Gloria went with one
boy for six months before her mother asked, "Who's that?"

One problem contributing to the family's lack of togetherness was that Oliver became an alcoholic when Warne Marsh was still an infant. Marsh later told Whitney Balliett that his father "never took a drink until he was thirty-five, and then he never stopped."[7] As his father's thirty-fifth birthday was May 5, 1928, six months after Warne was born, Warne was relating information that he could not have known for several years, but his father's drinking must have been common knowledge. Later that same year, on September 22, 1928, Oliver's mother, Mary (a.k.a. May, or Mae) Warne Marsh, died rather suddenly while still in her fifties, an event that may have caused the onset of Oliver's drinking.[8]

While his drinking did not prevent the two younger children, Gloria and Owen, from feeling affection for him—Gloria adored him and never thought of him as an alcoholic, though she knew he drank, while Owen loved to sit in his workshop and hold nails for him—it seems to have contributed significantly to Warne's early estrangement from his father. Gloria recalled a time when Warne refused to let his father drive him to a social event, complaining that his father wouldn't be able to drive straight. That Warne was acutely conscious of his father's drinking throughout his life is suggested by the emphasis he placed on it in telling others, like Balliett, of his childhood. Geraldyne Marsh, who married Warne in 1964, recalled Warne's telling her how his father had taken his first drink at a cocktail party and how "from that day he drank a fifth of gin [daily] to the day he died."

When he was not at work, Oliver Marsh seems to have spent most of his time in his workshop, making tables, chairs, and cabinets, or curled up asleep on a couch, sleeping off his liquor. He passed his expertise in carpentry on to Warne, who later would surprise his friends by making similar items. He once made a shower stall in Lennie Tristano's basement apartment for bassist Sonny Dallas. Another time, living in an apartment where his practicing disturbed the neighbors, he constructed a wooden box, with armholes, in which he could place his saxophone to muffle the sound as he played.

For her part, Elizabeth, who was a great reader, spent much time reading in her and Ollie's suite of rooms at the far end of the house. As Gloria remembered, "We would come home from school, and if her door was closed we weren't to bother her. . . . Days would go by and we wouldn't know if she was in there or not. . . . Our lives were very separate. . . . The house was beautiful, and my little friends would say, 'Oh, you live in that house? You're so lucky,' and they couldn't understand that all I wanted to do was visit their homes, because they had a regular family." Similarly, Owen recalled that his mother would "spend all day in her room, and she wouldn't know if I was home or not. . . . Warne and I had outside exits, and . . . the three of us didn't really meet that often."

"We really had a strange upbringing," summarized Gloria. When in later years she met the man she was to marry, Richard Oxford, "he thought we were the weirdest bunch he had ever met in his life. Of course he came from a very proper, together family." He also did not know the family until several years after Oliver's death in 1941. But the "separatism" of the Marsh household, their tendency to live separate lives under the same very large roof, with the children coming and going pretty much as they pleased after reaching a certain age, seems to have been constant from early on, though it may have been exacerbated by Oliver's death.

To compensate for the absence of closeness at home, Owen and Gloria adopted their Aunt Minnie Colman, Elizabeth's sister, as a substitute mother. Minnie's older daughter, Marian, was about the same age as Owen and Gloria, and the three grew up almost as siblings. But Warne, always the loner, did not join their circle.

The one person Warne was close to was his mother. According to his cousin Frances Mayer, she made it "very clear whom she preferred," spoiling him "terribly." "Warne was always allowed privileges that we weren't," said Gloria. "He was allowed to be away from the house, he had his own friends, he went places—I never knew where Warne was."

A primary bond between Warne and his mother was music. She recognized his talent from a very early age, when Warne was three or four: "I could tell from the minute he sat down with his ear and picked out everything at the piano, that that was it." Strangely, she did not arrange for him to have piano lessons until years later. When he was eight she bought him a piano accordion (an accordion with a piano keyboard, as opposed to a gypsy-type accordion with buttons but no keyboard) for Christmas.[9] "It was a whim of mine," she said. But Warne never took lessons on accordion and never, according to Owen and Gloria, acquired any great proficiency, apparently being content with what he could teach himself, with a little help from his mother.

Nevertheless, his natural talent asserted itself immediately on receiving the accordion that Christmas of 1935, the family's first in the new house on Laurel Canyon. His mother got out her violin, and after Warne strapped on the huge instrument and briefly familiarized himself with the bass buttons, she and he made a grand candlelight entrance playing "Silent Night." He "played around" with the accordion for a time, perhaps half a year, but never developed a serious interest in it.

Finally, at the age of ten, Warne began taking piano lessons.[10] As Owen recalled, all three children started lessons at that time. "I think I had half a lesson and then quit. My sister might have gone through six months with lessons, and Warne stayed with his. It wasn't anything serious, just learning how to read music. . . . By the time he had taken instruction for three months he was probably far ahead of the teacher." Warne progressed far enough to "pick up on the Magdalena Bach books," the easy student pieces Bach wrote for his young second wife.[11]

Bach and the piano not withstanding, it was not until Warne entered North Hollywood Junior High School and encountered the school band director, Earl Immel, that he discovered his true musical passion. He presented himself to Immel as an accordionist, not a pianist, perhaps because he wanted to be in the marching band. Immel, knowing there was no place for accordion in the band, suggested he take up another instrument. Would he like Immel's own instrument, the saxophone? Warne thought that was a good idea, and Earl Immel became his first saxophone teacher.

He started on alto. "His mother," said Immel, "bought him an alto, [but] he was pretty miserable on alto sax. He could get around on it all right, but it was not too good a sound, so [after maybe half a year] I again made a suggestion, that he try a tenor, and he took off on that. . . ."[12] His dexterity was very fast. He could play with anybody who'd been playing a year or two ahead of him right away."

Around the same time as he switched to tenor saxophone, Warne indicated a desire to play bass clarinet as well. "His folks," said Immel, "seemed to be able to buy him as many instruments as he wanted, when he wanted them. . . . Two weeks on the bass clarinet and he could play the literature we were playing."

Warne's mother remembered fondly a triumphant moment on bass clarinet. Earl Immel was also the director of the Los Angeles All-City High School Orchestra, and he recruited Warne for the orchestra as perhaps the only kid in town who could play bass clarinet, or who owned one.[13] At a concert in which the orchestra played Sibelius's "Valse Triste," Warne, Mrs. Marsh said, "just had this one note to play, but he had to count like crazy." She was sitting in the balcony with all the music teachers from the different schools, and when Warne came in correctly with his one note, there was gleeful celebration in the balcony.

Learning bass clarinet was probably a consequence of his mother's conventional idea of what one did to make a living in music. "I was supposed to be learning clarinet, and working towards being a studio musician. . . . Either classical music or studio work—in Hollywood, that's all you thought of. Jazz was not even discussed as a career."[14] In high school he even learned to play E-flat tuba, possibly as part of the same ambition.[15]

But if music was a bond between Warne and his mother, it served only to distance him further from his father, who, Warne said, "had no interest whatever in music."[16] Exactly when the withdrawal from his father began is not clear, but by the time of Oliver's sudden death on May 5, 1941, when Warne was thirteen and a half, Gloria thought that he and his father "had no relationship whatsoever."

Elizabeth Marsh recalled the day of her husband's death: She received a call from MGM, where Oliver Marsh was shooting tests for a new Jeanette MacDonald movie, informing her that he had been stricken during breakfast at the studio cafeteria. She rushed to the hospital, but Oliver Marsh died of a cerebral hemorrhage that same day. When she returned she told the children, "Your father's gone." They did not understand the euphemism, so she explained that he was dead. At that, she said, "They all went, very quietly, to their rooms, hiding emotion from me, to save my feelings."

One would assume that young Warne must have felt his father's death deeply, but, typically, he showed little emotion, to the extent that Gloria later wondered whether it affected him much at all. What is certain is that by this time in his young life music had become an all-consuming passion, one in which his father had had no share.

NOTES

1. "Injunction Sought against Cameraman," *Los Angeles Times*, 15 March 1926, 10 (Part 2).

2. John Douglas Eames, *The MGM Story: The Complete History of Fifty Roaring Years* (New York: Crown Publishers, 1975), 57, 115.

3. Cobbett Steinberg, *Reel Facts: The Movie Book of Records* (New York: Vintage Books, 1978), 23, 28.

4. "Sale of Rancho, Report Reveals," *Los Angeles Times*, 16 June 1935, 1 (Part 5).

5. Whitney Balliett, "A True Improviser," *New Yorker*, October 14, 1985, 113.

6. Ibid., 112.

7. Ibid.

8. "Funeral of Mrs. Marsh Tomorrow," *Los Angeles Times*, 23 September 1928, 2 (Part 2).

9. Warne told Whitney Balliett that he "took up piano and accordion when I was ten" (p. 111), but his mother insisted that she bought him the accordion for the first Christmas in the house on Laurel Canyon, which was in 1935 (not 1937, as Marsh told Balliett), when Marsh was eight.

10. Elizabeth Marsh, when I interviewed her in 1990, did not recall that Warne had ever had formal instruction on piano, but Owen and Gloria confirmed that he had, and their remembrance of the time conforms with Marsh's statement to Balliett that he took up piano when he was ten. However, in his liner notes to the Atlantic LP 1291, *Warne Marsh, with Paul Chambers, Philly Joe Jones, Ronnie Ball, and Paul Motian,* Nat Hentoff wrote that Marsh's first instrument "was the piano, which he studied from six to ten." Marsh may have said he started at six because he felt that he was "studying" piano all the years when he appeared to others to be casually doodling on it. Or possibly Hentoff misunderstood him.

11. Balliett, 113.

12. Marsh told Balliett, "The director of my high school band told me I didn't sound so good on alto and maybe I should get a tenor, so I switched when I was fifteen" (pp. 113–14). But once again his own purported account is probably inaccurate. Nat Hentoff, in his liner notes to Atlantic LP 1291, *Warne Marsh,* wrote, "At about twelve, [Warne] spent a short time with the alto, but took the advice of his junior high school teacher . . . and switched to tenor," which accords with Immel's recollection. At fifteen Marsh had already joined the Hollywood Canteen Kids as featured tenor saxophone soloist.

13. "Warne Marsh—A Conversation with Robert Ronzello," *Saxophone Journal* (Spring 1982): 11.

14. Les Tomkins, "The Warne Marsh Story," *Crescendo International* (May 1976): 21.

15. Balliett, 114.

16. Ibid., 112.

The Canteen Kid

At the time of his father's death Warne Marsh had been studying saxophone for a year and a half, and within another year and a half, by the age of fifteen, he was sufficiently accomplished to turn more or less professional. His prodigious progress in those three years was the result of endless hours of practice.

"Eight or twelve hours without stop was common," said Owen Marsh. "I'm just talking nonstop, practically. To my untrained, nonmusical ear, absolute toneless unmelodic riffs, just working his fingers. . . . And this would just go on and on and on, forever."

Probably by the time he took up saxophone, Marsh had moved out of the bedroom he had always shared with Owen and set himself up in the library, where he practiced and slept. One of the first things he taught himself was "Scatterbrain," a sprightly 1939 hit by Johnny Burke, Frankie Masters, Kahn Keene, and Carl Bean full of useful eighth-note arpeggio figures.[1] While he was practicing, his sister, Gloria, would sometimes enter the room to find a book, sit down, and read for an hour or two, and eventually leave with Warne still practicing. Among the jazz solos she heard him painstakingly learning from records was Coleman Hawkins's "Body and Soul." He later acknowledged, "[Hawkins] impressed me. I think that's the man I listened to most."[2] In those first three years of study he also learned Ben Webster's solo on Duke Ellington's "Cottontail." A friend loaned him her 78-rpm record of the piece, and when he returned it, it was white from wear.[3] Probably, besides other solos by Hawkins and Webster, he also learned solos by Tex Benecke, whom he called "my very first inspiration,"[4] and perhaps Corky Corcoran, the Harry James sideman by whom he was "entranced"[5] early on and from whom he took a few lessons while still in high school. Corcoran encouraged him in his love for Ben Webster but apparently taught him little, communicating mainly a dislike for Lester Young, based on the way Young often held his horn in unnatural positions. "We didn't get much done," Marsh later said. "I can't even recall what we did. The only thing I recall is that he ridiculed Lester Young to me. He said, 'Who can play the saxophone sticking [it] out there like that?'"[6] His principal teacher, after his junior high school teacher Earl Immel, was classical saxophonist Mickey Gillette, with whom he studied for perhaps as long as two and a half years.[7] Marsh said that Gillette, "who I understand performed with the San Francisco symphony at one time . . . was a teacher who never once picked up his horn and played anything for me. . . ."[8] At some point in his student days he worked with the saxophone books of the early virtuoso Rudy Wiedoeft. "I still have them somewhere," he said in 1982. He never heard Wiedoeft earlier, "but I recently heard a great record by him. I didn't know that he was that good."[9]

Sometime around Marsh's fifteenth birthday, probably in the fall of 1942, his first semester at North Hollywood High, he joined a youth band fronted by a young trumpet player of average talent named Chuck Falkner. Falkner had started his band around 1939, while still a thirteen-year-old student at Bancroft Junior High School in Hollywood. At first the band consisted only of a few fellow seventh- and eighth-graders at Bancroft: Betty Churchill and Don Walter on alto saxophones; Herb Cox, Mickey Potter, and Falkner on trumpet; Scott McKenna on trombone; Jack Tippenger and later Phil Ramacher on drums; and Jean Ambler on piano. Early rehearsals were at the homes of Churchill and Falkner.

Mrs. Falkner, Chuck's mother, was a "stage mama" type who envisioned Chuck and his younger sister Barbara in show business. She had started them singing and dancing at an early age, and with the formation of the band she became their de facto agent. Installing ten-year-old Barbara as the band's "canary," she started getting them little jobs, the first of which was a fashion show at the Broadway department store in Hollywood. At that point the only slow number they knew was "On the Santa Fe Trail," and they played it over and over for the parading models. As Chuck's older brother, who was in the music business in Chicago, sent them stock arrangements of hits recorded by Glenn Miller, Harry James, Count Basie, Jimmie Lunceford, Gene Krupa, and other popular big bands, they learned more tunes, added personnel, and adopted a high-sounding name: Chuck Falkner's Colonial Club Orchestra. Mrs. Falkner rented rehearsal space and got them more and better jobs, such as playing for parties at the home of child film actress Jane Withers and for benefits sponsored by the Hollywood American Legion.[10] They often played on weekends at a hot springs resort in the San Fernando Valley called Pop's Willow Lake, and they began playing at various ballrooms in and around Los Angeles, such as the Pasadena Civic Auditorium and the Rendevous Ballroom in Balboa.

Mrs. Falkner's main interest was not music but the promotion of her children, with Chuck Falkner cast in the role of big band front man. His function, as was common with commercial swing bands of the day, was not to contribute musically so much as to look good, at which he seems to have succeeded fairly well. A story about the band in *Down Beat* reported, "He's got a pleasant, youthful personality and fronts the band with professional ease plus just enough kid stuff to sell well."[11] A publicity photo of the band in its early days, before Marsh joined, shows Falkner in front of the band in checkered sport coat, tie, white pants, and white shoes, his right arm raised as if to conduct, smiling brightly out at an imaginary audience. Younger sister Barbara, dressed in chiffon and taffeta, sits to one side of the sax section as the band vocalist, smiling equally brightly.[12]

How Marsh came to join the band is not clear. The Falkners had moved from Hollywood to the North Hollywood area, and if Mrs. Falkner visited North Hollywood High in search of talent, or if Chuck Falkner enrolled there, they would have learned about Marsh, as by the time he graduated from junior high he was already something of a legend among his peers. Marsh's classmate and fellow saxophonist, Bob Hardaway, who joined Falkner's band somewhat after Marsh, has said he was in awe of Marsh from junior high school on, Marsh was so far ahead of everyone else.

Regarding Marsh's prowess in those years, his brother, Owen, told of how Warne and two other teenage saxophonists from North Hollywood High, Bob and Bill Cushman, who lived across the street from the Marshes, flabbergasted the audience at a music festival at another high school in the San Fernando Valley. After the other school's band had performed, Marsh's saxophone trio entered from the back and two sides of the auditorium, playing as they advanced down the aisles to the stage. "It was just like Supersax Junior, they came in and they blew them away. This audience just went nuts." Marsh, said Owen, thoroughly enjoyed the moment: "He was so tickled about that—he was big time and they were little guys."

In part because it was the period of World War II, when the ranks of working musicians were decimated by the draft and when whole bands sometimes joined the military as a unit, Mrs. Falkner soon succeeded in putting Chuck and his band in the public eye. Sometime after the onset of the war in December 1941, the band caught the attention of songwriter Harry Revel and began through his auspices to work war bond rallies and servicemen's shows. They also played for patriotic affairs at the homes of Bing Crosby and Mary Pickford. Film star George Raft and attorney Jerry Geisler, who had organized a USO (United Servicemen's Organization) show featuring wrestlers and boxers from the Hollywood Legion Stadium, hired the band for the show's tour of military bases. Geisler arranged for the band to join Local 47 of the Musicians' Union, even paying their fees, so that they could go on the tour.[13]

Around the start of 1943 the band began playing regularly at the Hollywood Canteen, the famous USO servicemen's club on Cahuenga near Sunset Boulevard; and in May, Chuck Falkner's Colonial Club Orchestra became the house band and was officially renamed the Hollywood Canteen Kids.[14] Jules Stein, president of the Music Corporation of America (MCA) booking agency, arranged for them to receive a weekly stipend from the Canteen and secured the services of studio arranger Walter Green to coach the band and help with the book,[15] which had already been augmented with original arrangements by Elliot Carpenter, formerly with Paul Whiteman, and young Neil Cunningham, who had joined the band on trumpet.[16] At the Canteen the band played two or three nights a week, filling in whenever a name band was unavailable, especially on weeknights, and alternating sets on weekends with famous bands like those of Harry James and Kay Kyser, who donated their services as a patriotic gesture. James and Kyser even gave the Kids their old band uniforms.[17]

The band was successful on yet another count, that of recruiting genuine talent. By all accounts Marsh was the outstanding talent in the band—"Oh yeah, obviously," said fellow member, trombonist Billy Byers—and he and baby-faced drummer Karl Kiffe were the band's principal soloists; but not only they but several others went on to forge careers in music. Bob Hardaway established himself in the Hollywood studios, becoming a member of the National Broadcasting Corporation (NBC) staff orchestra that played for the *Dean Martin Show* and occasionally subbing on *The Tonight Show* band. Byers, who joined the band at fourteen, recorded as a jazz trombonist and became an Emmy Award-winning composer/arranger, contributing arrangements to the Count Basie band among many others. A year or two after the Canteen Kids broke up in mid-1944, Kiffe joined the Jimmy Dorsey band for two and a half years, later settling in Las Vegas and working the hotel scene there.[18] Trumpeters Ollie Mitchell and Johnny Chech, saxophonist Ronnie Lang (another fourteen-year-old prodigy), and trombonists Dave Wells and Scott McKenna all continued as professional musicians.

In July 1943 the Canteen Kids made another breakthrough, being hired for a featured spot in Ken Murray's *Blackouts,* a sophisticated burlesque revue that had a long run at the El Capitan Theater in Hollywood, a few blocks from the Canteen. Shortly after they began at the *Blackouts,* Chuck

Falkner was drafted and Karl Kiffe was elected leader. The band had the closing slot, and Kiffe's drum solo at the end of the evening regularly brought down the house.[19] If Kiffe impressed the audience, the girls in the *Blackouts* made at least as deep an impression on Kiffe, to whom Murray once delivered an avuncular lecture after catching Kiffe peeking through a hole in the curtain of the girls' dressing area.[20] After the Kids left the *Blackouts* sometime in 1944, Kiffe continued to do a featured drum solo act in the show's 1944 and 1945 versions.

At the *Blackouts* the Kids were subjected to a demanding schedule: a show every night plus matinees on weekends.[21] They had little time for the Canteen anymore. Then around January 1944 they entered show business with a vengeance when they began making a Jane Powell movie called *Song of the Open Road*.[22] They had already, before Marsh joined the band, appeared in a Jane Withers movie called *Johnny Doughboy*, and after Marsh joined, they were featured in two shorts, *Junior Jive Bombers* and another featuring Kay Thompson and the Williams Brothers.[23] *Song of the Open Road*, one of Powell's first full-length films, was the film in which Marsh, according to his brother, Owen, appeared on-screen with a look that said, "I'm disappearing, I'm not here." The Canteen Kids appear as members of a corps of young people recruited to travel from farm to farm to help harvest crops during wartime. In one sequence the camera pans over the different sections of the band as Powell sings. In another they, including Marsh, are seen standing around the porch and yard of the farm as Powell does another number. Drummer Karl Kiffe is featured in two numbers and even has a line to speak. For other musical sequences music is supplied by Sammy Kaye's band or by off-camera studio musicians.

In late June and early July of 1944, the band did engagements at the Orpheum Theater in Los Angeles and the Golden Gate Theater in San Francisco, appearing on stage with Jane Withers. However, the Canteen Kids were actually in the process of breaking up. Marsh had already begun that spring to devote part of his time to another youth band made up of teenagers from Santa Monica and West Los Angeles and led by Richard Markowitz, who used the name Dick Allen. During the summer of 1944 the Dick Allen band, including Marsh, was in residence at the Sleepy Hollow Ballroom in Laguna Beach. Sometime before the end of the year Markowitz was drafted, but in early 1945 his band, now under the leadership of Jimmy Higson, a student at University of California at Los Angeles (UCLA), and going by the name of The Teen-Agers, landed the job of house band for Hoagy Carmichael's new weekly half-hour radio show. The program aired on NBC stations throughout the West Coast starting February 26, 1945. The job with Carmichael and the Teen-Agers lasted at least until the fall of 1945 and possibly into the spring of 1946, with Marsh as the featured tenor saxophone soloist. Years later Marsh told interviewers that the Teen-Agers were "all the work of a couple of sharp promoters." The band's agent, Van Alexander, said Marsh, "*was* the Teen-Agers."[24]

Soon after the Carmichael show began in February 1945, the sixteen-year-old prodigy André Previn joined the Teen-Agers as an arranger and featured pianist. His recollection of the experience, in his autobiography, was not flattering: "When I was sixteen years old, I began to write an arrangement or two for radio shows, [including] a truly deadly weekly half-hour with Hoagy Carmichael and a band simply known as The Teenage Band."[25] Previn was then on the verge of huge success. In June 1945 he signed with MGM to write movie scores, and in November he signed with MCA, beginning the career as a jazz pianist that preceded his illustrious career as conductor of some of the world's leading symphony orchestras.[26]

Previn and Marsh had actually met a year or two before Previn joined the Teen-Agers, and when Previn was fourteen, Marsh fifteen, and drummer Karl Kiffe sixteen, the three had made a private recording of "How High the Moon," a copy of which still exists. It shows that at that early stage all three had developed remarkable jazz expertise. As Kiffe remarked in 1990, "If we don't sound like Coleman Hawkins, Art Tatum, and Gene Krupa, I'll go on the wagon today." But if Previn at fourteen had the technique of an Art Tatum, if in his twenties and thirties he made a score of commercially successful trio albums, and if his early and continued fame stands in stark contrast to Marsh's lack of it, he was never, except as a teenager, the equal of Marsh as a jazz artist. Previn's recorded jazz playing, notwithstanding its commercial success, is lightweight compared to Marsh's.

From the time he joined Chuck Falkner's band at age fifteen, Marsh had led a heady life for a teenager, especially one so withdrawn and inwardly focused. He was always a difficult person to be close to. Yet he had his musician friends that he ran with, and girls were attracted to him. Pretty Betty Churchill, the only girl in that band and his section-mate on alto, had a long-lasting crush on him, and they quickly became a couple, holding hands in the back of the bus on band tours and dating throughout high school. At times, walking home from a movie, Marsh would become so absorbed in his own thoughts that he would be half a block ahead of her before realizing that she was not beside him. Probably his self-absorption was partially due to the fact that at fifteen he was already a habitual marijuana smoker, a habit that continued to the end of his life. Churchill knew that Marsh and his friends smoked pot, but she disapproved, and they never did it in her presence.

Marsh and Churchill sometimes double-dated with one of Marsh's classmates at North Hollywood High, Beverly Carpenter, and her boyfriend at the time, a trumpet player named Don Davies. Later, after Marsh had graduated from high school and served eighteen months in the army, Beverly and Marsh would have an affair and talk of marriage. Now, in high school, Beverly was one of a gang of jazz aficionados that included as its nucleus Marsh, Billy Byers, Karl Kiffe, Johnny Chech, and Neil Cunningham, all from the Canteen Kids, and Beverly's future husband, a talented trumpet player named John McComb.

Both Beverly, whose mother had friends who were nurses, and Byers, whose father was a doctor, were a source of pills, mostly Benzedrine, for the gang. She didn't smoke pot, but when they would go to a drive-in restaurant, often the one near Hollywood High at Sunset and La Brea, the guys would roll up the car windows and light a joint, and she would get a "contact high" from the smoke in the air.

Beverly Carpenter was a source not only for pills but for jazz. Her mother, because she played the ponies, listened all day long to radio station XEMO, "The Voice of Baja California," which regularly alternated a half-hour of race results with a half-hour of big band jazz, and from childhood Beverly was exposed not only to the likes of Glenn Miller, Benny Goodman, Harry James, Gene Krupa, and other top white bands but also to black bands like Count Basie, Duke Ellington, Jimmie Lunceford, Andy Kirk, and Erskine Hawkins. By the time she reached high school she had a record collection that was much in demand by Marsh and his fellow teenage jazz players. It was she who loaned Marsh Ellington's "Cottontail," from which he learned Ben Webster's solo.

Billy Byers's account catches the flavor of those years: "We used to hang out together when we weren't working and go down to the beach, Karl, Johnny Chech, Warne, and I. . . . We were a quartet that stuck together all the time, hanging out, drinking beer, chasing girls. . . . We went to the Club Alabam and the Cotton Club when we were little tiny tykes, and we were in the Palladium all the time, and we were in the joints down there on Central Avenue. . . . We were all over the place. . . . By the time we were sixteen we were all driving, and before that there was the Red Car [Pacific Electric streetcar]. . . . We heard Duke Ellington, Jimmie Lunceford—we were crazy about Jimmie Lunceford—Harlan Leonard, Cab Calloway, Count Basie, Earl Hines. . . . They let us in because those were the war years, there were a lot of sailors, there was not such a big deal about being black or white."

That being black or white was not a big deal would, of course, come as news to blacks in Los Angeles, who were routinely refused admission to white-run night clubs, even though their black friends were the star attraction on the bandstand. *Down Beat* chronicled an incident in 1943 in which a black friend of musicians in the Benny Carter band was denied entry to Zucca's Hollywood Club, where Carter was playing. An account of the incident by a local columnist provoked an angry reaction from the club's press agent, who felt the club was being unfairly singled out for what was a common practice. He claimed that white night club operators were "not worrying so much about the fact that the presence of Negroes will drive away white patronage" as about the possibility that "some boozed up white man . . . will insult some Negro patron, and . . . [the club operator would] have a nasty riot on his hands."[27]

Race was in fact a very big deal in society at large. There were still two Musicians' Unions in Los Angeles, Local 47 for whites and Local 767 for blacks. The issue of racially mixed dancing had caused an embarrassing row at the Hollywood Canteen just two weeks before Chuck Falkner's band was officially hired as house band. "It seems," wrote a *Down Beat* reporter, "that some white girl hostesses decided that there was no reason why they should not dance with Negro soldiers, and some white soldiers saw no reason why they should not dance with Negro girls. They did. Certain persons, evidently women acting as 'chaperones' of the hostesses, attempted to break up this practice. . . ." Subsequently the Canteen's board of directors was persuaded not to prohibit mixed dancing only after film stars John Garfield and Bette Davis "threatened to resign from the board and withdraw the support of the Screen Actors' Guild" if such a rule were passed.[28]

What Billy Byers referred to, looking back in 1990 at the changes in racial attitudes brought about during the previous forty-five years, was not race relations in general in 1943 but the welcoming attitude of blacks toward young white jazz musicians. This attitude was soon to change as a feeling grew among some black enthusiasts of the revolutionary new music of bebop—though not such creators as Charlie Parker and Dizzy Gillespie—that this was black music that whites could only imitate and exploit. In 1952 a letter appeared in *Down Beat* declaring that "Jazz is primarily a Negro art form." The letter went on to assert that when Goodman, Miller, and other popular white bandleaders came "trotting proudly over the ruins [of black big bands] . . . swing died! Again the art form was given new life [by Parker, Gillespie, et al.], and again America's color caste slipped into the picture [with Stan Kenton, George Shearing, Charlie Ventura, and Lee Konitz], and any other whites that could assimilate 'bop,' and bop died!"[29] In 1953 an unidentified black bebop musician told a German jazz critic, "You see, as soon as we have a music, the white man comes and imitates it. We've had jazz for fifty years, and in all those fifty years there has been not a single white man, perhaps leaving aside Bix, who has had an idea. Only the coloured men have ideas. But if you see who's got the famous names, they're all white."[30] A few years later a letter appeared in *Metronome* declaring that no "member of the Caucasian race has ever been and never will be anything in jazz. . . . Now all these punks like Dave Brubeck, Chet Baker and so on are supposed to be inventors in jazz . . . [but] jazz is more than a music—it's a way of life, that no white man has been blessed to live. . . . Your people do not have jazz in their heredity."[31] By the early 1960s, as militant Black Nationalism began to supersede the integrationism of Martin Luther King, white jazz players, far from being automatically welcomed, were often made to feel like interlopers, that jazz was a black music they had no right to play.

Playing jazz was one thing Marsh was not withdrawn about, and in 1944–45 he could be heard sitting in at some of the jazz clubs around town. Ronnie Lang, who was a year or two younger, remembered hearing him around that time at the Hangover Club on Vine Street and being duly impressed not only by his playing but by seeing the seventeen-year-old Marsh toss down a straight shot of whisky. Like Byers, Marsh experienced little, in those early years, of the reverse racism that entered jazz later. He told Whitney Balliett, "When I was seventeen [i.e., in 1944–45] I began sitting in with Dexter Gordon and Wardell Gray and Lawrence Marable."[32] In another interview he said, "There was Stan Getz and Zoot Sims, Wardell Grey. . . . It was lovely."[33] He was speaking not of Hollywood but of the scene on Central Avenue: "[T]he real jazz was being played in the coloured district, Central Avenue. That's where you had to go for all the action. . . . I grew up there—it was the one link to the East Coast, Kansas City, and where music was really being played."[34] Another musician that he heard and probably met in those early years was tenor saxophonist Allen Eager. "There was a club we used to play at, on Hollywood Boulevard. This was when Eager was 17 or 18, and I was 15 or 16. '43 and '44 . . . . I think he was from L.A., wasn't he?. . . He had a life in New York I didn't know about, because I was 16. I hadn't been out of L.A. He knocked me out when I heard him in L.A."[35]

According to Byers, he, Warne, and other more advanced players not only sat in on Central Avenue and Hollywood Boulevard but also started to get calls for studio recording dates, because as older musicians were drafted there were fewer and fewer left who could read and play well enough for the studios, and few blacks were hired.

Among the people Marsh met when he sat in at jazz clubs around town was a young undergraduate trumpet player and physics student at a local university.[36] They met outside a club on Hollywood Boulevard. Besides music, they shared at that time a fondness for marijuana. Their friendship spanned over forty years, and in the 1970s and 1980s he was at times Marsh's connection for a far more dangerous drug, cocaine, the easy availability of which was to prove regrettable.

Marsh summed up his feeling about Los Angeles in an interview: "In the 'thirties and 'forties . . . Los Angeles was no place for a musician. I didn't feel I was even serious about music until I got to New York. L.A. was like a frontier. When I was growing up, the popular music that you could hear on Hollywood Boulevard was Dixieland; the best thing I remember [there] was Errol Garner, working in a club before anyone knew him. . . ."[37]

In August of 1945 the war ended, and in the fall Marsh enrolled as a music major at the University of Southern California (USC), whose records list Marsh as a student from November 1945 to April 25, 1946. For at least part or possibly all of the time up until late April 1946, he continued to work with the Teen-Agers on the Carmichael show, as an extant broadcast tape on which he is the featured soloist on "Apple Honey" finds him being introduced as "Warne Marsh of USC." But on April 27, 1946, despite the fact that the war was over, he was inducted into the army. He has been quoted as saying he was drafted, but in one interview he phrased it differently: "I was inducted as a musician and was sent [to Camp Lee, Virginia] for six weeks of training unit. . . ."[38] His friend and fellow Tristano student Ted Brown, who met Marsh at Camp Lee, believes he enlisted, and after exactly eighteen months he was in fact discharged as "Regular Army," which would not have been the case if he had been drafted. It seems likely that, believing he would be drafted anyway, he made a deal with army recruiters whereby he would be assigned as a musician in return for enlisting.

Shortly after his arrival at Camp Lee he was placed in a newly organized Special Services dance band. It was at Camp Lee that he heard about the blind pianist Lennie Tristano and his method of teaching. His subsequent contact with Tristano was the pivotal event of his musical life.

NOTES

1. Whitney Balliett, "A True Improviser." *New Yorker,* October 14, 1985, 113.
2. Quoted in Terry Martin and John Litweiler, unpublished interview, October 14, 1973.
3. Beverly Carpenter McComb, interview, c. March 1991.
4. Francis Davis, "Warne Marsh's Inner Melody," *Down Beat,* January 1983, p. 17.
5. Balliett, 114.
6. Martin and Litweiler, op. cit.
7. Balliett, 114. Marsh told Balliett that he started with Gillette when he was sixteen, but he may have started the summer before his sixteenth birthday, when Gillette returned to Los Angeles after receiving a medical discharge from the

army. See Hal Holly, "Los Angeles Band Briefs," *Down Beat,* June 15, 1943, 4. Also relevant is Holly's "Los Angeles Band Briefs," *Down Beat,* February 25, 1946, 6: "Saw entire sax section of Jimmy Higson's 'Teen-Agers' ork [of which Marsh was a member] leaving Mickey Gillette sax school. They all study there."

8. "Warne Marsh—A Conversation with Robert Ronzello," *Saxophone Journal* (Spring 1982): 11.

9. Ibid., 16.

10. Information about Chuck Falkner's band, here and elsewhere, was obtained principally through interviews with Betty Churchill Conway (now Betty Nearhoff) and Don Walter, both original members of the band. Where such information comes from other sources, it is so indicated.

11. "MCA Sponsors Draftproof Band," *Down Beat,* June 1, 1943, 8.

12. Tom Nolan, "Playing in the Band," *Los Angeles Herald,* 14 July 1985, 8 (California Living).

13. Ibid., 8.

14. Ibid., 9.

15. "MCA Sponsors Draftproof Band," 8.

16. Cunningham's promising career was plagued by drug addiction, and he committed suicide in 1966. His Los Angeles County death certificate, dated January 21, 1966, gives his full name as Harvey Neil Cunningham. The cause of death was "Gunshot wound to the chest." Elected to Phi Beta Kappa in 1951 while a senior at UCLA, he held up a drug store with a toy gun to obtain narcotics in 1952. After seeing his picture on television as a wanted suspect, he attempted suicide by an overdose of cocaine and was subsequently arrested, convicted of robbery, and sentenced to a year in Los Angeles County Jail. He shot himself to death in his apartment at 616 S. Serrano Ave., Los Angeles, on January 21, 1966.

17. Nolan, 9. Also Betty Conway and Don Walter, interviews.

18. Nolan, 9. Also, "Coast Kid Signs As J. D. Drummer," *Down Beat,* August 15, 1945, 7: "Karl Kiffe, eighteen-year-old drummer who has been turning down offers from name bands since he was fifteen, has been signed by Jimmy Dorsey. . . . Kiffe recently closed a long run as a specialty act with the Hollywood stage show *Blackouts of 1945.*"

19. Nolan, 9. Also Conway, interview.

20. Ronnie Lang, interview.

21. Nolan, 9. Also Conway and Walter, interviews. Walter thought that the *Blackouts* and Canteen jobs overlapped for at least a year, but Conway, who kept a scrapbook, had the *Blackouts* job beginning June 13 and ending November 16, 1943. An item in *Down Beat* for December 15, 1943, mentions that the Canteen Kids band "has been featured for past several months in . . . *Blackouts of 1943,*" perhaps indicating that the band was still so featured in December. ("On the Beat in Hollywood," 9.)

22. "On the Beat in Hollywood," *Down Beat,* December 15, 1943, 9.

23. Nolan, 9. Also Conway, interview. I have been unable to locate the Thompson-Williams Brothers film and do not know the exact title. See "Warne Marsh's Recorded Legacy."

24. Martin and Litweiler, op. cit.

25. André Previn, *No Minor Chords* (New York: Doubleday, 1991), 10.

26. Barry Ulanov, "André Previn," *Metronome,* April 1946, 20–21.

27. "Niteries Facing Race Problem," *Down Beat,* March 1, 1943, 6.

28. "Canteen Heads Have Row over Mixed Dancing," *Down Beat,* April 15, 1943, 1, 5.

29. Leroy E. Mitchell Jr. "'Jazz Is Negro Music, Whites Merely Try to Profit from It': Reader," *Down Beat,* March 7, 1952, 10.

30. Quoted in Frank Kofsky, *Black Nationalism and the Revolution in Music* (New York: Pathfinder Press, 1970), 57. Also quoted by Francis Newton, *The Jazz Scene* (Harmondsworth, Middlesex, England: Penguin Books, 1961), 205. Originally in Joachim Ernst Berendt, *Das Jazz buch* (Frankfurt and Hamburg: Fischer Taschenbuch Verlag, 1953), 93–95. Although there is no question that jazz is the creation of black Americans, there has always been a mixture of white and black elements in the music. The notion, in particular, that white big bands merely appropriated and "whitified" what was originally developed by blacks is clearly simplistic. Gene Lees points out that white arrangers like Bill Challis and Will Hudson were composing and arranging for black big bands like Fletcher Henderson's in the 1920s (*Cats of Any Color: Jazz Black and White* [New York and Oxford: Oxford University Press, 1995], 201). And James Lincoln Collier maintains that the basic structure of big band jazz was invented in 1918 by the white composer and arranger Ferde Grofe (Collier, *Jazz: The American Theme Song* [New York: Oxford University Press, 1993], 166–72).

31. G. J., "Heredity Versus Environment," *Metronome,* April 1956, 12.

32. Balliett, 114.

33. "Warne Marsh," *Saxophone Journal* (Spring 1982): 11.

34. Les Tomkins, "The Warne Marsh Story," *Crescendo International* (May 1976): 21.

35. Martin and Litweiler, op. cit.

36. He prefers not to be named.

37. Tomkins, 20–21.

38. "Warne Marsh," *Saxophone Journal* (Spring 1982): 11.

Private Marsh

At Camp Lee Marsh played in the newly formed Second Group Special Services band for approximately nine months. As Camp Lee was a band training center, a number of bands already existed there, but this particular band was in process of being organized when Marsh arrived. According to Jim Lester, who was arranger and lead trombonist for the band, the instigator was a young lieutenant and trombonist named Tommy Thomas. When Lester arrived in the spring of 1946, he immediately ran into another recently arrived trombonist, Don McCrady, who told him he had met an officer Thomas, "who loves to play trombone." Said Lester, "I had some four-trombone arrangements with me; we got together with Tommy, who turned up another trombonist, and the four of us rehearsed these charts whenever we could. Tommy loved it so much he started thinking about a big band. What he had to do to make it happen I don't know, but he identified musicians as they came to the camp for basic training and saw to it that at the end of training they got assigned to his Special Services unit, for which he had obtained its own barracks. Phil Vinceguerro was already a sergeant while we were all privates, and Tommy made him the leader, but he was leader in name only. So gradually the barracks filled up, and beyond the big band there were singers and I believe a comedian."

According to the *Lee Traveller,* the base newspaper, the first nominal leader of the band was probably one Benny Campo, but Campo was discharged in May, when Vinceguerro must have taken over. Said to have been a guitarist in the Tony Pastor band, in later newspaper accounts he is referred to as Phil Vincent.[1] Marsh is never mentioned in these accounts.

Frequently mentioned, besides Vincent, were pianist Dick Mitkowski; trombonist Bruce Hendricks; tenor saxophonist Chuck Cerrito; trumpeter Paul Storberg; drummer Chubby Gale; and bassist Bill Riegel, who with Vincent made up a seven-piece combo that played for weekday dances at servicemen's clubs.[2]

Years later Lester sent Marsh a tape of the big band headed by Vincent. According to Lester, the personnel of the band included several people never named in the *Lee Traveller.* Fred Waters, who became Marsh's closest lifelong friend, was on lead alto, Marsh on jazz tenor, probably Cerrito on second tenor, and Gaynor Maxwell on baritone saxophone. The lead trumpet chair was filled by Herb Patnoe, with the jazz solos handled by Bill West. Lester played lead trombone and McCrady, second. The rhythm section included Jimmy Joyner on drums, Riegel on bass, and Mitkowski on piano, plus a guitarist, possibly Vincent.

Lester recounted how Lt. Thomas's birthday became the occasion for one of Marsh's infrequent forays into arranging, in which he had had no formal training whatsoever. "We all liked Lt. Thomas, so when one of his birthdays rolled around we decided to give him a surprise. The trouble was that we only found out about it the day before. What we did was this: Warne and I went to work, separately and at the same time, on an arrangement of 'Jeannie with the Light Brown Hair,' because Tommy's wife was named Jean. When we finished we got together again, and I threw together a modulation between the two choruses. Then I stayed up late copying out the parts, and at his party the next day the band played it for him, absolutely sight unseen—no time to rehearse. It worked well, and in fact it's on the tape [that Warne had]."

Lester has said that the tape he sent Marsh was the sound track of a film made of the band. Each number is introduced by a professional announcer, who at a point halfway through the program identifies the location as a hospital at Camp Lee. Presumably it is the tape Marsh mentioned to Francis Davis in 1983, when Davis asked him what he sounded like as a teenager: "Like Charlie Parker out of Ben Webster. . . . I've got a tape someone sent me from when I was 19 years old in the army at Camp Lee, Virginia, . . . of the Special Services band we were in."[3]

There are fifteen tenor solos on the tape, and Lester says they are all by Marsh. It is easy to hear the Webster influence, especially on the jump tunes, though Marsh's phrasing is more fluid, reminding one not only of Webster but also of Don Byas. This is especially true of his playing on "Opus 3," a slight variation on "Apple Honey," where Marsh's supple, fleet-fingered solo contains more notes than Webster would have played. But the muscular Websterish vibrato and the swing-era licks are obvious.

The influence of Parker is less noticeable. Though in the early 1940s Parker had made a name for himself with the Jay McShann, Earl Hines, and Billy Eckstine big bands and in jam sessions at Minton's Playhouse and Monroe's Uptown in New York, he recorded little until 1945, partly because of the recording ban imposed by the American Federation of Musicians from 1942 to 1944.[4] Marsh had apparently heard few of Parker's recordings until he got to Camp Lee. There, said Ted Brown, who was also at Camp Lee and met Marsh at that time, he was part of an informal group that liked to listen to Parker records and jam. According to Brown, Marsh was always the quickest to pick up Bird's lines and figures: "He could nail them right away."

One thing he may have picked up was the so-called bebop triplet, a few examples of which occur in Marsh's solos on "Cherokee," "Just the Way You Look Tonight," and "Exactly Like You." But the Parker influence is probably reflected more subtly in the harmonic sophistication of Marsh's playing and his tendency to play longer phrases on some tunes than was customary with swing-era musicians. What might seem to be a direct influence in "Exactly Like You," which begins with the exact same eight notes as Parker's "Cool Blues," is probably a coincidence, as "Cool Blues" was not recorded until February 19, 1947, a month after Marsh left Camp Lee. He may, however, have heard it performed live or on private recordings, perhaps not by Parker but by early Parker devotees. On "Cherokee" the most noticeable feature is not the bebop triplets but the specifically Marshian characteristic of preferring the upper reaches of the horn, a preference that here takes him into the altissimo register and makes it difficult to determine whether it is an alto or a tenor solo. The same tendency, though not so pronounced, is evidenced on several other solos.

Marsh's solos on several tunes—"Exactly Like You," "Just the Way You Look Tonight," "This Is Our Waltz," and "Hopeless Opus," a 16-bar jump tune, seem to indicate a Lester Young influence because of their lighter sound and linear melodic construction. But Marsh made it clear in later interviews that he was not influenced by Young until he was transferred to Fort Monmouth, New Jersey, and was able to hear Young in person in New York and study his music with Lennie Tristano. His teenage years, he said, "were my Ben Webster years. . . . Lester Young was more or less underground. . . . We kids weren't thinking Lester Young; we were thinking Duke Ellington."[5] Elsewhere he said, "I simply wasn't listening well enough to be drawn into Lester when I was younger. That's a fact."[6] On the other hand, he had been greatly impressed as a teenager by hearing and perhaps meeting and jamming with Alan Eager in Los Angeles in 1943–44, and although he later said that what he heard in Eager was Charlie Parker, not Lester Young, he may have subconsciously absorbed some of Eager's Prez-like phrasing as well.[7]

Marsh's first exposure to Lennie Tristano came by way of another musician at Camp Lee, trumpet player Don Ferrara. Ferrara had studied with

Tristano before entering the army and was still corresponding with him. He showed Tristano's letters to Marsh. "They were lessons," said Marsh, "and they seemed exactly what I wanted from a teacher, somebody who could unify what I'd already been exposed to in both classical music and improvisation."[8] In another interview he described in more detail what he found in Tristano's letters to Ferrara: "Oh, it was elementary. It was what a musician needs to know to be able to express himself in the language of music. . . . It was all the rudiments of music that actually you don't get when you go after playing dance band music and playing solos the way kids do. You don't get what classical music does offer if you stay with it long enough, which is polyrhythms and mixed meters and good harmony and ear training, the substance of music."[9]

It is not known whether Marsh also began a correspondence with Tristano at that time. What is known is that around January 27, 1947, as Marsh put it, "through the help of a friend in Personnel I got myself stationed up outside of New York," at Fort Monmouth, New Jersey, only an hour and a half bus ride from New York City.[10] What actually happened, according to Fred Waters's wife, Carol, was that Waters got hold of a lieutenant's uniform from the supply room, strolled into the camp records center, and shifted Marsh's records from a file for personnel to be shipped to Germany to one for transfers to Monmouth. Marsh's motive for going along with Waters's nervy shenanigan was probably in equal measure to avoid going to Germany and to be close to New York, where he could not only immerse himself in the New York jazz scene but also study with Tristano.

At Monmouth, a Signal Corps training center, Marsh played in the band that marched the trainees to class and, at the end of the day, back to the barracks. He also played in a small pick-up dance band along with Darwin Aronoff. Aronoff, an accomplished clarinetist who learned what saxophone he knew from Marsh in exchange for giving Marsh clarinet lessons, played lead tenor in the dance band because he was an excellent reader, with Marsh playing jazz tenor.[11]

Marsh, Aronoff recalled, was "quite virtuosic," on a level far above most of the musicians at Monmouth, with "an unusual dry sound" with little or no vibrato. On Aronoff's testimony, Marsh's sound had already changed from that heard on the tape of the Special Services band at Camp Lee, possibly as a result of his correspondence with Tristano. The marching band at Monmouth was described by Aronoff as "terrible," but it had the virtue of allowing its members a great deal of free time, including weekends from Friday night to early Monday morning, a situation of which Marsh took full advantage.

"By this time," he told Whitney Balliett, "I had heard Charlie Parker and Lester Young, and been completely turned around, I spent every spare minute in New York, listening to Parker and studying with Lennie Tristano."[12] In another interview he said it was "the finest thing my country ever did for me [that] they stationed me" near New York at that time. "This whole city made its impact on me, turned me on to the music. . . . [I]t was the flowering of bebop. I was hearing the best music the country had produced at the age of nineteen; I was studying with Lennie, and associating with Lee. . . . I just loved the early bebop when I heard it—it was such dynamic, substantial music."[13] The whole experience was pivotal for Marsh, as he made clear on another occasion: "I mean, at an impressionable age, to hear Charlie Parker live any night of the week . . . and study with Lennie . . . and be loose in New York City, and by the way, to not only get into Parker and Lester Young but also to hear Bartok for the first time. . . . You know it's just such a trip that it can easily shape your basic thinking. And it has mine."[14]

Nat Hentoff once wrote that Marsh studied with Tristano for only four months while at Fort Monmouth,[15] but in another interview Marsh indicated that he started studying with Tristano immediately after his arrival at Monmouth, which would make his period of study with Tristano closer to the full nine months he was there.[16] At this time he also studied clarinet with Joe Allard of Julliard.

Little more is known about Marsh's activities while in the army. Even his official service record contains only a few basic facts, as a fire in the National Personnel Records Center in St. Louis on July 12, 1973, apparently destroyed his file. Jim Lester said that at Camp Lee, Marsh was stoned on marijuana most of the time. Fortunately he was able to avoid the court martial and imprisonment meted out to Lester Young for using marijuana: there are no records of any disciplinary action against him. Barry Ulanov of *Metronome* once indicated that he had heard him as a "soldier musician," but did not remember when or where.[17] Although one would expect that he might occasionally have played open jam sessions in New York, in interviews he never mentioned it. Possibly Ulanov heard him at sessions with Tristano. His jazz-loving friend from high school, Beverly Carpenter, said he sent her acetates of such sessions that may have dated from this time.[18]

On October 26, 1947, his twentieth birthday, Marsh was discharged at Fort Monmouth from the 389th Band with the rank of Private First Class. He told Balliett that after his discharge he went back to college in California, but although he did return to Los Angeles, the University of Southern California has no record of his re-enrollment there.[19] He seems instead to have spent most of the next year gigging around town and jamming on Central Avenue. Ted Brown, the saxophonist whom he had met at Camp Lee and who would soon join him in New York as a fellow student of Lennie Tristano, remembered jamming with him at the Downbeat Club on Central Avenue with such early West Coast bebop stalwarts as Sonny Criss, Teddy Edwards, Roy Porter, and Hampton Hawes. They may have been joined at such jam sessions by trombonist Billy Byers, Marsh's friend from Canteen Kids days.

For a time Marsh played regularly in a combo led by Butch Stone at the Red Feather, located at Figueroa and Manchester. His colleagues in Stone's band included, at various times, Byers, drummer Karl Kiffe, trumpeter John McComb, and pianist Neil Cunningham, all friends from the pre-army years.[20] He played a few rehearsals and an engagement at the Trianon Ballroom in Southgate with Tom Talbert's thirteen-piece band, sharing the jazz tenor chair with the eccentric but highly regarded Steve White.[21] Jimmy Giuffre, who recruited him for an octet that played a few gigs in 1948, remembered remarking to Marsh on the difficulty of writing good inner lines in contrapuntal music. Marsh's typically dry comment was, "According to who is it a good line?" probably meaning that one should trust his own judgment as to what was good, not criticize himself by textbook standards. Sometime in 1948 he met altoist Hal McKusick, who remembered jam sessions in the guest house at Marsh's home in North Hollywood. Beverly Carpenter remembered the sessions and how Marsh and his musician friends liked to swim in the pool. The pool was green with algae, as Marsh's mother had been unable to maintain the pool and grounds of the three-acre estate, but they swam anyway.

But as Marsh said later, "My head was not in California."[22] Throughout his life he consistently spoke of the New York of the late 1940s and early 1950s as a jazz paradise, "just alive with music, a marvelous, stimulating place to be."[23] Just as consistently he spoke of Los Angeles as a wasteland: "If you wanted jazz, you left L.A. and went to New York. It was quite clear-cut then."[24]

His chance to get back to New York came late in July 1948. Buddy Rich's big band was just finishing a two-month residence at one of Marsh's teenage hangouts, the Hollywood Palladium. Marsh's friend and session mate, Hal McKusick, was lead alto in the band, and when second alto Nick Sands left and Rich turned to McKusick for suggestions on filling the chair, McKusick recommended Marsh. Did he play alto, Rich wanted to know. "No," answered McKusick, "but he has a beautiful delicate sound and he can play in the alto range on tenor." Rich, who according to McKusick wanted more of a bebop band and who was aware of the three-tenor sound of the Woody Herman sax section, agreed to hire Marsh, and McKusick transposed the entire second alto book for tenor, with possibly some help from Marsh. Marsh was skilled at sight-reading and transposing at the same time, so perhaps it wasn't necessary to write out everything. The other members of the saxophone section were Ben Lary (sometimes referred to as Ben Larry or Lowry), who took most of the tenor solos, either Buddy Arnold or Rich's younger brother Mickey, also on tenor, and Harvey Levine, baritone.[25] The band also included Terry Gibbs on vibraphone and Doug Mettome and Johnny Mandel in the trumpet and trombone sections, respectively.

Marsh's first appearance on a commercially available record was as a member of this band. He can be heard, at least as a member of the section, on the monaural *Buddy Rich and His Legendary '47–'48 Orchestra*, Hep CD 12. The liner notes to this record contain several errors and omissions. For one thing, the personnel of the 1947 and 1948 bands was quite different, so that the title should refer to "orchestras," not "orchestra." Also, altoist Nick Sands is mistakenly identified as "Eddie Sands" and should not have been included as a member of the band as of July 20, 1948, as by that time Marsh had replaced him; they never played in the band at the same time. Johnny Mandel is mistakenly listed as playing bass trumpet, whereas he actually played trombone in the 1948 band.[26] And except for Allen Eager, who played in the 1947 band but not the 1948 version, there is no attempt to identify the tenor soloists, except for one tune, Jimmy Mundy's "Queer Street," where it is suggested that a couple of insignificant 4-bar fills might be by either Marsh or Lary.[27] Finally, although three different personnel lists are given for recorded performances on July 20, July 27 (both at the Hollywood Palladium after Marsh joined), and October 28, 1948 (in New York), there is no systematic attempt to correlate tunes with those differing personnel and dates.

Of the tunes on this CD recorded after Marsh joined the band, only five have tenor solos: "Queer Street," recorded at the Hollywood Palladium in July 1948, according to the liner notes; "Fine and Dandy," "Robbin's Nest," "Four Rich Brothers," and "The Carioca," reportedly recorded in October 1948 by the same band that appeared at the Avalon Ballroom in New York.[28] Hal McKusick thought the "Queer Street" fills and the more extended solo on "Robbin's Nest" were probably by Lary, the one on "Four Rich Brothers," by either Marsh or Lary, the one on "Fine and Dandy," possibly by Marsh, and the one on "Carioca," probably by Marsh but possibly by Jimmy Giuffre. Judging solely by stylistic characteristics, all of the four extended solos show a marked Lester Young influence in melodic ideas, phrasing, economy of notes, and tone, and none sound like either the Warne Marsh of Camp Lee or Marsh on his first records with Lennie Tristano in March of 1949, less than six months after he left the Rich band in late 1948.

A week or two after Marsh joined, the band went on a three-month cross-country tour, heading first for Northern California, with Jimmy Giuffre replacing Mickey Rich or Buddy Arnold in San Francisco. The tour ended in New York in October. The band played an engagement at the

Avalon Ballroom on 42nd Street in that month, then moved to the new Clique Club on 52nd Street (which a year later would become Birdland).

In December Rich fired the whole band. As a story in *Down Beat* reported it, after Christmas, "Buddy Rich put his entire band on notice (the musicians were devout boppers who refused to play 'commercial junk' and told Rich so). . . ."[29] Marsh seems to have left the band before then, though he stayed with Rich for a brief time after the band arrived in New York. Ted Brown reported that Marsh was living in a hotel for a short time in that period, which he probably would not have been able to afford except as a member of the band. In an interview he characterized his time with the Rich band "as a means of getting from Los Angeles to New York and paying the way. . . . I quit the band two weeks out of New York."[30]

Marsh's recollection of his only major big band experience was laconically lukewarm: "There was always friction when I soloed, and gradually Rich parcelled out my solos among the other saxophones. Also, I sat right in front of his boom-boom-boom bass drum, which was the size of a small house. I ran into him ten years later, and I was amazed he remembered me."[31] Rich, he said, "could not really get with my playing. . . . He just couldn't hear me."[32]

NOTES

1. "Dance Band Sends Cots," *Lee Traveller,* 8 May 1946, 4.
2. Ibid. See also "Vincent Band Strictly Hep," *Lee Traveller,* 5 June 1946, 4.
3. Francis Davis, "Warne Marsh's Inner Melody," *Down Beat,* January 1983, 27.
4. Because of the loss of jobs for musicians, which the AFM attributed to broadcasting and recording, the union had called for royalties to be paid by record companies for each disc sold. The demand was backed by a ban on instrumental recording beginning August 1, 1942, and lasting roughly two years. Decca and Blue Note came to agreements with the union in September and November 1943, but industry giants Columbia and Victor did not settle until November 1944. See *The New Grove Dictionary of Jazz,* ed. Barney Kernfeld, Vol. 2 (London and New York: Macmillan, 1988), 359–60.
5. Robert Ronzello, "Warne Marsh—A Conversation with Robert Ronzello," *Saxophone Journal* (Spring 1982): 11. This article is bibliographically puzzling. Although the title mentions Ronzello, the interview itself is conducted by a person identified only as "D. W."
6. Terry Martin and John Litweiler, unpublished interview, October 14, 1973.
7. Ibid.
8. Brian Case, "Jaws, Teeth and Lower Lip," *New Musical Express* (England), 17 January 1976, 31.
9. Martin and Litweiler, op. cit.
10. Ibid.

11. Darwin Aronoff, interview.

12. Whitney Balliett, "A True Improviser," *New Yorker*, October, 14 1985, 114.

13. Les Tomkins, "The Warne Marsh Story," *Crescendo International* (May 1976): 21.

14. Ronzello, 13.

15. Nat Hentoff, liner notes to *Warne Marsh*, Atlantic LP 1291, 1958.

16. Ronzello, 11.

17. Barry Ulanov, "Symptoms," *Metronome*, February 1950, 34.

18. Beverly Carpenter McComb, interview. McComb, who married a teenage friend of Marsh's, trumpeter John McComb, in the early 1950s, said that Marsh sent her the acetates when he was studying with Tristano, but could not remember whether the year was 1947, when he was still at Monmouth, or 1948–49, after he had returned to New York as a civilian. The earlier date seems slightly more likely, as the love affair which the pair entered into on Marsh's return to Los Angeles after his discharge from the army broke up when he left again for New York in the late summer of 1948. Still, they may have remained friends, especially considering her interest in jazz. Unfortunately the acetates no longer exist.

19. Balliett, 114.

20. Beverly McComb and Butch Stone, interviews.

21. Tom Talbert, interview.

22. Balliett, 114.

23. Roland Baggenaes, "Warne Marsh," *Coda* (December 1976): 3.

24. Davis, 27.

25. Most of this information about the Rich band comes from interviews with Hal McKusick, Jimmy Giuffre, and Johnny Mandel. See also Alastair Robertson, liner notes to *Buddy Rich and His Legendary '47–'48 Orchestra*, Hep CD 12 mono. A photo of this saxophone section, with Jimmy Giuffre having replaced Mickey Rich or Buddy Arnold as the third tenor, appears in Robertson's liner notes, where the caption misidentifies Marsh and Lary, and another appears in Richard S. Sears, *V-Discs: A History and Discography* (Westport, Conn.: Greenwood Press, 1980), 618.

26. Mandel, interview.

27. Reportedly Rich paid "a lot of money" to Mundy for this arrangement, only to find that it had already been published and was available for $2 in sheet music stores!

28. Robertson, liner notes to Hep CD 12, cited in fn. 24.

29. "First Ten Years of Birdland," *Down Beat*, December 10, 1959, 20.

30. Martin and Litweiler, ibid.

31. Balliett, 114.

32. Martin and Litweiler, op. cit.

Tristano: Guru Extraordinaire

Marsh's principal aim in joining the Buddy Rich band had been to resume his studies with Lennie Tristano, and he must have done so immediately after the band reached New York at the end of October 1948, as by February 1949 he was appearing with Tristano at the Clique Club and by March he was in the recording studio with his mentor.

Born in Chicago on March 19, 1919, Lennie Tristano came to jazz from an extensive classical background. He had studied piano since he was four and had also learned to play cello, clarinet, and tenor saxophone. His eyesight was always weak. He was born during a flu epidemic and at age six suffered a serious attack of measles; both diseases affected his eyes. In 1928, when he became totally blind, he was sent to a state school for the blind and other handicapped students in northern Illinois. There he continued his musical studies, giving recitals, playing for parties, and eventually, from the age of twelve, performing in clubs and saloons off campus.[1]

After years of classical training with heavy emphasis on Bach and Beethoven, at nineteen Tristano entered the American Conservatory of Music in Chicago. "By day he practiced Bach; by night he played clarinet in a Dixieland band. . . . He played tenor saxophone and piano in Latin bands, but then it was back to the piano and Bach."[2] In 1941 he earned his Bachelor of Music degree and subsequently completed all requirements for a Master's except the final exams, but decided to forgo the $500 or so in fees for the degree and to make his way as a working musician in the barrooms of Chicago, mostly on tenor saxophone.[3]

While still at the state school, Tristano had become increasingly attentive to jazz. Two of his earliest influences on piano were Earl Hines, whom
he heard on broadcasts from the Grand Terrace Ballroom in Chicago, and
Teddy Wilson. Another important influence was Art Tatum. As a youngster he was particularly impressed by Tatum's treatment of Massenet's
"Elegie."[4] By 1944, Tristano recalled, "I had reached the point where I
could rifle off anything of Tatum's—and with scandalous efficiency."[5] He
credited Roy Eldridge, whom he had heard in person at the Three Deuces
in Chicago, for his "first electrifying musical experience. . . . [Eldridge]
profoundly influenced my musical development."[6] Other important influences were Louis Armstrong, Billie Holiday, and Lester Young.[7]

As early as 1937 Tristano had begun playing jazz in black clubs in Chicago, feeling "more at home there than anyplace."[8] In 1943, while playing at the Cave of the Winds on Madison Avenue, he met Phil Featheringill, a writer for *Metronome,* associate editor of *Jazz Quarterly,* and
sometime record producer, who became an enthusiastic booster. In the
same year Tristano encountered a fifteen-year-old tenor player named Lee
Konitz. His account of the meeting is memorable:

> I was playing at the Winking Pub in Chicago, and this kid comes up and
> asks to sit in. He was playing tenor saxophone then, and he was horrible,
> atrocious. He was playing with a mickey band at the Paradise Ballroom. I
> told him, 'Forget the tenor, play alto'. . . . Lee studied with me until I left in
> '46, about three years. We got together in New York again in 1948.[9]

Besides Konitz, other students in Chicago included composer, arranger,
and trombonist Bill Russo and pianist Lloyd Lifton. The latter continued
to study with Tristano for thirty years.

Tristano made his first recordings for Featheringill in 1945 with a group
that included another early booster, Woody Herman bassist Chubby Jackson. In mid-1946 Tristano moved to New York and took, if not the town,
at least *Metronome* coeditor Barry Ulanov by storm. He placed second to
Nat "King" Cole[10] among pianists in *Metronome's* annual poll, but that was
good enough for Ulanov to name him Musician of the Year for 1947.[11] He
had previously included Tristano in two Dixieland-versus-Moderns
"battle of the bands" broadcasts in the fall of 1947, along with Dizzy
Gillespie, Charlie Parker, Ray Brown, Max Roach, Billy Bauer, and John
LaPorta, the latter two both admirers and sometime students of Tristano's
from the Herman band. The two broadcasts were on the Mutual network's
Bands for Bonds series on September 13 and 20. Tristano also appeared
on a third Ulanov-organized Mutual broadcast November 8, 1947, with a
somewhat different modernist lineup that included Parker, LaPorta, Bauer,

Fats Navarro, Allen Eager, Tommy Potter, Buddy Rich, and Sarah Vaughan.[12]

Even as a fledgling teacher in Chicago Tristano had begun to formulate very definite ideas about jazz and the teaching of improvisation. First and foremost was his belief that jazz is a fine art, not entertainment, or dance music. Hand-in-hand with this basic tenet went a deep antipathy toward the various forms of commercial music that serious jazz musicians are wont to play to make a living, and toward the club owners and other representatives of the business world who force them to do so.

In an article written in 1944 for Featheringill's *Jazz Quarterly* he declared that "the variegated depravities infecting the Windy City's jazz and musicians have smothered every evidence of originality."[13] This state of affairs was a natural result, he wrote, of "the polluted, acquisitive nature of bookers and cafe owners, who have . . . instilled in the musicians the attitude that they must either conform, commercially, or starve, causing them to commit artistic suicide. Since the high brows refuse to admit that the jazz man is an artist . . . , the applied terminology, instead of being 'artistic suicides,' should be 'commercial casualties.' Any art form must be allowed to grow unhampered; for as soon as it becomes vitiated by the demands of the multitude, the infection spreads and the kill is effected."[14]

In this purist dedication to an art that refuses to traffic with the corrupting marketplace, Tristano was at one with the creators of high modernist art, and it is revealing that late in his life, discussing the emotion requisite to great jazz, he quoted from the famous final passage of Walter Pater's *The Renaissance,* in which Pater extols "the poetic passion, the desire for beauty, the love of art for art's sake."[15] When in 1985 Warne Marsh said, "I became convinced in the bebop days that jazz is a fine art, not a folk music for second-class Americans,"[16] he was echoing Tristano.

He was similarly reflecting Tristano's influence when he called jazz "the most significant music since the Baroque period"[17] and named Béla Bartók as the modern composer who had reintroduced "the interplay of fresh and original melodies."[18] Bach, the culminating genius of the Baroque, and Bartók were Tristano's favorite composers, and under his tutelage Marsh and other students studied Bach's two- and three-part inventions, even playing them in jazz clubs.

The English pianist Ronnie Ball, also a student of Tristano's, described one such occasion when Tristano's group was playing opposite Charlie Parker's: "Amid the noise of the crowd, the Parker boys finished and left the stand, and Lennie sent Warne Marsh and Lee Konitz up there. . . . Then, through the confusion, came the mellow strains of one of Bach's two-part inventions—melodic, precise. And in a few minutes the crowd was hushed. . . . Then Lennie went on with the rest of the boys and with a definite psychological advantage over the stilled crowd."[19]

That Bach and jazz were strongly linked in Tristano's thinking is indicated by his comment that "Bach's inventions need jazz musicians to execute them properly."[20] Indeed, the linkage of jazz to the highest musical expression extended beyond Bach to classical music in general. In his teaching Tristano stressed "that jazz is not an inferior music and that jazz musicians are expected to have greater command of their instruments than classical players."[21]

Besides the insistence on jazz as a fine art and the strong influence of his classical training, an unusual aspect of Tristano's teaching was his interest in psychoanalysis.

Tristano had read deeply in Freud—twenty-seven volumes, Barry Ulanov said—and his friend and student Steve Silverman, now a prominent psychiatrist, described him as "a born analyst," extraordinarily sensitive to his students' extra-musical, emotional problems. As an example of Tristano's psychological acumen, Silverman recounted an incident from his own early psychiatric practice, at a time when he was studying piano with Tristano. On duty in the emergency room of a hospital in Brooklyn, he was called upon to interview a black man whom an intern had diagnosed as depressed and possibly schizophrenic. Silverman found him indeed depressed and disturbed, but the diagnosis of schizophrenia was based on the intern's failure to understand a musical metaphor: "Man," the patient had said, "my whole life I've been able to get through the first eight, but I can never make it through the bridge." Recognizing the allusion to the common AABA song-form, in which each section is eight measures long and the B part is called "the bridge," and having on his mind his scheduled lesson with Tristano that afternoon, Silverman suggested that the patient might like to talk to Tristano. Being a jazz aficionado, the patient was thrilled. Silverman called Tristano and told him the problem, whereupon Tristano talked to the patient for forty-five minutes. Said Silverman, "Lennie knew exactly where the guy was—he completely cooled him out."

Tristano's tendency to see things from a psychoanalytic perspective was vividly and rather recklessly displayed in a statement reported by jazz historian and critic Ira Gitler: "In 1964, when asked what he thought of [John] Coltrane, [Sonny] Rollins, and [Miles] Davis, Tristano answered, 'All emotion, no feeling.' He replied to 'How do you distinguish between the two?' with: 'Well, say I believe that there is no real hysteria or hostility in jazz, their stuff is an expression of the ego. I want jazz to flow out of the id. Putting it another way, real jazz is what you can play before you're all screwed up; the other is what happens after you're screwed up.'"[22]

Tristano also saw the problem of audience in Freudian terms: "Everybody in this country is very neurotic now. They're afraid to experience an intense emotion, the kind of emotion, for instance, that's brought on by good jazz."[23]

In April 1951 the English bassist Peter Ind, a ship's musician aboard the *Queen Mary* who had met Tristano a year or two earlier, began taking lessons from him. He had sat in with Tristano's group at Bop City, and now he settled in New York and became a regular member of the Tristano circle. An intellectually curious, self-educated man, Ind had read with interest a book about Freud that was rather critical of him, and when he mentioned it to Tristano, Tristano urged him to read Freud himself. He did so, reading "almost everything that Freud wrote," and then, prodded by another Tristano student, drummer Jeff Morton, began to read the works of the controversial neo-Freudian Wilhelm Reich, starting with *The Function of the Orgasm.*[24] Though Tristano may have already been familiar with Reich, who had established his Orgone Energy Laboratory in nearby Forest Hills in 1939, it was apparently the enthusiasm of Morton and Ind that led to the Reichian influence on the Tristano circle. "I think it was Jeff," said Ind, "who started this whole scene and for a awhile it was a fact that almost everybody associated with the group at Lennie's was reading Reich."[25] The standard readings were *The Function of the Orgasm,* in which Reich propounded the theory that neurosis was the result of blocked sexual energy and maintained that the cure was the achievement of satisfactory orgasm, and *Character Analysis,* in which the focus was on the breaking down of resistance, or "character armor," in the therapeutic situation.

In this period, probably sometime in 1951, said Ind, Tristano's brother Michael came to New York to share Tristano's house. A trained psychologist, Michael was, in Ind's words, "very aware of Reich but he expressed doubts about whether he'd be able to give character analysis not having the training."[26] Despite his reservations, Michael agreed to try his hand at Reichian therapy, "so a number of us started in therapy with Michael Tristano and others went to different doctors that Reich had trained. At that time in New York there were about 20 doctors who had studied with Reich and the scene was very strong."[27]

Ind was deeply and permanently influenced by Reich's ideas, especially his later theories of beneficent cosmic, or "orgone," energy. He built several of his own orgone boxes, what Reich called Orgone Energy Accumulators. The orgone box was a six-sided affair roughly the size of a telephone booth, made of metal on the inside and wood on the outside. The idea was to sit in it and absorb orgone energy. "I found that I got the results he got," said Ind, "and I felt the feelings in the accumulator. . . ."[28] After the Food and Drug Administration charged Reich in 1954 with distributing a fraudulent therapeutic device, Ind said, "I started to doubt it. . . . So I did more and more experiments and then it got to the point where I couldn't doubt any longer. I realized that here were great discoveries that were being ignored. . . ."[29] Reich's ideas about beneficent and life-creating cosmic energy later led Ind to propound his own cosmology, challenging the scientific status quo, in a cogently reasoned book titled *Cosmic Metabolism and Vortical Accretion*. He also wrote an unpublished book about Reich.

Among other Tristano students who read Freud and Reich and underwent at least some therapy with Michael Tristano were pianist Sal Mosca, who stayed with Michael for several years, and Marsh, who told French interviewers that he had consulted with Michael "briefly."

Marsh's comments on jazz and psychoanalysis to his French interviewers are noteworthy. In the New York of the early 1950s, he said, there was a current of thought which viewed jazz and psychoanalysis as the two great cultural revolutions of the modern era. He was led, therefore to read Freud and Reich, but said his reading was more important to him than any visit to an analyst, just as the discipline that jazz requires had taught him more than any therapy. For anyone, he concluded, who wishes to be creative, "the first task is to know oneself, and this is also the goal of psychoanalysis."[30]

According to Steve Silverman, jam sessions at Tristano's studio, far from being competitive "cutting sessions," were unique for their atmosphere of psychological sophistication, most of the students either being in therapy, considering therapy, or at least sensitive to the non-musical, psychological difficulties of improvising.

Silverman's perception of Tristano as "a born analyst" is that of a long-time student and friend. Another mental health professional holds a less admiring view of Tristano as amateur psychologist.[31] This observer, who in the early 1950s was an enthusiastic young Tristano fan and is now a practicing psychoanalyst, attended two of Tristano's Saturday night jam sessions for his students and found them "very peculiar experiences." The studio would be darkened, with the blind Tristano, oblivious to the dark, padding about in bathrobe and slippers. After the playing, the lights would go on and Tristano would conduct a kind of therapy session with the whole group, visitors as well as students, during which he would give advice about everyday problems—love affairs, jobs, living arrangements. The future psychoanalyst felt a "messianic," "mind-control" quality in Tristano.

Whether Tristano was a Svengali, as many felt, or a born psychotherapist, his conviction that personal, non-musical problems could adversely affect the jazz improviser, and that psychotherapy could help free one to be more creative, marks him as a distinctly independent thinker in the jazz community.

It seems, however, that Tristano's understanding of psychoanalysis came entirely from books, not from actual therapeutic experience. When his marriage to Judy Moore began to unravel around 1954–55, he insisted that they both see an analyst. Judy agreed, and Tristano participated in one session in the classic style, lying on the couch. But while Judy continued, Tristano quit after the one session, fearing that analysis might interfere with his art.[32]

It is not uncommon for people whose initial enthusiasm for psychoanalysis stems from books to discover that the actual therapeutic experience is unsettling or intolerable, especially if they are strong personalities like Tristano. But in this instance Tristano found himself in the ironical position of having for years recommended to his students, for the good of their art, what he himself refused to undergo, for the good of his own art.

Whatever light that sheds on Tristano's character—Judy Tristano, later Judy Gilbert, said flatly that what he sought, in his personal relations, was control—it is clear that by introducing psychoanalytical concepts into his teaching and by playing the role of guru and father figure, Tristano created a special, cult-like atmosphere that, while strongly attracting some, repelled others. Hal Grant, born Harold Granowsky, the drummer on Marsh's first record with Tristano, was one who was repelled, ending his association with Tristano after about six months. He described Tristano as a magnetic personality, extremely intelligent, who loved to surround himself with students who needed a father figure. Many such students, for their part, would walk around with their eyes closed, to feel what it was like to be blind like Tristano, and would adopt Tristano's whispery style of talking, his preference for black coffee, his way of holding his coffee cup, even his way of sitting. Warne Marsh, said Grant, was one of those who adopted Tristano's mannerisms.

Another who chafed under Tristano's regimen was clarinetist and alto saxophonist John LaPorta. A member of Woody Herman's "First Herd," LaPorta had met Tristano in Chicago in 1946 when Tristano brought a piece of music to a Herman rehearsal. After Tristano moved to New York, LaPorta studied with him. He was almost the same age as Tristano, being seven or eight years older than Marsh and Konitz, but he felt that Tristano treated him "like a whipping boy," and he discontinued his studies around 1949 or 1950. In a subsequent conversation he told Tristano that he left because "you were never wrong, there was no space for me."

LaPorta felt very strongly that Marsh's self-imposed subjection to Tristano was a mistake. He recounted an incident at one of Barry Ulanov's informal Monday night literary seminars for Tristano and his students. Marsh and Konitz had just completed one of their first recording sessions, and they played cuts from it. On hearing one of Marsh's solos, Tristano shook his head and clicked his tongue. "What's wrong?" asked Marsh. Tristano, who according to LaPorta habitually referred to himself as "Lennie" or "we," said, "Lennie thinks you don't believe anymore." LaPorta thought that he was referring to some Lester Young quotes in the solo. To LaPorta, the quotes were perfectly appropriate. "I didn't find anything for him to be upset about—but it was a mind game that was going on. I said, 'Lennie, are you talking about those Lester Young quotes?' And he said, 'Yeah, Lennie doesn't think that Warne really believes; he's lost it in terms of what we're trying to do here.' I said, 'Would you prefer him doing some of your five-beat phrases?' Total silence. I looked at Warne, and he looked like he had been hit with a hammer. He just completely crumpled up."

LaPorta had always admired Marsh: "Of all the people there, including Lennie, I thought Warne was the greatest talent. I think Lennie had a great mind, but Warne had tremendous intuitive talent, creative talent. He was the creative one, to me." After the incident in Ulanov's Greenwich Village apartment, he talked to Marsh under a street lamp for two or three hours, advising him to leave Tristano. "I told him, 'Look Warne, you've got talent. Stand up on your own two feet, do your thing, and get away from this sickness. You've got talent, but you've got to stand up for it.' But I got nowhere. He was completely snowed by Lennie."

Steve Silverman, while denying that Tristano was a Svengali, conceded that he "set up the preconditions for idealization." Tristano, he maintained, was quite aware that his relation to many of his students involved what psychoanalysts call "transference," essentially a dependent, child-to-parent relationship, and, like a good psychoanalyst, knew that progress required that the student transcend his dependence.

That Tristano had some such understanding was suggested by Sal Mosca: "Lennie told me something years ago. He feels that one of the ways for a person to become independent is to move through a stage where you are dependent. . . . For instance, if you are studying with a teacher, just be completely, as much as possible, dependent on his direction . . . and through this almost total dependence, you will find your own independence."[33] Whether or not Tristano was rationalizing an inclination to dominate, he did constantly stress that the ultimate goal of his teaching was to enable the student to achieve his or her own musical individuality, free of imitation or dependence on others.

All of these factors—the self-conscious insistence on jazz as a fine art, the strong classical influence, the purist attitude toward commercial music, the Freudian orientation, the cultist atmosphere—served to set Tristano and his students apart from the Parker-inspired beboppers, despite the friendly relations between Tristano and such key figures as Max Roach and Parker himself. "Negro beboppers were not drawn to Lennie," wrote

Ira Gitler.[34] Neither were white beboppers, although altoist Phil Woods took enough lessons as a teenager "to realize what I didn't know."

For their part, many of Tristano's students were intent on separating themselves from the rest of the jazz world. "You were supposed to walk on the other side of the street" from the boppers, said Hal Grant. "The attitude was 'We have to stay to ourselves to maintain artistic purity.'" Tristano himself, in an article in 1947, had scolded the boppers for their "supercilious attitude and lack of originality" as well as for their "self-destructive habits," for example, their tendency, in imitation of Charlie Parker, to become addicted to heroin. As always, his language was vivid and provocative: imitators of Dizzy Gillespie were "little monkey-men [who] steal note for note the phrases of the master."[35]

Beyond all this, the fact was that Tristano's musical conception was significantly different from that of the boppers, however much he admired Parker. A principal difference was his notion of the role of the rhythm section. According to Jack McKinney, "He considered the drummer as a timekeeper, and he was particularly adverse [*sic*] to drum solos by bombastic players who make more noise than music."[36] He was also averse to drummers who accented beats 2 and 4, as most were in the habit of doing. He wanted a relatively even rhythmic flow from the drummer in order to accommodate his melodic ideas, which emphasized long lines that often superimposed different rhythms over the basic 4/4 pattern. Drummers who took too many liberties were apt either to get lost or to clash with what Tristano and his horn players wanted to do. As bassist Peter Ind put it, speaking from his extensive experience in Tristano's rhythm sections: "Lennie was doing things that were beyond the bop vocabulary, and he found that many drummers were not sensitive enough for his music. . . . Lennie would develop a phrase that had a melodic rhythm of say 7, and superimpose a rhythmic accent of 3 and then play this recurring pattern with an underlying pulse of 4/4—no wonder drummers got anxious! Bird and Pres played phrases that crossed bar lines, but Lennie had taken that several steps further, and unless the drummer really understood what he was doing, attempts to play fills in the usual way between the soloist's phrases led to some pretty weird clashes. Lennie would say, 'Just keep that pulse going, whatever you do don't interrupt the pulse.'"[37] Miles Davis made a similar point about Tristano and bass players: "He invents all the time, and as a result, when he works with a group, the bass player generally doesn't know what Lennie's going to do. . . . He should write three or four bass lines, so that the bassist can choose."[38]

Ind felt that the conception of the rhythm section advanced by Tristano and adopted by his horn players was an imposed theoretical idea that not only limited group creativity but wasn't even what they really wanted.

"What I think went wrong with that group around Lennie, and particularly so with Warne, is that what they wanted was something that wouldn't get in their way . . . but they weren't equally open and giving to the rhythm section. The greatest creativity . . . comes when everybody is listening to everybody else, and they spark each other. They thought they wanted a specific thing. It didn't fit the bill, and then they would be moaning because it wasn't working . . . and then maybe they'd hire somebody who didn't give a shit about what they were doing and just went his own way, and peculiarly enough, they liked that."

Additionally, Ind pointed out, there was a human cost: "I felt bruised by it all, because the rhythm section was treated like a commodity, and if the commodity was wearing out or substandard, it was just discarded and another one was put in its place."

Other differences between Tristano and the beboppers concerned the use of counterpoint and simultaneous improvisation, important elements of traditional New Orleans jazz which Tristano valued and the boppers did not; and, most obviously, that overall, un-bluesy tone or feeling of Tristano's music that made him a founder of the "cool" school and the center of a running controversy regarding emotion and intellect in modern jazz.

The technical aspects of Tristano's teaching began with listening to a select group of jazz masters. Tristano believed that only a very few musicians had been responsible for the important developments in jazz.[39] His pantheon consisted of seven players: Louis Armstrong, Earl Hines, Roy Eldridge, Lester Young, Charlie Christian, Charlie Parker, and Bud Powell.[40] These he considered "the major innovators in the history of jazz up until 1945."[41]

One may well be struck by the omissions in this list: Jelly Roll Morton, for instance, or Duke Ellington, or one of his own major influences, Art Tatum. As for Morton, Ellington, and other composer/arrangers such as Fletcher Henderson, Tristano argued that jazz is the art of improvisation, not of orchestration.[42] He did accord secondary niches to Billie Holiday[43] and to Billy Kyle as a precursor of Bud Powell,[44] and he acknowledged his own debt to Tatum.[45] But he never included Coleman Hawkins or any other saxophonist of that school, such as Ben Webster or Chu Berry, on his list, and the only trumpet player after Eldridge he considered worth studying was Fats Navarro.[46] Of his basic list of seven, the player for whom he felt the greatest affinity, because of his melodic inventiveness and purity of feeling, was probably Lester Young.[47]

Studying the solos of past masters was not new in jazz. What was decidedly new, however, was the emphasis Tristano placed on singing them. It was not enough merely to transcribe a solo from a record and then learn it on one's instrument. Before his students were allowed to do either, they were required to sing it perfectly. If the student were studying a solo by Charlie Parker, he had to sing it so well with the record that he could no longer hear Parker but only the rhythm section.[48] Sal Mosca said he spent a year and a half on Parker's solo on "Scrapple from the Apple" before Tristano allowed him to play it on piano. Steve Silverman described the resulting physiognomic experience as magical—"It gets into your bones."

An incident related to this training was recounted by Billy Bauer. On an occasion when Tristano's group shared the bill with Charlie Parker at Birdland, Miles Davis, a member of Parker's group, approached Bauer, Marsh, and Konitz to ask if they were familiar with a certain solo. By way of answer Marsh and Konitz sang it for him, in unison. Bauer did not remember whose solo it was, but Lee Konitz said in 1994 that it must have been by Parker or Lester Young, many of whose solos they studied under Tristano.[49]

Tristano insisted that the student know all major and minor scales, be able to identify "everything from the interval to the triad to the seventh, ninth, eleventh, and thirteenth chord," to identify keys, and "to play every piece in every major and minor key."[50] He placed great emphasis on rhythmic fundamentals: "We begin by patting hands before we get into the instrument. I use a metronome, but no one can be as true as a metronome. It takes a long time, and I just want my people to start with half notes, playing even with the metronome."[51] After students became comfortable with simple rhythms, they moved on to polyrhythms, such as superimposing three-, five-, or seven-note figures over a two- or four-beat base.[52] "Mixed meter," said Marsh, "is something we consciously train[ed] ourselves to use. Also, polyrhythms. . . . Beyond the study of harmony and ear-training, which is a part of learning to improvise, and rhythm, there are really only two other things that happen in creating a melodic line. That's phrasing, or meter, and mixed-meter, which is a complexity of meters."[53]

Tristano's major emphasis, however, was on melody. As Lloyd Lifton said, "We were trying to play an original line, rather than just what everyone else was playing—which was based upon Charlie Parker's music."[54] Tristano felt that "no one in jazz had given sufficient attention to melodic development. He thought the melodies of jazz could be just as memorable as an operatic aria."[55]

As a means to melodic development, Tristano had his students write out new melodies over the chord changes of popular songs as they would ideally like to improvise them.[56] These melodies, or lines, tended to use long phrases that ran over the bar lines, displacing the meter and phrasing of the original in odd ways. Compositions such as Marsh's "Marshmallow" and "Background Music" (based on "Cherokee" and "All of Me," respectively), Konitz's "Subconscious-Lee" (based on "What Is This Thing

Called Love"), and Ted Brown's "Featherbed" (based on "You'd Be So Nice to Come Home To") were exercises of this sort. Such exercises, said Brown, heightened one's awareness of the structure and possibilities of a tune, "filtered out a lot of junk," and made one think about what one wanted to say.

Late in his life Marsh elaborated at length on "Marshmallow" as an exercise in applied theory: "[I]t is, like a lot of those lines, one that we worked on for lessons. . . . This one is an exercise in polytonality, which are tonalities on top of tonalities. . . . You can make a pyramid of major seventh chords moving upwards in fifths. So, C Major [seven: CEGB] plus G Major seven [GBDF#], plus D Major seven [DF#AC#] gives you some notes that are quite different in the second octave. . . . Hindemith was doing it fifty years ago in classical music. That's his concept of polytonality. . . . A [major] seventh chord [e.g., CEGB] has got a major [CEG] and a minor triad [EGB] inside of it. There are, in other words, two harmonies within a major seventh chord, and they can both be used as tonal centers. In a [major] ninth chord [e.g., CEGBD] there are two seventh chords and then [you can add] the augmented 11th [F#] major sound, which is just looking at the notes C Major plus G Major seventh. They overlap; the scales overlap, and there is the theory right there. . . . You're in two keys. You can think in either one. The piano player can play in one, and the horn can play in another. . . . So that's what that song ["Marshmallow"] is; that line is an exercise."[57]

In the 1980s Marsh gave a seminar at Berklee School of Music in which he detailed Tristano's exercises for gaining tonal and rhythmic control of a motif. Starting with a simple, four-note motif, one would practice it forward, backward, and inverted on every degree of every major and harmonic minor scale, then on every degree of every chord of that scale, including such extensions as flat or sharp ninths and sharp elevenths. Then one would practice the motif in various polyrhythmic forms—three against two, two against three, four against three, three against four, etc. And finally one would practice what Tristano called displacement by starting the motif at different places in the bar—for example on beat one, on the "and" of beat one, on two, the "and" of two.[58]

The goal of Tristano's teaching, however, was always improvisation, not composition. "Tristano insists jazz is an improvised art, and his emphasis has not been upon composition; improvisation is instant composition."[59] However much jazz is characterized by bent notes, the blues scale, or the all-important swinging pulse, Tristano saw its creative essence as improvisation, the spontaneous creation of original melody.

Peter Ind reflected his years of study with Tristano when he cited the improvised melody as the basic challenge in jazz: "It's comparatively easy to go up and down on an instrument and sound like you've got complete mastery, but it's something else to develop a musical line and let it take you, and have the facility, . . . the musicality to follow it through and not lose it. Because what often happens with the jazz musician is that he gets an idea and it's beautiful but it gets out of hand, he can't hold it. His musicality or technique is not enough and he has to let it go. But being able to follow your ideas through—that's what jazz is really about."[60]

For Tristano, being a jazz improviser meant walking the edge between spontaneous creation and disciplined technique, being able simultaneously to conceive and execute original ideas, without relying on preconceived or habitual licks, patterns, or figures.

Tristano's music was often characterized by his detractors as "cold" and "intellectual," and an aspect of his teaching that should be discussed here is his thinking regarding the expression of emotion in music. He made an easily misunderstood distinction between emotion and feeling. "For my purposes . . . emotion is a specific thing: happiness, sadness, etc. But when I listen to the old Count Basie band with Pres, it is impossible to extract the particular emotion. But on the feeling level it is deep and profoundly intense. Feeling is practically basic to jazz."[61] He saw emotion as coming from the ego, or personality, and feeling from the id, a deeper level.[62] If one looks past the sloppy use of Freudian terminology, his meaning seems to be that what he calls emotion is superficial, even false, an egotistical or shallow appeal for audience response. The response it asks for is unearned because it comes not from the depth of the music itself but from something egotistically or sentimentally imposed on it. What he calls "feeling" appears to be simply the creative intensity of the music, the internal logic of the notes themselves. A critic, Al Zeiger, understood this aspect of Tristano's aesthetic perfectly: "The attempt to achieve a 'sweet' sound is no longer present in this music. The musical idea and its development is of prime importance. . . . It is a reaction against music that is sentimental and chiefly coloristic in nature."[63] The last statement referred specifically to the free jazz pieces "Intuition" and "Digression," but it applies equally to all of Tristano's music, and to his teaching. Jack McKinney stated it this way: "Tristano wants the student to be lyrical, but he does not want him to be effusive; he should develop beautiful melodies, but they cannot be saccharine. As any artist expresses himself melodically, he must walk a thin line between artistic expression and excessive emotion. Part of the art is in holding back the emotional expression. . . ."[64]

Marsh expressed a similar idea about ego and emotion. To the question of how the musician "should infuse emotion into his playing," Marsh replied, "He has no choice. . . . He has to let himself be the instrument of creating music, or he has to impose something of his personality on his playing. He can only go those two ways, and he's making an artistic mistake if he goes the second way. The second way is characteristic of all egotistical arts."[65] Again, the emotion, or in Tristano's terms the feeling, is in the music, intrinsically, not superimposed on it.

In another interview the same distinction is suggested, though not stated explicitly, in Marsh's comparison of Lester Young with Coleman Hawkins and Ben Webster: "Lester never wastes a motion, he's the most economical player I know, and that's art, that's artistic playing. Ben and Hawk are a little more emotional. The balance between emotion and substance is tipped towards emotion with both Ben and Hawk, but with Lester it's a perfect balance between emotion or feeling and the substance of his melodies."[66] Here Marsh confuses the issue by using "emotion" and "feeling" as synonyms, but it is clear that what he calls "the substance of his melodies" is the structural logic of the lines themselves, which is where Tristano locates intensity or feeling.

Marsh's approach to tone is obviously connected to this Tristanian antipathy to sentimental or egotistical playing. It is not true that Marsh used no vibrato, any more than it is true that Lester Young used none. It only seems like none in contrast to players like Hawkins and Webster. Marsh described Young's tone in exactly the same terms he used for Young's playing overall: "When I heard Lester Young, things really changed once and for all for me, as far as tone goes. Lester's tone is totally economical—he never wastes a bit of energy. Just on academic grounds, that appeals to me. To me, that's efficiency."[67] Asked how he felt about players who use a wide, pronounced vibrato, he replied, "Fixed vibratos do not sound like they are a part of the music. A great vibrato does sound like an inherent, integral part of the music. Like Charlie Parker's. Lester's is beautiful, Billie Holiday's is great. Roy Eldridge had a great one." What about the vibratos of Ben Webster or Johnny Hodges, the interviewer asks, do you consider them valid? "No," replied Marsh, "I don't, because it's emotional without necessarily relating to the substance of the music."[68] Marsh used vibrato sparingly, foregoing it entirely at times, varying it to fit his ideas and the particular song he was playing. As Ted Brown has noted, in up-tempo pieces he had a way of using vibrato at the very end of a note to push it to the next and generate rhythmic excitement.

Finally, one must confront the racial aspect of Tristano's music. One study describes the Tristano school as "a branch of the white modern jazz school on the East Coast. . . . The members of the Tristano school were few in number and, with the exception of drummer Denzil Best on some record sessions, included no Negro adherents."[69] The description is accurate, though somewhat misleading, considering that prominent black musicians like Charlie Parker, Max Roach, Miles Davis, and Charles Mingus voiced respect for Tristano's music.

Lee Konitz, when asked why he was drawn to Tristano's approach as opposed to Parker's, said, "I think one of the basic differences was that it was coming from the white viewpoint. My inspirations were black musicians, basically. . . . [But] Charlie Parker was remote to me—I just knew him through the few 78-rpm records that were available at that time—and Tristano was articulating the philosophy that certainly made a big difference. . . . I just felt that I could identify more with that approach. I thought that I belonged there. I've always, to this day, felt almost apologetic for intruding on the black jazz musicians' terrain. Because they have been the major figures. [But] of course I understand that we're all entitled to play theme and variations."[70]

Konitz believed that Tristano consciously thought of himself as the creator of a "white" type of jazz that drew not only on the innovations of black musicians like Louis Armstrong, Lester Young, and Charlie Parker but also on those of European classical composers like Bach, Bartók , and Hindemith. Saxophonist Lew Tabackin felt that the result was that Tristano "took the blackness out of the music."[71]

There is no question of racism here. Tristano repeatedly acknowledged the primacy of black musicians in the creation and development of jazz, and his models without exception were black. But in the face of a rising chorus of black cultural nationalism that declared that jazz was not merely historically but in its essence a black music, and that authentic innovation in jazz could only be made by blacks,[72] Tristano declared that the music was universal, and that the dominance of American blacks as major innovators was due to environment, not genetics: "[N]obody has a corner on music. Let's be logical. There are Negroes and/or slaves all over the world, but nothing like jazz ever happened anywhere but here in this country. . . . So you get to the point where you must realize this is an environmental thing. True, most of the great originators have been Negro. But that's because of environment. If Charlie Parker had been born in China, he would have been a great musician, I'm sure; but he wouldn't have invented bop."[73]

In the sense that the blues were noticeably in short supply in the repertoire of Tristano and his students, it is true that he "took the blackness out of the music." But one might say the same about one of Tristano's black models, Art Tatum, whose repertoire, like Tristano's, consisted mainly of popular songs of the 1920s, 1930s, and 1940s by white composers such as George Gershwin, Cole Porter, or Jerome Kern, and who seldom played the blues, at least on record. Billie Holiday's repertoire was similar. And it should be remembered that Tristano's great memorial to Charlie Parker on learning of his death, "Requiem," was a blues piece, albeit with an introduction drawn strictly from the classical tradition.

Like Tristano, Warne Marsh repeatedly acknowledged the seminal role of black Americans in the development of jazz while maintaining the authenticity of white contributions: "It really is curious the way jazz is underrated in its country of origin. Part of it is that its significance is over-looked because it's a black art—in spite of the fact that it has produced significant black musicians—by any standards Charlie Parker is a major artist; if you put him up alongside Bach or Bartók, he still is substantial. In America, though, there's the question of who's a first-class citizen and who's not, and can a second-class citizen produce fine art? And automatically, the assumption is: it's folk music, it's not art. . . . The American Negro has produced the folk music that's called jazz, and that's that. By this time you would think there were enough white musicians who have made a career of what the Negro started to give the lie to that."[74] And again: "What led up to bebop was 50 or 60 years of honest music by the American black. His day is yet to come as a musician. The musicians in America know what's going on but the people at large still regard jazz as folk music. . . . It's not art, it's folk music. That's what they think, and it's stupid."[75]

Marsh has occasionally been quoted as making remarks concerning whites and blacks in jazz that seem to have a racist tinge. Lew Tabackin reported that after his lone record date with Marsh, Marsh maintained that the only model for tenor saxophonists was Lester Young. When Tabackin asked, "What about Coleman Hawkins?" Marsh replied, "That's the black way of playing. They bend notes." The comment is absurd on the face of it. Not only were both Young and Hawkins black, but Marsh himself was strongly influenced by Hawkins and Ben Webster. Beyond that, he was in no way reluctant to bend notes, as any listener will hear. Probably the comment was expressive mainly of a desire to pick a quarrel with Tabackin, whose playing is heavily influenced by Hawkins, Webster, and Don Byas to the virtual exclusion of Lester Young.

Again, the English saxophonist Gary Windo, who studied with Marsh in the 1980s, reported that Marsh once said, "Whites should not play the blues, because blues are not a part of their experience." This is hardly a racist remark but simply an acknowledgment of cultural differences between whites and blacks. Marsh, of course, did play the blues, sometimes magnificently, sometimes perfunctorily. What he is really saying is that authenticity is basically a matter of personal integrity. It is easy enough for a white player to adopt conventional black mannerisms in playing the blues, but where does that leave him in his quest for authentic self-expression? If he is true to himself and his heritage, he will play the blues, if he plays them at all, as he plays everything else, in his own unique way, from the depths of his own experience. He will resist the temptation, which can be very strong, to pretend to be black and will search out his own individual and cultural identity.

Some such argument seems to underlie the comments of Marsh and Konitz as well as the virtual exclusion of the blues from the Tristano repertoire. Its basic assumption is that the essence of jazz lies not in its "blackness" but in its commitment to melodic improvisation. In practice, since Tristano's students almost without exception were white, this set of attitudes meant that Tristano's studio became a center for the serious study of what and how whites could authentically contribute to historically black music.

NOTES

1. John Francis McKinney, *The Pedagogy of Lennie Tristano* (Ph.D. dissertation, Fairleigh Dickinson University, 1978), 10–11. Also see Barry Ulanov, "Master in the Making," *Metronome,* August 1949, 14, 32.
2. McKinney, 12.
3. Ulanov, 32.
4. McKinney, 12.
5. Bill Coss, "Lennie Tristano Speaks Out," *Down Beat,* December 6, 1962, 20.
6. McKinney, 12.
7. Ibid., 13.
8. Ibid., 14.
9. Ibid., 79–80.
10. "Metronome's All Stars," *Metronome,* January 1948, 37.
11. "Musician of the Year—Lennie Tristano," *Metronome,* January 1948, 19.
12. Barry Ulanov, "Moldy Figs vs. Moderns," *Metronome,* November 1947, 15, 23. Also [Barbara] Hodgkins, "Winners Take All," *Metronome,* December 1947, 10.
13. Lennie Tristano, "What's Wrong with Chicago Jazz," *Jazz Quarterly* (Spring 1945): 23.
14. Ibid., 23.
15. McKinney, 31.
16. Whitney Balliett, "A True Improviser," *New Yorker,* October 14, 1985, 116.
17. Ibid., 116.
18. Ibid., 117.
19. Ronnie Ball, "Portrait of Tristano," *Melody Maker,* January 27, 1951, 5.
20. McKinney, 93.
21. Ibid., 121.
22. Ira Gitler, *Jazz Masters of the Forties* (New York and London: Macmillan, 1966), 243.
23. Bill Coss, "Lennie Tristano Speaks Out," *Down Beat,* December 2, 1962, 20.
24. Mark Gardner, "Peter Ind Talks to Mark Gardner," Part 3, *Jazz Monthly* (England) (April 1970): 17.
25. Ibid., 17.
26. Ibid., 17.
27. Ibid., 17.
28. Ibid., 18.
29. Ibid., 18.
30. Jean Delmas and Laurent Goddet, "Warne Marsh," interview, *Jazz-Hot* (Paris) (March 1976): 20. A transcript of the original interview, which would

necessarily have been in English, was not available to me. What is given here is my own rough translation or paraphrase of the French into which Marsh's comments were cast by the interviewers.

31. This informant wished to remain anonymous.

32. Judy Tristano Gilbert, interview.

33. Gitler, 227.

34. Ibid., 231.

35. Lennie Tristano, "What's Wrong with the Boppers?" *Metronome,* June 1947, 10.

36. McKinney, 67–68.

37. Gordon Jack, "Peter Ind Interview," unpublished, originally broadcast on BBC c. 1996.

38. Nat Hentoff, "Miles," *Down Beat,* November 22, 1955, 13–14.

39. McKinney, 35.

40. Ibid., 35–55.

41. Ibid., 55.

42. Ibid., 36.

43. Phil Schaap, interview.

44. McKinney, 36.

45. Coss, 20.

46. Schaap, interview.

47. McKinney, 44–45.

48. Steve Silverman, interview.

49. In his autobiography, *Sideman* (New York: William H. Bauer, Inc., 1997), 80; Bauer writes, "Miles Davis sort of slinks up and says 'You cats ever hear of John Coltrane?' Both Lee and Warne sang a whole chorus and Miles just walked away." But in a phone conversation September 16, 1997, Bauer conceded that the reference to Coltrane was probably wrong, a result of his being pressured to remember by his editor or ghostwriter. Although Coltrane was with Dizzy Gillespie's big band and sextet between 1948 and 1951, he had recorded almost nothing, except for bootleg records culled from radio broadcasts, before 1955. Tristano's group appeared at Birdland at its opening December 15, 1949, and probably played there at least once in the ensuing year, but Marsh and Konitz probably did not have enough exposure to Coltrane to memorize a solo.

50. McKinney, 64, 66, 69.

51. Ibid., 68.

52. Ted Brown, interview.

53. Terry Martin and John Litweiler, unpublished interview, October 14, 1973.

54. McKinney, 83.

55. Ibid., 96.

56. Ted Brown, interview.

57. Robert Ronzello, "Warne Marsh—A Conversation with Robert Ronzello," *Saxophone Journal* (Spring 1982): 16–17.

58. This information is taken from nine pages of handwritten notes by an unidentified Norwegian student in the class labeled "Lennie Tristano's Exercises, As Related by Warne Marsh."

59. McKinney, 8.

60. Mark Gardner, "Peter Ind Talks to Mark Gardner," Part 1, *Jazz Monthly* (England) (February 1970): 12.

61. Alan Surpin, "Lennie Tristano: Feeling Is Basic. . . . ," *Down Beat,* October 16, 1969, 30.

62. See Gitler, 243.

63. Al Zeiger, "Lennie Tristano: A Debt of Gratitude," *Metronome,* June 1955, 23.

64. McKinney, 75.

65. Martin and Litweiler.

66. Roland Baggenaes, "Warne Marsh," *Coda*, December 1976, 5.

67. Les Tomkins, "The Warne Marsh Story," *Crescendo International*, May 1976, 21.

68. Robert Ronzello, "Warne Marsh—A Conversation with Robert Ronzello," *Saxophone Journal* (Spring 1982): 16.

69. Alun Morgan and Raymond Horricks, *Modern Jazz* (London: Victor Gollanz Ltd., 1957), 80.

70. Konitz, interview.

71. Tabackin, interview.

72. See, for example, the influential LeRoi Jones (a.k.a Amiri Baraka), *Black Music* (New York: William Morrow, c. 1967), 13: "The white musician's commitment to jazz, the *ultimate concern,* proposed that the subcultural attitudes that produced the music as a profound expression of human feelings, could be *learned* and need not be passed on as a secret blood rite. And Negro music is essentially the expression of an attitude, or a collection of attitudes, about the world, and only secondarily an attitude about the way music is made. The white jazz musician came to understand this attitude as a way of making music, and the intensity of his understanding produced the 'great' white jazz musicians, and is producing them now." Jones's use of a phrase like "secret blood rite" and his use of quotation marks around the word "great" in the phrase "'great' white musicians" imply that the ability to play real jazz is a matter of race or genetics, not merely of culture. "Great white musicians" are not really great because they have *learned* to play jazz simply as music, not as something in their blood.

73. Coss, 20–21.

74. Tomkins, 23.

75. Baggenaes, 4.

Success and Seclusion

At about the time Warne Marsh joined Buddy Rich at the Hollywood Palladium in late July 1948, Lee Konitz left the Claude Thornhill band, which had disbanded, and resumed his studies with Lennie Tristano in New York.

Only three years after switching to alto, on Tristano's advice, Konitz had already acquired a reputation, and not only because of his year with Thornhill. As early as 1945 *Metronome*'s Chicago correspondent Phil Featheringill had written that the eighteen-year-old Konitz, whom he had heard with the Jimmy Dale orchestra, "has promise of being one of the great white altos."[1] Early in 1948 Konitz had finished ninth among altoists in the *Metronome* All Star poll with fifty-eight votes, and he had been mentioned by *Metronome* coeditor George Simon in the same breath with Clark Terry and Fats Navarro as one of those serious younger musicians "who don't blow their horns just so they can get a rise out of some fanatic followers."[2] At least as gratifying from Konitz's standpoint, probably, was Ella Fitzgerald's approving comment, during a Leonard Feather blindfold test, on a solo with the Thornhill band: "I remember that alto player."[3]

As for Lennie Tristano, Barry Ulanov of *Metronome* had been lavishing attention on him as the new messiah of jazz ever since the appearance of his first trio recordings for Keynote, "I Can't Get Started" and "Out on a Limb." *Metronome*'s review of April 1947 was a barely moderated rave: "For Barry Ulanov [the panel of reviewers also included George Simon and Barbara Hodgkins], these are the finest piano sides in the last ten years; they introduce the remarkable Mr. Tristano to records, a brilliantly resourceful musician who combines familiar pop figurations here with a linear construction and dissonances out of Hindemith and manages to integrate all of this and a driving beat successfully. . . . Here is a breath of fresh air in the stale winds of jazz."[4]

In the same issue Ulanov wrote "A Call to Arms—and Horns," in which Tristano, along with such already established figures as "Dizzy [Gillespie] and the BeBop crowd," "Woody [Herman]'s inspired band," and arranger/composers Ralph Burns, Eddie Sauter, and George Handy, is cast as a harbinger of things to come: "The jazz musician who plays with a full knowledge of his instrument and the advances of music in our time is taking shape today. Hooray, and Hi-yo Hindemith. . . . This is a new music, a fresh one, a rich one, not all of a piece, but entirely informed by the sound of Modern Music, all of it, from Hindemith, Bloch, Berg, Schonberg and Stravinsky through Ellington, Strayhorn, Gillespie and the great soloists of jazz in all its years."[5]

It seems certain that Tristano was the immediate inspiration for this outburst. This surmise is strengthened by yet a third piece in the same April 1947 issue of *Metronome,* an editorial in which Ulanov describes how, in checking his judgment of Tristano, he played the Keynote sides and some air checks for various musicians in Hollywood, where he was on assignment. "Sonny Burke gasped. . . . 'Too sensational. . . . The finest I have ever heard. Good God!'" André Previn "had laughed, as hysterically as this writer, shaking his head in the manner of an unbeliever, murmuring something about 'It can't be! It can't.'"[6]

From then until late in 1951 scarcely an issue of *Metronome* came out that did not contain some favorable mention of Tristano and/or his students, whether in news items, editorials, articles—even those on other musicians—reviews, blindfold tests, or letters to the editor. In January 1948 *Metronome,* probably in large part because of Ulanov's influence as co-editor, named Tristano "Musician of the Year,"[7] and a year later he was one of three "Influences of the Year," along with Lester Young and Sarah Vaughan.[8] The following July, Ulanov, announcing his critical criteria of freshness, profundity, and skill, wrote: "[U]ntil some of the later Ellington, until Charlie Parker and Lennie Tristano, there has been little if anything in jazz that could be called profound."[9]

In August Ulanov published a major piece on Tristano, "Master in the Making," not only revealing the close friendship that had developed between himself and Tristano but admitting to "a collaboration of sorts" to advance their common goals for jazz. The two had met in the summer of 1946 when Chubby Jackson brought Tristano, Billy Bauer, and Arnold Fishkin, Tristano's working trio at the time, to perform a classroom concert at the final session of Ulanov's summer course at Juilliard in "The Development and Theory of Jazz."

At that concert, Ulanov wrote, although the class ended, "my tutelage in the art began." A few months later Tristano's first trio record appeared, to be greeted by Ulanov's rave review. Looking back on it, Ulanov expanded on his earlier comments: "Here was a full, fresh demonstration that jazz could parallel the development of classical music in the twentieth century without actually deriving from it." Soon after the record appeared, Ulanov and Tristano "started to discuss his music and my work, the background and foreground of jazz and jazz musicians, the futility of current musical fashions and the fecundity of those we hoped we could make current. A collaboration of sorts began." At Tristano's apartment on East 73rd they talked "over endless cups of coffee," sometimes from early afternoon to after midnight, and not only about music. Ulanov, in addition to coediting *Metronome,* was a student of literature and the arts who around 1947 embarked on a Ph.D. program in fine arts at Columbia. He urged on Tristano classics such as *War and Peace* and Dante's *Divine Comedy,* which he said Tristano "took possession [of] . . . as delightedly as a child seizes a new toy."[10]

The all-consuming nature of Ulanov's championing of Tristano was amusingly brought out in a 1950 interview with Stan Kenton in which they discussed Ulanov's latest project, the New Jazz Society (NJS). Kenton, in a consummate display of cagey, super-sincere needling, tells Ulanov that a major question about the fledgling society is Lennie Tristano: "Lennie is respected, admired: his music has aroused passionate interest among many. But Lennie is only one modern musician. Nevertheless, for you he's been *the* modern musician." A lot of people, says Kenton, want to know whether Ulanov's enthusiasm for Tristano will dominate the organization. Ulanov, acknowledging that "for me Lennie is the most distinguished of the modern jazzmen," agrees that of course the purpose of NJS should be "to discover fresh talent and encourage every jazz experiment." The ever-voluble Kenton pronounces himself "thrilled" to hear that.[11]

Into this environment of growing and established reputations, including those not only of Tristano and Konitz but of the older members of Tristano's circle, Billy Bauer and bassist Arnold Fishkin, the twenty-one-year-old Warne Marsh arrived virtually unheralded. It is true that a "Warren" Marsh had finished thirteenth, with thirty-nine votes, in the tenor saxophone category of the latest *Metronome* poll, announced in the January 1948 issue.[12] If this poll result really referred to Warne Marsh, not the similarly named saxophonist Arno Marsh, and was not the result of some more bizarre mistake, it is quite remarkable, as Warne Marsh was still in the army at Fort Monmouth until October 1947 and in Los Angeles for the rest of the year. He had had no press whatsoever, except earlier as a member of teenage bands in Los Angeles, and no known exposure in New York except at Tristano's studio, where Barry Ulanov and a few others indeed might have heard him. He probably did some gigging and jamming around Los Angeles in November and December of 1947, but it is amazing that this limited exposure could have earned him a respectable place, just behind Ben Webster and Lucky Thompson and tied with his one-time teacher Corky Corcoran, in a national poll that closed before the end of the year. It was not unheard of for some local favorite to receive a significant number of votes, said Ulanov, but he wondered how he and other *Metronome* editors could have overlooked the misspelling of Marsh's name. Of course, if they had never seen it in print, as is likely, they may not have known the correct spelling. But to imagine Marsh as some sort of "local favorite" raises more questions than it answers.

At any rate, Marsh's reputation in October 1948 was minuscule compared with those of Tristano, Konitz, and the rest of their circle. On October 28 he was recorded on a radio broadcast as a member of the Buddy Rich band, but did not solo, and for the next six months, as for most of the preceding years, his name was not so much as mentioned in the jazz press.

When Tristano, Konitz, Bauer, Fishkin, and drummer Mel Zelnick were hired to play off-nights at the Royal Roost early in December 1948, Marsh was apparently not with them. Possibly he was with the Buddy Rich band at the new Clique Club, even though he stated that he left the band two weeks after its arrival in New York in late October. But Zelnick thought he might have sat in with the Tristano group, and he was with them six or eight weeks later when they too played the Clique Club.

After the Rich band closed around the end of December, the Clique Club tried a variety of attractions, including Sarah Vaughan, George Shearing, and an all-star bebop group led by bassist Oscar Pettiford, to compete with Charlie Parker and Charlie Ventura at the Royal Roost. None were notably successful at drawing customers away from the Roost, where Parker and Ventura were held over, and in a last-ditch effort to maintain a jazz policy the Clique hired Charlie Barnet's big band and the Lennie Tristano Sextet, this time with Warne Marsh as well as Lee Konitz, Billy Bauer, Arnold Fishkin, and young drummer Harold Granowsky. The Tristano-Barnet bill fared no better commercially than their predecessors, and on March 17, 1949, after trying Sally Rand's burlesque troupe for a week, the Clique Club, for three months the number two jazz center of New York, folded.[13]

The exact dates of the Tristano group's engagement at the Clique are uncertain. McKinney intimates that it was their performance there that earned them an offer from New Jazz, soon to become Prestige Records, to record on January 11.[14] But this session did not include Marsh, who was with the group at the Clique, and in fact was originally not Tristano's at all. "It was supposed to be [trumpeter] Tony Fruscella's date," Lee Konitz told historian Ira Gitler, ". . . and Bob Weinstock suggested that Tony and I get together. . . . Tony didn't want to do it, so Bob asked me if I would. I asked Lennie to take the date."[15] More than likely the engagement at the Clique began sometime in February and ended March 10, when the club turned from jazz to burlesque. In April, Ulanov wrote, "The Clique . . . has fired jazz from its premises . . . but not before permitting several thousand to hear the superb Lennie Tristano Sextet. . . . And while he was at the Clique, Lennie made some first sides for Capitol [and] saw his fine New Jazz records come out. . . ."[16] This account would place the New Jazz session before the engagement at the Clique.

That session, with Tristano, Konitz, Bauer, Fishkin, and Shelly Manne on drums, produced four titles, Konitz's "Subconscious-Lee" (based on "What Is This Thing Called Love,") and Tristano's "Progression" ("Idaho"), "Judy" ("Don't Blame Me"), and "Retrospection" ("These Foolish Things"), the latter two without Manne.[17] Reviews of "Subconscious-Lee" and "Judy" were laudatory. *Metronome* (probably Ulanov) wrote, "[T]hese two sides present some of the brightest new jazz of one of the brightest jazz newcomers."[18] Tom Herrick of *Down Beat* was equally enthusiastic: "[W]hat guitar and piano do together [on 'Judy'] is a wonderful thing. . . . 'Subconscious' . . . is a superb side almost without fault" on which Konitz plays "with the freedom of expression and mastery of fourth dimensional harmony that he could only hint at in his days with the Thornhill band." Herrick ended his review with, "Dizzy, the Bird, and a few others started it, but they've been caught up with."[19]

Marsh's first record date with Tristano was on March 4, for Capitol. The rest of the group was the same as on the January 11 session except that seventeen-year-old Harold Granowsky was on drums instead of Shelly Manne. Granowsky had recently come to New York from Indiana, directly out of high school. He had found an open session where he sat in with bassists Red Mitchell and Bill Anthony and had been referred by the latter to Tristano, who liked his playing.

This first record date provided the occasion for the only extant letter in which the habitually laconic Marsh is at pains both to convey information about his current life and to articulate personal feelings.[20] Although the letter is undated, the content indicates that it was written between March 4, the date of the session, and May 4, when Marsh says he will be eligible to join the New York local of the Musicians Union. A reasonable guess is that it was written around mid- or late-April, perhaps after the May 1949 issue of *Metronome* appeared with its review of the record. It is worth quoting in full:

Dearest Mother,

I've thought of you very much since I wrote you that letter. In a way I'm sorry I wrote it—sorry because I know that I must of [*sic*] hurt you. But you know how honest I was trying to be with myself. I hurt myself by hurting you, Mother. I do love you, else I wouldn't feel hurt. And you know, this isn't something I've figured out with my mind, like I've always tried to figure out my relationships with people—I love you, Mother.

I've moved into a room in the same building that Lee and his wife live in, and I have kitchen privileges, meaning I can use the community icebox and cook my own breakfast and lunch. Still eat supper with them. The new address is: 230 W. 76th Apt 68 N.Y.C. 23, N.Y. TRAFALGAR 47348[.]

Our record has just been released, so be sure to get it. Title is 'Crosscurrent,' and 'Wow!' And just because it says 'Bop instrumental' on the upper right of the label—doesn't make it Bop! Capitol just released a whole flock of modern jazz records in one week & deceided [*sic*] to call them all Bop. It's commercial music now, you know. A new night club has just opened in Manhattan—Times Square, in fact—called 'Bop City.' Ridiculous! Lennie has a previous record out on the 'New Jazz' label called 'Subconscious-Lee' that you might be interested in, although I wasn't with the group when they recorded it. We're really causing a lot of controversy in the jazz world. You'll have to read the reviews of these records. I'll send you the latest *Down Beat* & *Metronome,* which both have lots to say!

I'm trying very hard to retire at 2 and get up at 10, with partial success. I've also started to drink a pint of cream a day, since I really don't weigh enough. And a most astounding thing has been invented—dehydrated orange juice. Just add water and imagine yourself in California. Which I do every morning. I'd sure like to see you soon, Mother. My 'period of waiting' with the Union is up May 4th, but I don't have a spare hundred dollars. Why don't you plan a summer trip to New York? The weather will be the nicest for a couple of months.

All my Love,

Warne

It is indeed unfortunate that we do not have the earlier letter that "must of hurt" his mother and for which he apologizes. According to Marsh's sister, Gloria Oxford, their mother never wanted him to leave California, and she neither liked nor understood jazz. Mrs. Oxford thought the quarrel was probably over either money or Marsh's move to New York. His decision to move to New York could not have pleased her. The break with his mother follows a pattern discussed by psychoanalyst Erik Erikson. Erikson speaks of an "identity crisis" that Western youth undergo in their late teens or early twenties and that involves both "devotion" and "repudiation": "[Y]oung people offer devotion to individual leaders and to teams, to strenuous activities, and to difficult techniques; at the same time they show a sharp and intolerant readiness to discard and disavow," especially aspects of their parents' lifestyle.[21] Certainly Marsh offered devotion to Tristano and the difficult techniques of jazz that he taught, and the move to New York constituted a definitive break with his demanding and domineering mother.

Perhaps the most intriguing aspect of Marsh's affirmation of love for his mother is his statement that it "isn't something I've figured out with my mind, like I've always tried to figure out my relationships with people." It appears that Marsh was aware of a split between his analytical mind and his emotions. Harold Granowsky, the drummer on "Wow" and "Crosscurrent," remarked that "a lot of people thought Warne was emotionally dead, a walking zombie," perhaps because he habitually processed his relationships intellectually rather than reacting with spontaneous emotion.

Certainly Marsh's remarks about bebop show how intent the Tristanoites were on distancing themselves from the horde of Charlie Parker and Dizzy Gillespie imitators, which is apparently what the word "bop" signified to them. It also seems to have signified to Marsh the inroads of commerce on jazz. Of course he knew that Parker's and Gillespie's music was not in itself "commercial," in the sense of being created to please the public and make money. What he considered "ridiculous" was the use by Capitol of the fad word "bop" to turn the new jazz into a marketable commodity.

Marsh may have had the *Metronome* review of "Wow" and "Crosscurrent" in hand when he wrote his mother. Athough George Simon "was not pleased by the acceleration of the "Wow" release [i.e., the bridge or B section] and found Lee's playing cold," Ulanov, predictably, loved everything—"a wealth of solos, offering a fine debut for Warne's tenor." Unlike Simon, he waxed particularly enthusiastic over "Wow"'s double-time bridge passages, "which increase velocity with a brilliant excursion into first 3/8, then 5/8, then back to 3/8 time against the basic 4/4." Konitz's solo on "Crosscurrent" he found "particularly warm."[22] In *Down Beat,* whose review appeared later in May, Michael Levin lauded Konitz's alto as "flowing, formal, and full of life and energy," while finding Tristano "highly interesting and as cold as iceberg lettuce." The doubled-up reed passages, he says, "will arouse interest. . . ." He does not mention Marsh at all.[23]

Levin's review was typical of the treatment Marsh was to receive from both *Down Beat* and *Metronome* for the next six years. Whether in mention of Tristano's students or in record reviews, Konitz was almost always named first, with Marsh mentioned in a kind of echo when he was not, as in this case, ignored. The same pattern prevailed on their early records together, where Konitz's solos typically preceded Marsh's.

In the case of this first record, such treatment was justified. Both of Konitz's solos are superior to Marsh's. His tone and attack have more bite, his lines more rhythmic variety, his conception more energy. There are suggestions of passion in his inflections, the warmth that Ulanov heard. Marsh's tone, by contrast, has a restrained, deadpan quality, and his lines seem almost academic, smoothly correct but unimpassioned, consisting almost entirely of legato eighth notes. However, they have strong structural and melodic logic. If one finds an added interest, it lies in the very lack of emotion, as if something this intellectually correct, this well executed, must contain somewhere the emotion that it withholds.

Late in his life Tristano told Jack McKinney that he had rehearsed his sextet for a year because he wanted one "that would have the delicacy and precision of Bach."[24] Neither Konitz nor Marsh had been continuously available that long, but Tristano may have been including the time when Marsh was still in the army and before Konitz joined the Thornhill band. Marsh himself said that after he returned to New York in October 1948, "We worked our butts off. Lennie was strong on competence in individuals and groups. Discipline. So a lot of work went into those Capitol sides. About four months."[25] At any rate, the group that recorded "Wow" and "Crosscurrent" could truly be said to have the Bach-like qualities Tristano was after, especially in the tour de force bridge of "Wow." The word "wow," incidentally, was said to be Tristano's favorite expression, "pronounced in a breathy undertone whenever he was deeply impressed."[26] Reportedly, it was also Barry Ulanov's response on first hearing the piece; hence the title.

On May 16 Tristano again took his sextet into the recording studio for Capitol, with drummer Denzil Best replacing Granowsky, who soon dropped permanently out of the Tristano clique. Two of the results, "Marionette" and "Sax of a Kind," were judged eminently satisfactory and were soon released. *Metronome*'s review, which appeared in September, praised "brilliant piano playing by Tristano and some fine sax playing by Lee Konitz and Warne Marsh," adding that "the delicacy and facility of this sextet continue to amaze and delight. . . ."[27] *Down Beat*'s review, appearing a month later, commended "a quality of warmth that [the group] has heretofore lacked on records." Konitz was "superb, Warne Marsh's tenor saxing just a little behind."[28]

The trouble began with the tracks that were eventually released as "Intuition" and "Digression." As Ulanov, who was present at the session, described it, "After two hours of more orthodox recording, five men grouped themselves around two microphones [there were six men on the

conventional recordings, but Best, at Tristano's request,[29] did not partici-
pate on drums on the free pieces] and began to make permanent the most
audacious experiment yet attempted in jazz. . . . The experiment was to
create a spontaneous music, out of skill and intuition, which should be
at once atonal, contrapuntal and improvised on a jazz base."[30] In other
words, they recorded the first free music by jazz musicians, without pre-
set melody, rhythm, or harmony.

One can imagine the consternation in Capitol's control booth. Ulanov
reported that two of four free pieces were erased, the remaining two being set aside for an "indefinitely postponed" release date.[31] That date
would not arrive until late 1950, probably precipitated by the fact that disc
jockey Symphony Sid Torin had already begun playing unauthorized copies of the record over the air, no doubt accompanied by some negative
publicity about Capitol's failure to release them.[32]

In September 1949 Ulanov hailed the Tristano group's unreleased free-
form recordings for Capitol as "the high point of all jazz until now, possibly the breaking point that will send jazz far away from its too well-
tested paths and far along the speculative road that every art form has
had to follow to achieve greatness."[33] This new jazz of Tristano's, he wrote,
"rests upon the pillars of all of music, the great supports that buoyed the
polyphony of Bach and gave depth to the elegance of Mozart. It marks a
strong parallel to the development of the twelve-tone structure in classical music in the twentieth century. . . ."[34]

What Ulanov knew, but did not say, was that neither "Intuition" nor
"Digression" is "free" in the sense of being totally unstructured in advance. In each there is the same order of entry: piano first, setting tempo
and mood, followed by alto, bass, guitar, and finally tenor saxophone.
"Intuition" has approximately the same tempo, and even similar figures,
for most of its length, as "Sax of a Kind," which they had just finished
recording. "Digression" is taken at a ballad tempo and reminds one, in
its shape and tonalities, of Tristano's earlier recording of "Yesterdays."

Although each instrument is heard as an individual voice, there are no
solos in the usual sense, nor is there a traditional rhythm section. The effort is to blend in and contribute to an evolving whole. Bauer introduces
a stark counter theme on "Intuition," but for the most part the performances are seamless. The feeling, however, as Ulanov's reference to
twelve-tone composition suggested, is far less jazz than twentieth-century
classical, which partially explains why the free jazz movement did not
really start until Ornette Coleman came on the scene some ten years later
with a more blues-based approach.

Tristano's group had been performing such free pieces as a regular part
of their studies. Said Marsh, "From the time that Lennie started us doing

it, we did it regularly. Two years. And I tell you, the first times were perhaps the best. They were so spontaneous, they were unbelievable, man, just three lines going." There was no attempt to incorporate Schoenberg's twelve-tone theory, no use of tone rows: "None of that shit," said Marsh.[35] Ronnie Ball described the way the group played free pieces at Birdland in December 1949: "[T]he boys start with no set chord formation, no key signature—and use just their own imagination and creativeness. Either Lee or Warne will start off on his own, play a few bars; then the others join in. It's a kind of musical telepathy."[36]

Marsh's next venture into the recording studio was on June 28, 1949, for New Jazz, not with Tristano but with Konitz as leader, joined by Fishkin on bass, Best on drums, and fellow Tristano student Sal Mosca on piano. For this session Marsh contributed one of his rare compositions, the devilishly difficult, up-tempo variation on "Cherokee" titled "Marshmallow," which he described as an exercise in polytonality.[37] Years later musicologist Frank Tirro hailed the piece as a "masterpiece of melodic writing."[38]

Both Konitz and Marsh have excellent solos. Konitz, leading off with a burst of eighth notes and continuing in a breakneck vein, plays with logic and biting intensity. Marsh's solo, at least equal and in my view superior to Konitz's, is masterful in its control and elegant in its structure, marking a distinct advance over his earlier recorded work. Rhythmically varied, unified by effective use of sequential figures, it rides a torrent of eighth notes in the bridge to a climax, then subsides with short sequential echoes of an earlier cadence-ending figure. Its emotion is of a piece with its structure, not as apparent as Konitz's fiery inflections, but deeper, despite its controlled, "cool" surface.

Curiously, Marsh dropped "Marshmallow" from his repertoire and never recorded it again.

The other piece issued from this session, Arnold Fishkin's "Fishin' Around," based on "I Never Knew" but with a different bridge, was cited by Marsh in 1982 as containing one of his best early solos, a judgment shared by Lee Konitz. Less spectacular than "Marshmallow," it is taken at relaxed medium tempo.[39] There appears to be no theme, only a chord progression, the two saxophonists improvising jointly on the first and last choruses. Marsh's solo, following Konitz's, again makes judicious use of sequential figures and contrast to create a strong sense of structure.

For whatever reason, the tune required several takes, none of the outtakes surviving. "In a final effort," wrote Ira Gitler, "to get a relaxed groove . . . all the lights in the studio had been extinguished. Then came the painstaking deliberation of which version to pick. Al Haig . . . was there [at Apex Studios on West 52nd St.] for one of his practice sessions.

He poked his head into the studio long enough to view the situation and sarcastically suggested, 'Why don't you call the witch doctor?'"[40] Which, according to Gitler, they ultimately did, playing the various takes for Tristano over the phone.

On September 8 Tristano's group was scheduled for the opening of Birdland, at the site of the old Clique Club, along with Charlie Parker, Bud Powell, Stan Getz, and singer Harry Belafonte. However, the club was refused a liquor license at that time, and owner Monte Kay, having already contracted with the musicians, rescheduled them for the Orchid Room, formerly the Onyx, on 52nd Street.[41]

On September 27 Marsh again recorded under Konitz's leadership for New Jazz. This time the drummer Jeff Morton, a new addition to the Tristano circle, joined Sal Mosca and Arnold Fishkin in the rhythm section. The tunes were Konitz's "Tautology," based on "Idaho," and "Sound-Lee," based on "Too Marvellous for Words."

On "Tautology," especially, Marsh came into his own with perhaps his finest recorded solo to date. Again there is great rhythmic and phrasal variety and significant use of sequential figures. Notable also is his freedom with bar lines, especially in the second eight bars of the first chorus, where an eight-bar phrase climaxes with four sequential figures involving rising triplet arpeggios, ending not at the start of the bridge but one bar into it. The second chorus begins with another eight-bar phrase, the climax of the solo, consisting of five bars of gradually rising groups of eighth notes carrying over into another sequence of rising triplets. In each of these long phrases the triplet passages momentarily shift the meter to a 3/4 feel against the basic 4/4, and each is a superlative example of what Whitney Balliett called "the sound of surprise."

Marsh's solo on "Sound-Lee," though impressive, is not quite as exciting as the one on "Tautology." Both sides, however, got very good reviews. In *Down Beat* Mike Levin wrote, "More of the precise, exactly balanced sounds of the Tristano group. Konitz still impresses as a fabulously fleet and fertile alto man. Some equally good tenor work by Warne Marsh, too."[42] This is the whole review, with Marsh still an echo, though an "equal" echo, of Konitz. In *Metronome* Ulanov, though preferring the more harmonically complex "Sound-Lee" as "on a higher plane musically," commended "the ever-improving Warne Marsh" for his "Tautology" solo.[43]

On November 1, on a rare road trip, Tristano's sextet, with Joe Shulman replacing Fishkin on bass, opened for two weeks at the Silhouette in Chicago. *Down Beat* correspondent Pat Harris noted that "the few Tristano disciples were waiting," but otherwise "the red carpet was barely visible." The "popular reaction" to Tristano, she wrote, "appears to be more than apathy." Instead it was "a bitter and hostile revulsion," which Harris attributed to the yearning for "a secure and simple past for our music." For her own part, she found the sextet "the most cohesive and purposeful unit we've ever heard . . . it is meaningful and significant music."[44]

From Chicago the Tristano group reportedly moved on to Milwaukee for a two-week engagement at the Continental, and sometime in November they squeezed in a concert at John Hancock Hall in Boston, sharing the bill with the Mary Lou Williams Trio.[45] For this concert Barry Ulanov was on hand to introduce the Tristanoites, later pronouncing it in print "a brilliant evening" of "dignity and joy." Tristano's group "was 'up' for the occasion, and when it came to its last number, played its heads and hearts off in the free improvisation they have aptly thought to call Intuition."[46]

On December 15, 1949, Birdland belatedly opened, with a lineup billed as a retrospective of jazz and featuring Tristano, Charlie Parker, Dixieland trumpeter Max Kaminsky, Lester Young, Stan Getz, and Oran "Hot Lips" Page.[47]

In his review John S. Wilson wrote that the Tristano group "pulled off the greatest surprise of the evening" in being more accessible to the average listener, a change he attributed to Jeff Morton's drumming. With Morton's "steady, flowing beat" as support, "the very gentle wisp-like meandering of Warne Marsh on tenor and Lee Konitz on alto, which frequently used to give the impression of just wandering off into space, now hold together. . . ." Noting Tristano's "rather adamant attitude in the past about compromising with his audiences," Wilson suggests that if this was compromise, it was one Tristano should be happy with.[48]

A recording, not issued until 1979 and titled *Lennie Tristano Quintet: Live at Birdland, 1949*, Jazz Records JR-1CD, is from either this engagement or one of several that the Tristano group played at Birdland in 1950. If it is in fact from 1949, it would have to be from the two-week engagement beginning December 15. Arnold Fishkin, who recorded the set, thought that it could have been in 1950. He was lucky, he said, to get what he did, because his new Revere tape recorder was plugged into the wrong voltage and began to smoke after five numbers, burning itself out. At some point later the beginning of the tape became damaged, but not before two copies had been made, one on tape and one, by Lloyd Lifton, on a wire recorder. On the version originally issued in 1979 by Jazz Records on LP, the beginning of Lifton's wire recording, with inferior sound, was spliced onto Fishkin's tape. For the CD, issued in 1990, the beginning of the tape copy of the original was spliced in in place of Lifton's beginning.

Marsh is the sole horn man here. Konitz was on the gig but was late, missing the first set, which was the one Fishkin recorded. Tristano, Bauer, Fishkin, and Morton were the others.

The record begins in progress with Marsh's two-chorus solo on "I'll Remember April." Almost immediately, in the fourth bar, Marsh displaces the meter, creating tension between his line and the expected flow of the song, and in bars eight and nine, where an important harmonic change takes place, he leaves almost the whole two bars empty, beginning his next phrase at the end of bar nine. A major aspect of Marsh's originality was this freedom with the harmonic meter. He comes back on line in the second sixteen bars. The solo is characterized by wide but natural-sounding intervallic leaps and, again, by use of sequential figures. Marsh's other extended solos, on "Indiana" and "All of Me," are also substantial and display similar characteristics: sequential figures, unusually wide intervals, surprising changes of direction, and manipulation of the harmonic meter, sometimes unexpectedly curtailing a harmonic sequence and sometimes extending phrases beyond where one expects them to end. (Musicians often speak of "playing across the bar lines." What they mean is playing across certain bar lines where the harmonic meter suggests a phrase should end, or, in other words, not being confined to the existing phraseology of the song.) In all there is an unusual air, not so apparent on the earlier records, of relaxed spontaneity, as if Marsh did not know where the line was going until a split-second before his fingers played it. And his playing is, as Wilson observed, very gentle, though Wilson's other terms, "wisp-like" and "meandering," do not do justice to the intelligence and purposefulness of Marsh's lines, however spontaneous and intricate.

Unfortunately, the sound quality leaves much to be desired, especially in its failure to capture Marsh's true sound. A more disturbing defect is the monotonous, metronomic playing of the rhythm section. Doubtless drummer Jeff Morton was doing exactly what Tristano wanted, but the absence of any rhythmic variety or excitement gives the performance a feeling of sterility, detracting from the fine playing of Marsh and Tristano.

Reviewing the record in 1991, Francis Davis wrote: "Try to imagine how bop might have evolved if its rhythms and dynamics had failed to keep pace with its harmony (or, maybe another way of putting it, if all of its leading figures had been white), and you've pretty much described the music on *Live at Birdland 1949*." The virtues of the record, Davis continued, were "ceaseless melodic invention, a healthy disregard for bar lines, rigorous and frequently surprising piano-sax-and-guitar counterpoint, . . . and the unlikely but seductive combination of rectitude and abandon that make Tristano a genre unto himself."[49]

Leaving aside Davis's gratuitous and stereotypical suggestion that white rhythm sections can't swing, much the same could be said about another belatedly issued live recording from the same period, *Wow: The Lennie Tristano Sextet*, Jazz Records JR9CD, dated "c. 1950." Again the recording was made by another member of the group, guitarist Billy Bauer, on his Webcor wire recorder; again the fidelity is terrible, capturing nothing of the nuances of Marsh's sound; and again, although Marsh, Tristano, and Konitz play with energy and imagination, the unidentified drummer and bassist give Tristano what he wants, a dull, uninspiring, metronomic pulse.

The year 1949 was an eventful one for Marsh, climaxing on Christmas night with the Tristano group's participation in a Carnegie Hall concert, from which "Sax of a Kind" and "You Go to My Head" were recorded and issued by the International Association of Jazz Record Collectors (IAJRC 20).[50] The concert included not only Tristano's group but Bud Powell, Max Roach, Miles Davis, Serge Chaloff, Sonny Stitt, Stan Getz, and Sarah Vaughan. In his liner notes to the record Bill Miner noted that "family doings, holiday cheer and the like must have kept critics and reviewers at home—for nary a mention of this memorable event can be found in the jazz periodicals of the day or in New York's major daily newspapers!"[51]

Marsh continued to study with Tristano in New York until the fall of 1955, but though four live performances with Tristano, including those just mentioned at Birdland and Carnegie Hall, were recorded, with the usual poor fidelity, and were eventually issued on discs, after May 1949 Marsh never again entered a recording studio with his mentor, not through any fault of his own but because of Tristano's purist reticence to join in the growing recording frenzy until he had something new to say. For different reasons, after the "Tautology" date in September 1949, it was not until 1955 that Marsh, with Konitz as leader, recorded again for immediate release and for a major jazz label, although in 1950 the pair participated in a 45-rpm single for London Records with singer and pianist Hadda Brooks.[52]

One reason for the virtual non-existence of Warne Marsh on records between 1949 and 1955 was his own purist reticence. As British critic Mark Gardner put it, "At one juncture he had subscribed to an almost isolationist view, believing that study would produce the answers to everything." Gardner relates the story of a fan who, on hearing Marsh and Konitz practicing together, asked why they didn't record. "'Lennie says we're not ready to record yet,'" replied Konitz.[53] But it was Marsh, not Konitz, who took Tristano's judgment to heart. Billy Byers, Marsh's old friend from Canteen Kids days, told a similar story, this one relating to Marsh's acceptance of Tristano's purist attitude toward commercial work. Like Marsh, Byers had settled in New York in 1949. For the next five years, he recalled, "I was very busy. I was writing for *Your Show of Shows*, and after that I was doing some record dates, writing record dates, and I saw that Warne was living in abject poverty, working at Macy's in order to play jazz five hours a week. . . . I said, 'Look, Warne, I've got a date you can come to. You're not a great clarinet player, but you can play in the chalumeau register, you can mumble a couple of long notes, and nobody will know you're not a great clarinet player, and you'll make $41.25 in three hours.' He said, 'No, I can't do it. Lennie won't let me.'"

Following Tristano's dictum that if one could not support himself playing serious jazz, it was better to take a day job than to muddy one's creative springs by playing commercial music, Marsh did indeed take low-paying day gigs, usually temporary clerical work, to support himself. He did work at Macy's for a time, as Lee Konitz confirmed, where he amused himself by teaching parrots to say "motherfucker." A gig "that didn't work at all," said Marsh, "was as a messenger. The guy fired me after about two days because he characterized the way I walked as being more or less a slouch or a stroll, and I was supposed to run around, you know?"[54]

But he was playing jazz far more than the five hours a week hyperbolically assumed by Byers. There were occasional engagements with the Tristano group: on March 19, 1950, they did a concert at Orchestra Hall in Chicago; in May and December they were back at Birdland; in April 1951 they played the Blue Note in Chicago; and shortly afterward they were once again at Birdland. In addition he was playing regularly in jam sessions with Tristano. Tenorist Ted Brown, who like Marsh began studying with Tristano in late 1948, would see Marsh and Konitz from time to time at jam sessions in a hall or studio that Tristano's students had rented for the occasion, and Marsh may occasionally have participated in other sessions, such as those at Jimmy Knepper's basement apartment at 136th and Broadway. Knepper did not remember Marsh at what became known as "The Apartment," but Brown remembered seeing both Marsh and Konitz there.

On June 1, 1951, Tristano, who until this time had been teaching at his home in Flushing, Long Island, opened The Lennie Tristano School of Music at 317 E. 32nd Street in Manhattan. "The school marked a clear break in his [Tristano's] career; from this time forward he was a teacher first and a performer secondly," wrote Jack McKinney. "There was no time for work in the clubs, and for a period in the middle of the 1950s Tristano did not play a professional engagement for three years."[55] Presumably the three years McKinney referred to were roughly 1952–55. Tristano began playing at the Sing Song room of the Confucius restaurant in the summer of 1955.

The new studio, formerly a furniture showroom over a garage, was discovered by Tristano's wife, Judy, and financed by pianist and Tristano student Phyllis Pinkerton, who reportedly invested $10,000 of her inheritance in the school.[56] According to *Time* magazine, which ran a piece on

Tristano two months after the school opened, Tristano had enrolled "some 35 pupils" in his school and planned to begin recording on his own label.[57]

The work of converting the former showroom to a teaching, recital, and recording studio was largely done by Tristano's students and friends. Recording engineer Rudy van Gelder assisted with the recording facilities, and the physical labor of erecting walls and installing drapes, rugs, and soundproofing was mostly performed by students.[58] Marsh, Konitz, Ted Brown, trumpeter Don Ferrara, trombonist Willie Dennis, and others would arrive nightly for several months to labor with hammer and screwdriver, until one night Tristano said, "Why don't we play a few tunes?" signaling that the Lennie Tristano School of Music was ready for business.[59]

Jam sessions were scheduled every Wednesday evening for less proficient students, and Saturday evenings on into late Sunday morning for the more advanced players. Tristano would play in the Saturday night and/or Sunday morning sessions. Frequent visitors included Charlie Parker, Charles Mingus, Roy Haynes, Kenny Clarke, and Max Roach. Roach's comments convey a sense of the scene: "Lennie was in New York City, and he was downtown. And Charlie Parker and Monk and all of us were uptown. Lennie had a school. And of course, Dizzy and Bird and Monk, that was the other school. But they were two different schools. And of course, we intermingled. I played a lot, jammed a lot with Lennie during that time, a lot of us did. . . . The thing that was so wonderful about Lennie and Lee Konitz and Warne Marsh was that . . . we were uptown, which was blacktown, and they were downtown, which was white. But they had something that was significant that was totally different from what we were doing, that you could respect and appreciate, and they respected and appreciated the things we were doing. It was really a happy medium kind of thing, 'cause a lot of people were imitating the things that we were doing. So if we wanted to be refreshed, we'd have to turn to Lee and Lennie and them."[60]

Leonard Bernstein sometimes came to listen. Bernstein expressed great admiration for Tristano: "I've heard a lot of his work, heard him fiddling around with motives and with rhythms, with ways of reaching something fresh. This is wonderful, and I hope he will continue to experiment. Eventually he may come up with something marvelous. Tristano is an enormous talent, but I don't think he's the last word, or that he's arrived yet."[61]

Another visitor was Stan Getz, who came at least twice to sit in. One Getz visit was unnerving to Marsh. "Warne had been playing his ass off," recalled Ted Brown, but seemed inhibited after Getz's arrival. But Peter Ind recalled another session "when Stan Getz was completely intimidated by Warne Marsh, who was so far ahead of him harmonically—but then

Warne was ahead of nearly everyone ideas-wise."[62] After the opening of the school, Marsh seems to have devoted himself almost exclusively to studying and occasionally performing in public with Tristano, with perhaps some teaching thrown in. In November 1951 he ran an ad in Metronome:[63]

How many students he may have attracted is not known, but it was undoubtedly this period that Mark Gardner referred to as "almost isolationist," with regard to playing in non-Tristano settings, or recording in any setting. Even the performances with Tristano all but disappeared. After 1952, Marsh told an interviewer, "The band didn't work together again till '58 through '60, which was when the Half Note opened."[64]

Konitz, on the other hand, was quite busy, and quite visible, during the early 1950s. In March 1950 he had participated in the famous "Birth of the Cool" sessions with Miles Davis, Gerry Mulligan, and Gil Evans, and in April he had recorded again for New Jazz, with fellow Tristanoites Bauer, Fishkin, Mosca, and Morton. Between 1950 and 1956 he recorded nine LPs under his own name, as well as recording as a featured sideman with Stan Kenton and the Gerry Mulligan group.

During these years, again unlike Marsh, Konitz received a generous amount of press, especially in *Metronome*. Barry Ulanov had done a profile of him as early as December 1948; in February 1949 *Metronome* had named him an "Arrival of the Year"; and in the June 1950 *Metronome* he shared with Stan Getz the title of "Musician of the Year."[65] In March 1951 he was the subject of a blindfold test, delivering himself of such remarks as "I sure get tired of listening to the blues" and "I believe that Lennie's is the only group that is actually trying to improvise."[66] In September *Metronome* ran a highly laudatory piece on the "Lee Konitz School" of altoists, which the writer maintained included Paul Desmond and Art Pepper. The piece, which was unsigned but bore the earmarks of a Ulanov contribution, ended with this encomium: "Lee's facile mind . . . has begun already to move jazz as we know it into forms as yet unforseen. . . . He may play the Pied Piper who, with his colleagues, will expatriate [expatiate? *sic*], elongate and make concrete a jazz form that is comparable to, yet not a copy of, 'classical' music."[67]

Marsh's contrasting lack of press visibility is nowhere more tellingly revealed than in an accompanying article, in the same issue of *Metronome,* on the "Getz-Young School" of tenor saxophonists. The article names nearly every player one could think of, from Zoot Sims and Allan Eager to the now forgotten Bob Graf and Buddy Wise, before adding, "Though never a bopper, young Warne Marsh often gets the Young-Getz sound."[68]

Although in February 1950 Ulanov had suggested that a fully matured Marsh should "some day [become] a profound artist," only once did Marsh receive anything like the raves that were regularly accorded Konitz.[69] In late 1951, in a *Metronome* review of the Tristano group at Birdland, Bill Coss wrote, "Warne Marsh was a little short of amazing. His tone was constant, beautifully controlled, matching color with thought, charming in his frequent simplicity. He gave the group some of the warmth that Billy Bauer used to contribute. This was the highlight of the evening to me, Warne playing better than he has for a long time." Konitz, on the other hand, seemed to Coss to have stood still for the last six months, playing "only a few great things." New addition Willie Dennis was "a definite also-ran this night," and the group as a whole "was a distinct disappointment."[70]

As unusual, for *Metronome,* as his praise of Marsh was Coss's resounding denunciation of Tristano: "The Tristano music, proudly announced as purely intellectual," was merely pretentious. "[I]t paints no picture, creates no clear impression and must, of necessity, grow tedious to [most listeners]. . . . I submit that through Tristano's pedantic, admitted refusal to use his human powers both of emotions and of tremendous thought to communicate to other men . . . there has been produced an unhealthy musical attitude, a limiting of creativity, a sophomoric cult and an ever-broadening, in-grown, other-world snobbishness that has no justification in relation to reality. In short, Lennie Tristano has failed to justify his position as an artist."[71]

Tristano must have been more than a little taken aback by this blast from the magazine that Barry Ulanov had made into his most enthusiastic supporter. The explanation, probably, was that Coss had only recently joined the *Metronome* staff, and Ulanov was on an extended leave of absence in Europe, completing research for his doctoral degree in Renaissance literature and the arts.[72]

A not particularly striking exception to Marsh's absence from the recording scene occurred in April of 1951 when arranger/composer Tom Talbert, Marsh's old friend and employer from Los Angeles, called him for a record date for Cosmopolitan with Kai Winding and Billy Taylor.[73] Marsh usually tried to avoid this kind of commercial date, but he probably needed the money and perhaps felt some obligation to Talbert. Two of the four tunes released, "Deep Purple" and "You're Blase," were vocals by Melvin Moore, a capable singer along the lines of Billy Eckstine. On both, Marsh takes competent eight-bar solos, characteristically moving the meter around on "Blase." On Talbert's instrumental original "I'm Shooting High," Marsh's twenty-four-bar solo is rhythmically fuzzy at times. His improvisation on "The Moonshower," while hardly spectacular, makes considerably more sense than Talbert's unmemorable melody. The whole atmosphere is commercial, however tasteful, with little room for blowing, and the record has at best a historical value.

At least the Winding-Talbert records were released, though they seem to have received no reviews. Another recording, *Lennie Tristano Quintet: Live in Toronto 1952*, privately recorded at a concert July 17, 1952, was infinitely more substantial, but was not released by Jazz Records until 1982. On this recording, with a rhythm section of Tristano, Peter Ind on bass, and Alan Levitt on drums, Marsh is in excellent form. For the first time one hears the intensely swinging, "bubbly" quality that characterized his best playing of the 1950s. The sound is still light, but the notes pop out with a rhythmic authority that could not be even marginally described as "wisp-like," especially on the driving minor tune "Lennie's Pennies." With Konitz and Tristano in equally good form, this record, despite the amateur recording quality, probably best represents the Tristano group of the early 1950s, while Tristano was still actively performing and before Konitz left, in the fall of 1952, to join Stan Kenton.

Konitz's decision to accept Kenton's offer was the first step in what was viewed as apostasy by Tristano's more cultish followers. As Konitz recalled the situation, "Because I had a family, I was compelled to work, and I wanted to work as a musician, so I was more willing to do that than all the rest of those people. I mean, they really kind of ridiculed me for joining Stan Kenton's band . . . that I was joining this heavy-footed band that was kind of smacking of commercialism or whatever."

That Marsh may have disapproved along with others is suggested by the fact that when Konitz appeared with Kenton at the Hollywood Bowl late in 1952, Marsh, though in town visiting his mother, failed to come hear him. Konitz felt hurt: "I kept saying, 'Jeez, why doesn't this guy come in and hear what I'm doing?' No interest." This despite Konitz's having praised Marsh in print earlier that year: "[F]or me, after Lennie the craziest [i.e., most impressive] musician around today [is] Warne Marsh."[74]

Possibly Marsh's failure to check out Konitz at the Bowl was due less to lack of interest than to conflicts with his own playing activities during his brief visit home. One occasion, when he appeared with Shelly Manne, pianist Hampton Hawes, and bassist Joe Mondragon at The Haig, just off Wilshire in downtown Los Angeles, is documented by a private recording made December 23, 1952, but not released until 1979.

Warne Marsh/Live in Hollywood is especially interesting as a rare example of Marsh's work with major players outside of the Tristano orbit. Hawes's punchy, hard-edged, rhythmically precise style, complemented by Manne's intense groove on brushes and ride cymbal, was a world away from Tristano's rhythm sections and from the more diffuse, more varied approach to time that Marsh had developed under Tristano, from his sudden twisting dives in and out of the flow, his inclination to emphasize subtlety over drive, notes over rhythm. Yet some worthwhile music resulted from this seeming mismatch.

On the up-tempo "Fine and Dandy" Marsh, though sometimes lagging behind the beat, allows himself to be caught up in the insistent flow of Manne's ride cymbal and turns in an excellent solo, as he does in the similarly up-tempo "I Got Rhythm" and "Buzzy." On the latter, a Charlie Parker blues, he achieves structure and unity by building several choruses around a simple triadic figure. In general, though, he sounds more comfortable at the more relaxed tempos of "All the Things You Are," "I'll Remember April," and especially "I Can't Believe That You're in Love with Me," where the Lester Young influence is distinctly present. Perhaps his most impressive solo is on the ballad "You Go to My Head." In all of his work here the so-called bebop triplet and the grupetto, or turn, favored by Tristano and Young, are much in evidence, both of them devices that he eventually abandoned. Again the amateur nature of the recording is apparent, but Marsh's extended solos on this record provide a tantalizing example of what could happen when he allowed himself to play with more mainstream musicians.

NOTES

1. Phil Featheringill, "Chicago Telescope," *Metronome*, October 1945, 14.
2. George Simon, "Simon Blows His Top—About Bop," *Metronome*, February 1948, 24.
3. Leonard Feather, "Ella and Her Fella," *Metronome*, October 1948, 28.
4. Barry Ulanov, "Lennie Tristano Trio," *Metronome*, April 1947, 32.
5. Ulanov, "A Call to Arms—and Horns," *Metronome*, April 1947, 15, 44.

6. Ulanov, "Checking a Judgment," *Metronome,* April 1947, 50.

7. "Musician of the Year—Lennie Tristano," *Metronome,* January 1948, 19.

8. "Influences of the Year: Lester Young, Sarah Vaughan, Lennie Tristano," *Metronome,* February 1949, 18.

9. Ulanov, "What's Hot and What's Not," *Metronome,* July 1949, 30.

10. Ulanov, "Master in the Making," *Metronome,* August 1949, 14–15. In an interview, Ulanov said Tristano did his reading at that time by listening to recordings for the blind.

11. Ulanov, "Stan Kenton Joins the New Jazz Society," *Metronome,* May 1950, 25.

12. "Metronome's All Stars," *Metronome,* January 1948.

13. "The First Ten Years of Birdland," *Down Beat,* December 10, 1959, 20. See also "Crowd Gives Enthusiastic Welcome to Extreme Bop by Pettiford All Stars," *Down Beat,* January 28, 1949, 1; "Boppers Taking Breather in NYC," *Down Beat,* January 28, 1949, 1; "Clique Bop Folds; Gals Take Over," *Down Beat,* April 8, 1949, 1; "Clique, Bop (City)," *Metronome,* April 1949, 6, 8.

14. John Francis McKinney, "The Pedagogy of Lennie Tristano" (Ph.D. dissertation, Fairleigh Dickinson University, 1978), 93.

15. Ira Gitler, *Jazz Masters of the Forties* (New York and London: Macmillan, 1966), 234.

16. Ulanov, "Things Are Looking Up Now," *Metronome,* April 1949, 42.

17. Bruyninckx gives a fifth title, "Tautology," but the version on Prestige 7004 that he cites was recorded in September 1949 with Sal Mosca on piano.

18. "Lennie Tristano Quintet," *Metronome,* April 1949, 40.

19. Tom Herrick, "Diggin' the Discs with Tom," *Down Beat,* April 22, 1949, 14.

20. A photocopy of the letter was given to me by Marsh's mother on April 24, 1990.

21. Erik Erikson, *Young Man Luther* (New York: W.W. Norton and Co., 1962), 41–42.

22. "Lennie Tristano," *Metronome,* May 1949, 39.

23. "Lennie Tristano," *Down Beat,* May 20, 1949, 14.

24. McKinney, 93.

25. Robert Ronzello, "Warne Marsh—A Conversation with Robert Ronzello," *Saxophone Journal* (Spring 1982): 12.

26. Bruce Turner, *Hot Air—Cool Music* (London: Quartet), 117.

27. "Lennie Tristano," *Metronome,* September 1949, 38.

28. Mike Levin, "Lennie Tristano," *Down Beat,* October 21, 1949, 14.

29. Francis Davis, "Tristanoites: The Legacy of Lennie Tristano," *Village Voice,* 4 June 1991, 51.

30. Ulanov, "The Means of Mastery," *Metronome,* September 1949, 14.

31. Ulanov, ibid.

32. Ulanov, "Tardy Triumph," *Metronome,* December 1950, 38.

33. Ulanov, "The Means of Mastery," *Metronome,* 26.

34. Ulanov, ibid., 14, 26.

35. Ronzello, 12.

36. Ronnie Ball, "Portrait of Tristano," *Melody Maker,* January 27, 1951, 5.

37. See fn. 57, "Tristano: Guru Extraordinaire," p. 77, above.

38. Frank Tirro, "The Silent Theme Tradition in Jazz," *Musical Quarterly* (July 1967): 329.

39. Ronzello, 17.

40. Gitler, 226.

41. "The First Ten Years of Birdland," 20.

42. Mike Levin, "Lee Konitz," *Down Beat,* December 2, 1949, 14.

43. Barry Ulanov, "Lee Konitz," *Metronome,* December 1949, 33–34.

44. Pat Harris, "Tristanoites Work Hard to Get to Hear Lennie," *Down Beat,* December 2, 1949, 4.

45. "Where the Bands Are Playing," *Down Beat,* November 18, 1949, 17.

46. Barry Ulanov, "A Concert in Boston," *Metronome,* December 1949, 42.

47. "Birdland Again Sets Opening," *Down Beat,* January 13, 1950, 13. See also "Birds, but Not of a Feather," *Metronome,* February 1950, 8.

48. John S. Wilson, "Birdland Applies Imagination to Jazz," *Down Beat,* January 17, 1950, 3.

49. Davis, 51.

50. Bruyninckx gives the date as December 24, 1949, but this is incorrect. Both McKinney (p. 196) and Bill Miner's liner notes to IAJRC 20 state that the concert was Christmas night, December 25.

51. Bill Miner, liner notes to *Stars of Modern Jazz Concert at Carnegie Hall, Christmas, 1949,* IAJRC 20.

52. Lee Konitz, interview.

53. Mark Gardner, liner notes to *Warne Marsh: Live in Hollywood,* Xanadu LP151.

54. Ronzello, 13.

55. McKinney, 99, 100–101.

56. Ibid., 100.

57. "Schoenberg of Jazz," *Time,* August 27, 1951, 84.

58. Leonard Feather, "A Sound Test," *Down Beat,* October 31, 1956, 31.

59. Ted Brown, interview.

60. "Max Roach Talks Tristano with Ed Scarvalone," transcript of broadcast on WKCR, New York City, January 22, 1979.

61. Leonard Bernstein, "The Jazz Scene Today," *Down Beat,* June 17, 1953, 6.

62. Gordon Jack, "Peter Ind Interview," unpublished, originally broadcast on BBC c. 1996.

63. *Metronome,* November 1951, 19.

64. Terry Martin and John Litweiler, unpublished interview, October 14, 1973.

65. Barry Ulanov, "Conscious Lee," *Metronome,* December 1948, 17.

66. "Lee Looks Them Over," *Metronome*, 13, 23.

67. "Lee Konitz School," *Metronome,* September 1951, 13.

68. "Getz-Young School," *Metronome,* September 1951, 15.

69. Barry Ulanov, "Symptoms and Symbols," *Metronome,* February 1950, p. 34.

70. Bill Coss, "A New Look at Lennie," *Metronome,* November 1951, 13.

71. Ibid., 13, 22.
72. "Metronome Ticks On," *Metronome,* August 1951, 8–9.
73. Tom Talbert, interview.
74. Nat Hentoff, "Scanning," *Down Beat,* July 2, 1952, 19.

Warne Marsh solo on "Marshmallow" ("Cherokee"), recorded June 28, 1949, LEE
KONITZ, New Jazz 807/Prestige 7004 & 24081, transcribed for tenor saxophone by
Andy Fite, as published in WARNE MARSH RECORDED SOLOS (William H. Bauer
Inc., Albertson, N.Y. 11507).

Analysis

ANALYSIS OF WARNE MARSH'S SOLO ON "MARSHMALLOW"
("CHEROKEE"), RECORDED JUNE 28, 1949,
LEE KONITZ QUINTET, **NEW JAZZ 807/PRESTIGE 7004,**
BY SAFFORD CHAMBERLAIN

This early Warne Marsh solo illustrates what critic Lawrence Kart meant when he described Marsh as a "compulsive structuralist." Marsh never wandered aimlessly through the changes; rather a typical Marsh solo was built around a series of motivic sequences, each motif being developed in several variations. This highly disciplined aspect often stood in contrast to more freely flowing transitional passages.

Here the first section (bars 1–32) is highly structured; the multinoted bridge (bars 33–48) is free flowing; and the last section (bars 49–64) integrates features of both previous sections. Overall there is a strong thesis-antithesis-synthesis pattern.

To see how this works we can look at a few specifics. The first phrase (bars 2–3) establishes a pattern for the whole first section, a stately, unhurried (though the tempo is very fast), quarter-note based motif whose shape is repeated exactly in the second phrase (bars 4–5) and referred to in various forms throughout the section.

The last two bars of the opening section (bars 31–32) emerge naturally out of what has gone before but also begin a transition to the bridge, with bar 33 outlining in parallel fashion the bridge's opening chord. Then begins the long, six-bar outburst of rapid-fire eighth notes (bars 34–40) that constitutes the release from the restraint of the first section. The last phrase of the bridge (bars 41–48) signals an intent to return to the more deliberate, quarter-note feeling of the opening, but the transition is not fully realized until bar 57, where rests, held notes, and brief motivic phrases ease us to closure.

This solo shares some features with Charlie Parker's famous "KoKo," also based on "Cherokee," recorded four years earlier, November 26, 1945. However, it stands in striking contrast in its overall feeling to both Parker's solo and the usual run of Parker-influenced, up-tempo bebop solos. Describing "KoKo" in *The Smithsonian Collection of Classic Jazz*, Martin Williams wrote, "KoKo . . . is a torrential, virtuoso improvisation, yet in its use of space, rest, and silence and in its initial juxtaposition of short tension-phrases and flowing, melodious release-phrases, it is also a beautifully paced performance." I find similar characteristics in Marsh's solo. Where it principally differs is in its deliberate, compositional air. Parker's solo, while beautifully structured in its own terms, is mostly what Williams calls "torrential," with the bridge being the more deliberately patterned section, while Marsh, who of course knew Parker's solo, places the torrentiality of his bridge in a setting of stateliness.

Hello Prez, Goodbye Lennie

One of the most exciting, briefest, and least noticed of Marsh's pre-1955 recordings was his solo on the *Metronome* All Stars recording of July 9, 1953. Considering his low profile in these years, he had done surprisingly well in *Metronome*'s annual poll, finishing fourth behind Stan Getz, the runaway leader, Flip Phillips, and Lester Young for three consecutive years, 1951–53. It is true that in 1953 his vote total of 135 paled beside Getz's 910, and probably a truer measure of his reputation was the *Down Beat* poll for the same year, in which he finished eleventh with ninety-eight votes to Getz's 1,164. Nevertheless the polls testify to the impact of his playing despite his relative seclusion. For the All Star date Barry Ulanov, unable to secure the services of Getz or Phillips, paired Marsh with his idol, Lester Young, and Marsh, following Roy Eldridge's lead solo, turned in a stunning sixteen bars on the up-tempo version of "How High the Moon." There is no rhythmic fuzziness here, nor any kind of fuzziness. Following Eldridge could have been no easy task, but Marsh's solo is easily the most inspired on the record, Eldridge included. John LaPorta, who was on the date on clarinet, said, "I was glad I didn't have to follow Warne. He played like Bach, total melodic flow, no licks." Marsh later reported to Susan Chen that Lester Young commended him with a laconic "Yeah, Prez." Said LaPorta, "That says it all for Lester. I think they were both Prez. I felt fortunate to be there."

Unfortunately for Marsh the record was never reviewed. *Metronome* ran an account of the recording session that mentioned Marsh favorably but bundled him in amid references to Eldridge, Kai Winding, and Lester Young: "Roy Eldridge led the ensemble on trumpet and blew some stupendous solos. Kai Winding, who has become almost a fixture on these dates, played fine trombone, while the tenor sax honors were divided between Lester Young, who made his *Metronome* All Star debut on this date, and Warne Marsh. Both played great horn, the former playing several solos and filling in often behind Billy's [Eckstine's] singing, the latter showing off especially well on the up-tempoed Moon."[1] *Down Beat* reviewed the ballad-tempo vocal releases of "St. Louis Blues" and "How High the Moon" featuring Eckstine, but somehow the instrumental sides got lost in the cracks.

Other Tristano students continued to get more press than the reclusive Marsh. Early in 1951 *Down Beat*'s Chicago correspondent Jack Tracy did a profile of pianist Lloyd Lifton, urging readers to "add his name to your list of probable future stars."[2] Lifton and fellow Tristano student Bill Russo at this time were cowriting a regular column of analysis of transcribed solos for *Down Beat* called "Music Off the Record." In February 1952 Nat Hentoff did a piece on clarinetist Bob Wilber as "one of Lee Konitz's most enthusiastic students."[3] And early in 1953 *Down Beat* carried a profile of Ronnie Ball.[4]

After the *Metronome* All Stars recording, Marsh spent the next two years in virtually total seclusion, studying with Tristano. By the end of 1954 he had dropped nearly out of sight in the annual polls, finishing fourteenth with twenty-nine votes in *Down Beat*'s poll and going unlisted in *Metronome*'s. In March 1955 a *Metronome* letter-writer from Ohio asked, "Where is Warne Marsh?" a query left unanswered by the editors.[5] In June, Bill Coss took note of Marsh's reclusiveness in discussing new directions on the tenor saxophone. Marsh, he said, "really should" lead the way, "but probably won't because he shares Lennie's seclusion."[6]

On June 14 Marsh, thanks to Lee Konitz, finally broke his recorded silence, making his most important record since 1949, indeed one of his most important ever, *Lee Konitz with Warne Marsh,* Atlantic LP 1217. Once again Konitz was the leader, and the group included fellow Tristanoites Sal Mosca, Billy Bauer, and, on one track, Ronnie Ball. But a significant difference from earlier recordings was Konitz's choice of Oscar Pettiford on bass and Kenny Clarke on drums. The more one listens to the record the more crucial one feels Clarke and Pettiford to be. Pettiford, especially, comes through as a spiritual center.

One measure of Pettiford's and Clarke's influence is the performance of all concerned on the bassist's slow blues, "Don't Squawk." As has been noted, the Tristanoites were little drawn to the blues. But here Marsh in particular seems affected by the gentle sound and lovely melodic conception of Pettiford's opening two choruses, and he responds with an ingenious solo that is both highly personal and full of traditional blues feeling, characterized by intervallic leaps into the altissimo register and by his unique dry, wry sound. It is this sound, more than anything else, that gives this solo its striking ironic edge. As critic Al Zeiger had recently pointed out, a central aim of Tristano's music was to expand the emotional range of jazz, to "incorporate other than happy and sad emotions," and this involved jettisoning "the lush sensuous sounds of previous jazz, along with the sentimentality associated with them."[7] Marsh's sound on "Don't Squawk" perfectly illustrates this endeavor. At the same time as he exploits blues licks, Marsh uses his sound to comment on the tradition, distancing himself from sentimentality and self-pity. Indeed, his performance teeters on the verge of parody, suggesting though never descending into it.

Mosca and Konitz also contribute excellent, lyrical solos, though not as daringly ironic as Marsh's, while Bauer's sensitive comping blends beautifully with Pettiford's bass and Clarke's subtle ride cymbal. On the whole, "Don't Squawk" is a superb blues statement such as was rarely achieved or even attempted by the Tristano circle, and much of the credit must go to Pettiford and Clarke, neither of whom had played with this exact group before.

"Don't Squawk," in fact, seems the lodestone of the entire record, drawing everything into its force field. Pettiford and Clarke, with their more direct feeling for the blues, infuse even such typical Tristanoite lines as the master's "Two Not One," Ball's "Ronnie's Line," and Marsh's "Background Music" with a warmer, less austere feel, while on more mainstream tunes like "Topsy," "Donna Lee," and "There Will Never Be Another You" the congeniality of the rhythm section spurs Marsh and Konitz to deliver classic solos, Marsh's remarkable for their ingenuity, Konitz's for their lyricism. On the album's only ballad, "I Can't Get Started," Marsh's solo is startlingly original, again utilizing surprising intervallic leaps and exploiting the altissimo register, while Konitz's opening chorus is a melodic gem. On this track, as on "Topsy," Mosca lays out on piano, and Bauer's comping makes a significant contribution.

As impressive as are the solos, the album is perhaps most arresting for the joint improvisation on out-choruses by Marsh and Konitz. Except for Gerry Mulligan's groups, little like this had been heard from modernists since the ascendance of bebop. The rapport between the two is little short of magical, especially on "Started" and "Another You." This challenge to usual bebop procedures was never taken up by mainstream modernists, though the avant-garde has continued to explore it.

This album, widely considered a classic of cool jazz, seems as fresh in the 1990s as when it was first released. Yet the earliest review, by an unnamed reviewer in *Metronome,* possibly Bill Coss, must have been terribly disappointing, especially as the reviewer utterly misunderstood what happens on the out-chorus of "Donna Lee" and, what was worse, extended his misunderstanding to a criticism of Kenny Clarke's drumming over the whole album. "Pettiford has to fight Kenny Clarke throughout," he asserts, backing up his judgment with "dig his [Clarke's] last break in Donna—and see how scrambled the horns get then."[8] What actually happens is that Marsh and Konitz deliberately begin on the "and" of beat one, rather than the "and" of two, and continue playing off-meter until the very last phrase, where they throw in two extra eighth notes to bring the ending back on track. Clarke, meantime, holds the time exactly where it's supposed to be. Konitz, confirming that this was deliberate, said that he and Marsh had often played the tune this way before. He also said that they did not bother to tell Clarke what they were going to do in advance.

Hearing the tension between horns and rhythm section, the reviewer attributed it to defective drumming rather than to the Tristanoish joke perpetrated by Marsh and Konitz. This was doubly unfortunate, as it persuaded him to begin his review with the lukewarm characterization, "A competent, swinging album," before finally admitting that the perceived conflict between Pettiford and Clarke was "the only real criticism of the album, one you will like." This reviewer also misidentified "Two Not One" as based on "Perdido" rather than "I Can't Believe That You're in Love with Me," and "Background Music" as "Maybe That's Why I Love You" instead of "All of Me."[9]

Shortly afterward Jack Tracy of *Down Beat* gave the album the top rating of five stars: "I have never heard Lee and Warne recorded this warmly before. Perhaps it is due to a rhythm section that spurs and swings, rather than acting as a metronome. . . . [T]here is a personality and relaxedness present that offers a stronger bond of communication than I have ever heard. . . . This is a provocative album, one with virility and lasting music."[10] Tracy obviously heard no conflict between Pettiford and Clarke.

June 1955 was a banner month for Lennie Tristano as well. He had begun, in late May or early June, playing in the Sing Song Room of the Confucius restaurant at 237 W. 52nd Street, his first club engagement in several years, and this led to his first long-playing record, indeed his first of any sort since 1951, titled *Lennie Tristano,* Atlantic LP 1224. Five of the tunes were recorded live at the Confucius, with Konitz, bassist Gene Ramey, and drummer Arthur Taylor. The other four, "Line Up," "East Thirty-Second," "Turkish Mambo," and "Requiem," were tremendously impressive performances, unlike anything Tristano or anyone else had ever recorded. But because Tristano had made use of the new technology of multitaping, they provoked a huge controversy. They also had a provenance markedly different from that of the live club recordings.

Connie Crothers, a student and close associate of Tristano's from 1962 to his death in 1978, has said that originally all material for the record was to come from the engagement at the Confucius. Performances were taped over the course of one or several evenings, but Konitz was dissatisfied with much of his playing, approving only five tunes for release.[11] At this point Nesuhi Ertegun, who was producing the record for Atlantic, came to Tristano's studio, wandered around, and noticed some practice tapes that Tristano had made. From these tapes, which Tristano had perhaps not originally intended for release, came the four controversial tracks that completed the record.

When the record came out, Barry Ulanov's liner notes virtually invited controversy. He began by defending Tristano against previously leveled charges of coldness and inaccessibility: "Uncompromising he may be. . . . But remote, inaccessible, recondite he is not. . . ."[12] Almost in the same breath he proceeded to defend Tristano's performance against the criticism, which he seems to have anticipated, that it was somehow antijazz: "This is jazz, no mistaking it for anything else. It meets all the requirements: it is improvised, brilliantly adding ideas to ideas all the way through; it swings, rapturously. . . . And so it is to the jazz in this record that I suggest you listen, forgetting, if you can, any preconceived notions about what Lennie Tristano represents in modern music. . . ." After a passage to the effect that it is the music itself that reveals the artist, and that this is "particularly true of jazz, where a performer composes as he blows, if he is a genuine jazz musician," Ulanov casually, almost incidentally, reveals that the recording has been technologically manipulated: "Lennie has fooled with the tapes of *East Thirty-Second* and *Line Up*, adjusting the bass lines Peter Ind (on bass) and Jeff Morton (on drums) prepared for him to the piano lines he has superimposed upon them." Exactly what "fooled with" means is never explained, and Ulanov rushes to refute the notion that there is a contradiction between such manipulation and the idea, which he has just expressed, that improvisation, the performer composing as he plays, is basic to jazz: "But the mechanical adjustment of tapes is not what you hear. What comes through first of all and last of all is the jazz, uninterrupted and pulsating and overpowering jazz. . . ."

The controversy that Ulanov's apologetics tried to avert, but probably encouraged, climaxed in the summer of 1956 in *Down Beat*'s "Letters to the Editor" column. There pianist John Mehegan asserted that Tristano must have recorded the piano parts of "Line Up" and "East Thirty-Second Street" at a slower tempo, "probably a perfect fifth down," and then speeded up the piano tape until it matched the prerecorded rhythmic accompaniment. His implication, which had already been voiced by others, was that Tristano's procedure was unethical and the resulting music aesthetically invalid, especially as improvised jazz.

Marsh, then at home in California, quickly came to his mentor's defense: "I feel obligated to point out that John Mehegan's eloquent appraisal of

Lennie Tristano's recording technique on *Line-Up* and *East Thirty-Second* is eloquently incorrect. . . . However, I don't hope to be able to illustrate this to John as long as he insists upon regarding Lennie's music as a personal challenge, rendering him incapable, of course, of simply listening to the music."[13] Typically laconic, Marsh did not trouble to explain exactly how Mehegan had erred.

Tristano's own response was disingenuous and evasive. In 1956 he told Nat Hentoff, "I understand some people say that making a record like the one I made isn't fair because I couldn't play the numbers that fast in a club. Well, I'll learn the record so I can play it at that tempo 'live.'" The record sounded good to him, he said, and "it's the music that matters."[14] John LaPorta recalled that Leonard Bernstein asked Tristano about his procedure, insisting that in certain passages he must have overdubbed himself because otherwise his two hands would bump into each other. Tristano's coy reply was, "It's all there in the music." Twenty years later, in the summer of 1975, Tristano described the multitaping of "Line Up" and "East Thirty-Second" to an anonymous interviewer. Explaining that he "always had a problem" with rhythm sections, he said, "I recorded the rhythm section first, so the rhythm won't mess up. . . . Many critics claim that I speeded up the tape of my piano. But what I did was to record the rhythm section first and I record[ed] my piano on that. There was no gimmick as critics say. Besides I did not play the piano that fast [i.e., the tempo on the record is not exceptionally fast]. If you insist, I'll show you that I can play much faster than that record."[15]

Aside from the fact that this explanation came twenty years after the fact and was never published in English at all, it apparently wasn't true. Although Barry Ulanov stated in 1997 that he "could not imagine that [Tristano] would have hidden something like that from me,"[16] he appears to have done just that. Sal Mosca has said that it was common knowledge among Tristano's students that he had, in fact, reduced the speed of the rhythm track by half and recorded the piano over it at half-speed. He must then have doubled the speed of the whole tape. The bass and drums would then be at real time and pitch, while the piano part would be an octave higher and twice as fast as originally recorded. Ted Brown said that at a lesson Tristano had played an early pressing of the pieces in question for him. His first reaction was, "That sounds speeded up." Tristano denied it. Later Brown played the record at half-speed, 16 2/3 rpm. At that speed, which made everything an octave lower, the bass and drums sounded distorted, but the piano sounded as it should sound in that register, convincing him that Tristano had played the piano part at half-speed in the lower register. He said that Peter Ind, who had state-of-the-art equipment similar to Tristano's, came to the same conclusion. So did Alan Broadbent, a later student.

The question remains—why did Tristano consistently, but so evasively, deny the truth? His statements that he could play "much faster than that" were beside the point. Brown felt that the tapes in question were simply experiments, devices for practice never intended for release. At the time, said Brown, Tristano was emphasizing to his students the value of practicing improvising on tunes at much slower tempos than they would use in performance. He did this himself, and Brown was certain that he had practiced with the rhythm tapes that Ind and Morton had provided, both at the real tempo and at half-speed. But though one can readily imagine Tristano practicing "Line Up" with the rhythm tape at half-speed, it is not so easy, unless he planned to speed up the tape, to imagine him practicing with his right hand in the bottom register of the piano, where he would never play a right-hand line in performance. And if he planned to speed up the tape, the next question is why? Just out of curiosity, or to prepare them for release? If the latter, when? Before or after Ertegun expressed his interest? In other words, how much and what kind of purpose went into the preparation and release of these performances?

Given all the circumstances, Tristano's motives for denial remain obscure. Even played at half-speed, real time for the piano, his performances on "Line Up" and "East Thirty-Second" are impressive. One persuasive explanation, suggested by Alan Broadbent and others, is simply that Tristano enjoyed playing mind games with people, especially the jazz critics of the time. Or perhaps, ardent champion of live improvisation as he professed himself to be, Tristano could not bring himself to admit to an essentially compositional procedure incompatible with that ideal, no matter how successful as composition. He could say, "It's all there in the music," but he couldn't bring himself to explain the details.

Whether Marsh understood this when he came to Tristano's defense is an open question. In failing to specify exactly where Mehegan's analysis went wrong, he indulged in the same evasiveness as Tristano. It is even possible that Tristano solicited him to write his letter and that along with Tristano's other students, he knew that Tristano was lying. He could say that Mehegan was wrong because he knew that Tristano had recorded the piano an *octave* below the rhythm track, not a *fifth* below as Mehegan had said.

The other two tracks that filled out the LP, "Turkish Mambo" and "Requiem," were only peripherally involved in the controversy. Ulanov's notes had admitted that "Turkish Mambo" contained "three lines, played—and recorded—one on top of the other," and he had declared that "Requiem" was "not really of any mechanical or electronic interest except in the paired piano lines that merge and separate from time to time."

Tristano himself gave an account of the recording of "Requiem" to the same anonymous interviewer cited earlier: "Let me tell you about

'Requiem.' It was March in 1955. Dizzy Gillespie called me and told me that Bird died. When I heard that, I couldn't say anything. Parker was [a] good friend of mine. He was the most wonderful and one of the greatest musicians I've ever known. So, that night, all I did was just play piano. About five hours later, I started recording the piano by myself and recorded 'Requiem.'"[17] Though Tristano did not elaborate on the actual recording process, overdubbing is obvious ten bars from the end, where a third hand would be required for the tremolo that is interjected at that point. A recent British publication asserts, without supporting evidence, that he recorded all of it at half-speed "so that, when played back [at normal speed], it would have an other-worldly ring to it."[18]

Aside from the multitaping controversy, a question raised by Tristano's record and the long engagement at the Confucius, which lasted through the summer, is why Marsh, always a favorite student, never appeared with him and Konitz, either on the record or at the restaurant. According to Crothers, Tristano had originally wanted Marsh for the Confucius engagement, but Marsh had told her, years later, that he had not felt ready. Another explanation, offered by Ted Brown, is, if true, a poignant instance of mundane reality intruding on art. It seems that Tristano had begun keeping company with a woman who until then had been going with Marsh, with the consequence that Marsh studiously avoided the Confucius. Whatever the case, Marsh's absence at the Confucius and on the record prefigured his immanent departure from New York.

A month after his June recording, Marsh appeared with Konitz at the Newport Jazz Festival, accompanied by an unfamiliar rhythm section of West Coast pianist Russ Freeman, Bob Carter on bass, and the Boston-based Buzzy Drootin on drums. Jack Tracy in *Down Beat* had nothing specific to say about Marsh's playing.[19] *Metronome*'s reviewer felt that "Konitz and Marsh never did catch fire, although the indication was there."[20]

In August 1955 Marsh put an end to his studies with Tristano and headed back to California. Both Marsh and Konitz participated in a Hollywood Bowl jazz concert on August 15, along with Buddy de Franco, Cal Tjader, Shelly Manne, Billie Holiday, and others. A *Metronome* review mentioned only Konitz, but Konitz confirmed that Marsh also was there, recalling that he and Marsh appeared for the rehearsal at the Bowl wearing short pants and were told by the conductor, Leonard Bernstein, that that would not do for the concert.[21] They had to leave the rehearsal to change, with the result that although they played most of the concert, they did not play in Billie Holiday's segment.

On departing New York for Los Angeles, Marsh left behind most of the belongings in his apartment, including Ted Brown's chess set. They were confiscated by his landlady.

The Tristano circle had already begun to break up. Konitz had long since asserted his own independence. In the spring of 1955, at the memorial concert for Charlie Parker, who died March 13, Jeff Morton had met the sculptress Julie McDonald, who was close to Parker and had sculpted a bust of him. She and Morton had subsequently taken up residence at her home in Pasadena, a suburb of Los Angeles. Others, like Ronnie Ball and Peter Ind, were in demand outside of the circle. With the engagement at the Confucius, which ran into the fall of 1955, Tristano could no longer conduct weekly sessions for his students, and he was having problems with the lease at 317 East 32nd Street. Konitz and Marsh left in August. The following June, Tristano closed his school in Manhattan and began teaching at his home on Palo Alto Street in Hollis, Long Island.[22] The building on East 32nd Street was demolished around 1962, when a huge apartment complex called Kips Bay Towers was erected, taking up two whole blocks.

Marsh had studied with Tristano for eight years, counting his time at Fort Monmouth. In that period he had generally avoided commercial work, recorded very little, received a minimum of press, and rarely performed except with Tristano or members of his circle. Yet he had gained the respect of discriminating fans, critics, and fellow musicians, including, according to Tristano, Charlie Parker: "The only person I felt Bird was sincere about in his praise was Warne Marsh. . . . We were playing in one of those dives when Bird tapped me on the shoulder and asked, 'Who's that kid?' I told him it was Warne, one of my students. Bird said, 'You watch that kid: he's got it.'"[23] In August 1955 Marsh may have felt it was time to put Bird's judgment to the test and move out on his own.

NOTES

1. "Metronome All Stars Record!" *Metronome,* September 1953, 13–15.
2. Jack Tracy, "Bright Future Predicted for Creative Chi Pianist," *Down Beat,* March 23, 1951, 6.
3. Nat Hentoff, "Former Dixieland Stalwart Bob Wilber Now a Pupil at Lennie Tristano School," *Down Beat,* February 8, 1952, 7, 18.
4. Leonard Feather, "Another British Pianist Scores Here," *Down Beat,* February 11, 1953, 18.
5. Sid Kelly, "Marsh Fire," *Metronome,* March 1955, 13, 35.
6. Bill Coss, "The Heart of the Matter," *Metronome,* June 1955, 19.
7. Al Zeiger, "Lennie Tristano: A Debt of Gratitude," *Metronome,* June 1955, 23.
8. "Lee Konitz, Warne Marsh," *Metronome,* January 1956, 36.
9. Ibid.

10. J[ack] T[racy], "Lee Konitz with Warne Marsh," *Down Beat*, January 11, 1956, 25.

11. Crothers thought the recording continued for several evenings, but Lawrence Kart says in his liner notes to Mosaic MD6-174, *The Complete Atlantic Recordings of Lennie Tristano, Lee Konitz & Warne Marsh,* that only one night was recorded. In 1981 Atlantic released SD2-7006, *The Lennie Tristano Quartet,* a double album of further titles from the Confucius.

12. Barry Ulanov, liner notes to *Tristano,* Atlantic 1224, c. 1956.

13. Warne Marsh, letter to the editor, *Down Beat,* July 11, 1956, 4.

14. Nat Hentoff, "Multitaping Isn't Phony: Tristano," *Down Beat,* May 5, 1956, 11.

15. Anonymous, "Interview with Lennie Tristano." This interview, in the form of an unsigned typescript, was among Marsh's papers. It was published in Japanese in *Swing Journal,* July 1976. My quotes are from the English typescript. The interviewer may have been the editor, Kioshi Koyama, an admirer of Tristano.

16. Interview. In his liner notes to Mosaic MD6-174, Lawrence Kart stated that Tristano had recorded himself at half-speed on "Line Up" and "East Thirty-Second." When I apprised Ulanov of Kart's statements, he said he had asked Tristano about it and that Tristano had denied it.

17. Anonymous, "Interview with Lennie Tristano."

18. Ian Carr, Digby Fairweather, Brian Priestley, *Jazz: The Essential Companion* (New York: Prentice Hall, 1987), 506.

19. Jack Tracy, "Newport!" *Down Beat,* August 24, 1955, 13.

20. "Newport Jazz Fest," *Metronome,* September 1955, 15.

21. Fran Kelley, "That Hollywood Bowl Concert," *Metronome,* November 1955, 20.

22. Ted Brown, interview.

23. "Lennie Tristano," *Down Beat,* October 30, 1958, 42.

♫

Back Home

At about the same time as the Hollywood Bowl concert, Marsh played an engagement with Konitz at Jazz City, but his activities for the next six or eight months went unrecorded in the jazz press.[1]

Sharing with his mother the family home in North Hollywood, he had no financial worries, and he seems to have adopted a mildly bohemian lifestyle, turning up at sessions and parties in Venice, where the Beat scene publicized by Lawrence Lipton was in full swing.[2] A student, guitarist Tom Runyan, recalled that one of the first times he heard Marsh play was in the mid-1950s at the home of a painter in Venice.

Marsh also was in contact with the circle of musicians and others around Lenny Bruce, especially Joe Maini and his beautiful wife, Sandra. He and Joe were frequent ping-pong partners. He seems also to have had some part in what Sandra, speaking of her relationship with Joe, called "the world's dirtiest love affair," as Joe reportedly once caught the two in bed.[3] This was not the contretemps it would have been in conventional society, as Sandra was a prostitute and Joe was known to shop her around to his friends, sometimes in order to get money for reeds.

Other acquaintances were altoist Med Flory, who with his wife, Joanie, ran a kind of continuous open house for musicians at their home in North Hollywood; altoist Herb Geller and his wife, pianist Lorraine Geller; trumpeter Joe Burnett; bassists Buddy Clark and Red Mitchell; pianist John Bannister, a frequent partner at chess and scrabble; and singer Bobbi Lynn. Lynn, at that time married to pianist Pee Wee Lynn, worked with Lenny Bruce in Honolulu in 1956, substituting for Bruce's estranged wife, Honey, when she failed to show up for the gig.[4] A friend of Bruce, Maini, and the

Florys, she met Marsh around that time. According to her, she and Marsh spent "hundreds of hours" with the Mainis.

It was probably shortly after his return to Los Angeles in August 1955 that Marsh began rehearsing and playing occasional gigs with a pianoless trio that included such important Los Angeles-based players as bassist Leroy Vinnegar and various drummers—Shelly Manne, Frank Butler, and Larence Marable among others. Vinnegar, who settled in Los Angeles in 1954, said he met Marsh through Konitz and worked with him at such L.A. clubs of the later 1950s as Zardi's and Jazz City, both on Hollywood Boulevard.

One wonders about the omission of piano in this, Marsh's first serious attempt to launch himself into playing situations outside the Tristano circle. Possibly the absence of any piano player helped him to be free of Tristano. Tristano was, in fact, a busy and sometimes intrusive accompanist.

In May 1956 an item in *Down Beat* mentioned that Los Angeles drummer Rick Jones was "finalizing plans for the Warne Marsh and Herb Geller units to hit the Orient shortly."[5] Marsh's unit may have included Vinnegar, but the tour to the Orient apparently never took place. Marsh did record a 45-rpm single with Jones on drums and Ronnie Ball on piano somewhat later, in the summer or fall.

Ball, a fellow Tristano student, arrived in Los Angeles in the spring of 1956 as a member of the Kai Winding-J. J. Johnson quintet, and with his arrival a West Coast branch of the Tristano school of playing gradually emerged. At first Ball, Marsh, and possibly drummer Jeff Morton began playing Tuesday night sessions at a hangout for Samoan and Tahitian immigrants, Whisling's Hawaii at 6507 Sunset Boulevard, near Wilcox. Featuring thunder effects for its homesick South Pacific clientele, the club was described by Los Angeles writer Carolyn See as a "dank hole" reeking "of cigarettes and defeat."[6]

See, then a graduate student in English at UCLA, later a book reviewer, novelist, and memoirist, was a jazz night regular. She recalled how, on session nights, "skinny and somber" young jazz fans, "dressed entirely in black, hungry and intent, never cracking a smile," drifted in to supplant melancholy three hundred-pound Samoans in their flowered shirts. "One by one, jazz musicians [slid] quietly in, absent-minded, vacant. . . . The bassist could be Red Mitchell, pale and jovial, sometimes moved to whisper, 'Nice to see ya!' Or sometimes the black mountain, Leroy Vinnegar. . . . The pianist [was] usually Ronnie Ball, destined to be unmemorable because the hope was always, would Hampton Hawes show up tonight? 'The Legendary Joe Albany' . . . was always rumored to be somewhere in town. Then, quiet as a cat in a cat cemetery, a slight, beautiful, slim-to-scrawny tenor player would mosey out, carrying his horn, wearing a white businessman's shirt far too large for his thin boy's neck, and begin distractedly to search around for, and fiddle with, his reeds."[7]

This was Marsh. His playing, See wrote, was "careless perfection." But many times she and her graduate school friends would make the trip to hear him only to be disappointed, because "Warne wouldn't show." She implied that his absences were due to his use of "drugs that none of us could have named,"[8] and she later wrote that Marsh "was on heroin at the time, as were Art Pepper, Chet Baker, and a few more."[9] In a conversation with me, she said that because her sister had been a heroin addict, she knew the signs, and that "on many occasions" she had seen Marsh "nodding out" or "unable to speak." But while Marsh may have been using heroin then on an occasional basis, there is no indication that he was ever addicted to it. For one thing, he disliked needles. For another, heroin was frowned upon by Lennie Tristano and his circle. Finally, close associates such as Lee Konitz, Ted Brown, Alan Levitt, and Marsh's wife, Geraldyne, while speaking freely about Marsh's use of other drugs, such as methamphetamine or cocaine, have consistently denied that he was at any time addicted to heroin.

In August 1956 another Tristano student, saxophonist Ted Brown, arrived on his honeymoon to visit his family in Long Beach. He found Marsh working with a quintet at The Haig, a club off Wilshire in the shadow of the old Ambassador Hotel near downtown Los Angeles. The group included Ball, guitarist Don Overberg, bassist Ben Tucker, just out of the air force, and a fourth Tristanoite, drummer Jeff Morton. Morton and his wife, Julie McDonald, were living in McDonald's home in Pasadena, where every Tuesday and Thursday afternoon Marsh rehearsed his new quintet. Within a short time after Brown's arrival, Overberg left to accept a lucrative offer from singer Peggy Lee, and Brown took his place, giving the group, in which all but bassist Tucker were Tristano-trained, a distinctive two-tenor front line.

Private, low-fidelity recordings of the group, some with Overberg and others with Brown, as well as several commercial recordings, show that See's characterization of Marsh's playing at this time as "careless perfection" was not an exaggeration. On such furiously up-tempo tunes as the privately recorded "Limehouse Blues," "Three Little Words," "The Best Thing for You," and "Featherbed," Marsh's roaring solos are phenomenal for fleetness, facility, and an exhilarating, highly personal swing, more exciting than anything he had yet put on record. There is nothing of the tentative, dreamy, "wispy" quality of some of his playing with Tristano, who had tended to dominate the proceedings. In these recordings everyone seems to be having more fun than Tristano was in the habit of encouraging.

On August 31, apparently before Brown had been fully integrated into the group but after Overberg had left, Marsh, Ball, Morton, and Tucker participated in a jazz concert at the Pasadena Civic Auditorium. Besides Marsh's quartet, which was assigned the closing slot, traditionally the high point of a concert, five other groups representing a cross-section of L.A. jazz were on the program: Art Pepper, with a rhythm section of Ball, Tucker, and Frank Capp; Bobby Troup; the Pete Jolly Trio; Buddy Collette with Hampton Hawes, Red Callender, and drummer Gene Gammage; and the Dave Pell Octet featuring Lucy Ann Polk and trumpeter Jack Sheldon.

Reviewing the concert, *Down Beat*'s West Coast editor John Tynan wrote of Marsh's quartet: "This group is new to the coast both in organization and musical conception. Unabashed disciples of Lennie Tristano, Marsh's men nevertheless speak with eloquent voices of their own." He especially commended Marsh's "fluent, swinging tenor" and, on the opening blues and "Crazy He Calls Me," "the spare beauty of Ball's middle register solos." He concluded, "The Marsh group is on the west coast to stay, and its influence cannot but soon be felt."[10] In all his years in New York, working in the shadow of Tristano and Konitz, Marsh had seldom received this kind of appreciation.

With the Tuesday night sessions at Whisling's Hawaii still happening, Brown and Morton decided to query the owner, Bill Whisling, about playing on weekends. As a result the Warne Marsh Quintet became a fixture at the club from September 1956 to April 1957, playing Thursday or Friday through Sunday. They even persuaded Whisling to rename the place, putting up a sign proclaiming it a "Modern Jazz Room." *Down Beat*'s Tynan had dutifully kept track of Marsh since his return to Los Angeles, several times inserting items in the magazine's "Strictly Ad Lib" column. On October 3 he noted that "Warne Marsh's new group, with Ronnie Ball on piano, may go into the Topper at Whittier and Rosemead."[11] Whether this gig materialized is uncertain, but on the same day that the notice appeared the group went into the recording studio for Marsh's first date as a leader. A second session was held October 11, and the results were issued by Imperial Records, first in monaural as *Jazz of Two Cities* and later in stereo as *Winds of Marsh*. The two cities referred to were Los Angeles and New York, and the title suggests Marsh's ambivalence: he considered New York his aesthetic home, the locus of his education in jazz, while Los Angeles was not only his birth home but the place where his education truly flowered, independently of his mentor Tristano.

As Ted Brown recalled the sessions, Albert Marx, the producer, "had two different tape decks set up, one for mono and one for stereo, and we each had two microphones," so that the monaural and stereophonic recordings were done simultaneously. This resulted in a certain duplicity in the packaging of *Jazz of Two Cities*. The cover proclaimed it "recorded in stereo," which was true in that the two tapes were recorded at the same time—but the tape used was the monaural one.

Additionally, some of the material on *Winds of Marsh* was different. For *Jazz of Two Cities* Marsh and Ball did some editing, splicing in Marsh's solo from an alternate take on "Ear Conditioning" and Ball's solo from another take on "Lover Man." For *Winds of Marsh* the record company chose to use the original takes of these two tunes in their entirety, with no splicing, as well as alternate takes of "Jazz of Two Cities" and "I Never Knew." All this was done without consulting Marsh, and to friends he angrily labeled *Winds of Marsh* a "bootleg" record.[12] Ironically, his solo on the *Winds of Marsh* version of "I Never Knew" is at least equal if not superior to that on *Jazz of Two Cities.* In my opinion it is one of the best he ever recorded, and it is arguable that the solos that Marsh and Ball spliced in on "Ear Conditioning" and "Lover Man" are inferior to the less predictable ones on the original takes.[13] Also, the stereophonic fidelity of *Winds of Marsh* captures the bite of Marsh's sound much better than the monaural *Jazz of Two Cities.* All the alternate takes are included in the 1996 CD release on Capitol, *Lennie Tristano and Warne Marsh: Intuition.*

Comparing Marsh's work on these records with his earlier recordings, what is most noticeable is the passionate, authoritative swing on such tunes as "Smog Eyes" (Ted Brown's line on "There Will Never Be Another You"), "Ear Conditioning" (Ronnie Ball's line on "Look for the Silver Lining"), Ted Brown's title tune (based on "Play, Fiddle, Play"), and especially Marsh's own up-tempo arrangement of "I Never Knew" (modeled on a 1943 version of the tune recorded by Lester Young, Johnny Guarnieri, Slam Stewart, and Sid Catlett). Marsh and Brown, trading eight-bar solos and improvising contrapuntally on the bridge and final eight bars, contribute a beautifully simple and touching performance of "Lover Man." Brown's best solo is on the original take of "I Never Knew," the one issued on *Jazz of Two Cities,* but his playing overall is less flowing and less vigorous and exciting than Marsh's, which is in a class of its own. Nevertheless, one of the special attractions of the records is the improvised interplay between the two tenors, which rises almost to the level of the interplay between Marsh and Lee Konitz on their 1955 Atlantic LP. A minor defect is that the two tenors combine with Ball's habitual middle and lower register solos to create a somewhat monotonous sameness of sound. Another weakness is the inclusion of "Tchaikovsky's Opus 42, MT3," which had been converted to a popular song under the title of "These Are the Things I Love." This was an unfortunate lapse in taste—the piece takes up a good deal of space and adds little of value. Possibly Marsh's choice of this tune was a tribute to his mother, whose taste ran to light classics. Or possibly he just liked it.

In his review of *Jazz of Two Cities* Nat Hentoff noted the Tristano influence "in the penchant for long lines and the kind of airy but wiry phrasing and logical, flowing conception that marked those Capitol sides like Marionette and Sax of a Kind." Both tenors, he wrote, "blow with admirable technical ease, empathic, and stimulating ideas and good if coolish sound. . . . Their time is also precise and subtle." As for the complex Tristano-style lines, Hentoff commented that they "project a certain amount of brittleness . . . as if they were more a problem to solve than a story to tell."[14]

At the time, Lennie Tristano praised *Jazz of Two Cities* as "one of the best records made in recent years, from the standpoint of originality, swing, drive, improvising, and charts."[15] On the basis of Marsh's playing alone Tristano's judgment is justified, and the group as a whole is arguably the best that Marsh ever led.

One tune on the album, Marsh's difficult high-note exercise on the changes of "All the Things You Are" that he called "Dixie's Dilemma," memorialized Marsh's only known brush with the law. Marsh had recently been consorting with a seventeen-year-old girl named Dixie, once showing up to give a lesson with Dixie in tow, at which time she had proffered a handful of Benzedrine pills to the student, Tom Runyan. One evening, as Ted Brown recounted the story, an unusually tall man and woman of rather square, nonjazz appearance entered Whisling's while the band was on a break, shooting pool, and inquired if any of them knew a girl named Dixie. Others in the band, more wary and street-wise than Marsh, professed ignorance. When Marsh, honest to a fault, said, "Yeah, I know her," the couple, who were plainclothes police, arrested him on a charge of statutory rape—i.e., consensual sex with a girl under eighteen—and hustled him off to jail. He was released the following day after his mother posted bail, and charges were eventually dropped after it became known that the underage Dixie had slept not only with Marsh but with most of the Charlie Barnet big band. As Brown suggested, the dilemma was more Marsh's than Dixie's. Marsh's comment to Brown was, "If I had known she was a statue, I wouldn't have fucked her."

On October 24, two weeks after the second session for Imperial, the quintet went into the studio for Kapp Records, recording four tunes: "Ben Blew," a blues; "Time's Up," based on "Indiana"; "Earful," a Ronnie Ball line on "I'm Getting Sentimental Over You"; and Marsh's line "Black Jack," on the changes of "Blue Lou."[16] The approach at this session was somewhat different from the previous one. Instead of Marsh, Brown, and Ball being featured more or less equally, as on the Imperial record, each was the principal soloist on one track.

On his own feature, "Black Jack," Marsh delivers four dazzling choruses of a rhythmic and melodic intensity seldom approached since the Lester

Young of the 1930s. One or two phrases are, in fact, virtual quotes from Young's early style, but rhythmically the solo has a drive and split-second abandon that belongs strictly to Marsh at his most inspired. A particularly telling moment occurs at the beginning of the fourth chorus, when Marsh lets two and a half bars of silence go by before picking up the melodic flow with a brilliantly quirky, rhythmically daring figure. His composed line, played in unison with Brown, is of a piece with his solo, fresh and swinging.

Brown, on his extended solo on "Earful," plays well in his own relaxed Lestorian groove, but overall the contrast with Marsh is noticeable. Ball, who is rhythmically much closer to Marsh, is similarly overshadowed by Marsh's brilliance. On the up-tempo "Time's Up," Ball's three fine aggressive, middle register choruses at the beginning are dramatically upstaged by Marsh's dynamic eight-bar break into a key-change and the astonishing single chorus that follows.

Despite the excellence of Marsh's contributions, the Kapp record, titled *A Modern Jazz Gallery,* was probably not heard by many potential or actual Marsh fans because of the way it was marketed, in a two-LP set showcasing a potpourri of West Coast jazz. This packaging was producer Albert Marx's brainchild, the purpose being to permit radio disc jockeys to play six different groups without ever having to change records or even lift the tone arm.[17] Accordingly, not only was Marsh's quintet sandwiched in among the small groups of John Towner and Billy Usselton and the big bands of Med Flory, Russ Garcia, and Marty Paich, but their four contributions were parceled out two to each disc. A record buyer would have had to be a Warne Marsh fanatic, of which few then existed, to purchase a two-record set to hear perhaps five minutes of Marsh.

A Modern Jazz Gallery did receive reasonably good reviews. Nat Hentoff wrote that the best of three small groups was "the relatively new California-based Warne Marsh unit, which creates linear interest, has a growing pianist in Ball, and a superior tenor in Marsh." But Hentoff was "not yet convinced that the sameness in sound due to the two-tenor setup is compensated for by the empathy between Brown and Marsh."[18]

Jack Maher, who devoted more attention to Marsh's group than to any of the others, also considered it "probably the most distinctive" of the small groups. Like Hentoff, Maher attributes to both Marsh and Brown "fluidity, fine technical assurance, and imagination," and like Hentoff he ignored not only Marsh's brilliance on "Black Jack" and "Time's Up" but also his un-Tristano-like drive and swing, though he did say that "the basicness of these so-called intellectual musicians will surprise some."[19]

The Kapp session was followed a month later by one with Art Pepper. In June 1956 Pepper had been released from the federal penitentiary at Terminal Island, a former naval prison in Los Angeles harbor. For all but

about six months of the previous three and a half years he had been in-
carcerated for possession of heroin, spending fifteen months in the drug
treatment program of the U.S. Public Health Service Hospital in Ft. Worth,
Texas, nine months at Los Angeles County jail, and ten months at Terminal Island.

On August 31 Pepper's and Marsh's groups had appeared on the same
concert program at the Pasadena Civic Auditorium. Pepper's group had
included two members of Marsh's rhythm section, Ronnie Ball and Ben
Tucker, and earlier that month Pepper had used Tucker for a record date
for Tampa, which suggests that they might all have encountered each
other before that at Marsh's sessions at Whisling's. Later in the fall Pepper and Marsh began to play together at The Haig. Wrote John Tynan, "Art
Pepper's Sunday afternoon and Tuesday night sessions [at The Haig] are
becoming the talk of the town, with Warne Marsh and Ronnie Ball regulars on stand."[20]

In his autobiography, *Straight Life,* Pepper stated that in this period he
was again a heavy user of heroin, and he declared that by January 19, 1957,
when he recorded *Art Pepper Meets the Rhythm Section* for Contemporary,
he had not touched his horn in six months. He even described the deplor-
able disrepair of his alto.[21] But Pepper may have been thinking of another,
perhaps later, time, for whatever the extent of his habit or the condition
of his instrument, his assertion that he had not been playing was not at
all true. Since his release the previous June he had not only played at various jazz venues around town but had made fourteen records. He had also
recorded several unissued titles with Marsh, some of which were later
included on *The Way It Was.* Though not released until 1972, *The Way It
Was* included five tracks recorded with Marsh at Contemporary's studios
on November 26, 1956. The entire date, with four extra titles, was subsequently issued on a Japanese CD, *Art Pepper with Warne Marsh* (Contemporary CD-VDJ-1577).

Pepper's remarks for the 1972 release are worth quoting:

> Not long ago, listening to some unreleased tapes at Contemporary, we came
> across a session I'd done with Warne Marsh. Warne is a very great tenor
> player who studied with Lennie Tristano. . . . We used to enjoy jamming
> together and decided to record with a group he had in Los Angeles. We
> didn't do enough for an album, so it never came out, but hearing those tapes
> again after 16 years brought back a lot of memories.[22]
>
> I remembered in 1956, when I did the date, everything was happening in
> L.A. Jazz City was going; there were clubs all over; there were jam sessions.
> Jazz at that time was like a musical conversation. The musicians listened to
> each other, complemented each other. The audiences were responsive and
> friendly—consequently the musicians played warmly and played well.

I heard a lot of that in those old tapes, which I liked very much. . . .

I loved the way that Warne Marsh played chords, the scales that he used, the notes that he picked, the way he played time, his phrasing. He knew his horn forward and backward. He played a lot like Miles in that he always seemed to find the right note. . . . The way he plays time is very different, very involved.[23]

It is a pity that the session with Pepper was not released at the time. Given Contemporary's status and distribution capability, plus Pepper's popularity, it would undoubtedly have enhanced Marsh's reputation and helped to free him from the by-then obligatory coupling, so far as the jazz press was concerned, with Konitz.

Pepper and Marsh clearly stimulated each other, and while Marsh's solos on the session do not rise quite to the level of "Black Jack" and "I Never Knew," overall the music is as satisfying as most of *Jazz of Two Cities* and *A Modern Jazz Gallery*. One reason may be the substitution of Gary Frommer on drums in place of Jeff Morton, and another may be that Ronnie Ball does not play so exclusively in the middle register, and when he does, he blends better with Pepper's higher-voiced alto. The principal reason, however, is that Pepper is Marsh's strongest front-line partner since Lee Konitz.

In the last few bars of their jointly improvised duet on the opening chorus of "Tickletoe," for example, Marsh and Pepper generate an electrifying send-off to Marsh's rhythmically jagged yet hard-swinging solo that follows. Their improvised theme statements on "I Can't Believe That You're in Love with Me" and "All the Things You Are," where they pass the lead back and forth, as well as their eight- and four-bar exchanges on out-choruses, surpass what Marsh and Brown had achieved, fine as that was. This is so despite the fact that Pepper, like Brown, is noticeably more diatonic, more harmonically conservative than Marsh, less accustomed at this point to seek out unusual, nonchord notes.

Marsh's and Pepper's rhythmic differences, also quite noticeable, provide a fascinating contrast. Pepper's characteristically buoyant, dancing time-feel appears to be achieved by sometimes playing the eighth notes almost classically even, sometimes just a hair behind the beat, and by tonguing them separately, with fairly uniform accents. Marsh, on the other hand, "swings" his eighth notes more radically, in a long-short manner, at the same time establishing an accentual pattern that is usually heavier on beats one and three, but on which he plays variations that sometimes seem to "turn the time around."

The Way It Was drew a rave five-star review from *Down Beat*'s John Litweiler in 1973. Calling Marsh an "ideal partner" for Pepper, Litweiler wrote:

Pepper and Marsh are an even hipper team than the classic Marsh-Lee Konitz pairings, and it's a sin that they haven't worked together frequently. Their rhythmic and harmonic bases were fairly similar (both swing-era), and their art was (and is) defined by inflection, accent, tonal variation and nuance. They share the Tristano ideals of heavy swing and total improvisation, and they are immense emotionalists; but otherwise, no two musicians could be more different. Pepper's perfect formalism is totally complemented by Marsh's romantic sensibility: the granite alto structures meet the emotionally spontaneous tenor's eternal search for the beautiful melody, the perfect phrase.

  Marsh here often presents the peculiar rests, momentary odd logic, and incredible insights into rhythm, accent and nervous dynamics that characterize his best work. Pepper's 'Can't Believe' is a delightful tribute to his early mentor, Benny Carter, and the opening notes of 'All the Things' envelop you in that special tension; the rhythmic contrast and asymmetric accenting move subtly but irrevocably to a final strain broken by fast lines and a lightning conclusion—'two measures too early.' At the end of the first chase chorus Pepper, whose resilient structure really makes the piece work, climaxes with eight unbelievable measures. . . . The Ball-Tucker-Frommer rhythm section . . . contrary to Pepper's own opinion, [is] probably the most empathetic he ever used. Interestingly, both Pepper and Marsh were here in Chicago recently, and both played like angels. A Pepper-Marsh reunion, now, would be more welcome than ever."[24]

At the time of Litweiler's review, he and Terry Martin interviewed Marsh, asking him, "Do you think Art and yourself could work together these days?" Marsh replied, "Art stays in trouble as much as he can. . . . I'm not sure where he's at, but something's happened again. Every time he goes to LA, it does. He knows too many people in LA, and he gets in trouble. He should leave that town forever. I loved the liner notes he wrote on that album 'The Way It Was. . . .'" Elsewhere in the interview, apropos of the mutual admiration between Pepper and Lee Konitz, Martin asks, "What do you think Art could gather from Lee?" Marsh responds, "The point is, he won't do it. He doesn't take care of business—He leaves himself to the mercy of whatever happens to himself. You can't grow that way." To Martin's comment that Pepper has "tremendous natural gifts," Marsh answers, "Of course he does. But that's more common than the ability to do something with it by far."[25]

It is interesting to speculate on what might have happened if Marsh and Pepper had continued to play together. They did, in fact, travel to San Francisco that fall, possibly accompanied by Ball, Tucker, and Frommer, for an engagement at the Blackhawk.[26] And they did record together one more time.

By December 21, when the Marsh quintet plus Pepper went into the studio for Vanguard to record their second complete LP, *Free Wheeling,* there were a number of distractions. For one thing, Marsh had signed an exclusive contract with Imperial as leader of the group, so that the recording was made under the nominal leadership of Ted Brown. For another, the Pepper connection had begun to cause friction. A would-be agent associated with Aladdin Records, with whose subsidiary, Intro, Pepper had recently signed a contract, had begun hanging around, but his interest was primarily in Pepper. He had perhaps a secondary interest in Marsh, but none in the group as a whole. Pepper liked Tucker and would use him on his *Modern Art* record date for Intro a week later, and he had found Ball acceptable for his Contemporary session with Marsh, but he had other drummers, such as Gary Frommer or Chuck Flores, whom he favored over Jeff Morton. As a consequence of all this, both Brown and Morton had begun to feel devalued.

There were other distractions as well. The entire session, according to Brown, was "uptight." There were too many people in the studio, among them Lee Konitz, John Tynan, Pepper's would-be agent, Ronnie Ball's wife, and Albert Marx, the producer, who insisted that they record one of several songs published by his own company. Pepper was fretting because his car had been repossessed at three o'clock that morning.[27] Although Brown was the ostensible leader, Marsh was counting off the tempos and calling the order of solos, a fact that probably contributed, along with the undercurrent of bad feeling generated by the Pepper situation, to the "uptight" atmosphere Brown mentioned.[28]

Pepper had stopped by Whisling's the previous Sunday to sit in, and they had given him the music for the recording session, scheduled for the following Friday. In the studio they briefly rehearsed the more intricate lines with Pepper while the engineers were setting up. They paid no attention to the songs Albert Marx had handed them, recording everything else first. When the time came to record one of the tunes published by Marx, they decided on Walter Gross's "Once We Were Young," and Marx required them to do seven takes. One of the last notes of the lead, played by Brown, was a high G in the altissimo register, held for two bars. By the time Marx was satisfied, Brown's inner lip was "hamburger."[29]

Although Brown is the only horn soloist on two of the nine tracks, the ambiguity of his status as leader is suggested by the fact that on the first tune on the record, Ball's "Aretha," Pepper and Marsh each play two choruses while Brown does not solo at all. He plays spiritedly on Marsh's "Long Gone" and the up-tempo "Avalon," one of his two features, but there is a certain choppiness in his phrasing and some repetition of ideas. His most fully realized solo is his chorus on "Foolin' Myself," which leads into sixteen bars of excellent interplay with Marsh. Pepper plays with crisp authority on each of the four tunes on which he solos.

Marsh solos on only five tunes. He is at his best on the up-tempo "Long Gone," based on "Long Ago and Far Away," the ballad "Crazy She Calls Me," and especially "Broadway," where his profoundly Lestorian solo is so beautifully structured that Pepper, following him, sounds melodically diffuse. Lee Konitz, who was in the studio, made special mention of "Crazy She Calls Me" in Nat Hentoff's liner notes: "Warne somehow has previously been hesitant in playing ballads; they haven't been his strong point. This time he did two takes, and both sounded like two gems. I'd always loved the way he played ballads when he laid into them, and he does on this."[30]

In August 1958 Mike Gold wrote that *Free Wheeling* "deserves more attention than it will get. . . . The Tristano approach has been disgracefully neglected by jazz musicians, critics, and record company a & r men." Gold found the record "not fully rewarding" despite "eloquent moments for both tenors." Brown, he added, is "less the master of his own thought than Marsh." Commending Pepper for his contribution, Gold gave the album three and a half stars.[31] In *Metronome*'s yearbook *Jazz 1959,* the record was named in a long list of records "of special value" for 1958 with this comment: "Magnificent solos by Marsh and Ball, good solos and exceptional group work by Brown and Pepper and strong, plunging rhythm by Tucker and Morton, all of it subordinated to an unusual amount of group improvisation. . . ."[32]

Although the *Free Wheeling* session ended the quintet's recording career, Marsh and his fellow Tristanoites continued playing at Whisling's through the spring of 1957. "The exciting Warne Marsh quintet appears to have found a home at Bill Whisling's," wrote John Tynan in February.[33] In the same issue of *Down Beat* appeared an ad that continued to run in each issue through May 2:

In March *Down Beat* published Tynan's review of the group's performance on two successive Fridays. Imprecisely stating that they had been together "almost a year"—the nucleus of the group seems to have been formed in July, only eight months earlier— Tynan praised them as "one of the most clearly individual groups in jazz . . . the strong men in the quintet are Marsh and Ball, exceptional soloists who can, and frequently do, swing like mad." The group's attitude was marked, he noted, by "an uncompromising conviction that they are playing their own unique brand of jazz."[34]

The group occasionally did other gigs, including a New Year's Eve at UCLA, at least one Monday night appearance at The Lighthouse, and a performance in January 1957 on Bobby Troup's regular half-hour *Stars of Jazz* television series. Private tapes with good sound exist of the latter, but with half the time devoted to Ann Richards's singing, the group had no chance to stretch out. Marsh solos briefly on "Ad Libido" (based on "Somebody Loves Me," although the same title was used for a minor version of "Long Ago and Far Away" on the later *Music for Prancing*) and his own "Background Music" (an "All of Me" contrafact).

But the end, both of the group and of their eight-month sojourn at Whisling's, was approaching. John Tynan reported in May that Whisling's was up for sale. As Marsh had built "a steady following," there was "hope that the new owner would continue a jazz policy," but Whisling's was soon to close down as a jazz venue.[35] In early summer there was some talk of after-hours sessions on Sundays, with Ronnie Ball presiding, but if it did indeed happen, it didn't last long.[36]

Not only did the group lose its steady venue, but Marsh had begun talking about "reforming."[37] In mid-April, Ted Brown, already bruised by the friction with Art Pepper and realizing that Marsh had lost interest, decided to return to New York. At some point prior to his departure, the group had entertained the idea of working their way back to New York as a unit. They had all driven to a consultation with an agent in Hollywood to discuss lining up engagements across the country. As leader, Marsh signed a ninety-day contract and was responsible for following through. But according to Brown, he never called the agent, and the agent never called him. Thus a combination of circumstance and Marsh's professional passivity resulted in the break-up of the group. Had Marsh been the kind of leader who recognized the value of keeping a group together and who had the aggressiveness to find work for it, a Dave Brubeck or Phil Woods type, he might have made a much more significant impact with this exciting group. Ironically, in later years Marsh commented on a similar failing of the leaders of bebop: "Look how close they came—when Charlie Parker had Bud Powell and Max Roach. Just the 3 of them, if they had stuck together, would have put bebop on the map, would have established it alongside of classical music."[38]

One of Marsh's close associates in this period was Donald Specht, a studio pianist and arranger, whom he met at a casual gig with bassist Buddy Clark. Specht, from Minneapolis, was already familiar with the Tristano material, having taken much of it off records. Marsh liked Specht's "arranger-style" piano, and in the summer of 1957 the two, occasionally joined by Clark, would meet at Specht's Echo Park apartment several times a week, not so much to jam as to take tunes apart and see what unconventional things could be done with them. They would try familiar tunes in different keys, experiment with interludes, work out alternate turnarounds. On one occasion they started noodling on a theme from Bartók's *Concerto for Orchestra* and ended up composing, score in hand, a piece they called "Bartok's Tune." Marsh once nonchalantly called it at a session led by a piano player who had been reluctant to allow Specht on the stand. Not knowing "Bartok's Tune," the pianist relinquished his chair.

"Warne tried his whole life," said Specht, "to demolish bar lines," and he wrote out for Specht the first eleven bars of Tristano's "Lennie-Bird," a "How High the Moon" contrafact, to illustrate how a series of three partially subdivided quarter-note triplets beginning on beat two caused an illusory downbeat a fraction of a beat after the actual beginning of the second bar. Specht considered Marsh like Coltrane in his penchant for "starting phrases in cockeyed places." Specht and Marsh also indulged frequently in Marsh's favorite pastimes, chess and scrabble. Marsh was highly skilled at both. Once after Specht had studied a Bobby Fischer book and had used one of the youthful chess master's gambits, Marsh looked at him quizzically and remarked, "You've been reading, haven't you?"[39] In scrabble, said Specht, he would seldom settle for average scores of seven or nine points, preferring to go for fifteen. It was a chancy thing to challenge him on a word—nine times out of ten the dictionary would prove him right. In both games he was a cutthroat competitor. If he lost, as he did only occasionally, he would insist on a rematch. To Specht, mind games and problem solving were important indexes to Marsh's character.

After the demise of Whisling's as a jazz venue, Marsh, who for a time shared a house in West Los Angeles with Ronnie Ball and his wife, Rita, continued working around town. Tynan reported late that summer that he and Ball "looked likely to open at the Hillcrest," on Washington near La Brea, and in September they were at The Haig.[40] Also in September the pair, plus Red Mitchell on bass and Stan Levey on drums, recorded an LP, *Music for Prancing,* for Mode.

This record exudes an atmosphere of quiet professionalism, due in part, no doubt, to the presence of Mitchell and Levey. Mitchell is superb both in his walking ensemble lines and in solo, while Levey, frequently using only brushes, supports but never intrudes on the soloists. Ball, playing in a higher, more normal register than was previously his wont, turns in one of his better performances on records. And Marsh seems completely comfortable, dealing with ballads and extreme up-tempos with equal ease. The record's only flaw is that it is a little too cool and restrained, despite moments of intensity. This may have resulted from a lack of enthusiasm on the part of Levey, who said in an interview that Marsh, whose time-feel he described as "floating," was not his favorite type of player.

Interestingly, the record contains only one tune that evinces an obvious Tristano influence, Ball's "Ad Libido," a minor adaptation of "Long Ago and Far Away" probably inspired by Tristano's "Lennie's Pennies." But where Tristano's minor version of "Pennies from Heaven" comes off seamlessly, Ball's "Ad Libido" encounters an awkward harmonic transition between the first eight bars and the second. Marsh negotiates it skillfully, but it remains a slight obstacle for the listener.

The other original composition on the record, Marsh's "Playa del Rey" (named after a Los Angeles beach adjacent to Venice), does not sound at first like a Tristano-influenced line at all. Yet it is in the Tristano tradition, being an ingenious transformation of "I'll Remember April," as Marsh suggests by quoting the opening phrase of that tune at the very end. Both are basically forty-eight-bar tunes, except that where "I'll Remember April" has the form ABA, with the sixteen-bar bridge sandwiched between the two sixteen-bar A sections, "Playa del Rey" has the form AAB, with the bridge following two repetitions of the A section. In addition Marsh's tune includes an eight-bar interlude leading into solos (but omitted between choruses by the same soloist).

While "Playa del Rey" clearly derives from "I'll Remember April," it is not easy to hear the relationship. This is because two harmonic substitutions in the beginning give "Playa" a completely different sound that conflicts with the melody of "April." Where the first eight bars of "April" in the key of F would consist of four bars of F major 7 (F-A-C-E) followed by four bars of F minor 7 (F-A♭-C-E♭), the first eight bars of "Playa" can be construed as four bars of E minor 7 (E-G-B-D) plus four bars of D# minor 7 (D#-F#-A#-C#), two apparently quite different chords. The difference, however, is deceptive in that they can also be construed as the upper extensions of F major 13#11 (F-A-C-<u>E-G-B-D</u>), with B as the #11, and E major 13#11 (E-G#-B-<u>D#-F#-A#-C#</u>), with A# as the #11. The melody of "Playa del Rey" is built on these upper chords, and for simplicity they were probably thought of, and noted, as E minor 7 and E♭ (D#) minor 7. Still, their source is the upper extensions of the F major chord with which "I'll Remember April" begins. Dropping down a half-step to E major and using the same upper extensions, one gets a chromatic progression that fits logically with the rest of the first sixteen bars of "I'll Remember April," yet produces a strikingly different flavor.

Another indication of "Playa del Rey's" close relation to "I'll Remember April" is the rhythmic structure of the opening theme, which mirrors a common bebop approach to "April" by shifting from Latin to swing at the bridge. While the melody doesn't have the linear complexity of a typical Tristano-influenced tune like Ball's "Ad Libido," "Playa del Rey" is the most interesting composition on the record. As with his earlier "Marshmallow," Marsh dropped it from his repertoire, probably for the same reason—both would have required rehearsal time, unlike the standards he came to rely on.

The restrained heat generated by "Playa del Rey" is even more evident on the other madly up-tempo piece on *Music for Prancing*, "It's All Right with Me." Marsh's double-timing and creative ideas here, all the while maintaining reference to the contours of the original melody, are one of the highlights of the record. Others are the two ballads, "Everything Happens to Me" and "Autumn in New York." On the first, Marsh plays off of Mitchell's lovely walking line with evident appreciation, and his interplay with Ball at the end is the essence of taste. On "Autumn," Marsh's solo is reminiscent, in its spontaneous, intensely personal emotionality, of his moving performance on "Crazy She Calls Me" on the *Free Wheeling* album.

Music for Prancing was a record that should have solidified Marsh's reputation. If it wasn't a five-star performance, due to its cool restraint, it surely deserved at least four stars. But because of Mode Records' corporate weirdness, it was never even reviewed. Several months after it was recorded, *Down Beat* reported that "Mode's recording license has been revoked [by the Musicians Union], we're told."[41] This was a consequence of musicians not being paid for recording sessions.[42] And in September 1958, to the question of what had happened to Mode Records in the previous six months, the magazine answered that it had been taken over by a holding company, Sonic Industries, which had formed a new corporation, Mode Records, Ltd. The new Mode had tried mass distribution through "high-volume, retail chain outfits," initially Thrifty drug stores in California. The results had been good, so Mode would now proceed with mass distribution on a large scale.[43] Unfortunately, *Music for Prancing* seems to have been shuffled aside in all this corporate maneuvering.

Only on its reissue in 1985 did the record receive the kind of attention that was due in 1957: "Here is Marsh . . . making what might appear to be patently conventional music, but subtly turning the session into a veritable tour de force as he demonstrates his almost uncanny ability to sustain a flow of rich improvisational ideas. Lestorian in attack, Tristanian in intent and execution, Marsh was . . . a master thinker and tactician on the tenor. Too cold; too brittle; not enough dynamic variety—so scolded some observers at the time. We all know better now."[44]

Late in 1957 Mode reportedly produced another Marsh record. *Down Beat* announced that Mode was "recording a date led by pianist Ronnie Ball that includes tenor man Warne Marsh; Rolf Erickson, trumpet; Red

Mitchell, bass; Don Overberg, guitar; and Stan Levey, drums."[45] Although no such record has yet been released, Peter Jacobson, who now owns the Mode library, believes the session did take place, probably in October or November 1957, and has indicated he may release the record on his VSOP label once he confirms the existence of the master tapes.

Before Marsh left California, he had begun playing with pianist Joe Albany, then living in Laguna Beach. On a fall afternoon in 1957 he and Albany got together for an informal session at the home of sound engineer Ralph Garretson in Long Beach. Bassist Von "Bob" Whitlock, whom Garretson had known since boyhood and who had been rehearsing with Albany, was present, and Garretson himself participated on brushes. The session began around noon and continued into the wee hours of the morning.[46] Garretson was at the time hoping to break into remote recording, along with his partner Richard Stambaugh. They had acquired some excellent equipment, and Garretson recorded part of the proceedings in stereo, a technology that was new at the time.

Sometime later, after Marsh had returned to New York, he told Lennie Tristano about the session. When Tristano expressed interest in hearing the tape, Marsh called Garretson, who sent him a copy.[47] This tape, or a copy of it, was apparently given by Marsh to Bill Grauer of Riverside Records.[48] Quite unexpectedly, without contacting Garretson or Stambaugh, and using not the original stereophonic tape but the copy, Riverside put out a monaural LP, *The Right Combination,* under Albany's name, with Marsh as sideman.[49] Riverside had obviously decided to capitalize on Albany's status as a virtually unrecorded, underground legend without bothering to obtain the master tape. The liner notes, written by Orrin Keepnews, are devoted almost entirely to Albany, Marsh being cursorily described as "prominent in the circle of 'far out' jazzmen around pianist-teacher Lennie Tristano."[50]

Despite the poor sound, unrehearsed endings, and, on two tracks, chopped-off beginnings, the playing by both Marsh and Albany is excellent. Albany's style is fuller, more orchestral in texture than Ronnie Ball's, and his percussive touch and headlong rhythmic approach are reminiscent of Bud Powell. Marsh is impressive throughout but especially so on the double-time section of "Body and Soul." Unfortunately this is one of the tunes whose beginning is missing, the tape picking up Marsh's solo at the bridge.

Whitlock, who was fresh out of Brigham Young University and had never met Marsh before, recalled being "a little surprised" by his playing in this first encounter. Having in mind Marsh's earliest records with Tristano and Konitz, he found him "much looser. . . . I kind of felt like he was an incarnation of Lester Young. . . . I think probably Warne was rebelling against being regarded as cold and [being] identified with that whole [Tristano] thing. . . . He was very facile, and he had a whole lot of different tonal colors in his playing . . . almost inaudible at times, very introspective, introverted, but then in very quick order very outgoing, like shifting gears, and I thought that was neat—nothing boring about his playing." He found Marsh, like Albany, masterful at "shifting meters," exploiting a kind of "rhythmic counterpoint." Most of all, Whitlock was impressed with the way Marsh listened to him and Albany: "I'd be playing a line and I'd hear him playing something very much related to it."

Martin Williams gave the record four of five possible stars in his review. "Interesting, enlightening, and rewarding music," he wrote, "and a rare chance to hear improvisation taking place for its own sake rather than for microphones, polls, or somebody's beer license." Williams devoted most of his attention to the recording circumstances, the poor sound, and Albany, but had this to say about Marsh: "Marsh's temperament fits well and I think he plays with more sureness and firmness than his most recent recordings have shown. And when, like Albany, he is trying something out, he is trying *something* out, not losing his way or searching around for an idea. Hear 'Body and Soul.'"[51] The most recent record that Williams had heard when he did the review was Marsh's next, with Paul Chambers, which, as we will see, Williams very much disliked.

Marsh's association with Albany and Whitlock continued for perhaps six or eight weeks that fall, as they played Sunday afternoon jam sessions at the Galleon Room in Dana Point, near Laguna, with drummers that included Nick Martinis and Red Martinson.[52] One of these sessions has been preserved on a good quality tape that Marsh's widow, Geraldyne Marsh, has made available to Peter Jacobson of VSOP Records for eventual release.

Marsh, perhaps restless away from Tristano and undoubtedly longing for the more intense Eastern scene, was about to return to New York. On November 13 he and Ronnie Ball departed for the East Coast, telling John Tynan there was "not enough work here."[53] Supposedly a more immediate cause was a phone call from a girl he knew in New York. Wrote Nat Hentoff, "She was in a night club where Horace Silver's quintet was playing, had him listen to the music, and he was on his way back."[54]

NOTES

1. Lee Konitz, interview.
2. Lawrence Lipton, *The Holy Barbarians* (New York: Julian Messner, 1959).
3. Tom Runyan, interview.
4. See Albert Goldman, *Ladies and Gentlemen—Lenny Bruce!!* (New York:

Random House, 1974), 172. By her own account to me, Lynn was the replacement singer mentioned but not named by Goldman.

5. "Strictly Ad Lib," *Down Beat,* May 2, 1956, 28–29.

6. Carolyn See, "One Soul Sings, Some Listen," *Los Angeles Times,* 2 January 1988, 8 (Part II). Ms. See has insisted to me that the correct spelling of the club owner's name is "Whislin," but I have preferred "Whisling," the spelling consistently used in *Down Beat.* See also gives the year as 1958, but by the summer of 1957 Whisling's Hawaii had changed ownership and abandoned its jazz policy, and by December 12, 1957, Marsh had moved back to New York, where he played mainly at the Half Note during 1958–59.

7. See, ibid.

8. See, ibid.

9. Carolyn See, *Good Luck and Hard Times in America* (New York: Random House, 1995), 101.

10. John Tynan, "Caught in the Act," *Down Beat,* October 17, 1956, 8.

11. "Strictly Ad Lib," *Down Beat,* October 3, 1956, 46.

12. Susan Chen, interview.

13. Aside from the obvious pun on "air conditioning," Ball's "Ear Conditioning" may obliquely refer to Charlie Parker's "Air Conditioning," a take of a blues recorded November 17, 1947. Two other takes of the same blues were titled "Drifting on a Reed." But "Ear Conditioning" is not a blues, and there seems to be no direct musical relationship between it and the Parker tune.

14. "Warne Marsh," *Down Beat,* March 21, 1957, 27.

15. Quoted in Ira Gitler, *Jazz Masters of the Forties* (New York and London: Macmillan, 1966), 247.

16. "Time's Up" was included on *Warne Marsh Groups: Noteworthy*, Discovery DSCD-945, under the title "Up Tempo," "Earful" was included as "Decisions," and "Black Jack," as "Casino."

17. Ted Brown, interview.

18. Nat Hentoff, "Modern Jazz Gallery: West Coast," *Down Beat,* February 20, 1957, 26–27.

19. Jack Maher, "Kapp Jazz Festival," *Metronome,* May 1957, 34.

20. "Strictly Ad Lib," *Down Beat,* December 12, 1956, 37.

21. Art Pepper and Laurie Pepper, *Straight Life* (New York and London: Schirmer Books, 1979), 192.

22. They did enough, as the Japanese release shows, but perhaps did not like enough of what they did.

23. Art Pepper, liner notes to *The Way It Was,* Contemporary OJCCD-389-2.

24. John Litweiler, "Art Pepper," *Down Beat,* December 20, 1973, 28.

25. Terry Martin and John Litweiler, unpublished interview, October 14, 1973.

26. Nat Hentoff, liner notes to *Warne Marsh,* Atlantic LP 1291.

27. Ted Brown, interview. Pepper does not mention the record date in *Straight Life*, but it is possible that the "repossession" Brown spoke of was actually an incident Pepper describes, when, after an argument, his live-in girl friend Diane had driven off in her car, his only transportation at the time, taking all his clothes with her. Pepper does not specifically date the incident, but it appears in his book

on page 191, immediately before his account of his Contemporary record date
with Philly Joe Jones, Paul Chambers, and Red Garland on January 19, 1957. On
the other hand, since Pepper's memory of not having played for six months does
not belong to this time period, the incident with Diane and her car may also not
belong here.

28. Lee Konitz, quoted by Nat Hentoff in his liner notes for *Free Wheeling*,
Vanguard VRS-8515.

29. Ted Brown, interview.

30. Konitz, quoted in Hentoff, liner notes for *Free Wheeling*, Vanguard VRS-8515.

31. Mike Gold, "Ted Brown," *Down Beat*, August 21, 1958, 20.

32. "Discography of the Year," *Jazz 1959*, Metronome Yearbook (New York:
Metronome Corp., 1959), 107.

33. "Strictly Ad Lib," *Down Beat*, February 20, 1957, 37.

34. John Tynan, "Warne Marsh Quintet," *Down Beat*, March 21, 1957, 10.

35. "Strictly Ad Lib," *Down Beat*, May 2, 1957, 39.

36. "Strictly Ad Lib," *Down Beat*, June 27, 1957, 40.

37. Ted Brown, interview.

38. Martin and Litweiler.

39. In 1958 Fischer, at age fifteen, became the youngest U.S. chess champion
in history. His book, *Games of Chess* (New York: Simon and Schuster, 1959), was
published the following year.

40. "Strictly Ad Lib," *Down Beat*, August 8, 1957.

41. "Strictly Ad Lib," *Down Beat*, February 20, 1958, 39.

42. Peter Jacobson, interview. Jacobson now owns the Mode library.

43. "Jazz a la Mode," *Down Beat*, September 4, 1958, 12.

44. Alan Bargebuhr, "Reissues," *Cadence*, July 1985, 55.

45. "Strictly Ad Lib," *Down Beat*, December 12, 1957, 52.

46. Von (Bob) Whitlock, interview.

47. Ralph Garretson, interview.

48. Orrin Keepnews, interview.

49. Ralph Garretson and Richard Stambaugh, interviews.

50. Orrin Keepnews, liner notes to *The Right Combination*, Riverside LP 12-270.

51. Martin Williams, "Joe Albany," *Down Beat*, February 5, 1959, 22.

52. Von (Bob) Whitlock, interview. See also "Strictly Ad Lib," *Down Beat*, October 31, 1957, 40.

53. "Strictly Ad Lib," *Down Beat*, December 26, 1957, 42.

54. Nat Hentoff, liner notes to *Warne Marsh*, Atlantic LP 1291.

Warne Marsh solo on "Broadway" recorded Dec. 21, 1956, FREE
WHEELING, Vanguard VRS 8515, transcribed for tenor saxophone
by Gary Foster.

Analysis

One is struck, first, by the extreme simplicity of the opening, as Marsh outlines the second inversion of the F triad, using mostly quarter notes. In the first two bars he plays the same three notes in the same order, adding a simple touch of rhythmic variety in the second bar by syncopating the first three notes. When he moves to the B♭7 chord in the third bar he exactly repeats the rhythmic structure—three quarter notes plus two eighth notes—of the first, now outlining the second inversion of the B♭ triad.

Starting with the last beat of bar 3 the quarter-note feel gives way to an eighth-note passage, harmonically less simple, that carries the phrase over the bar line into bar 5, where Marsh pauses dramatically, letting his opening statement sink in. This extended four-and-a-half-beat rest encourages us to feel the first five bars as one phrase, though it can be argued that the eighth-note rest in bar 2 makes it two phrases.

The next phrase, beginning with the pickup in bar 6 and ending with the half-note in bar 10, while continuing to develop an immediately accessible and logical melodic line, involves us in some typical Marshian harmonic and rhythmic complexity. The handling of the changes of the two "turnaround" bars (7 & 8) is deft and canny. The easy chromatic descent from the 2nd to the major 7th of the F chord of bar 7 leads into a surprisingly wide intervallic leap upward from the flat 9 (E♭) to the root

126

(D) of the D7($\flat$9) chord. The next four downward-moving notes have a decidedly indirect relation to the Gm7 chord—they actually include three notes of the G$\flat$ triad (D$\flat$, B$\flat$, and G$\flat$) and only two (B$\flat$ and F) that belong to Gm7. This is interesting in that G$\flat$7 is the "tritone" of the next chord, C7, and is often substituted for it.

The four notes at the end of bar 8 are the crux of the whole phrase. They accomplish three things: they very simply identify the C7 chord by using two of its most important notes, E and C; they echo the upward leap of bar 7; and, most impressively, they displace the meter. A more conventional player would probably have played two different notes on the last beat, replacing the two Cs with perhaps a G and a B, so that the downward passage initiated by Marsh's two Cs would begin on beat 1 of the next bar, which is also the beginning of the second 8-bar section of this AABA tune. This of course would shift the passage in bars 9 and 10 over a beat, and the last two notes would fall on beat 1 of bar 11 instead of beat 4 of bar 10. The point is that Marsh's two Cs start a sub-phrase that *feels* like something that should start on beat 1, at the beginning of the next section, not the end of the last one. So strong is this feeling that if one is playing the passage, one may be tempted to leave out a beat and miscount the rests in bars 11 and 12. Marsh, of course, knows exactly where he is, finishing out the section with the same engaging simplicity with which he began the solo.

The next section, the bridge, is organized around the roughly parallel figures of bars 17 and 21, where the notes are different but stand in the same relation to their respective chord-scales: in bar 17 the phrase starts with the 4th of the C minor scale (F), leaps up to the 9th (D), down to the 4th (F) and 3rd (E$\flat$), and back up to the root (C). Similarly, the pickup to bar 21 is the 4th (E$\flat$) of the B$\flat$ minor scale, followed by the 9th (C), the 4th (E$\flat$) and 3rd (D$\flat$), and the root (B$\flat$). The melodic, harmonic, and intervallic structure is basically the same. The surprise is in the way the two phrases starting at bars 17 and 21 are developed. The phrase at 17 is in the mode of charming simplicity with which the solo began, but the phrase at 21 is not only harmonically and melodically far more complex but also is extended two bars beyond where we expect it to end. The expectation is instilled by the phrase at bars 17–20, whose development ends after three bars. The development of bars 21–26 extends for five-plus bars, ending with a convoluted two-bar passage full of surprising turns and intervallic leaps. This phrase is the climax of the solo. The two phrases at bars 27–30 and 31–33 are a winding-down from complexity to radical simplicity again. But the last phrase is not quite so simple as it sounds, involving both the syncopation of the note on beat 4 of bar 31 and the echo in the last four notes of the four notes of bar 30.

In short, this one-chorus solo is a little masterpiece, comparable in its lyricism, its combination of simplicity and complexity, its mastery of structure, and its sheer singability to the great one-chorus solo by Lester Young, which the band segues into after solos by Art Pepper and Ted Brown. The performance as a whole is a heartfelt tribute to Young, and this is particularly true of Marsh's solo, which even contains, in bars 17 and 21, a figure from Young's "Jive at Five" solo of April 2, 1939, with the Count Basie band.

♫

Lennie Again

On December 12, 1957, Marsh was in the New York studios of Atlantic Records to record, as leader, with two mainstays of the highly regarded Miles Davis rhythm section, bassist Paul Chambers and drummer Philly Joe Jones. The date, according to Nat Hentoff's liner notes, was arranged and supervised by Lennie Tristano.[1] One suspects that Tristano and Marsh had been in communication while Marsh was still in California, and that Marsh's return to New York was mainly because of Tristano and this record date, not a phone call from a girl or lack of work on the West Coast. Doubtless Tristano's immediate motive was to showcase Marsh, always a favorite pupil, on a major label with members of the most celebrated rhythm section of the day.

Although Chambers plays on all six tracks, Jones, with Ronnie Ball added on piano, plays on only two tracks, "Too Close for Comfort" and "It's All Right with Me," both recorded December 12. The other four numbers, "Yardbird Suite," "My Melancholy Baby," "Just Squeeze Me," and "Excerpt" (a contrafact of "I'll Remember April") were recorded January 16, 1958, with Paul Motian on drums and no piano.

On first impression, Marsh and Chambers do not seem to fit well together. Repeated listenings suggest that much of the problem originated in Atlantic's control booth, in that Marsh, Ball, Jones, and Motian all seem underrecorded in relation to Chambers, whose bass sounds domineering. But beyond this, Chambers seems never to enter into Marsh's conception. It is as though he is too used to players like John Coltrane and Sonny Rollins to hear what Marsh is doing. In itself, Marsh's playing is on a very high level, at least as high as his work with Joe Albany a couple of months

earlier, if not higher. All of the numbers, except perhaps "Just Squeeze
Me," have moments of heat and brilliance, especially "Too Close for Comfort," "It's All Right with Me," and "Excerpt."

Given the general excellence of Marsh's playing, it is hard to understand
the severity of Martin Williams's review, which appeared before his review of Marsh's record with Joe Albany. Awarding the record only two
and a half stars (out of five) in *Down Beat*—anybody of integrity and professional skills could normally count on at least three stars—Williams
wrote: "To be sure I wasn't being misled by Paul Chambers' and Philly
Joe's fine musical energy, I played Tristano's Marionette again. There, and
here on Comfort and It's All Right, Marsh approaches a balance between
coolness and liveliness that Getz has, in his different way, achieved. Admitting that such reactions can be highly subjective, I think the other tracks
here sometimes come close to ambling reticence or enervation. Certainly
his work on Charlie Parker's Yardbird dramatizes the rhythmic problems
of this branch of 'cool' playing: imposing an occasional foray into a more
boppish rhythmic territory on a basically quarter-note rhythmic conception is not always successful. And although Melancholy Baby opens very
well, Marsh's return after Chambers' solo sounds almost like a retreat—
melodically, rhythmically, and emotionally veiled."[2]

This was by far the worst review Marsh ever received. To Williams's
credit, it was also the first to attempt any sort of serious consideration of
his playing. But it raises a number of questions. It is curious, to begin with,
that Williams uses "Marionette" as a standard of comparison rather than,
say, "Tautology" or "Marshmallow," or almost anything from the 1955
Marsh-Konitz record with Oscar Pettiford and Kenny Clarke, which he
should have been familiar with, or *Jazz of Two Cities* or *A Modern Jazz Gallery*, both of which had been reviewed early in 1957 in *Down Beat*. Williams says later in his review that the rhythmic setting on the Tristano
Capitols was "nearly ideal" for Marsh at that point, but that in the present
instance, when his playing had become more personal, "Marsh chose his
company badly." Actually Tristano probably had considerable, perhaps
decisive input into Marsh's choice. Aside from that, it is hard to imagine
rhythm sections more nearly ideal for Marsh than that of his own quintet, with Ben Tucker and Jeff Morton, or the earlier Pettiford-Clarke combination. Still, if in this case Marsh chose his colleagues badly, why does
Williams go out of his way to praise Chambers and Jones? It is as much
the job of a rhythm section to accommodate a horn player as it is his to
choose players who will. Or, if it was simply an unfortunate matter of
incompatibility between highly individual players, as Williams finally
suggests, to excoriate Marsh's playing to this extent seems inappropriate.

Most puzzling were Williams's remarks about "Yardbird Suite" and
"Melancholy Baby." The notion that bebop differed from older jazz in

being based on an eighth-note rather than a quarter-note rhythmic conception was first introduced by Andre Hodeir in his important study *Jazz, Its Evolution and Essence,* published in the United States in 1956: "Cozy Cole's ideas of rhythm are based on the quarter note, Kenny Clarke's on the eighth. . . . Between the even cymbal strokes by which the regular beat is maintained, the snare and bass drums give out either muffled or clear percussions . . . on subdivisions of the beat. Thus the accentuation, in modern jazz, falls between beats."[3] But what dramatic conflict Williams heard between Paul Motian's bebop rhythms and Marsh's alleged quarter-note conception in "Yardbird Suite" is a mystery. There are a couple of half-strangled notes in Marsh's second solo, but they would seem to be the result of Marsh's commitment to spontaneity rather than to any rhythmic cross-purposes.

Again, when Williams, after conceding that "Melancholy Baby" "opens very well," complains that Marsh's second solo is "almost a retreat—melodically, rhythmically, and emotionally veiled," it is hard to find any justification for such negative criticism. Marsh plays the same way in his second solo as he does in his first—there is no dramatic difference, and his exchanges with Jones are particularly lively and inventive.

Williams's basic criticism, disregarding the details, is that Marsh is not sufficiently "assured." By this term, he says, "I don't mean hard, aggressive, hostile, or any of those descriptions that are now being spuriously thrown around, with disgruntled inflections, by musicians of the cool style." What he means, he explains, is the assurance exemplified by more established "cool" musicians like Stan Getz, Art Pepper, and Paul Desmond, and he closes by saying that Marsh's playing on "Excerpt" (a brilliant excursion on "I'll Remember April," consisting only of Marsh's solo, without theme statement or ending) "seems to show" that Marsh is capable of this kind of assurance. But if "Excerpt" shows this, so too do "Too Close for Comfort" and "It's All Right with Me," which Williams accords only a grudging nod in passing to his more heartfelt negative remarks.

The more one considers the inconsistency, inaccuracy, and severity of Williams's criticism, the more likely it seems that, under the guise of criticizing Marsh, he was defending his own preconceptions. As he recognized, Marsh's playing had developed into a far more personal expression than in 1949, and it was an expression quite different from that of highly praised and influential contemporaries like Sonny Rollins, John Coltrane, and Stan Getz. Marsh's conception had little to do with any of these players, although he was closer to Getz by virtue of their common affection for Lester Young. As Von Whitlock suggested, Marsh's playing combined deep introspection and intellectual and rhythmic ingenuity with outbursts of passion that were the more moving by virtue of the restraint

they had to overcome. And it was an expression totally committed to
Tristano's exaggeratedly purist notion of improvisation. This last, I think,
is what put off Williams, generally considered an important and able critic.
Marsh was the kind of player, by that time, who could stun with his brilliance but who would never, under any circumstances, fill the gaps of
inspiration with cliches. In his playing he was honest to a fault.

By midsummer of 1958 Marsh was back on familiar Tristanoite ground,
ensconced with Lee Konitz at the newly opened Half Note "indefinitely."[4]
Konitz had opened at the club in March with a quartet that included Billy
Bauer, bassist Peter Ind, and drummer Ed Levinson.[5] Still there in late
April or early May, Konitz talked of adding another horn player, possibly trumpeter and Tristano student Don Ferrara.[6] The added horn player,
however, soon turned out to be Marsh, and he, Konitz, and club co-owner
Mike Canterino launched a campaign to persuade Lennie Tristano to join
them. As an enticement, Canterino installed a new Steinway piano.
Tristano tried it out but found it wanting, so Canterino turned it in for
another one, chosen this time by Tristano himself.[7]

Early in August, Tristano agreed to a "trial weekend, with intentions
of staying on if things work out well."[8] Things apparently did, as he continued playing long weekends, Thursday through Sunday, through October.[9] For most, possibly all, of this extended stay at the Half Note he was
joined by Marsh. The occasion was noted in the *Metronome* yearbook for
1959: "Lennie Tristano came out of long retirement late last year [1958] to
play an extended engagement at New York's Half Note. Bassists and
drummers came and went like the wind, but the two basic voices—
Lennie's and tenorist Warne Marsh's—were singularly and correctly always there, perhaps somewhat confined because of the fluctuating rhythm
sections, but, still, potently engaged in inspired examples of empathy
combined with startling clarity, all of it done in a warmer, more basic
manner than in the recent past."[10] Late in September the group included
Marsh, Henry Grimes on bass, and Paul Motian on drums.[11] This line-up
was captured in a radio broadcast of August 9, 1958, later issued as a bootleg record, Bombasi 11:235. The same material, with slightly different titles,
was reissued on *Lennie Tristano: Continuity*, Jazz Records JR6.

Finally, on February 3, 1959, Tristano was reunited on stand at the Half
Note with both of his two star students, Marsh and Konitz.[12] Curiously,
what has been issued on records of this engagement does not include
Tristano, and the first fruits, not issued until 1974, barely included Konitz.

The story is complicated. According to Konitz, the engagement at the
Half Note "wasn't Warne's gig or my gig. We were working there as a
quintet with Tristano; but Lennie was taking Tuesday nights off to teach.
On the nights we recorded we had asked Bill [Evans] to sit in for Lennie."[13]
These proceedings, with Evans on piano, Paul Motian on drums, and

Jimmy Garrison on bass, were recorded in stereo on February 24 and possibly March 3, 1959, by Peter Ind,[14] who by prior agreement turned something like one hundred minutes worth of tapes over to Verve Records.[15]

In the normal course of things, Verve, having commissioned Ind to make the tapes, would have released the record within a year or two. Nothing, however, was normal. The Verve tapes languished in the Verve vaults for an incredible thirty-five years until 1994, when a two-CD set of twelve tunes recorded by Ind was issued as *Lee Konitz: Live at the Half Note*, Verve 314-521-659-2.

Ind, however, had recorded much more than the twelve tunes finally released by Verve. This is known not only by the testimony of Ind but by the fact that in 1974 and 1977 Revelation Records released Marsh's solos, with almost everything else edited out, on some forty-five songs by the same group at the Half Note, including most of the material later included on the Verve set. And at some point not long before the Verve issue, a set of four ninety-minute cassette tapes had begun circulating among Marsh cognoscenti containing, in complete form, all of the Verve CD material, most of the Revelation material, and some tracks never released on either label.

What happened with the Verve tapes is easily explained: the company simply sat on them for thirty-five years, presumably not seeing a market for them during the hegemony of rock. How the Revelation records came about, on the other hand, is a story that one is tempted to say could never have happened to anyone but Warne Marsh.

According to Peter Ind, Marsh and Konitz wanted Tristano to help them choose what to release on records, and either they or Ind, at their request, supplied Tristano with *monaural* copies of all of Ind's tapes. The copies, like the Verve masters, likewise languished, in a remote corner of Tristano's attic, until the early 1970s, when they were discovered by Connie Crothers in an unmarked cardboard box, covered with dust and cobwebs. Crothers reported that when Tristano listened to the tapes, which he had forgotten about, he was enthralled. Remembering that Marsh had mentioned at the time that he was not particularly happy with his playing, Tristano asked Crothers to edit out everything but Marsh's solos in order to send the edited tapes to Marsh as a gift, evidence of the high quality of his playing.[16]

By that time, 1973, Marsh was living in Pasadena, California, teaching both privately and at a local music store, Berry and Grassmueck. The supervisor of the store's teaching program, and the man responsible for bringing Marsh into the program several years earlier, was altoist Gary Foster, a Tristano-Marsh-Konitz admirer from Kansas who had met Marsh in California in 1966. When the quarter-track, 7½ inches-per-second monaural tape arrived from Tristano, Marsh and Foster sat down to listen to it in Marsh's teaching cubicle. The sound quality was terrible, the rhythm section barely audible, and the absence of theme statements, endings, and other context sometimes forced them to identify hard-to-recognize tunes by playing possible changes on the piano while listening to the tape.

A mutual friend of Marsh and Foster was John William Hardy, a jazz enthusiast and co-owner of Revelation Records. In 1969 Hardy had issued Marsh's first record as a leader in eleven years, with Foster as sideman. A highly regarded zoologist and college professor, Hardy and his partner Jon Horwich operated Revelation on a shoestring. Seeing in Marsh's Half Note tape the opportunity for a low-cost record of a major but neglected artist, Hardy obtained Marsh's consent to issue it. Said Marsh in a contemporary interview, "Bill Hardy, he now has a tape that was made in 1958 [actually 1959] at the Half Note that Lee Konitz was the leader of for Verve Records. It was never released, and my solos were taken off of it and made into a series of tracks, enough for an album. Lennie Tristano edited it and thought it was worth putting out, so I gave it to Bill."[17] Hardy issued the material in two installments under the title *Warne Marsh: The Art of Improvising.* Volume 1, Revelation 22, appeared in 1974; Volume 2, Revelation 27, in 1977.

The title was suggested by Marsh in a letter to Hardy, included in the liner notes to Volume 1: "I've been trying ideas for liner notes that would put the art of improvisation—a splendid title—and jazz, and classic music all in perspective with each other. I get as far as describing improvisation as a new genre of music—not the improvising of a solitary great composer in Bach's time—but ensemble improvising as an art form; however, to estimate the role of improvisation in classic music, particularly in its inception, when I'm convinced improvising was *the* motivating power, and to estimate improvisation in jazz, obviously considerable, but rejected by traditional thought, or at least suspect as art. . . . I'm trying to put into words the part spontaneous playing plays in the progress of music—you try it!"[18]

Besides this interesting expression of the importance Marsh placed on improvisation, the liner notes contain two statements by Hardy that were at best injudicious. He says that "[Marsh's] teacher, Lennie Tristano, regards the present material as among his highest achievements," and adds that Tristano "felt that the music [recorded at the Half Note] was valuable only for Warne's solo periods."

The problem with these statements, especially the one that implicitly denigrated the contributions of Konitz and Evans, is that according to both Foster and saxophonist Lenny Popkin, then a student and close associate of Tristano, Hardy never talked or corresponded with Tristano. His knowledge of Tristano's opinions was at best secondhand, through Marsh.

One unhappy result of his statements was that for twenty years Lee Konitz nursed an unwarranted resentment against Tristano. As Konitz said in the liner notes to the Verve release, "I was very angry when Lennie cut me out of those Revelation albums."[19] Only in 1994, presumably after reading Konitz's remark, did Crothers and Popkin tell him the true history of *The Art of Improvising,* and that Tristano had never intended the edited tape to be released.

Another result was that Marsh's playing, in itself remarkable, was presented in a format so devoid of presentation values that few except a tiny cult of mid-1970s Marsh students and devotees could appreciate it. One reason for the dauntingly poor sound quality of the Revelation records was that they were made from a monaural copy of stereophonic tapes. This is probably why Bill Evans, who admittedly laid out a lot behind the soloists, is so far in the background when he does play—he was recorded on another microphone. Another reason is that the monoaural version was at least a third-generation copy. That the stereophonic originals were, as Peter Ind claimed, "absolutely top-notch" was proven true by the excellent fidelity of the Verve release, where the rhythm section, including Evans's brilliant piano, is as fully present as the horns, not a ghostly off-stage apparition.

In his liner notes to Revelation 27, Hardy wrote, "Make no mistake: Warne Marsh is a giant, the equal in stature of Parker, Coltrane, Gillespie, Armstrong, . . . and Lester Young." Reviewer John Litweiler of *Down Beat* heartily agreed with him. In an extraordinarily detailed review, Litweiler ignored the deficiencies of fidelity and context and gave the record five stars, saying it contained "some of the finest tenor playing of modern times." He noted that in the 1950s, critics "were abusing the entire Tristano school for their rhythmic lackings and Marsh particularly for being a 'hesitant player'. . . ." On the contrary, Litweiler found no hesitancy whatsoever: "What we hear here is supremely self-confident music, an absolute commitment to Marsh's peculiar aesthetic of total spontaneous improvisation, and an extraordinarily high level of melody that permitted no conventional or trivial material."[20]

Litweiler went on to describe Marsh's harmonic freedom, referring to specific cuts on the record, which included more than one version of several tunes: "What is most immediately shocking about this collection is Marsh's harmonic inventiveness. . . . Listen to his substitution of a completely unusual mode for the changes in half a strain of the first Scrapple [from the Apple]. . . . you realize how liberally he's treated the chords when a snatch of theme appears near the end of the second Scrapple. Where is the 12-bar 1-4-5 outline of Blues, the obvious changes of Lunar [Elevation], what's happening in the third It's You [or No One], etc.?

. . . The first Indiana opens with a bit of theme (a rarity in this set) before becoming pure Marsh, but the second Indiana achieves atonality before the cut-off final chorus."

Litweiler dealt similarly with the rhythmic aspects of Marsh's playing: "Marsh's time is unbelievable, perfect. . . . He may conceive of the beginning of a long phrase in one rhythmic pattern, suddenly invent a totally curious accent or hold a note when least expected, then conclude the phrase in an entirely different sense, the whole covering perhaps ten measures without a breath ('Song for You'). . . . Spotted throughout the record, in fact, are nonstop phrases that utterly demolish all conventional signposts (bar lines, changes, etc.) and move with the melodic and rhythmic thrill of [Cecil] Taylor or Bud Powell."

After noting the variety of Marsh's "sonoric inflection," Litweiler concluded: "Surely the concept of freedom in jazz was meant to indicate precisely this kind of spontaneous—yet internally perfectly logical—collection of surprises. Despite the excellence of his other recordings and his current eminence as the major soloist of Supersax, this is very nearly the definitive Marsh record, the 'distilled essence' of one of the most brilliant and significant creators of our time."

The descriptions of Marsh's playing by Bill Hardy and Bob Blumenthal, in their liner notes to the Revelation and Verve albums, respectively, are perceptive. Hardy, having warned the record-buying public that *The Art of Improvising* "is not for everybody," suggests that for listeners "involved in ear training . . . we can think of no finer test of your ability to hear chord changes than here. Marsh is seldom obvious in his approach to the chord; his solos are without cliché; he almost never, except in an oblique way, ever states the melodic theme of these pieces. . . ."[21] Blumenthal's description approaches the heart of Marsh's method: Marsh "is indeed at his best, piling phrase upon permutation upon tangent in a stream of melodic creation. . . . Marsh creates long ribbons of improvisation, in which each phrase simultaneously responds to its predecessor and anticipates a further response. Ideas are taken into different keys, beats are displaced, and entire accent patterns are reversed; musical matter is spawned from continually dividing melodic cells."[22]

Although it could be argued that the Revelation records, because of their total lack of presentation values and consequent tiny audience, did as much harm as good for Marsh's reputation, Marsh himself was totally unaware of that possibility, citing Revelation 22 as "the best picture of my playing on record. . . . That's the only record I can honestly say I think I played my best on."[23] Interestingly, he had not thought so highly of his playing at the Half Note until Tristano sent him the tape, another indication of Tristano's immense influence on his life.

Had Verve issued its Half Note material in 1959 instead of 1994, and had there been reviewers like Litweiler or Blumenthal around, Marsh's recording career might not have vanished, as it did for the next ten years. As things stood, he made one more record on May 12 and 13, 1959, as a sideman on *Lee Konitz Meets Jimmy Giuffre* for Verve, soloing on three tracks. The playing of Marsh, Konitz, and Bill Evans is superb. Marsh contributes excellent solos and exciting exchanges with Konitz on "When Your Love Has Gone" and a blues, "Cork 'n' Bib," and a stunningly oblique, original solo on "The Song Is You." Giuffre's arrangements for the band, which consists of a five-man saxophone section—no brass—plus rhythm, with Konitz playing lead alto, are gorgeous, and the record will strike many listeners today as a classic.

Unfortunately, *Down Beat*'s anonymous reviewer, awarding the record only three and a half stars, seemed to expect a more conventional, brass-powered, big band sound. Most of his negative criticism was for Giuffre's writing: "In the misty puffs of sound that Giuffre creates on paper, one keeps hoping a well-defined fist will jab out of the fluffiness. That it never does . . . is the essential fault of this album." Konitz's blues, "Cork 'n' Bib" (brilliantly arranged by Giuffre, a fact unnoted by the reviewer) was cited as "the best track. . . . Pianist Evans emerges from the strange tangle of talents as best man, with Konitz and Marsh following."[24] The "tangle of talents" included Konitz, Marsh, old friend Hal McKusick on second alto, fellow Tristanoite Ted Brown on second tenor, and Giuffre on baritone, a truly extraordinary saxophone section.

After the Konitz-Giuffre sessions, Marsh appeared again with Tristano and Konitz at the Half Note in July.[25] Their performance elicited a complaint from Jack Maher that much of their material "seemed rather pale and dated," that they "seemed bent on resurrecting the past." Their playing, he felt, lacked the "excitement and joyousness" they had conveyed in the past.[26]

Tristano played three more engagements at the Half Note and one at the Showplace, another Greenwich Village club, in the next seven months. Konitz was with him on at least three of these, but Marsh's name is not mentioned in the notices.[27] He was definitely with Tristano's group for a gig at Basin Street East, for which he had recruited bassist Sonny Dallas.

It was Dallas's first experience with Tristano. Originally from Pittsburgh, Dallas had recently come to New York and begun playing sessions and working with the likes of George Wallington, Phil Woods, Paul Motian, Bob Brookmeyer, and Nick Stabulas. At a session he met Marsh, who liked his playing and told Tristano. Having heard the stories about Tristano's conflicts with rhythm sections, he had no great desire to become one of the scores of bassists Tristano had hired and fired. But when Marsh told him Tristano's group was opening at Basin Street East and invited him to join them, he needed the work and agreed to give it a try. He did not know the Tristano lines, but he knew the standards they were based on, and he knew how to keep his place. On the gig it turned out that that was all Tristano was asking for, and he became Tristano's regular bassist for the next ten or eleven years. He concluded that all the stories about Tristano's wanting unimaginative, metronomic rhythm sections must have been made up by bassists and drummers who got lost when Tristano launched into his customary polyrhythmic excursions. All Tristano ever wanted, said Dallas, was for his rhythm sections to swing and keep their place. He maintained that Tristano never restricted drummers, unless they were in the habit of emphasizing beats two and four in a "corny" way.

Sometime after the Basin Street East gig, Marsh returned to California. In those days, 1958–60, he was, Dallas said, "playing his ass off—I thought he was the greatest tenor who ever lived." But except for the occasional gigs with Tristano, he rarely worked, and in California he could live cheaply with his mother.

While Marsh was at home in California, Tristano's quintet was booked for two weeks at a club in Pittsburgh, Dallas's hometown. Tristano contacted Marsh, who agreed to meet the group, which included Konitz, Dallas, and a drummer, possibly Paul Motian or Roger Mancuso, in Pittsburgh. According to Dallas, Marsh played so brilliantly that Konitz, stepping to the microphone after a Marsh solo, would simply stand bemused, then walk back to his place without playing a note. This happened so frequently, said Dallas, that as the first week drew to a close the club owner complained. Customers wanted to hear Konitz, whose reputation at that time was at least as great as Tristano's, but Konitz was not playing.

Said Dallas, "I never heard anything like it. I'll never forget seeing how one man, Warne, could shock and stifle another great musician like Lee."

Konitz himself, speaking to Ira Gitler about the difficulty in general of following solos by Tristano and Marsh, confirmed, if not Dallas's account of this specific incident, at least the existence of similar ones: "I have the feeling sometimes, playing with Lennie and Warne—whom I admire a great deal, my favorite players in a lot of respects—where I just knew I couldn't play after what I had just heard. I felt cool enough in some way not to have to play. . . . [I]n a healthy playing situation . . . if a cat is saying it, at any given moment, you're not obliged to say more—or anything. He can have it."[28]

Tristano's quintet, with Marsh, Konitz, Dallas, and Roy Haynes on drums, played at the Famous Door in Toronto in November 1959;[29] Marsh was still in New York on December 19, 1959, and February 22, 1960, for jam sessions at Peter Ind's; and the following July he appeared again with

Tristano and Konitz at the Half Note.[30] But after two more known sessions at Ind's on August 9 and September 8, 1960, Marsh once again abandoned New York, retreating to California to endure nine years of almost total obscurity.

NOTES

1. Nat Hentoff, liner notes to *Warne Marsh,* Atlantic LP 1291.

2. Martin Williams, "Warne Marsh," *Down Beat,* January 8, 1959, 31–32.

3. Andre Hodeir, *Jazz, Its Evolution and Essence*, trans. by David Noakes (New York: Grove Press, 1956), 218–219.

4. "Strictly Ad Lib," *Down Beat,* July 24, 1958, 52.

5. "Konitz a Winner," *Metronome,* June 1958, 10.

6. Dom Cerulli, "Lee Konitz," *Down Beat,* May 15, 1958, 16.

7. Mike Canterino, interview. See also "Lennie Tristano," *Down Beat,* October 30, 1958, 17; and Bob Blumenthal, liner notes to *Lee Konitz: Live at the Half Note,* Verve CD 314-521-659-2, May 1994.

8. "Strictly Ad Lib," *Down Beat,* September 18, 1958, 8.

9. "Strictly Ad Lib," *Down Beat,* October 2, 1958, 51; and November 13, 1958, 54.

10. "The Small Groups of 1958," *Jazz 1959,* Metronome Yearbook (New York: Metronome Corp., 1959), 13.

11. "Lennie Tristano," *Down Beat,* October 30, 1958, 17.

12. "Strictly Ad Lib," *Down Beat,* February 19, 1959, 47.

13. Bob Blumenthal, liner notes to *Lee Konitz: Live at the Half Note,* May 1994, Verve CD 314-521-659-2. Konitz's account is disputed by Connie Crothers, who maintained in an interview with me, December 7, 1994, that Tristano never taught on Tuesdays. But Crothers's close association with Tristano did not begin until 1964, and she is hardly objective.

14. Blumenthal, ibid.

15. The twelve tracks on *Lee Konitz: Live at the Half Note* contain approximately one hundred minutes of music, and Michael Lang, who supervised the production of the album, told me that this was all the material Verve had. Lang's statement was confirmed to me by Phil Schaap, at the time in charge of Verve's vault holdings.

16. Connie Crothers, interview.

17. Terry Martin and John Litweiler, unpublished interview, October 14, 1973.

18. Warne Marsh, liner notes to *Warne Marsh: The Art of Improvising,* Vol. 1, Revelation 22.

19. Blumenthal.

20. [John] Litweiler, "Warne Marsh," *Down Beat,* January 16, 1975, 29.

21. John William Hardy, liner notes to *The Art of Improvising,* Vol. 1, Revelation 22.

22. Blumenthal.

23. Roland Baggenaes, "Warne Marsh Interview," *Coda*, December 1976, 5.

24. "Lee Konitz-Jimmy Giuffre," *Down Beat*, November 12, 1959, 40.

25. "Strictly Ad Lib," *Down Beat*, July 23, 1959, 37.

26. J[ack] M[aher], "Low Calorie Diet," *Metronome*, September 1959, 10.

27. "Strictly Ad Lib," *Down Beat*, September 17, 1959, 47; October 1, 1959, 52; October 15, 1959, 44; October 29, 1959, 46; November 12, 1959, 51; November 26, 1959, 66; and March 3, 1960, 38.

28. Ira Gitler, *Jazz Masters of the Forties* (New York and London: Macmillan, 1966), 245.

29. "Strictly Ad Lib," *Down Beat*, November 26, 1959, 67.

30. "Strictly Ad Lib," *Down Beat*, July 21, 1960, 69.

The Lost Decade

Some eighteen months before Marsh gave up on New York to return to California, when he was still playing engagements at the Half Note with Tristano and Konitz, Dan Morgenstern published a piece on "Modern Reeds" in *Down Beat*. In the section on tenors, Morgenstern discussed the contributions of Coleman Hawkins, Lester Young, Stan Getz, Zoot Sims, Brew Moore, Al Cohn, Sonny Rollins, John Coltrane, and others. In a separate section on younger followers of Lester Young he expatiated on Bill Perkins, Richie Kamuca, Bob Cooper, Bill Holman, Phil Urso, Selden Powell, and Dick Hafer. Nowhere in the article was Marsh's name so much as mentioned.[1]

Such was the depth to which Marsh's reputation had sunk, at a time when, as private tapes and belatedly issued records showed, he was at the height of his powers. By the time he was settled again in California around the beginning of 1961, he had gone unlisted in both the *Down Beat* and *Metronome* polls.

One can only speculate on his reasons for giving up on New York at this time. He probably could have continued playing with Tristano three or four times a year, and it is hard to imagine that he could not have found other venues besides the Half Note. Perhaps the lack of offers to record bothered him, or simply the general failure of the jazz world to recognize his prowess in this period of increasing recognition for contemporaries like Coltrane and Rollins. Most likely what tipped the balance was the fact that in California, living with his mother, he could play his music but be relieved of the task of making a living at it.

Whatever the reasons, his return to California was clearly a retreat. He seems to have made little effort to perform publicly or form a group, and one of the first things he did was enroll, probably at his mother's expense, in a course in television repair at a private technical school.[2]

He settled into his old social circle of musicians in or near North Hollywood—Fred and Carol Waters, Joe and Sandra Maini, Med and Joanie Flory, Herb and Lorraine Geller, Joe Burnett, John Bannister, Buddy Clark, Jim Aton, Jerry Guerrera—and he renewed his relationship with pop-singer Bobbi Lynn. She had broken her foot, which was in a cast, and Marsh kept her company, playing scrabble and chess with her. One evening he showed up, scrabble box under his arm, and said, according to her, "Okay, you win, I want to marry you." She already had one child and was pregnant with another, not Marsh's, and told him she needed to think it over. Ultimately, realizing that Marsh was not a good bet for supporting a wife and two children not his own, she declined. In 1963 she married a nonmusician she described as "anti-show-business."

Lynn described Marsh's relationship with his mother as comfortable and close: "They had great camaraderie. His mother idolized him. She would pat his hand, and he would respond by putting his arm around her. If he were going out, she would lay $10 on the table and say, 'You'd better take this.'" Lynn got the sense that Marsh had never really had to worry about money, which made him careless with it. The family home, she said, was like a set from a 1940s movie—"When you stepped out of the car and into the estate, it was another time zone, a haven, like nothing from outside could harm you."

In 1961–62 another woman, Anita Leonard, came briefly into Marsh's life. They met at a party at the home in Venice of a well-known Beat painter, Bob Alexander, known locally as "The Reverend Baza" because he was an ordained minister, the founder of a Beat church he called the Temple of Man. "[He] took his vocation seriously," wrote a historian of the Venice West scene, "and a steady stream of proselytes, runaways, visionaries, and completely unclassifiable people flowed through his house on Cabrillo Avenue."[3] Anita Leonard had arrived with a friend of Joe Maini, but she and Marsh "wandered off into the night" together, probably after she approached him, as she said Marsh never initiated such meetings. "He was hanging out in my apartment, writing music while I was going to work." He lived with her for awhile—"We would play scrabble and chess all night." Marsh told her he was in love with his mother. "He said he was attracted to her sexually and everything. He recognized that it was a problem for him with women. She didn't like me at all. We never met, but we used to talk on the telephone, and she didn't like that he wouldn't come home."

Though Marsh did not play much in public, he could never stop playing. He renewed his musical relationship with Don Specht, played occasionally with pianist Forrest Westbrook in Santa Monica, and in early 1962 was a daily participant in midnight-to-morning jam sessions at bassist Pat "Putter" Smith's. Smith, the younger brother of Carson Smith, the original bassist in the Gerry Mulligan Quartet, had met Marsh through Joe Maini in 1958 or 1959 and played with him at a few "casuals" (routine jobs like parties, dances, or wedding receptions). In 1962 he had an isolated house on Fenn Street, on a hillside above the Pasadena freeway. One had to drive a mile down a dirt road to get to it. Here, for the first six months of 1962, he hosted all-night sessions at which most of the jazz players in Los Angeles played at one time or another. Some would come to play and stay two or three days. The rhythm section, besides Smith, usually consisted of guitarist Dave Koonse, pianist Ronnie Hoopes, and drummers Mike Romero or Alonzo Garibaldi. Marsh, said Smith, was always on "speed"—methamphetamine, dexadrine, or benzedrine—"what everyone was using at the time." Smith, on "speed" himself, was practicing twelve hours a day and "probably getting nothing out of it." Marsh showed up every night for several months. He was, said Smith, a "very devoted improviser."

As a person, Smith thought Marsh was deficient in many ways. He was not, he felt, a kind person—"he had lots of enemies"—and was "a real womanizer, totally without ethics in that regard," given to sexual flings with other people's wives or girlfriends. He would use people, especially younger ones who studied with him. "He was my hero," said Smith, "but I wouldn't let him use me." A seldom-noticed characteristic that Smith observed was that Marsh "wouldn't display weakness—and we all have weaknesses."

Musically, Smith loved Marsh's playing. "He was so interesting because of the way his phrases were made, it wasn't predictable." For example, Smith said, if there were two 4/4 bars in which the chord changed at the beginning of the second bar, Marsh would not play four beats on the first chord and four beats on the second but might play three beats on the first and five beats on the second, or vice versa, which created "a certain stress that I love." And Smith loved the fact that Marsh was a "very highly developed melodic player" who did not resort to "sheets of fourths" or other pre-set patterns. "Melody," said Smith, "is everything. All the great compositions are wall-to-wall melody."

Professionally, Smith felt that Marsh "couldn't bear the responsibility of real success. I would see him start to get an audience, then he would cut out. . . . It happened so predictably that I felt like it was part of a plan."

Sometime around 1962 Marsh moved to Las Vegas—Smith thinks he joined the Les Elgart band briefly to get there. In Vegas he lived with guitarist Don Overberg and his wife, Dee. According to Overberg, he came with the intention of "giving a go" at being a "legit," or working, musician. Overberg got him a job in Earl Green's band at the Dunes Hotel, playing for a revue, "Vive les Girls." Marsh lasted perhaps a week before he either quit or was fired. Said Overberg, "It just wasn't his cup of tea." But instead of returning to Los Angeles, Marsh stayed on with the Overbergs for six months to a year. For a month or so he worked for an old friend from pre-army days in Los Angeles, Jake Gerheim. Gerheim, a trumpet player and alumnus of the Alvino Rey band, met Marsh in 1945 through John McComb and later took a few lessons from Lennie Tristano on Marsh's recommendation. In Las Vegas he ran a business that made electronic instruments for the atom bomb tests at the nearby Mercury Project, and he hired Marsh to wire them.

But Marsh's main activity in Las Vegas was playing almost daily sessions with Overberg and bassist Roy Shain, another Vegas resident who had met Marsh in the early 1950s in New York. It was a time, said Shain, when jobs were so plentiful in Las Vegas that musicians could not play all the jobs they were offered, but by his own choice Marsh never worked again after his experience at the Dunes. Probably he received living expenses from his mother.

Around 1963 Marsh returned to Los Angeles, where he sat in on a Monday night at Shelly's Manne Hole with fellow saxophonist Lou Ciotti, who was filling in for Joe Maini that night. Ciotti had heard and admired Marsh's early work but was disappointed with his playing at Shelly's. "I didn't think he played well at all," said Ciotti. Marsh, he felt, was "at a disjointed point" in his life. A little later they met again at the North Hollywood apartment of bassists Buddy Clark and Jim Aton and became friends, often playing chess, cribbage, bridge, and backgammon at the apartment, a favorite hangout. But Marsh still seemed not to feel like playing, and he apparently worked little more in Los Angeles then than he had in Las Vegas. Alan Levitt, a drummer who had studied with Tristano and recorded with Konitz in the 1950s, reported going to hear the Gerald Wilson big band in Los Angeles around this time and seeing Marsh, who was in attendance, in a stupor, so high he could barely talk. Levitt thought he was going to pass out.

In the fall of 1963 Marsh turned up in Monterey, probably because Konitz was living in the area, in Carmel Valley. Here, on October 30, he met Geraldyne Elmore, who would soon become his wife. She remembered the date because it was her twenty-fourth birthday.

Geraldyne, a brash, attractive, fun-loving, garrulous girl, was born in 1939, the daughter of Charles Franklin Elmore, a sometime teacher and

California oil field worker with family roots in Missouri, and Lena Rosselli, a native of the Monterey area whose Italian ancestors had lived there for three generations. In 1943, during World War II, her father died, and her mother, who did not remarry for nine years, went to work as a dental assistant at nearby Ft. Ord, a hub of military activity. The job of raising three-year-old Geraldyne fell to her Italian-speaking maternal grandmother, Mary Rosselli, originally from Genoa, Italy.

Geraldyne became a jazz fan as a nineteen-year-old living in San Francisco in 1959. She heard, and hated, some of the jazz-and-poetry sessions conducted by Lawrence Ferlinghetti, Allen Ginsberg, and other Beat poets. Then, in a North Beach bar, someone played a Charlie Parker record on the jukebox, and she was hooked. She became such a regular at Jimbo's Bop City, an after hours club in the Fillmore district, that they gave her a free pass.

In the fall of 1963 she was living in Pacific Grove, near Monterey, with an artist friend and his wife—"hiding out," she said, from an abusive boyfriend with whom she had recently broken up. The artist had put some sketches of her on display in his gallery. When another friend of his, singer and pianist Bob Dorough, came to town and saw the sketches, he asked to meet the model. Arrangements were made for Dorough, Geraldyne, the artist, and his wife to go to the Outrigger, a club on Cannery Row in Monterey where Lee Konitz was playing. As it happened, Warne Marsh was there, sitting in with Konitz. Marsh was single, Dorough was not, and Geraldyne and Marsh ended the evening together. After about a month of seeing each other, Marsh returned to Los Angeles, but within a few days showed up again on her doorstep carrying a bottle of Lancers wine. They drove down to Paolo Colorado Canyon, near Big Sur, and there the thirty-six-year-old Marsh asked her to marry him and "be the mother of my children."[4]

She said yes, but the marriage itself was not to take place for several months. On Christmas day, 1963, they were in a motel in Los Angeles. Marsh went to visit his mother, leaving Geraldyne in the motel and not telling his mother about her. After Christmas they set out for New York, driving day and night, carrying on a running game of scrabble. They stopped briefly in Houston, Missouri, to visit Geraldyne's relatives from her father's side. It was a musical family, said Geraldyne, and when Marsh took out his tenor to practice one of the aunts said, "Aren't you putting a little too much air through that horn?" As they neared New York Marsh kidded Geraldyne that Lennie Tristano, being blind, would want to touch her all over when they met. Once in New York they headed for Tristano's four-story home in Jamaica, Long Island. There, to Geraldyne's great relief, Tristano merely shook her hand. She and Marsh took up quarters in Tristano's basement.

Geraldyne's impression, from talking to Lou Ciotti and others who had spent time with Marsh in the year or two before their meeting in 1963, was that Marsh had not been doing much serious playing. As to his being in a "disjointed" state of mind, she didn't think he was depressed: "Bored, maybe, stoned a lot, because he didn't get to play enough. He was just lying around, hanging out, playing chess, taking a lot of pills, downers, like Placidil, maybe sessions here and there. Maybe he was feeling sorry for himself. He had this crazy idea that he could quit playing for awhile and then pick up his horn and play great. When we got to New York, even Lennie told him, 'Hey, man, you're just goofin' around, getting high all the time. Just play your horn, Warne.' After that Warne started practicing every day. I would hear Lennie on the fourth floor and Warne in the basement."

Soon after arriving at Tristano's, Marsh had a seizure because of drugs. "We were playing badminton in Lennie's yard and all of a sudden he started moving in frames [jerkily, as in a malfunctioning movie] and fell down. I said, 'Warne, if you're joking, don't do it, it's not funny,' and he began to convulse. I screamed so loud Lennie heard me on the fourth floor. He came flying down and told me to go in the house and call an ambulance. He said later he thought Warne was going to die and wanted me to go inside so I wouldn't see it. I kept trying to open Warne's mouth and he kept biting my fingers. He had taken an upper and a downer. I didn't know his habits then. When he told me, I said, 'I want it understood between us that you let me know what you're taking, so that if anything happens at least I'll know what to do.'"

At one point while living at Tristano's, Marsh took "some electronic kind of job in a factory, and when he'd come home he was so miserable" that Geraldyne begged him to quit. She went to work for an answering service "because I couldn't stand how unhappy he was."

On April 11, 1964, they drove with Tristano and others to City Hall to be married. The ceremony took "about three seconds," and the ring Marsh tried to put on her finger was too small. Afterward one of the party threw rice at them and they all went to a bar for champagne. On the way back to Jamaica, Tristano asked, "Have you got the marriage certificate?" Geraldyne had left it in the bar, and after taking Tristano home, Marsh drove back to Manhattan to retrieve it. When he finally got back to Tristano's house, a student, Jack Block, was waiting for him. Marsh had forgotten about the scheduled lesson, but gave it, still with rice in his hair. Later that evening he and Geraldyne went back to the Half Note in Manhattan, where Zoot Sims was playing.

Tristano had made his second, highly acclaimed LP, *The New Tristano,* for Atlantic in 1962. In an interview after the release of the record he re-

sponded to a question about his current students, "No, I don't have a
Warne Marsh now. Nobody does. Warne had and has the fantastic ability
to thrill me the way Prez or Roy, [Charlie] Christian or Bird, maybe a few
others had."[5] Tristano had played infrequently in public since the Half
Note gigs of 1958–60, but now, with the arrival of Marsh, he reformed the
quintet with Marsh, Konitz, bassist Sonny Dallas, and drummer Nick
Stabulas.

The quintet played the Half Note in early June 1964, and on June 6 they
recorded a live half-hour segment from the club for *Look Up and Live,* a
Protestant religious program. Aired on August 9 over CBS, this recording reveals Tristano playing with great energy and brilliance, in the
manner of his 1962 recording. Konitz is equally inspired. Marsh has a brief
solo on "317 E. 32nd Street," but his solos on "Subconscious-Lee" and
"Background Music" are canceled out by the narrator's voiceover. By
Sonny Dallas's account, Tristano unexpectedly counted off "Background
Music" behind the narrator because time was running out. Frantically
raising his voice over the band and Marsh's solo, the narrator urges his
audience not to impose some arbitrary religious meaning on the music
but "to listen, to listen, to listen, and perhaps music like this will beguile
us into praying."

Later in June the group played at Le Coq d'Or in Toronto, and in October they were back at the Half Note, with Roger Mancuso replacing
Stabulas on drums. Don Heckman, reviewing the group for *Down Beat,*
was struck most by the "exceptional character of Konitz' playing," saying that Konitz had become "one of the most consistently creative alto
players on the scene." As for Marsh, "[his] peculiarly constricted tone is
alternately attractive and repellent. In ballads it tends to grate on the ears,
but its bassoonlike edge cuts through nicely in the faster tempos." This
"minor annoyance" of tone, however, was "more than compensated for
by his exceptionally complex rhythmic lines. I found myself continually
feeling that Marsh had lost control of the meter or the harmonic sequence
and then suddenly surprised to find that he had turned the time around
or delayed or anticipated but always came out perfectly in the end." He
concluded, "Again, as with Konitz, one can only regret that Marsh has
been heard so much more rarely than many lesser players."[6]

In the same issue of *Down Beat* Dan Morgenstern did a piece on Konitz's
return to New York after two years in California. In the course of the interview Konitz put in a plug for Marsh: "Warne is a very neglected
player. . . . He is a real improviser. He's never been appreciated sufficiently."[7]

Early in 1965 the Tristano quintet played the Jazz Workshop in Boston.
At that point the reunited quintet broke up, reportedly because Konitz

demanded more money.[8] Marsh, who spent hours trying to persuade Konitz to reconsider, summed the situation up this way: "In 1965, Lee, Lennie and I put the band together, briefly, and started to work. This was largely because we finally had all the offers for work we needed to keep a band together—which we did not have in the early 'fifties. . . . But Lee quit, for reasons he felt were substantial; and of course, as it turned out, they *are* substantial—he needed the particular training he felt necessary."[9] What Marsh meant by "particular training" is unclear, except perhaps as it refers to Konitz's increasing willingness to play in a great variety of contexts.

In the fall of 1965 Tristano accepted an invitation to tour Europe as a soloist, giving televised performances in Stockholm and Paris in November, and Marsh and Geraldyne moved back to Los Angeles.[10] Marsh returned to the East Coast briefly in the spring of 1966 for a one-week engagement at the Cellar Club in Toronto with Tristano, Dallas, and Mancuso but without Konitz. It was Marsh's last known club date with his mentor.

A curious sidelight of the Cellar Club gig was a review in the *Toronto Telegram* that quoted Tristano to the effect that the divorce of jazz and dance music was a mistake. "'The greatest jazz musicians played for dancing,' said Lennie discussing the decline of jazz, 'but when tables and chairs replaced the dance floor the wane in jazz began.'"[11] This from one of the prime exponents of jazz as an art form, as music to be seriously listened to for its own sake! Perhaps something got lost in the editing.

Meanwhile, Geraldyne had become pregnant. Tristano urged her and Marsh to stay in New York and have the baby there, but after the breakup of the quintet Marsh insisted that they return to Los Angeles, probably because it would be easier to obtain financial help from his mother. "I felt," he said later, "if I was going to give time to a family, settle down, that I could do it more effectively in L.A. than I could in New York. Nothing was really happening in New York; there was neither the group I was a part of, nor was there a real club scene—certainly not one attractive enough to make a musician want to stay there."

In June 1965 Geraldyne gave Caesarian birth to Siamese twins, joined at the chest. They died at birth and were hustled off by attendants without her ever seeing them. On seeing his wife wheeled out of the operating room, Marsh fainted.[12] Elizabeth Marsh, visiting her daughter-in-law in the hospital, informed her, according to Geraldyne, "Nothing like this has ever happened on my side of the family."[13] Marsh never talked about the experience.

Sometime before the birth of the twins Marsh sat in with pianist Clare Fischer and Lee Konitz at the Lighthouse.[14] In 1965 he was playing regularly at drummer John Tirabasso's Friday morning sessions, which continued for several years. Other regulars were Lou Ciotti, Frank Strazzeri, Putter Smith, Dave Parlato, Abe and Sam Most, Jimmy Zito, John Gross, Hart Smith, Sal Nistico, Frank de la Rosa, and Dave Koonse.

Late in 1966 Ciotti called Marsh for Ace Lane's rehearsal band, and in Lane's garage studio he met altoist Gary Foster. Foster, long an admirer of Marsh, Konitz, and Tristano, had already, as early as 1964, dialed Marsh's phone number as listed in the union directory but received no answer. On December 2, 1966, Foster was scheduled to work a dance job with Keith Williams, Marsh's old associate from Canteen Kids days, at the Balboa Bay Club. At the last minute Williams called to ask him to bring another tenor player. Foster called Marsh for the $50 gig, and they drove to Balboa together. On the way back Foster posed some technical questions and asked if he could take some lessons. Marsh responded, "I think you're a good enough musician to work it out for yourself, and that would be a better way to do it."

Shortly afterward Marsh called Foster at the Pasadena music store, Berry and Grasmueck, where Foster taught, to ask if he felt like playing. Foster had lessons scheduled till 10 p.m. but went to Marsh's place in the San Fernando Valley afterward. Marsh set the metronome at a slow tempo and asked him to improvise on a tune normally played much faster. Foster did so, and after he had played a few choruses Marsh joined him. They played all night, beginning a routine of playing in this manner once or twice a month.

Clare Fischer had begun rehearsing a big band that included both Foster and Lou Ciotti, and in January 1967, on their recommendation, Marsh joined the band, playing in the saxophone section for half of the album *Duality* as a replacement for Dave O'Rourke.[15] At about the same time, Marsh and Ciotti formed a quartet with bassist Jim Krutcher and drummer John Tirabasso, using primarily material written or inspired by Tristano in their repertoire. This group worked every Sunday afternoon at the Brass Ring on Ventura Boulevard for six months. On one occasion Foster subbed for Ciotti, and this was the beginning of the quartet that later would record Marsh's first record as a leader in eleven years. Late in 1967 Marsh, Foster, Tirabasso, and bassist Dave Parlato began rehearsing at least once a week, Fridays at Tirabasso's.

From around 1966 Marsh had been supplementing his income by cleaning swimming pools, but toward the end of 1967 Foster, who was then in charge of the instructional program at Berry and Grasmueck, offered Marsh a teaching job at a significantly higher hourly rate. Marsh accepted, though he may still have done some pool cleaning in 1968 and 1969.[16]

In 1968 both Marsh and Foster began working frequently with Matty Malneck's small dance band, and on May 12 Clare Fischer's big band, with Marsh, Foster, and Ciotti in the saxophone section, played its first job at

Donte's in North Hollywood. This excellent band, featuring compositions and arrangements by Clare Fischer and his brother Stewart, was fairly active during the year, playing at Donte's on June 23, August 1, October 6, and December 15.[17]

On August 16 and 17, two weeks after the birth of Marsh's first son, Casey—the name was originally K.C., for Kansas City, but evolved into the more conventional form—the Fischer band recorded the *Thesaurus* album for Atlantic. Marsh soloed on two numbers, "Miles Behind" and "Lennie's Pennies." The latter also featured Foster, both solo and in unison with Marsh on the dizzyingly complex Tristano line. On this, Marsh's first studio recording on which he solos since the *Lee Konitz Meets Jimmy Giuffre* album of 1959, his playing is startlingly original, though the buoyancy and rhythmic abandon of his best playing of 1955–60 is missing. Fischer, a notorious stickler where time is concerned, has said, "It always bothered me that Warne hung back on the beat," and that tendency is discernible in his solos on this record. Not everyone, however, found it bothersome.[18]

Reviewing the record for *Down Beat*, Lawrence Kart had little good to say for the arrangements, the band, or most of the soloists, except for Marsh. The album, he wrote, was "an earnest though generally unsuccessful effort, but it does contain superb solos by Warne Marsh . . . that will fascinate anyone who cares for the Tristano tradition or Lester Young of the '50s. . . . Both solos are gaunt, startling explorations of the furthest reaches of orthodox time and harmony, and they recall Tristano's claim that Charlie Parker once named Marsh as the only man who was doing something new on the saxophone. Certainly these solos once more place him in the front rank of tenor men."[19]

Although the Fischer band played five engagements in the first seven months of 1969, three at Donte's and two at the Lighthouse, Fischer was soon to lose interest because of the difficulties of booking and recording it. In 1970 the band played at Donte's on March 15 but worked little during the rest of the year. Its last performance was probably December 9, 1970, again at Donte's. But Marsh's career, thanks in no small part to his friendship with Gary Foster, was about to shift into what for him was high gear.

NOTES

1. Dan Morgenstern, "Modern Reeds—And How They Grew," *Down Beat*, May 14, 1959, 16–18, 38.

2. Tom Runyan, interview.

3. John Arthur Maynard, *Venice West: The Beat Generation in Southern California* (New Brunswick, N.J., and London: Rutgers University Press, 1991), 185.

4. Geraldyne Marsh, interview.

5. Bill Coss, "Lennie Tristano Speaks Out," *Down Beat,* December 6, 1962, 21.

6. Don Heckman, "Caught in the Act," *Down Beat,* November 5, 1964, 17.

7. Dan Morgenstern, "Lee Konitz: No Compromise," *Down Beat,* November 5, 1964, 16.

8. Sonny Dallas, interview.

9. Les Tomkins, "The Warne Marsh Story," *Crescendo International,* May 1976, 20.

10. John Francis McKinney, *The Pedagogy of Lennie Tristano* (Ph.D. dissertation, Fairleigh Dickinson University, 1978), 110–11.

11. Dave Caplan, "Tristano's Jazz—A Bit on the Surrealistic Side," *Toronto Telegram,* 23 March 1966.

12. Geraldyne Marsh, interview.

13. Ibid.

14. Gary Foster, interview.

15. Ibid.

16. Ibid. Also Cliff Ingraham, interview.

17. Foster, interview.

18. Marsh had played in the section, without soloing, on the second recording session for Fischer's album *Duality,* Trend/Discovery DS 807, in January 1967. He was substituting for David O'Rourke, who played on the recording session of June 20, 1966.

19. Lawrence Kart, "Clare Fischer," *Down Beat,* April 4, 1969, 22.

A Second Career

For Marsh the most important event of 1969 was the recording on September 14 and October 25 of *Ne Plus Ultra*, Revelation 12, Marsh's first studio recording as a leader since the dates with Paul Chambers in 1957–58. His sidemen, with whom he had been rehearsing at least weekly for nearly two years, were Gary Foster, alto; Dave Parlato, bass; and John Tirabasso, drums. Along with the two solos on Clare Fischer's big band recording, *Ne Plus Ultra* marked the rediscovery of Warne Marsh by at least a portion of the jazz press. Greatly abetted by his later visibility as the major soloist of the popular Supersax, he was in process of emerging from the doldrums of the 1960s into a relatively busy second career.

Reviews of *Ne Plus Ultra* in both *Down Beat* and the English publication *Jazz Journal* were laudatory. In the latter Steve Voce called it a classic. "The playing of the four men is of the highest level. . . . Certainly it is intellectual jazz of the highest order but its rewards are consequently deeper. It is the kind of music that musicians feel that nonmusicians should be incapable of appreciating but somehow the nonmusicians usually do."[1]

In *Down Beat* Harvey Pekar gave it four and a half stars, denying the fifth star only because Marsh was not given enough solo space. "His playing is relaxed and creative. He is ceaselessly inventive, and his work is harmonically and melodically fresh and rhythmically unpredictable. . . . He constructs solos well, sometimes building relentlessly, piling climax upon climax. . . ." About the freely improvised piece "Touch and Go," which Marsh and producer John William Hardy had perhaps included as a reminder to Ornette Coleman and the free jazz avant-garde of the 1960s that Tristano had recorded the first free pieces in 1949, Pekar wrote, "It is

152

not only a free selection but also one of the most interesting and well put together free selections ever recorded." He concluded by calling the record "one of the most important jazz LPs to be issued in the past year."[2]

Equally important in the rehabilitation of Marsh's reputation was the release on Peter Ind's new Wave label of material recorded in Ind's New York studio a decade earlier. On May 2, 1969, Marsh had mailed a laconic postcard to Ind, then living in England: "Release Record, Send Tape— Warne." When the record was released soon afterward as *Warne Marsh*, Wave LP-6, the cover, conveniently for discographers, showed a photo of the card, complete with dated postmark. The record is now usually referred to under the title *Release Record, Send Tape.*

Reviewing it in the spring of 1970, the English critic Mark Gardner wrote: "Marsh is a thorough original. Nobody else sounds remotely like him, except perhaps his old buddy Ted Brown and two British musicians—Charlie Burchell and Bobby Wellins. Warne has a certain dry and expressive tone that is entirely his own. When all is right—as on *Warne Marsh* (Wave LP6)—he is one of the most satisfying players in the jazz idiom. . . . [T]his is all joyous music with I Remember You capturing especially memorable improvisation by a great neglected saxophonist. . . . Much more could and should be said about Marsh and this magnificent sample of mature playing. . . . Get the record and all will be clear."[3] Another English critic, Victor Schonfield, declared that "I Remember You" was "one of the great jazz solos,"[4] and two months later Steve Voce also echoed Gardner's enthusiasm: "Completely devoid of showmanship, trademarks or gimmicks, [Marsh] is probably one of the greatest tenorists of the last quarter century, and ranks with Hawkins, Lester Young, Getz, Rollins and Coltrane."[5]

Very possibly Marsh never saw these reviews, though Ind may have sent word of them. It was a kind of recognition that was still, ten years after his death, withheld by all but a few jazz critics in the United States.

By this time Marsh had begun working in a quartet with Foster, Parlato, and Tirabasso, specializing in the Tristano repertoire. On November 22, 1970, they played for Pete Douglas's Bach, Dancing, and Dynamite Society in Half Moon Bay, just down the coast from San Francisco, and on January 11, 1971, they played the first of a number of Monday night performances at the Ice House in Pasadena. On July 23 Marsh, Foster, and pianist Ron Hoopes, who taught with them at Berry and Grasmueck, began playing weekends at The Gilded Cage in Arcadia, near Pasadena. The bassist was usually Dave Parlato or Paul Ruhland, and there were a variety of drummers, including Tirabasso, Stix Hooper, and Harvey Mason. In the fall Marsh and Foster played six Monday nights with similar fluctuating personnel at Jazz West, on Ventura Boulevard in the San Fernando

Valley, and on November 21 they played for the postearthquake reopening of Ray Avery's Rare Records store in Glendale.⁶

The year 1971 also saw the birth of Marsh's second son, Jason, on April 9.

Following up on the critical, if not monetary, success of *Ne Plus Ultra,* on May 9, 1972, Bill Hardy of Revelation Records recorded an informal jam session at Clare Fischer's home with Marsh, Foster, Fischer, Ruhland, and Tirabasso. The evening, said Foster, was "uneventful." None of the players thought of the occasion as a recording session, Foster even using it to try out a new mouthpiece. The main reason for taping it was Hardy's desire to test his new Stellavox SP-7 recorder, a Swiss machine weighing only eight and a half pounds that "completely changed [his] concept of location recording." Despite the fact that none of the principals thought the results worthy of release—whenever anyone asks Foster to autograph the record, he offers to buy it back—Hardy issued the material under the ponderously cute title *Report of the 1st Annual Symposium on Relaxed Improvisation* (Revelation 17). The extent of the relaxation was suggested in a cover photo showing Marsh, Foster, and Fischer holding drinks and grinning like fraternity brothers at a picnic.

In his four-star review in *Down Beat,* John Litweiler began by noting the contrast between the seriousness of the *Ne Plus Ultra* date and the loose feeling of this one: "Marsh's attitude reminds you of Richie Allen [a well-known baseball player] between pitches. . . . Yet there is certainly no lack of tension from this most customarily intense of improvisers. There is the brilliantly extended and elaborated theme statement in *It Could [Happen to You],* and a classic love of life that pervades the entire solo. . . . The first chorus of his *Mellowtone* solo is very mid '40s Youngish, but his *Yesterdays* solo is uncharacteristically fragmented, due probably to the rhythm section's complete misunderstanding of his doubletiming intentions. A very satisfying night for Marsh. . . ." Litweiler's remarks about Foster and Fischer were markedly unappreciative: "[O]n the whole Foster's ideas are a weak and somewhat disorderly version of later Konitz. . . . Foster stands midway between Marsh's spontaneous flow of melody and Fischer's general vulgarity, with no real style to call his own. . . ."⁷ Clearly the four stars were for Marsh only.

But however much Foster may have been overshadowed by Marsh as a player, he was the best friend Marsh ever had in terms of advancing his career. In 1967 Foster had been responsible for Marsh's joining Clare Fischer's band, and now, in July of 1972, he was responsible for Marsh's first contact with Supersax. While working with guitarist Laurindo Almeida at Donte's, Foster was asked by bassist Buddy Clark to fill in for tenor player Pete Christlieb at a rehearsal. Christlieb, who built racing cars in his spare time, had been injured by a piece of hot metal that pierced his eardrum and was unable to play for six or eight weeks. Foster declined, but suggested Marsh, thus launching Marsh's five-year association with Supersax.

The idea for Supersax, which was to play Charlie Parker solos orchestrated for a five-man sax section, originally had grown out of altoist Med Flory's friendship with Joe Maini.[8] Inspired by Maini, who knew a number of Parker solos by heart, Flory wrote arrangements of Parker's solos on "Star Eyes," "Blues for Alice," and "Just Friends" back in the late 1950s. As members of Terry Gibbs's big band, said Flory, "We used to do them with Joe Maini, Richie Kamuca, Charlie Kennedy, Bill Hood and myself with a rhythm section." Lou Ciotti was sometimes in the section as well.[9]

In December 1971 Flory and Clark, who had begun writing his own arrangements of Parker solos, brought together a group including Flory and Bill Perkins, altos; Richie Kamuca and Bill Hood, tenors; Jack Nimitz, baritone; Conte Candoli, trumpet; Jake Hanna, drums; and Ronnell Bright, piano, for the first Supersax rehearsal. Jay Migliori soon replaced Kamuca, and Pete Christlieb replaced Hood.[10] Rehearsals were held in Perkins's garage studio on Birmingham Road in Burbank.

Christlieb soon left, he said, not only because of his injury but because "there were too many notes to read and not enough blowing"—it was too much like the commercial things he did in the Hollywood studios. Marsh, after subbing for Christlieb at rehearsal, remained as a regular member of Supersax. But had not Foster recommended him, Marsh probably never would have been asked to join the band. When Flory spoke to Perkins about Marsh's joining, he said, "He doesn't play very good, but he's available."[11] Flory was being facetious, as he often was, but he was also reflecting a commonly held opinion. "Warne's playing wasn't too widely appreciated by musicians around L.A.," said Perkins. "He wasn't respected by the typical musician because he wasn't into versatility, or to when the red [recording] light goes on. Then one night we turned him loose on 'Cherokee,' and from that point on his playing was very much appreciated by the group."

Flory's attitude toward Marsh was somewhat ambivalent. On the one hand, he recognized Marsh's originality. "He was always completely free, out there, the Zen of jazz. When he soloed, everybody would just sit and dig. I liked Warne because you never knew what he was going to do, where he'd take you. Everything was just totally now, what jazz is. Personally he was kind of detached, sort of fey, his life was prosaic, humdrum. But when he played, he knew no boundaries, he was completely open."

The only time he ever saw Marsh flustered, he said, was a Sunday afternoon in December 1974 when Stan Getz sat in with Supersax at Hungry Joe's in Huntington Beach. As the rest of the band played their orchestration of Parker's solo on "Moose the Mooche," Flory could see Getz's hands trembling with excitement as he waited to play. When he did, "He was rollin' it, so great, playing like he never played on records." Following Getz, Marsh seemed to "freeze," according to both Flory and Lou Levy, who was on piano. But for all Getz's prowess, said Flory, he was never as "surprising" as Marsh, who "never touched the same base twice."

Despite Flory's respect for Marsh's originality, however, his idol and model was Charlie Parker, not Lennie Tristano, and when, after five years, Marsh left the band, Flory's choice for a replacement was Don Menza, a very different kind of player.

After eleven months of rehearsal, Supersax gave its first paid performance in November 1972 at a marathon concert sponsored by the Blue Angel Club at Pasadena's University Club. Others on the ten-hour-long program included Joe Venuti, Joe Pass, Ruby Braff, Abe Most, Nat Pierce, Jimmy Rowles, Herb Ellis, Sonny Criss, Mavis Rivers, Ronnell Bright, Red Norvo, Flip Phillips, John Best, and Ray Sherman.[12] Shortly afterward Supersax made what is usually considered their public debut at Donte's in North Hollywood. By this time they had arrangements of sixteen Charlie Parker solos.[13] Reviewer Harvey Siders complained that Marsh's "characteristic tenor lag" on "The Bird" made him "want to goose him to catch up," but acknowledged that "solo honors belonged to [Jay] Migliori and Marsh for their long, exciting tenor dialogue" on "KoKo."[14]

Mauri Lathower of Capitol Records also heard Supersax at Donte's that night, with the result that early in 1973 the band recorded its first album for Capitol, *Supersax Plays Bird*. According to Flory, they recorded all the tunes for the album as they had played them at Donte's, with solos by Marsh and other saxophonists, but Lathower insisted that they rerecord the entire album without saxophone solos. From that point on, no Supersax studio recording would include saxophone solos. Released in May, the record won a Grammy for Best Jazz Performance by a Group in 1973.

Supersax played Donte's repeatedly during 1973. "The success of Super Sax and its Bird-like mission," reported *Down Beat* in mid-March, "has been so phenomenal, the group will soon be installed as the permanent Sunday attraction at Donte's."[15] Two months later the magazine reported that Sundays at Donte's during April indeed "belonged to Super Sax, except for one."[16]

On June 17 they achieved major visibility as part of George Wein's Newport Jazz Festival West in the Hollywood Bowl, playing on a program that included such stars as Dizzy Gillespie, Art Blakey, Sonny Stitt, and Mary Lou Williams. Later that summer, on July 29, they played the Concord Summer Jazz Festival in Northern California, and on September 22 they performed at the Monterey Jazz Festival. For a period that fall they were the regular Thursday night attraction at Chubby Jackson's short-lived club in the San Fernando Valley, The Estate, and in October they were on tour again.

Marsh's attitude toward Supersax at this time was positive, even excited. When the group played in Chicago in October, interviewers John Litweiler and Terry Martin asked, "How do you feel about Supersax?" "I love it," replied Marsh. "It's a challenge, and it's very satisfying. . . . [T]he material is a constant challenge. We simply don't play it the same way twice. It's the equivalent of demanding an improvising situation all the time. We have the Charlie Parker melody in mind, [and] the harmony part, which is a trip of its own to negotiate. . . . The very structure of how we present a piece is still growing." Asked if the group might introduce material other than Parker's, Marsh answers, "Yes! The possibilities are really fantastic. It's a fine saxophone section, really. However, we're not halfway through Parker yet. We're playing it very much better than we did when we made the album. . . . There's a distance to go there yet, also, in achieving just exactly what Charlie Parker achieved." By that, he explains, he means capturing "every nuance" of Parker's tonal inflections.

In the interview Marsh sounds equally excited about the commercial viability of the group: "It's of a caliber that Willard Alexander's buying it, ABC is buying it on the west coast, so both coasts are being booked with a fine manager. Capitol Records is paying for this whole trip, and they want two more albums right away. So the prospects are working not only [this] country, but Europe and Japan."[17]

Supersax did in fact make its second recording for Capitol, *Salt Peanuts,* late in 1973. The title track was arranged by Marsh—he had told Martin and Litweiler that the opportunity to arrange for the band was part of the attraction of Supersax, and he had written two other arrangements of Parker solos, "Now's the Time" and "Billie's Bounce." Like Supersax's first album, *Salt Peanuts* was nominated for a Grammy. Sadly, again there were no saxophone solos.

Supersax continued to be quite active over the next two years. At the end of 1973 they played New Year's Eve and two succeeding nights at Shelly's Manne Hole. Early in 1974, after they were awarded the Grammy for their first record, they made an extended road trip, to New York and Philadelphia. In the summer they were part of another tour sponsored by Belvedere Cigarettes, a Canadian company. Others on the tour, which included Toronto, Winnipeg, Vancouver, and Detroit, were Carmen McRae and the big bands of Woody Herman and Maynard Ferguson. At the Toronto concert Supersax astonished the audience by playing their set despite the fact that their music had not arrived, relying on their memory of the extremely demanding charts. Back in California, they played at

Donte's six or eight times, at the Playboy Club in Century City for a week in October, and several times near the end of the year at Hungry Joe's in Huntington Beach.

The next year marked Marsh's first trip overseas, as Supersax made a six-city tour of Japan, playing concerts from January 7 to January 15, 1975, in Tokyo, Yokohama, Nagoya, Kanazawa, Osaka, and Fukuoka. In a letter home from the Tokyo Hilton Marsh wrote: "The concert in Yokohama last night was a sellout, and I think they liked us—1500 very quiet & polite people (at $7.00 per person—we're being vastly underpaid) and the band was treated to [a] Kobe steak dinner afterward that was a gas. Med's funny—standing up there trying to carry on with his shtick & nobody understands anything except the actual titles of the tunes, at which point they'd start clapping whatever context Med used a title in. He started introducing 'Star-Eyes,' 'I won't tell you when this tune was written'— (the last of the fun wars) [i.e., World War II]. Exactly nine people cracked up." Marsh asks his wife to call Frank Severino and Jim Hughart for his upcoming gigs at Donte's January 21 and 28, adding that if Severino can't make it he'll use Supersax drummer Jake Hanna.

Returning to Los Angeles January 19, 1975, Supersax played at its usual haunts around Los Angeles, including Donte's at least five times during the year and at least once each at the Lighthouse, the Parisian Room, the Pilgrimage Theatre, and, in San Diego, the Catamaran Lounge.

Considering the frequency of Supersax's appearances, especially in California, the number of reviews is disappointingly small, and the number of them mentioning Marsh as soloist borders on the nonexistent. Reviewing the band's performance at the Playboy Club in 1974, Leonard Feather was full of praise for the ensemble, but bemoaned the fact that the soloists, "excellent though they are, cannot match Bird's genius." The one exception, he added, was Flory: "He captures more of the passion and sense of creativity than any other member, yet he was featured in only one solo. To retain the Parker essence, the other members' work ought to be curtailed and Flory should give himself more time to stretch out."[18] Flory was and is a fine player, but in big bands he usually functioned as lead alto rather than jazz soloist, and this may be the only time in his career that he was favorably compared as a soloist with Parker. It was also the only time that anyone wrote of him as Supersax's major soloist, a role more often accorded Marsh. In Feather's defense, it may be that Marsh didn't solo in the set he heard. As a rule, each saxophonist would get one solo per set, amounting to an average of three solos in a three-set performance. But sometimes he would get either more or fewer, depending on Flory's attention to detail and choice of numbers that night. Daniel Fiore, a guitarist and record store owner from Connecticut who knew Marsh, reported hearing Supersax at a club in Manhattan on an occasion when Marsh did not play a single solo all night.

In 1975 Feather somewhat modified his stance toward the band's soloists. Reviewing the band's appearance at the Pilgrimage, he commented, "Every chorus, whether arranged or adlibbed, bore the stamp of a creative act; even the non-Parker improvised solos, though not centrally important, stood up well. . . ." Still reluctant to compare Marsh to Parker, he at least reported the audience response: "It was a rare joy to hear waves of applause greeting the tenor sax of Warne Marsh, the alto-and-baritone battle between Joe Lopes and Jack Nimitz."[19] *Coda* reviewer Fred Bouchard, after commending Frank Rosolino for his trombone solos and Flory for his "tight-lipped lead alto" at the Catamaran Lounge, took a more usual view, writing that "Warne Marsh, not unpredictably, took solo honors with oblique, brilliant Bird references woven into *Blue 'n Boogie* and a wonderful excursion in his squirming, lemony tones on *Salt Peanuts* that drew a standing ovation."[20]

Feather seems never to have taken to Marsh. The closest he had come to praising him was in a review of Marsh's own quartet at the Pilgrimage Theatre in the fall of 1972, just after Marsh joined Supersax: "Marsh is a tenor saxophonist who in the late 1940s became Lennie Tristano's sideman and disciple. The precepts instilled by Tristano, who advocated a cerebral, nonviolent approach to swinging, still are detectable in his lean, supple lines." In Gary Foster, added Feather, "Marsh has a mirror-image foil. . . . This spontaneously combustive pair achieves a delightfully easy interplay in its unison or counterpoint choruses, with surging dynamic accents like billowing zephyrs of sound."[21] Feather usually had the good sense to avoid such billowing poeticisms. That he indulged himself in this review of Marsh and Foster is as curious as the terms "cerebral" and "nonviolent," sometimes appropriate in Marsh's earlier career but seldom in this period, when his playing with Supersax was more aptly described as "shot out of a cannon."[22] As Pete Christlieb said, "It defies reason that anybody could do what he did at those tempos." In 1977, after Marsh had left the band, Feather wrote that "Warne Marsh has been replaced by Don Menza, for whom this is an ideal setting. His contribution to 'Salt Peanuts' was limber, swinging and perfectly controlled."[23] This was more direct praise than he had ever accorded Marsh.

Marsh continued with Supersax through 1976, but from about 1974 to 1977, mainly because of his exposure with the group, he was able to devote more and more time to his own projects, even spending the greater part of one year in Europe, shuttling back and forth to meet commitments in the States. One such occasion was in February 1976 when, after about two months in Europe, he returned for a Supersax engagement at Ratso's in Chicago. A tape exists that includes not only Marsh's solos but also a rendering by the entire band of "I'll Remember April," with back-to-back solos by Marsh and guest Zoot Sims. Out of this visit also came Marsh's first full album under studio conditions and for immediate release since 1969 (*All Music*, Nessa N-7, discussed in a subsequent chapter). Then he was off again to England and the continent, shuttling back briefly for an April 5 engagement with Supersax at the Playboy Club in Los Angeles, a performance documented by a tape of an hour-long radio broadcast over KBCA-FM.

Finally, sometime in 1977, Marsh broke his connection with Supersax, partly, according to both Ted Brown and Gary Foster, on the advice of Lennie Tristano, who considered Supersax too commercial. Med Flory's comments on Marsh's being replaced by Don Menza were typically double edged: "We were sorry to see Warne go, of course. You know he was fixing TV sets in the San Fernando Valley before he got back into playing again. He is a marvelous musician and a really lyrical cat—but maybe he should have played a few strip joints. Menza, on the other hand, is a real killer—He goes for the throat. Whereas Warne is a summer picnic in the woods, Menza is charging the battlements."[24] No doubt Flory was intent on countering any notion that the band was diminished by the loss of Marsh. Still, it is hard to avoid the impression that Menza, an aggressive hard-bop player, was more to Flory's taste.

Other members of Supersax had no such ambivalence. Altoist Joe Lopes considered Marsh without question the major soloist of the group, even taking some lessons with him. Lanny Morgan, who replaced Lopes in mid-1975, expressed similar admiration: "I was always on the edge of my chair, listening to Warne. He sort of became one of my heroes during that period. If you put ten tenor players up there with Warne—Sonny Rollins, Sonny Stitt, Coltrane, Richie Kamuca, Bill Perkins—Warne, most of the time, is the one who's going to go where people least expect him to go. . . . Once you got used to Trane, and heard him for awhile, it was kind of predictable . . . but Warne was really very individual, he seemed to be constantly thinking and exploring. Like everyone he had certain personal cliches, like those turns the Tristano people liked to use, like Warne used in his 'Background Music.' But I would hear him do that one way one night and then put it in a completely different place another night. When most people would start on the first beat, he'd start on the fourth or second beat. There are a lot of people who don't like that, even some in the group [Supersax], but I thought it was just wonderful. I always listened when Warne played."

In 1991 former Supersax member Bill Perkins recalled that shortly before Marsh's death, after he had returned to California in 1985, "I was saying to myself that I wanted to study with Warne. I could have learned a lot from him. Then he died before I got around to it." Harmonically, he said, for thirty years Marsh had been doing things with chordal extensions and voice-leading in improvisation that younger players were just discovering, and he was "par excellence" at rhythmic displacement. "He could put the time across bar lines with absolute impunity, create long lines with sequential material that would go right across the rhythm." On hearing on the radio, around 1985, Charlie Parker's "KoKo" followed by Marsh's "Marshmallow," both based on "Cherokee," Perkins said, "I was astounded. I realized that 'Marshmallow,' in its way, was equally outstanding." He summed up his feelings about Marsh as "a series of regrets, that I wasn't more attuned to listening and learning from him" earlier.

NOTES

1. Steve Voce, "Warne Marsh—The Best Is Yet to Come," *Jazz Journal* (October 1970): 25.

2. Harvey Pekar, "Ne Plus Utra," *Down Beat,* October 1, 1970, 22–23.

3. Mark Gardner, "Seven Ways," *Jazz Journal* (March 1970): 37.

4. Victor Schonfield, "Warne Marsh," *Jazz Journal* (February 1986): 29.

5. Steve Voce, "Late Warne-ing," *Jazz Journal* (May 1970): 12.

6. Gary Foster, interview. Foster is the source of much information about Marsh in California in 1966–77.

7. John Litweiler, "Warne Marsh/Clare Fischer/Gary Foster," *Down Beat,* October 10, 1974, 22–23.

8. Leonard Feather, "Blindfold Test," *Down Beat,* November 22, 1973, 31.

9. Mike Hennessey, "Retracing the Bird," *Jazz Journal* (September 1978): 8.

10. Ibid., 19. Also, Foster, interview.

11. Perkins and Flory, interviews.

12. "Strictly Ad Lib," *Down Beat,* January 18, 1973, 43.

13. Leonard Feather, "Blindfold Test," *Down Beat,* November 22, 1973, 31. Also, Harvey Siders, "Caught in the Act," *Down Beat,* February 15, 1973, 30.

14. Siders, 30–31.

15. "Strictly Ad Lib," *Down Beat,* March 15, 1973, 38.

16. "Strictly Ad Lib," *Down Beat,* May 24, 1973, 35.

17. Terry Martin and John Litweiler, unpublished interview, October 14, 1973.

18. Leonard Feather, "Supersax: A Lot of Bird in the Band," *Los Angeles Times,* 2 October 1974, 11 (IV).

19. Leonard Feather, "Supersax: Old Gold with New Luster at Pilgrimage," *Los Angeles Times,* 30 April 1975, 12 (IV).

20. Fred Bouchard, "Supersax," *Coda* (June/July 1975), 37.

21. Leonard Feather, "Dual Concert at Pilgrimage," *Los Angeles Times,* 24 October 1972, 17 (IV).

22. Ted Brown, interview.

23. Leonard Feather, "Supersax Opens Monday Series," *Los Angeles Times,* 15 January 1977, 7 (II).

24. Hennessey, 19.

Warne Marsh solo on "I Remember You," recorded Dec. 19, 1959, WARNE MARSH, RELEASE RECORD, SEND TAPE, Wave (E) LP-6, transcribed for tenor saxophone by Safford Chamberlain from a draft by Rob Lockart.

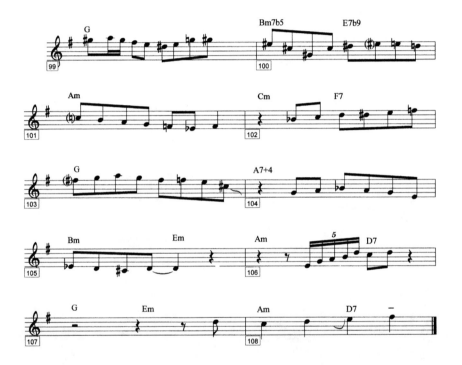

Analysis

ANALYSIS OF WARNE MARSH'S SOLO ON "I REMEMBER YOU,"
RECORDED DECEMBER 19, 1959, *WARNE MARSH:*
***RELEASE RECORD, SEND TAPE*, WAVE (E) LP-6,**
BY ROB LOCKART

Hearing recordings of master improvisers in a more "live" situation, such as this recording from an informal session in Peter Ind's New York studio, is always my favorite opportunity to listen to that player stretch his ideas. Such is definitely the case in these three choruses by Warne Marsh on the standard "I Remember You."

On first listening one is most intrigued with the rhythmic shadings, especially the flourishes in bars 48–52, 73–75, and 89–93. The exactitude of the execution made me conclude that these flourishes are based on the quarter-note triplet, to imply a sort of brief metric modulation. This technique of temporarily shifting time divisions, though still not common practice, is somewhat more widely used today, yet this recording was made in 1959, and in fact Warne had been using this technique since his earliest recordings in 1949. He was truly ahead of his time.

Harmonically, as well, Warne shows us that he was hearing things in quite a forward fashion, as in the use of the tri-tone substitution of an A♭ chord over a D7 in bar 36 and bar 60, and the use of a D♭ over a G7 in bar 84.

In addition to the harmonic richness, Warne is very creative in how he uses dissonance, anticipating or delaying harmonic resolution. For instance, in bar 17 the C# chord over the C major 7 resolves to the C in

171

beat 4, and the G# chord in bar 45 on beat 4 is an anticipation of the C# minor 7 in the next bar.

But this solo is not a math project. Everything Warne plays here is something that comes from within, and the interest is in the balancing of these ideas with rhythmic interest and unique melodic shapes. And above all, it is *swinging*.

♪♪

A Taste of Europe

The years 1974–1976 were probably the busiest of Marsh's career. Since it was his habit to wait passively for jobs to come to him rather than aggressively solicit them, there is little doubt that most of this activity, probably even his first ever European experience, was due to his exposure with Supersax.

An exception was a February 22, 1974, concert at Occidental College with Gary Foster, Dave Parlato, and John Tirabasso. Arranged by John William Hardy of Revelation Records, who included the Bobby Bradford-John Carter group on the bill, this concert probably had more to do with Hardy's personal admiration for Marsh and his promotion of all of these players for his record label than with Marsh's new visibility with Supersax. But a December 1974 gig at Hungry Joe's in Huntington Beach would seem to have been a direct result of several Supersax appearances at the club in the same period, and Supersax's frequent appearances at Donte's probably opened things up for Marsh's own group at Donte's as well as a new club on Ventura Boulevard, The Times. Throughout most of 1975 his quartet, with Lou Levy on piano, Jim Hughart or Fred Atwood on bass, and usually either Dick Borden or Frank Severino on drums, was booked frequently at The Times and Donte's.

An unusual recording session that may have been an outgrowth of the Supersax connection was with the gypsy violinist Elek Bacsik for Bob Thiele's Flying Dutchman label. Titled *Bird and Dizzy, A Musical Tribute*, the album included on several tracks Med Flory and Buddy Clark of Supersax, as well as trumpeter Oscar Brashear and on most tracks Mike Wofford, piano, Shelly Manne, drums, and Chuck Domanico, bass, who constituted Thiele's regular West Coast rhythm section at the time. According to Wofford, it was probably recorded in 1974, possibly as early as 1973, at TTG Studios in Hollywood, with the personnel largely chosen by Thiele. Bacsik lived in Las Vegas and probably had little if any knowledge of Marsh's work.

Marsh plays on five tracks but solos only on "Moose the Mooche" and "Groovin' High." Startlingly inventive and beautifully logical and melodic, these solos are among his finest on record. Leonard Feather's comments in the liner notes about his playing were perfunctory and misleading: "Marsh's pipelike sound and smooth sense of time govern his two choruses [on "Moose the Mooche"], recalling the fusion of bop and cool jazz that date[s] back to his association with the Lennie Tristano school back around 1949."[1] Marsh's sound is beautifully captured here, and it is not at all "pipelike" but rather slightly rough, almost gutteral, thrilling in its sense of strength and individuality. His manipulation of time and meter, while smooth enough, is most impressive for its twisting ingenuity.

Besides the increased playing opportunities, other heartening events were Peter Ind's re-release of the *Release Record, Send Tape* album, Wave LP 6, originally issued in 1969, and the impending release of a new album from tapes made by Ind in 1960. Ind wrote to Marsh on June 6, 1975, enclosing contracts for both the reissue and the new album (Wave LP 10, *Warne Marsh: Jazz from the East Village*). In the letter Ind also notes that he has been in contact with Gerry Teekens, of Rare Jazz Records in Holland, who has heard that Marsh may be coming to Europe with Supersax and "who is very keen on recording you." Although Teekens did not record Marsh on his upcoming European tour, he was helpful in other ways, and in the 1980s, after Teekens had started his Criss Cross label, he would issue some of Marsh's most important records of that period.

Before departing for Europe Marsh played two quite different concerts. On October 4, 1975, he appeared at Carnegie Recital Hall in New York with Tristano protégés Connie Crothers, piano; Roger Mancuso, drums; and Joe Solomon, bass. The event was probably arranged by Lennie Tristano in order to promote Crothers, and Marsh's feeling for Tristano was such that he probably couldn't have brought himself to refuse the gig even if he had wanted to. A private tape reveals it as a very strange affair. Crothers's virtually atonal harmonic and heavy-handed style had nothing in common with Marsh's strictly tonal conception and sense of swing, despite her professed admiration for him. On one tune, "317 E. 32nd Street," Marsh seems to be trying to fit in with Crothers's crashing, dissonant chords, but for the most part he seems simply to shut her out of his mind. When she occasionally abandons her pretentious dissonances for a single-note phrase or two, she sounds like the Tristano of twenty years earlier.

Despite the fact that she and Marsh seem worlds apart, Marsh described the concert a few months later in glowing terms: "My most vivid recent musical experience is having heard and performed with Connie Crothers in concert in New York City last October. She is 34 and has studied with Lennie twelve years and she is a fascinating musician. She's one of the three or four musicians I've played with who can evoke a better performance out of me than I could give were I playing alone."[2] After listening to the tape, most listeners will be hard-pressed to account for Marsh's praise except as an extreme example of Tristano's influence on him.

The following month, after an engagement back in Los Angeles at Donte's, Marsh, Gary Foster, Atwood, and drummer Jake Hanna flew to Northern California to play a concert on November 16 at the College of the Siskiyous near Mt. Shasta and the Oregon border. Arranging for the date and joining them on piano was their former colleague Ron Hoopes, who had relocated in the Mt. Shasta area to teach at the college. The concert, documented on private tape, was especially notable for one of Marsh's best ballad performances of the period, on "Lover Man." It may be that Hoopes, a gentle and deeply religious man, was in part responsible for the unusually tender mood of "Lover Man." More typical of mid-1970s Marsh were his fluent, many-noted, aggressively inventive solos on "Featherbed" and "Two Not One." The sound on the tape is so echoey that it's hard to get a good read on his tone, but it appears to be somewhat mellower, less strident than it often was in 1975.

Private tapes of many of the performances at The Times and Donte's that year, both with Supersax and his own group, show that the Warne Marsh of the 1970s was a considerably different player than the Warne Marsh of the 1950s. He had a heavier, harder sound, and in general the gentleness, the lyricism, and the thrilling buoyancy of the best of the earlier work was missing. He could be astonishing when pouring out a torrent of notes on up-tempo tunes like "Cherokee" or "Salt Peanuts," on which he regularly soloed in live performances with Supersax, or "Subconscious-Lee" or "Little Willie Leaps," which he played frequently in clubs with his own groups. But he seldom sounded good on ballads. Undoubtedly crucial elements of his sound are missing on the tapes, even those with fair fidelity. But the harder, more aggressive approach, his peculiar way of attacking and bending notes, and his frequent refusal to use vibrato could result in an unpleasantly demanding effect, and his phrasing could sometimes seem forced and graceless.

An example of the difference in his playing is a May 1975 performance of "I Remember You" at The Times, captured on tape. It is unfair to compare it with the inspired version of the tune on Peter Ind's Wave LP-6, which English critic Victor Schonfeld called "one of the great jazz solos." Yet while that degree of inspiration cannot be expected every time out, it is legitimate to note certain general characteristics of the two solos. In contrast to the earlier, the later one seems marked by a dogged effort to avoid cliches at any cost rather than by the joyous élan of spontaneous discovery, and on two or three occasions Marsh plays himself into a corner from which he extricates himself only with a certain awkwardness. There is a kind of grim determination about it, and it signals qualities in Marsh's work of the later 1970s and 1980s that cause an admirer and colleague like Peter Ind to call 1955–60, not the later years, Marsh's peak period. That said, it is also true that the best of the later work is absorbing in its own right.

Within days of the concert in Northern California, on November 19, Marsh arrived in Copenhagen for the start of an extensive Scandinavian tour at the behest of the Danish Jazz Exchange. It was Marsh's first trip to Europe, and like other American jazz musicians, from Sidney Bechet and Coleman Hawkins to Kenny Clarke and Dexter Gordon, he was to find there a measure of artistic respect and monetary reward far surpassing anything he had experienced in America. His pleased response to Europe is reflected in a letter to Geraldyne written December 4:

> Playing with Lee [Konitz, who had just joined the tour] is shapping [sic] up fine. He's lapping up working with me again, and I've got him covered. There's a big demand for the two of us together, and a bigger demand for the old Tristano-Konitz-Marsh band. Big money is being mentioned if we could put that band back together. Although this is still an exploritory [sic] trip for me and Lee, I can already feel we're going to be big business in europe [sic]. Every job has been a sell-out, & the audiences really dig the music.

The tour at first involved fourteen performances and a radio broadcast at various venues in Denmark, Sweden, and Norway, culminating with four days at the Club Montmartre in Copenhagen. All the performances were originally to be with local musicians, but for the final engagement at the Montmartre the promoters were able to add Konitz, who was then spending much of his time in Europe.

The performances in Copenhagen launched a spate of records. Two of these, Volumes 1 and 3 of the Jazz Exchange series, were recorded at the Club Montmartre December 3–5 with a Danish rhythm section of Niels-Henning Orsted Pederson, bass; Ole Kock Hansen, piano; and Svend Erik Norregard and, for one tune, Alex Riel, drums. Volume 2 of the series was recorded December 27, when Marsh and Konitz played a return engagement at the Montmartre with a rhythm section of Peter Ind, bass; another Tristano alumnus, Alan Levitt, drums; and Ind's former student Dave Cliff, guitar.

Dave Parlato at Ne Plus Ultra *recording session, Herrick Chapel, Occidental College, Los Angeles, Sept. 14 or Oct. 25, 1969. Photo courtesy of John William Hardy.*

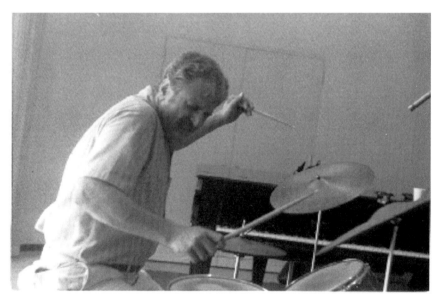

John "Terry" Tirabasso at Ne Plus Ultra *recording session, Herrick Chapel, Occidental College, Los Angeles, Sept. 14 or Oct. 25, 1969. Photo courtesy of John William Hardy.*

Supersax at John Anson Ford Theatre, Los Angeles, c. early or mid-1970s. L to r: Lou Levy, Buddy Clark (back row), Conte Candoli, Jake Hanna (back row), Jay Migliori, Warne Marsh, Med Flory (standing), Joe Lopes, Jack Nimitz. Photo by Ray Avery.

*Geraldyne and Warne Marsh on their wedding night in front of the Half Note,
where they went to hear Zoot Sims. New York City, Apr. 11, 1964.
Photo courtesy of Geraldyne Marsh.*

*From left, Ted Brown, Warne Marsh, Ronnie Ball, and Jeff Morton at Bobby Troup's
"Stars of Jazz" television show, January 1957. Bassist Ben Tucker is out of the picture.
Ray Avery, who took the photo, gives the year as 1958, but his must be incorrect,
as the group had completely broken up by the fall of 1957.*

Warne Marsh in his garage studio in Pasadena, CA, Dec. 15, 1976.
Photo by Mark A. Weber.

Warne Marsh at his favorite pasttime, c. early 1970s, in his home in Pasadena, CA.
Photo courtesy of Geraldyne Marsh.

Art Pepper, left, and Warne Marsh at Donte's, Jan. 26, 1977.
Photo by Mark A. Weber.

From left, Lee Konitz, as; Nick Stabulas, d; Warne Marsh, ts; Sonny Dallas, b (behind Marsh); Lennie Tristano, p. Sept. 7, 1959. Photo by Duncan Schiedt. Schiedt noted the occasion as the Stars of Birdland Tour, but Sonny Dallas thinks it was the Newport Jazz Festival USA Tour.

L to r: Jon Paal Inderberg, Terje Venaas, Warne Marsh, Torgrim Sollid at Storyville Jazz Club, Molde, Norway, Feb. 18, 1981. Not shown: Erling Aksdal, piano, Espen Rud, drums. Photo by Torbjørn Farstad, courtesy of Torgrim Sollid.

L to r: John Lowe, Bill Perkins, Warne Marsh, Gary Foster, Lou Ciotti at Thesaurus *recording session, TTG Studios, Los Angeles, CA, Aug. 26 or 27, 1968. Photo courtesy of John William Hardy.*

L to r: Warne Marsh, Clare Fischer, Gary Foster at Fischer's home in Los Angeles during recording of Report of the 1st Annual Symposium on Relaxed Improvisation, *May 9, 1972. Photo courtesy of John William Hardy.*

Lee Konitz's first recording session as leader for New Jazz/Prestige, New York City, June 28, 1949. L to r: Sal Mosca, piano; Lee Konitz, alto sax; Warne Marsh, tenor sax; Arnold Fishkin, bass; Denzil Best, drums. Photo by Don Schlitten.

Tom Talbert band, Trianon Ballroom, Southgate, CA, April 1948. Saxes, l to r: Warne Marsh, Benny Godfrey, Elmer Koeling, Steve White, Don Davidson; back row, l to r: Bob Stone, bass; Roy Harte drums; Harry Brainerd, trombone; Bob White, trumpet; Gene Norton, trombone; Lou Ohberg, trumpet (face obscured). Out of picture: John McComb, trumpet. Photo by Tom Talbert.

L to r: Buddy Jones, b; Lennie Tristano, p; unknown, d; Lee Kontiz, as; Warne Marsh, ts; Willie Dennis, tb. Date, place, occasion unknown. Photo courtesy of Geraldyne Marsh.

Lee Konitz, left, and Warne Marsh in New York's Central Park, June 1955. This photo, by William Claxton, was used as the cover for the Atlantic LP Lee Konitz with Warne Marsh, *recorded June 14, 1955.*

Marsh at the Modern Jazz Gallery *session, Los Angeles, CA. Oct. 24, 1956. Photo by William Claxton.*

*Ted Brown, left, and Warne Marsh
at the* Modern Jazz Gallery
*session for Kapp Records, Los
Angeles, CA, Oct. 24, 1956.
Photo by William Claxton.*

Ronnie Ball, left, and Ben Tucker at Modern
Jazz Gallery *session, Los Angeles, CA,
Oct. 24, 1956. Photo by William Claxton.*

Ronnie Ball at the Modern Jazz Gallery
*session, Los Angeles, CA, Oct. 24, 1956.
Photo by William Claxton.*

Ben Tucker at the Modern Jazz
Gallery *session, Los Angeles, CA,
Oct. 24, 1956.
Photo by William Claxton.*

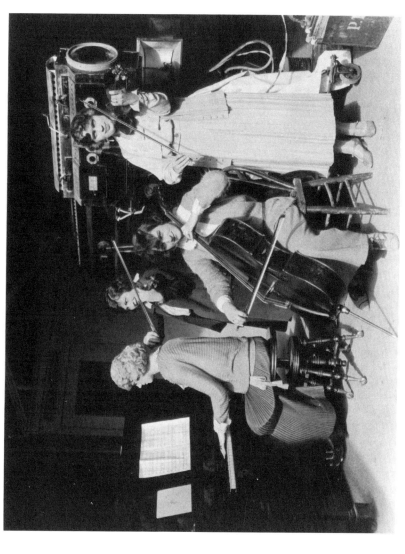

Elizabeth Marsh, Warne's mother, second from left, as "sideline" musician on studio set during silent film era. c. 1920–27. Others unidentified. Photo courtesy of Owen Marsh.

Elizabeth and Warne Marsh, c. 1928–30.
Photo courtesy of Owen Marsh.

Warne, Oliver, and Gloria Marsh,
c. 1929–30. Photo courtesy
of Owen Marsh.

Warne Marsh, age 17–18, soloing
with The Teen-Agers on the Hoagy
Carmichael Show, c. 1945–46.
Photo courtesy of James D. Higson.

Gloria and Warne Marsh,
ages 3 and 5,
c. 1931–32. Photo courtesy
of Owen Marsh.

Warne Marsh, age 17, Dec. 25, 1944. Photo by Herberts Studio, North Hollywood, CA, courtesy of Owen Marsh.

*Hollywood Canteen Kids at the Hollywood Canteen, c. 1942. Saxes, l to r: Don
Walter, baritone; Warne Marsh, tenor; Bill Cushman, alto; Betty Churchill,
alto; Morton Friedman, tenor; drums, Karl Kiffe; bass, unknown; trombones,
l to r: Billy Byers, Chris Martin, unknown; trumpets, l to r: Don Cowan,
Johnny Chech, Don Davies, Harry Matthews. The barely visible pianist at
lower left may be Neil Cunningham. The jackets were donated by Harry James.
Photo courtesy of Betty Churchill Nearhoff.*

*Second Group Special Services Band, Camp Lee, Virginia, 1946. Standing in front:
Rosalyn Hughes, vocals; Phil Vinceguerro, leader. Front row, l to r, seated:
Dick Mitkowski, piano; unknown, guitar; Warne Marsh, unknown, Fred Waters,
probably Chuck Cerrito, Gaynor Maxwell, saxophones. Middle row, standing, l to r:
Bill Riegel, bass; probably Bruce Hendricks, Jim Lester, Don McCrady, unknown,
trombones. Back row, l to r: Jimmy Joyner, drums; probably Paul Storberg, Herb
Patnoe, unknown, Bill West, trumpets. Photo courtesy of Geraldyne Marsh.*

On the whole, Marsh's playing on these records suffers somewhat by comparison with Konitz's, especially on the earlier ones with the unfamiliar, and rather loud, Danish rhythm section. Again, Marsh's sound is probably poorly represented as a result of being recorded live, in the club. But his note choices sometimes seem coldly intellectual, the notes chosen not because they are expressive or aesthetically pleasing but simply because they could be made to work harmonically. His phrasing sometimes seems ungainly, his sound unrefined. If he is at times moving, in spite of such shortcomings, it is partly because there is also a certain urgency in his manifest determination to go beyond whatever he had done before, to discover the new even if it meant perpetrating the ugly along the way. Konitz, on the other hand, is the epitome of cultured and controlled sound, graceful swing, and freshly inventive lyricism, not only on the Jazz Exchange recordings but on the private tapes and other recordings with Marsh during this European period. Marsh himself commended Konitz's playing in this period as "the best he's sounded to me in twenty years," adding, in response his interviewer's question, "Because he's with me? I get that feeling, this time."[3]

Of the tunes recorded with the Danish rhythm section December 3–5, Marsh's best performance is on "Just Friends" on Volume 3. Here his solo is melodic and unforced. However, his low notes lack authority, he lags slightly behind the beat, and there is even here some stridency in his tone. Konitz's solo, on the other hand, is beautifully lyrical and inventive, without any of Marsh's rough edges of tone and time, and this same contrast between roughness (Marsh) and refinement (Konitz) is observable in varying degrees throughout Volumes 1 and 3. One often finds in Konitz's solos here a loving quality, a kind of secret sweetness. The characteristic feeling of Marsh's work is imperfectly controlled aggression.

During this early December engagement at the Club Montmartre, the audience response was so enthusiastic that Konitz contacted Peter Ind in London with the thought of arranging a tour. Ind called Alan Levitt, then living in Paris, and a former pupil, guitarist Dave Cliff. With invaluable help from Gerry Teekens, Marsh's Dutch admirer, the group was able to line up bookings in Holland, England, Belgium, France, and Italy that would take up much of the next eight months.

The first of these was in early December at the BIM-huis in Amsterdam. As Ind told Alun Morgan, he, Cliff, and Levitt flew to Amsterdam, where they met Marsh and Konitz, "and we played our first gig together that night. No rehearsals, nothing. . . . It was hair-raising but it came off. And when we did our second date [in another town] the following night we found that a lot of Dutch fans who'd heard us in Amsterdam had driven over a hundred kilometers to hear us again."[4]

On December 18 they were in London, where they played a concert at the Covent Garden Community Theatre in the Seven Dials area. Reviewing the concert in *Coda*, Michael James devoted most of it to Marsh: "Not only is he a magnificent saxophonist but, more important, one of the few players since Parker's death to have risen to the challenges posed by that departed master. . . . The bounding aggressiveness and remarkable rhythmic flexibility of his playing, based on tremendous facility of execution, unprecedented control in and beyond his instrument's upper register and extraordinary tonal consistency throughout the range, struck the audience that much the more forcibly for their not so far having been altogether captured on record. Another aspect of his work to seize one's attention was his ability to articulate phrase patterns of very considerable length and dense rhythmic content, often implying double time yet also running his lines over and across that very implied beat further to intensify the solo's substance."[5]

James ended his review with an encomium to Marsh's dedication and integrity: "When one thinks of the multiform pressures to which jazz musicians are exposed, especially in today's climate, it is not in the least surprising that so many eventually dilute their styles, either by jettisoning hard-won individuality so as to conform to a fashionable stereotype . . . or, perhaps more understandably, by grafting commercially useful procedures on to their own medium. That Marsh has compromised in neither of these ways, but instead has worked assiduously over the years to broaden and intensify a truly personal form of expression speaks as eloquently for his integrity as it does for his musicianship."[6]

Three days after the Covent Garden appearance Marsh and the rhythm section, without Konitz, played another concert at Queens Theatre in Sittingbourne, Kent, arranged by British critics Alun Morgan and Mark Gardner. Gardner's review, also in *Coda*, described Marsh as "a dedicated and astonishingly creative artist at the peak of his powers," adding that "none of Warne's records does complete justice to his superb sound."[7] To Morgan, who as early as 1961 had written that Marsh was "one of the greatest of jazz improvisers since Charlie Parker," the concert was "absolutely staggering.[8] I've never been in the presence of so much musical invention in my life, before or since. . . . It was all pure music all the way through, and I wished it would go on forever. . . . At the end he was forced to play an encore. . . . I was standing in the wings to make the closing announcement. He'd finished [the encore, 'Background Music'] with a tremendous flourish, and he sort of fell back into the wings into my arms. I said, 'Is that it?' and he said, 'I can't play another note.' And he couldn't, he'd put so much into his playing that night. There he was playing in a place he'd never been to, in the middle of winter, to a small audience in a decrepit cinema, and he played his heart out, as if he'd been playing at Carnegie Hall. . . . It was superb music from start to finish."⁹

Morgan remembered with amusement explaining that he needed to know beforehand when the intermissions would be, so that he could alert the bar staff. Marsh gently reproved him, saying, "Alun, you're putting alcohol ahead of music." But he did comply, following his announcement of the last tune of the first set with a dryly sardonic addendum: "Alun, I know you're out there somewhere. You can get the bar ready now."

In his review of the Sittingbourne and Covent Garden concerts, Morgan wrote that Marsh's fingering was astonishing "in its accuracy at the kind of tempos he seems to enjoy. . . . the ability to surprise, excite, and even amuse the listener is ever present in a Marsh solo. . . . Warne's phrasing can be the most logical you will hear in jazz, almost as if 32 bars have been worked out beforehand. Then suddenly, when you least expect it, the logic of the phrase patterns is given a new slant, the accents are no longer tied directly to the rhythmic pulse and the improvised line goes snaking across the top like a car skidding on an icy road. But unlike a skidding vehicle the driver . . . is perfectly in control."¹⁰

The day after the Sittingbourne concert, December 22, found the quintet in Whitley Bay, Northumberland, some fifty miles south of the Scottish border, playing at the Corner House Pub. At the end of that week they were again in Copenhagen for a return engagement at the Montmartre Club.

The live recording made there, Volume 2 of the Danish Jazz Exchange series (Storyville SLP-4026), is certainly the best of the three albums. The previous three-week tour of Holland and England with their own more sensitive and sympathetic rhythm section—Levitt's cymbal work is especially noteworthy—had resulted in much tighter ensembles, and Marsh plays with considerably more control, especially in terms of sound. The difference is apparent on "Kary's Trance," where Marsh opens with an unaccompanied introduction and three flowing, relaxed choruses before Konitz joins him in playing the theme. On "Two Not One" some of Konitz's restraint and delicacy seems to have rubbed off on Marsh, as he starts softly and gradually builds one of his best solos of the series. Both here and on "Darn That Dream" the joint improvisation by Marsh and Konitz is lovely. Konitz contributes a masterful solo on "317 E. 32nd Street," complete with a surprising yet perfectly logical quote from "Chicago," which would be hard for anyone to follow, but Marsh's solo, beginning again in a restrained manner and building to double-time passages, is almost equally impressive.

While in Copenhagen, Marsh took the opportunity on December 28 to record in Storyville's studios with bassist Niels-Henning Orsted Pedersen, whose playing he loved, and with Cliff and Levitt. A separate session the next day was with only Pederson and Levitt. This quartet and trio material, containing some of Marsh's finest playing of the 1970s, had still not been released in the United States in early 1997, though Storyville finally issued it in Europe in 1996. Part of its interest is that it includes many tunes not in the usual Tristanoite repertoire and never before recorded by Marsh: "After You've Gone," "Without a Song," "You Don't Know What Love Is," "The More I See You," "Be My Love," and others, even a blues in G♭. Marsh's playing is uniformly excellent, with tone, time, and fingers under perfect control, and Pedersen matches him virtually note for note at no matter what tempo. Since it is a studio recording, the fidelity for once is first rate.

On December 30 the Marsh-Konitz quintet played a concert in Nantes in the south of France, on a program that also included French pianist Martial Solal, who joined the quintet for several numbers before playing a solo stint. French critic Jean Delmas reviewed the concert for *Jazz-Hot*, devoting most of his attention to Marsh: "Rescued from silence by the ambiguous grace of the frustrating Supersax, Warne Marsh had not been heard for a very long time. This man of ungainly elegance, perfectly accompanied by Al Levitt and the former Tristano student, the Englishman Peter Ind, gives us the full measure of the acrobatic intelligence that can be heard on his best records. What is surprising are the rhythmic risks, that is, his unbelievable capacity to push to its furthest limits the escape from the bar lines discovered by Lester [Young], the architecture of time taught by Tristano, the freedom of rhythm that he admired so much in Parker."[11]

By March 15, 1976, after a quick trip to Chicago for the aforementioned Supersax engagement at Ratso's and subsequent record date (discussed in the next chapter), Marsh was again in London for a concert at the Shaw Theatre with Konitz, Ind, and Levitt. Recorded live, it was issued on Ind's Wave label as *Lee Konitz/Warne Marsh: London Concert*, Wave LP-16. "Body and Soul" and "Star Eyes" are notable for beautiful joint improvisation by Konitz and Marsh, and Marsh plays especially good solos on "Background Music," "All the Things You Are," and "Easy Living." But again there are times when his tone and phrasing seem heavy and graceless compared to Konitz, whose solo on "Background Music" is extraordinary and whose ebullient, skipping lead voice in the joint improvisations refuses ever to allow the performance to sag.

British critic John Postgate, in a review of the reissued *London Concert* and *Warne Marsh: Release Record, Send Tape* in 1986, commented, "If Konitz is among the coolest of jazzmen, then Marsh is positively frigid. . . ."[12] This seems unjust to both players in this period. But Postgate added, more appropriately, that Marsh was "relaxed to a degree that enables him to float over bar lines seemingly on the edge of disaster, with convoluted phrases that resolve miraculously. Sometimes he goes over the top and the miracle is more clumsy than impressive, but that is part of the game. Like Pee Wee Russell . . . his music relies on tension shared with the listener." He concluded, "this kind of jazz is an acquired taste; it has tedious spells and it sometimes lacks the drive of more formal sessions . . . but it is deceptively accomplished and can yield exquisite recompositions as, for example, their rendering of 'Body and Soul.'" Adrian Macintosh, who heard the group several times during their English tours, remarked on "the [earlier] critics of their music, and their claims that it was insipid and lacking in guts. My feeling then and now is that this music belongs to the most potent and intense to reach these shores in years."[13]

Some years later Marsh told a student that he had "taken something," a drug, that night. When the student marveled that he could play what he did under the influence of a drug, Marsh said, "Come on, I could get out of bed in the middle of the night and play that stuff."[14] The remark suggests a certain *hubris*—excessive pride—the fatal flaw of Greek tragedy.

The London concert seems to have been part of an extended tour of England conducted by Marsh, Cliff, Ind, and Levitt in February and March 1976. A review by Chris Sheridan in *Down Beat* finds the quartet playing at the Warren Bulkeley Hotel in Stockport, near Manchester, probably before the London concert. Wrote Sheridan, "[E]ncountering the extraordinary talents of Warne Marsh in such a place is like finding Sinatra working in your neighborhood bar. It was also redolent of hearing Charlie Parker in the flesh. . . . Only three other living tenor saxophonists are capable of making music at the inspired level consistently inhabited by Marsh. . . . Warne has always been a subtly complex musician, but his style has developed continually throughout his career. It is now more emphatic and exultant than it was; and his tone, which always had more bite than bark, is now more umbrous, even gritty. He also deploys greater tonal flexibility, moving between the familiar, luminous sonority and an almost Rollinsian irascibility. And his sense of swing now floats less than it swaggers."[15] One of the tunes Marsh played at this gig was "It's Only a Paper Moon," which never appears in his recorded repertoire.

Late in May 1976 Marsh was once more in London at Ronnie Scott's, again with Konitz, Ind, and Levitt. From this engagement emerged another live recording, *Lee Konitz Meets Warne Marsh Again* (or *Warne Marsh Meets Lee Konitz Again*—the album actually has both titles) on Pausa. Both saxophonists acquit themselves well on this LP. Both have fresh, inventive solos on "Two Not One" and "All the Things You Are," and Konitz's masterful solo on "Star Eyes" is only marginally superior to Marsh's excellent effort.

Apparently the time not accounted for between early December 1975 and May 24, 1976, was spent fulfilling bookings in Belgium, France, and Italy that Ind or Gerry Teekens had arranged earlier. For the Italian part of the tour Marsh was joined by his wife, Geraldyne, who accompanied the group to Milan, Bergamo, Torino, and Pescara. She remembered the trip as being in 1975, in which case it could only have been between December 9, when Marsh wrote her from Amsterdam, and December 18, when he played the concert at Covent Garden Community Theatre in London. In an earlier letter from Copenhagen Marsh had said, "I don't know about Italy yet," so the trip was in the works. But it may not have occurred until after the December 30 concert in Nantes, France.

After the engagement at Ronnie Scott's in May, Marsh seems to have returned home to California, but his stay there was brief. He was soon back in New York, where on July 1 and 2 he played two concerts for the Newport/New York Jazz Festival with Konitz, Sal Mosca, bassist Eddie Gomez, and drummer Elliot Zigmund. This same group seems to have performed in June and again on July 7 at Storyville, as there are private tapes bearing those dates. On July 10, however, Marsh and Konitz were back in Europe at the Blue Bird Jazz Club in Kristianstad, Sweden, for a festival, and two days later Marsh and Konitz performed again in Copenhagen. From there, on July 12, Marsh wrote Geraldyne the following account:

> Sweetheart—It's 7:50 a.m. and I'm doing deep breathing exercises and singing long tones because there's nothing else to do at this hour. The sun rose at 4:30 AM! and I've been awake ever since reading and waiting for breakfast, served at 7:15. Lee's asleep in the next room. . . . I read two complete novels from the time I left L.A. until we arrived at Ahus, Sweden, about 4 p.m. Saturday, slept two hours, and played our concert, rather well, including about seven encores, for a full house of about 500 people, who simply started stamping their feet and and clapping until we got back on. We finished them off with a Bach 2-part invention; then I got as drunk as I could, enjoyed some of the local music, and collected one thousand-two hundred-fifty American dollars cash!! Amazing!

In the letter he mentions that their next concert will be July 18 at The Hague, near Amsterdam. Gerry Teekens, he says, has offered him the use of his house in Enschede, Holland, for the intervening six days. With all that free time before the concert, he says, he will need something to do, "like practice or write."

The concert at the Hague may have been the last on the tour. Later that month, on July 28, 1976, Marsh was back home playing on the steps of the Pasadena city hall with Gary Foster, Fred Atwood, and drummer Peter

Donald, the first European experience having ended after more than eight busy months.[16]

NOTES

1. Leonard Feather, liner notes, Elek Bacsik: *Bird and Dizzy, A Musical Tribute,* Flying Dutchman BDL1-1082, stereo.

2. Roland Baggenaes, "Warne Marsh Interview," *Coda* (December 1976): 4. Although the date of publication would seem to indicate that the concert occurred in October 1976, the article was apparently written when Marsh was on tour in Europe in 1975, so that Marsh's "last October" refers to October 1975.

3. Les Tomkins, "The Warne Marsh Story," *Crescendo International* (May 1976): 20.

4. Alun Morgan, liner notes, *Warne Marsh/Lee Konitz Quintet: Live at the Montmartre Club*, Jazz Exchange series, Vol. 2, Storyville SLP-4026, December 27, 1975.

5. Michael James, "Heard and Seen, Warne Marsh," *Coda* (March 1976): 37.

6. Ibid.

7. Mark Gardner, "Warne Marsh," *Coda* (March 1976): 37.

8. Alun Morgan, "Warne Marsh," *Jazz Monthly* (June 1961): 7–9, quoted in Alun Morgan, "Warne Marsh—All Music," *Jazz Journal* (February 1976): 4.

9. Morgan, interview.

10. Morgan, "Warne Marsh—All Music," 4–5.

11. Jean Delmas, "Warne Marsh-Lee Konitz-Martial Solal a Nantes," *Jazz Hot* (Paris) (February 1976): 26–27. My translation.

12. John Postgate, review of *London Concert*, Wave LP-16, and reissue of *Warne Marsh: Release Record, Send Tape,* Wave LP-6, *Jazz Journal* (February 1986): 28.

13. Adrian Macintosh, "Lee Konitz-Warne Marsh-Al Levitt-Peter Ind," *Jazz Forum*, No. 49 (1977): 47.

14. John Klopotowski, interview.

15. Chris Sheridan, "Caught . . . ," *Down Beat*, April 8, 1976, 35.

16. Gary Foster, interview.

♪♪

Warne (Coming) Out

Marsh's attitude toward recordings was in keeping with his general disdain for the commercial aspects of his profession. Recalling the early years with Tristano, he said, "Recorded material played a very little part in our lives in the forties and fifties. . . . what really held importance was our daily lives and performing live. . . . That's the way that this music grew up. It didn't grow up in recording studios. . . . At best [recordings] are simply a record of one day in the life of . . . you know?"[1] In 1976 he told another interviewer, "Record dates I can live without. I did a studio recording recently and it was not an acoustic recording, it was a mechanical recording. And when you divide musicians, when you put them 20 feet apart and try to record them through engineering the musicians are not getting a blend in the first place. And there's no way in the world an engineer is going to fabricate good music from music that was not performed well . . . and yet they seem to think they can do it. The whole philosophy is wrong, it's a product of our hi-fi psychology. They have sophisticated equipment, they have everything but good acoustics, you see, but string quartets, for example have not grouped themselves in tight little circles for 300 years for no reason. . . . The best performances are still going to be live performances when the band happens to be set up well and the club has some [good] acoustics. . . . [R]ecording's incidental to me, it's a way of offering the music to a larger audience but I never like to think of it as an end in itself. You notice that Lennie Tristano records very rarely."[2]

One wonders if there is not in Marsh's attitude, with its final appeal to the authority of Tristano, an element of rationalization for his professional passivity. Certainly live performance is at the heart of any music, but just as certainly it would be well-nigh impossible to preserve and nurture a jazz tradition in an industrial society without recordings. Unlike classical music, jazz cannot be notated accurately, and, contrary to Marsh's assertion, it grew up side-by-side with recording technology. Furthermore, Marsh here completely ignores the fact that his own early training with Tristano focused heavily on learning recorded solos, including all the nuances of tone and inflection, by Lester Young and Charlie Parker.

Fortunately, Marsh's stated opinions did not prevent him from recording when the opportunity presented itself, and in the years 1974–78 he made the impressive total, for him, of fifteen records as leader or co-principal, not counting two Supersax records, where he does not solo, or the one with Elek Baksik, where he solos only twice. Not all were released—two with Pete Christlieb were not released until after his death, and two with Nels-Henning Orsted-Pedersen have only recently been released—and only two were for major labels. But they were well-reviewed and important both for their substance and Marsh's reputation.

The records from the European tour were mostly from live performances, with some loss of fidelity. On the other hand, all but one of the eight records Marsh made in the United States between 1976 and 1978 were done under studio conditions. The first of these was *All Music* (Nessa N-7), made in Chicago, February 20–21, 1976. Independent producer Chuck Nessa took Marsh and the Supersax rhythm section of Lou Levy, Fred Atwood, and Jake Hanna into the studio to record Marsh's first full album done under studio conditions, and for immediate release, since the *Ne Plus Ultra* LP of 1969.

Actually, according to Nessa, the Supersax gig at Ratso's was itself the indirect result of Nessa's desire to record Marsh. Nessa had only recently reactivated his label with a recording by Chicago saxophonist Von Freeman. Now, with the encouragement of fellow Marsh admirers in Chicago—Lawrence Kart, Terry Martin, and Harriett Choice, then the jazz writer for the *Tribune*—he contacted Marsh at home in California, learned that Supersax would be on the road in February, and with the help of Choice, who had the ear of the owner of Ratso's, succeeded in bringing Supersax to the club.

It was the first time Choice, who had admired Marsh's playing of the 1950s, had heard him live. Her review of Supersax having piqued his interest, they struck up a lasting friendship. He had never heard Frankie Trumbauer, whom Lester Young credited as a major influence, and they stayed up all night at her apartment listening to her collection of Trumbauer and Bix Beiderbecke. He took the opportunity to grill her about Chuck Nessa as a record producer, and she assured him that anyone recorded by Nessa was lucky.

Nessa gave Marsh free reign. Originally Marsh's idea was to record and improvise on Charlie Parker solos, in the manner of Supersax, but by the time of the first session Marsh had determined to use his familiar repertoire of Tristano-type favorites—"317 E. 32nd Street," "Subconscious-Lee," "Background Music," "It's You or No One"—plus an original blues, a ballad, and Lou Levy's "Lunarcy," a reharmonized version of "How High the Moon." Over the two days, February 20–21, multiple takes were recorded of all except Marsh's own "Background Music." Immediately after the lone take, Marsh turned to the control booth and said, "That's the one that's replacing 'Ko-Ko,'" referring to one of the Parker pieces in the original plan. Several takes of Johnny Mandel's ballad, "A Time for Love," were attempted, but none were successful, and at the urging of Nessa and others in attendance, Marsh substituted another Tristano favorite, "Easy Living." All of the issued material was from the second day of recording, except for Levy's introduction to "Lunarcy." The second-day takes were successful despite a problem with the piano brought about by a failure of the air-circulation system. The recording studios were in an old Chicago skyscraper, the Carbide and Carbon Building, with a self-contained air supply. With the failure of the system, the piano could not be kept in tune. As Nessa was on the phone trying to locate another studio, Marsh and Levy poked their heads in and said, "Screw it, let's play."

All of the outtakes from both days, said Nessa, have been preserved, and he hopes one day to issue the material in a two-CD set. This would be especially valuable for the blues, "On Purpose," which evolved gradually over the two days, and another number that everyone felt was a superior take but which was incomplete because Atwood, the bassist, made a mistake and stopped playing.

Though certain notes on the piano had a tinny, out-of-tune sound, reviewers of *All Music* either ignored it or failed to notice. Jon Balleras gave it a five-star review in *Down Beat*. "Time was," he wrote, "when this tenorist was looked upon by some as a rather bloodless player, a kind of dedicated musical scientist. But Marsh's high energy section work with Supersax and his recent small group releases have underscored the inadequacy of the old critical mythology. . . .The Warne Marsh contained in *All Music* is simply one of the most warmed-up and wound-up players imaginable. Marsh is formidable. This is true not only of his stylistic depth, spanning Young and Hawkins to Parker and beyond, but also of his almost absolute command of tension and release and melodic development. Marsh's phrases seem set in perpetual motion. Once conceived, they develop in an intuitive, freely associative way, carried along by the momentum of their own inner logic. Additionally, Warne has developed a heightened control of saxophone tone; there are all sorts of interesting colorations to listen to here. . . . These constantly shifting colors are augmented by an occasional squeak, presumably intentional, for emphasis."[3]

It is doubtful that Marsh ever intentionally squeaked, and the influence of Hawkins and Parker, while certainly present, is so only in a very general sense. As for tonal colorations, they are definitely there, and Balleras's description of Marsh's melodic procedure is cogent.

To my ears Marsh is most satisfying on "On Purpose" and "Easy Living." His tone overall is controlled and full of nuance, almost mellow. His double-timing on "Lunarcy" is also impressive, as are his two solos on "Subconscious-Lee." Levy's playing, while bright, swinging, and energetic, seems rhythmically jerky, not really his best.

It was probably this same spring that Marsh played a concert with Sal Mosca at Sarah Lawrence College in Bronxville, New York. The date given on the Interplay record *How Deep, How High,* issued in 1980 and including two tunes from the concert, is April 25, 1977, but Paul Altman, a saxophonist and student of Sal Mosca's who produced the concert while still an undergraduate at Sarah Lawrence, graduated in June 1976. Mosca has agreed that the correct year was probably 1976, and this is also the recollection of Ted Brown, who attended the concert. Marsh had been in England for the London concert on March 15 and would be there again in May, but he seems not to have been averse to bouncing back and forth between Europe and the States that year, and a concert in New York on April 25 does not conflict with any known engagement.

Altman's account of producing the concert provides some insight into relationships not only between Mosca, Marsh, and Tristano but also the gulf between Tristano followers and the rest of the jazz world at that time. When Altman first suggested to Mosca that he do a concert with Marsh, he assumed that Mosca, if agreeable, would contact his old friend and colleague. Mosca, however, requested Altman to arrange things with Marsh. When Altman called Marsh in California, Marsh agreed to play but wanted nothing to do with the details, saying, "Lennie Tristano will be my agent. Just do whatever Lennie says." When it came to selecting a drummer, Mosca suggested Shadow Wilson, unaware that Wilson had died in 1959, some two years after recording with Mosca on a Lee Konitz date (*Lee Konitz Quintet,* Verve MGV8209). Mosca's ignorance of Wilson's death seventeen years earlier suggests the extent of his self-imposed seclusion from the world of regularly performing jazz artists.

Even before Altman attempted to track down Wilson, Mosca's suggestion was superseded by Tristano's recommendation of Billy Higgins as drummer. Altman felt that he could offer Higgins a fee of $125. Since at the time that was a more than adequate amount for a two-hour concert, he felt that Higgins would probably have accepted. Tristano, however, insisted on a different approach. Altman was to first ask Higgins how much he would charge, report back to Tristano, and then offer Higgins the $125 that Altman was really prepared to pay. As it turned out, Higgins, offered what looked like a blank check, asked for a munificent fee of $300. Hearing this, Tristano laughed and directed Altman to offer him $125. Higgins declined. Altman felt he was justifiably insulted by Tristano's procedure.

Other drummers were considered, including Connie Kay of the Modern Jazz Quartet, and in the end Altman was able to procure drummer Roy Haynes, who had recorded with Lee Konitz in 1959 (*You and Lee,* Verve MGV8362). The bassist was Sam Jones.

Altman reported that Tristano had originally agreed to sell tickets to his students but later reneged. Despite this setback, the concert sold out. Although Altman felt that throughout these proceedings Tristano did not act entirely in Marsh's best interests, Marsh's readiness to defer to Tristano was characteristic.

The *How Deep, How High* album included only "Background Music" and "She's Funny That Way" from the concert. Though both suffer from echoey sound, as if recorded from the audience, both contain some brilliant playing. Marsh is particularly dynamic on "Background," seemingly stimulated by Mosca's unconventional comping. In his own solos on both tunes Mosca takes great liberties with meter and harmony. There is some clashing of Mosca's chords with Jones's bass line at the beginning of "Background"; and in the last eight bars of Mosca's solo, when his harmonic and rhythmic improvisation reaches its climax, Jones simply quits playing. But however eccentric, Mosca's performance is brilliant, making one lament his decision to concentrate his career on teaching.

The same might be said about the four piano-tenor duo tracks on the album, recorded at Mosca's Mt. Vernon studio in February and August of 1978. All four tracks—"The Hard Way" ("You'd Be So Nice to Come Home To"), "Noteworthy" ("Lover Man"), and two versions of "Somebody Loves Me"—contain remarkably contrapuntal, brilliantly lyrical, totally individual playing by both men. Mosca considered Marsh's performance on "Noteworthy" a "magnificent example of nuance of tone," in which every note is uniquely expressive. Their instincts for responding to each other make these tracks particularly memorable.

How Deep, How High was rather indifferently reviewed. Barry McRae wrote in *Jazz Journal,* "Mosca is especially percussive and jaunty [on the duo tracks], and throughout he shows an excellent sense of rhythmic displacement. Marsh, for his part parades his long buoyant lines, and both find plenty to say about the tunes in hand. . . . [On the concert tracks] Jones and Haynes . . . [give] greater urgency to their playing. Marsh's best solo is arguably the driving effort on *Background Music. . . .* Those who like the more meandering quality of the 'school's' most pure form will prefer the duo titles. . . ."[4] To speak of the duo tracks, with their beautifully structured melodic lines, as "meandering" does them a serious injustice.

Back in Los Angeles, at about this time Marsh began working occasional one-nighters, when in town, with bassist Jim Krutcher at the Redondo Lounge in Redondo Beach, a practice he was to continue until late 1977. Others who worked there with Krutcher included Pete Christlieb and Art Pepper. In October Marsh played at the Sand Dance Club in Long Beach with Fred Atwood on bass, Alan Broadbent on piano, and Nick Ceroli on drums, documented by a private tape dated October 3.

A major recording that same month, October 13–14, was *Tenor Gladness* with the rising tenor saxophonist Lew Tabackin. The others on the date were bassist John Heard, drummer Larry Bunker, and, unofficially on one number, pianist Toshiko Akiyoshi, who also produced the record and contributed two of the compositions. This was the session at which Marsh rather ill-humoredly engaged Tabackin in a dispute about the relative merits of Lester Young and Coleman Hawkins.

Marsh's evident distaste for Tabackin's style, with its full tone and pronounced vibrato, stemmed in large part from the precepts of Lennie Tristano, who "argued that his saxophonists should use a flat uninflected tone so that their lines would stand or fall on the quality of their construction and not on emotional colouration."[5] The same point was more invidiously made by Jack Sohmer in his *Down Beat* review of *Tenor Gladness*: "Marsh's tone, in its cultivated objectivity, its remote dispassion, seemed [in 1949] even further removed from the heart of jazz than did Konitz'. It was shorn of both vibrato and body, for those were artifacts of an expressiveness alien to the Tristano philosophy. Since the center of harmonic and rhythmic gravity was held to reside in the intellect, the Tristanoites thought of tone as a mere vessel through which more important stuff was meant to course. Accordingly, emotional expressiveness was discouraged in favor of intellectual scheme plotting, as Marsh outdistanced even Konitz in his flight from telltale inflections. The result was a detached, seemingly disembodied sound, curiously metallic and orderly, and only faintly suggestive of human origin."[6]

On *Tenor Gladness* Marsh's tone is hardly as dispassionate as all that, but Sohmer's remarks accurately suggest the pronounced contrast with Tabackin's "full-blooded, passionate and virile" sound.[7] The contrast, indeed, was a major element in Akiyoshi's desire to record them together: "The reason I had been waiting to hear Warne Marsh and Lew Tabackin perform together was that I felt that both of them are essentially true jazz players and at the same time everything about them is entirely opposite."[8]

Though he later characterized it as a "romantic" notion,[9] Tabackin was similarly intrigued with the idea of recording with his opposite: "We simply wanted to point out the differences between our approaches."[10]

Those differences were so pronounced, wrote Sohmer, that "the best moments on the record occur when either one or the other is not playing; their concerted efforts lack coordination and direction. . . . Tabackin's assertiveness of delivery, his peremptory way with the beat, his prolix journeys through the changes—all are simply too much for the introspective and highly organized Marsh. There is no way that he can match Tabackin in swinging, yet his own approach seems painfully inadequate by comparison."[11] Having delivered this resoundingly negative evaluation of Marsh, Sohmer essays to say something positive, only to collapse again into negativity: "This is not to say that Marsh's playing, because it lacks the compelling urgency of Tabackin's, is any the less interesting for it. On the contrary, he is an intriguing musician, and particularly in the area of phrasing. But his idiosyncratic tone, as well as his intonation, might yet offend by virtue of their unorthodoxy; with due respect to Marsh's reputation and ongoing participation in Supersax, it can only be assumed that the noted perversity is intentional."[12]

A more appreciative view of *Tenor Gladness*, particularly of Marsh's playing, was offered by Chris Sheridan in *Jazz Journal*: "I have seen this album panned for flaws derived from an alleged incompatibility between the tenors, yet found the contrast between Marsh's acoustics and Tabackin's bearlike jousting quite viable. . . . [T]he alternative versions of *Basic* . . . are powerful tours de force, and Marsh, though particularly enigmatic at times, moves continuously in surprising directions without sacrificing his unerring momentum and clarity of purpose. . . . An often exciting, sometimes untidy record well worth investigation."[13] It should be noted that the two tracks titled "Basic #1" and "Basic #2" are not "alternative" versions of the same thing, as Sheridan seems to imply. "Basic #1" is a blues, while "#2" uses "I Got Rhythm" changes.

Many listeners might agree that by most criteria Marsh comes off second best on this record. The virtuoso Tabackin, with his aggressive attack, fleet fingers, full-bodied tone, on-top-of-the-beat time feel, and conservatory-schooled mastery of the changes, sounds in complete, authoritative control. Yet despite his sometimes amazing virtuosity, his note choices are predictable and his manner somewhat annoying. In this context he reminds one of the muscle-bound beach bully strutting his stuff before the alleged ninety-seven-pound weakling. Yet Marsh, solid but not brilliant in tone, lagging slightly behind the beat, and once or twice half-fluffing a note, comes off as much the more original player. Hardly a ninety-seven-pound weakling, he is rather a wiry daredevil acrobat, more intent on surprising himself than anything else, at times answering Tabackin's py-rotechnics with a stunningly inventive and individual response. A good example is in his second solo on "March of the Tadpoles," where he fol-lows Tabackin's dazzling double-timing with a much trickier passage, working the turns of the theme into an echo of Chopin's "Minute Waltz." And on "Easy Living," where Tabackin does not play and Marsh is ac-companied by an unidentified pianist (who is undoubtledly Akiyoshi), he delivers one of his most lyrical ballad solos.

An oddity of the record is that the theme of Akiyoshi's "Hangin' Loose," based on the Tristano favorite "Mean to Me," is played by Tabackin alone, both at beginning and end, though Marsh has a fine three-chorus solo. Since Marsh plays in unison with Tabackin on the other Akiyoshi origi-nal, "March of the Tadpoles," one wonders why he didn't on this one.

In February 1977 Marsh and Lee Konitz resumed their musical collabo-ration, playing a week at the Jazz Showcase in Chicago. John Litweiler's full-page review in the *Chicago Reader* was warmly appreciative:

> It's fair to say that Art Pepper is Konitz's only equal among white alto saxists; and among tenormen, the visceral swing, melodic ingenuity, and organizing instincts of Marsh combine to generally surpass such rivals as Stan Getz and Zoot Sims. Needless to say, Marsh and Konitz are among the 70s' very finest creators on their instruments. Konitz sounded better to me at the Showcase than he has in any of his Chicago dates of recent years. . . . Among players whose careers began in the 40s, only Marsh and Sonny Rollins have shared such disrespect for formulas, and perhaps be-cause of their shared background and intermittent reunions, Konitz never seemed as free as he was this week with Marsh. . . . Among the contrasts between the two are Marsh's more relaxed swing, his much more varied sax sound and dynamics (Konitz is unusually even), and the added complexity in Marsh's lines. Lawrence Kart, I believe, mentioned this tenor saxist's ca-pacity for playing amazingly long lines without pausing to breathe, then allowing only a single beat's pause for air before the next phrase. Such lines appeared in almost every solo Marsh played at the Showcase, and, in fact, a 'Sound-Lee' solo consisted almost entirely of these lengthened lines, as if Marsh was discovering too much melody to be bothered by such details as inhalation. While his lines also eschewed superfluity, his livelier rhythmic instincts determined that melodies would be etched in more abrupt curves and angles. His art is less consonant than Konitz's, and though Lester Young's tenor sax styles were important in the early schooling of both Konitz and Marsh, the latter's frequent recalling of Younglike lines was notewor-thy this time. . . . The intensity of the duets, solos, and chases, the beauty of the cascades of melody, the mercurial vitality of the musical shapes as they evolved, are probably beyond the power of words. Marsh's style in particu-lar is immediately engaging and accessible. . . .[14]

Some four months later, February 28 through March 2, 1977, Marsh and Konitz made another high profile album as guests of the Bill Evans Trio, which then included Eddie Gomez, bass, and Eliot Zigmund, drums. Produced by Evans's manager Helen Keane for Fantasy, the record received only three and a half stars from *Down Beat* reviewer Jon Balleras. He found the record uneven, shifting "disquietingly between loose, sometimes even raucous sax solos and the precise, inbred sound of Evans' trio."[15] The word "raucous" probably refers to Marsh, whose playing is marked by a certain rough abandon, especially on some climactic high notes on "Eiderdown" and "Speak Low." Balleras was justifiably appreciative of the joint improvisation on "Night and Day": "Here Konitz and Marsh open with [a] stunningly interwoven, unaccompanied *soli* wrought with happy, chancy meetings as they volley the head back and forth. . . ."[16] On the other hand, he commits a gaffe in misidentifying Konitz's ballad feature: "The first chorus of *Goodbye*, a piano-alto duet, is graced not only by Konitz' subtle melodic paraphrases but also by Evans' floating passing chords. . . . A superb accompaniment for a superb soloist. . . ." He obviously meant to name Konitz's actual ballad, "When I Fall in Love." Marsh is featured on "Ev'ry Time We Say Goodbye," and although his intonation is sharp, it is one of his most memorable ballad solos.

Marsh, unfortunately, did sometimes have intonation problems, not because of a faulty ear but because of inattention to the condition of his saxophone. He was in the habit of leaving his mouthpiece, reed still attached, on the neck. Instead of removing the reed to wet it before playing, he would dip the mouthpiece in water. Once at Donte's, hearing that Marsh was sharp, Gary Foster asked him to "pull out," that is, move the mouthpiece further toward the end of the neck. Marsh responded that he couldn't pull out, because the mouthpiece had melded with the cork. Years earlier, on his way to Las Vegas for a week's work with Louis Bellson's big band, Marsh had stopped to borrow Foster's tenor because he had torn the cork off the neck of his own trying to remove the mouthpiece.[17]

The day after the last *Crosscurrents* session, Marsh sat in with Evans's trio at the Great American Music Hall in San Francisco, and on this same visit to the Bay Area he played two nights with Konitz at the Keystone Korner. On one of these nights they were accompanied by George Cables on piano, James Leary on bass, and Eddie Marshall on drums, and on the other by Marshall, bassist Harley White, and pianist Art Lande. Wrote one reviewer, Marsh and Konitz "reminded anyone who may have forgotten that they are two of the greatest melodic improvisors in jazz, past or present. . . . Marsh's and Konitz's thematic inventions unfurl with fine drive and momentum now, and their intelligence is colored with an exquisite sensuality—to especially stunning effect in ballads like 'What's

New' and 'Lover Man.' In short, the old 'cool' now simmers with a radiant, glowing fire."[18] Phil Ellwood, writing in the *Examiner,* focused on Konitz, saying of Marsh, "[He] has had far less exposure in recent years and his tone showed it, but his knowhow and easy knowledgeable swing contributed mightily to all the ensemble efforts." In a sign-of-the-times anecdote, Ellwood noted that the then up-and-coming young guitarist Pat Martino, booked opposite Marsh and Konitz at Keynote Korner, had *not* said, as Ellwood had previously reported, that "he did not want to play with 'old time beboppers' . . . on the same show." What he said, or meant to say, was that he and his manager-wife "thought it inappropriate that an electric artist like Pat who is headed for big success should have an older-fashioned acoustic jazz group booked with them."[19]

Both appearances, at Great American Music Hall and Keystone Korner, are documented by private tapes that include performances of tunes from their album with Evans: "Speak Low," "Every Time We Say Goodbye," and "Night and Day."

A week later, March 13, 1977, found Marsh and Konitz reunited again for a concert in Edmonton, Alberta, Canada, with a Canadian rhythm section of Wray Downes, piano, Shelly Gjersten, drums, and Dave Young, bass. Reviewing the performance in *Coda,* Kellogg Wilson wrote, "As an individual soloist, Konitz disappointed me since I thought his playing was below the generally high quality he has established in his recordings. . . . My impression of Marsh, however, was that he played much better than I recalled from his recordings. In fact, he played so well that I now consider him to be a major figure. He is clearly influenced by Lester Young but is much more original than, say, the early Stan Getz in that regard. . . . I hope that Marsh can be recorded suitably. Even 85% of the quality of his in-person playing would still result in a very important recording date."[20]

Around this time, spring of 1977, Marsh made one of his finest recordings of the 1970s, *Warne Out,* with bassist Jim Hughart and drummer Nick Ceroli. Hughart had first met and worked with Marsh in Minneapolis in 1958–59 and played with him again in the late 1960s in Los Angeles. The three had begun jamming together earlier in the spring at Hughart's "Model A" studio in Granada Hills, a San Fernando Valley suburb. The material on the album was recorded by Hughart May 14–15 and June 5, 1977, and issued by Toshiya Taenaka on his Interplay Records.

Pete Welding began his five-star rave review in *Down Beat* by puzzling over the title: "Marsh neither is 'worn out' nor is his music particularly 'outside.'"[21] But Marsh's wife, Geraldyne, who coined the title, had a third meaning in mind, that Marsh was "coming out."[22] The title aside, Welding found the record "an utterly marvelous set of performances . . . by one of the handful of masterly, truly original musicians curently active in jazz.

Marsh is of a rare breed, a player who never coasts . . . but who constantly tests and challenges himself. . . . Certainly he's playing with greater power, vigor and confidence than at any time in his career. . . ." The *All Music* album for Nessa was "a stunning album," but "*Warne Out* takes that several notches higher, thanks primarily to the greater freedom and daring of his playing. . . ." The performance of "Lennie's Pennies," he wrote, like those of "Duet" ("All the Things You Are") and "Ballad" ("I Should Care"), was "nothing short of incredible. . . . You are not likely to hear better, more invigorating, exploratory, committed, inspired, interesting or fully realized saxophone playing anywhere than in this perfect album. *Warne Out* contains some of the most exciting, commanding, utterly astounding music I've ever heard. . . . [I]t is, I am certain, destined to become a classic. . . . Marsh is a titan, and this set of performances comes closer to indicating the full extent of his accomplishment than any recording he's made so far."[23]

Welding was John William Hardy's recording engineer for two of Marsh's earlier albums on Revelation, *Ne Plus Ultra* and *Report of the 1st Annual Symposium on Relaxed Improvisation*, and may be suspected of bias, but he is on solid ground in viewing *Warne Out* as Marsh's finest album of the 1970s. Here there is none of the stridency that marred even some of his more impressive efforts of the period. He seems completely comfortable with the unobtrusive yet fully alive backing provided by Hughart and Ceroli, and his serpentine lines uncoil effortlessly and with perfect logic, not only on the three tracks mentioned by Welding but on all the others: "Loco 47" ("This Can't Be Love"), "Liner Notes" ("You Stepped Out of a Dream"), "Warne Out" ("It's You or No One"), and "Warne Piece" (a 12-bar blues).[24]

Welding's enthusiasm for *Warne Out* was echoed by Steve Voce in England: "Marsh remains one of the most inventive communicators of the last four decades. His beautiful sound, faultless technique and logical yet lightning stream of ideas leave one breathless with admiration."[25] Voce did voice a cavil concerning one of the overdubbed tracks: "On 'Duet' his lines are so different that they conflict, and it is not possible to follow both at once, making one wonder whether it was a good idea." But he considered *Warne Out* "a great album."

As for the listener's following the two overdubbed lines on "Duet" and "Warne Piece," it is not really that difficult. The counterpoint is all the more incredible when one knows that in making the overdub, Marsh listened only to the rhythm track, not to his own first solo—this according to the testimony of Hughart, who was both bassist and recording engineer.[26] That the two lines fit together as well as they do is a matter not of accident but of the consistency of Marsh's improvisational approach, and of his melodic memory of what he had played the first time.

The liner notes of the original LP credit Marsh as composer of all except one piece, Tristano's "Lennie's Pennies." This is both correct and incorrect. The other pieces were all improvisations on standards whose themes were never stated. As lead voice, Marsh spontaneously created the initial melodic lines that took the place of the written melodies. But titles were needed, and since each piece was essentially a group effort, Marsh suggested that whoever came up with a title should have composer credit. Hence, on the actual LP, though not the liner notes, Ceroli was cited as composer of the two tunes that he titled, "Loco 47" and "Warne Piece."

 Marsh, Hughart, and Ceroli continued to play together, and by September 1978 they had been joined by saxophonist Pete Christlieb, who had become a great admirer of Marsh. Their sessions resulted in several records. The first, and with respect to Marsh's reputation the most important, was *Apogee,* produced for Warner Brothers, for immediate release, by Walter Becker and Donald Fagen of the well-known Steely Dan group.

Marsh's records usually arrived in the stores unheralded, in record jackets as unprepossessing as Marsh's thrown-together wardrobe—Med Flory liked to make fun of the way he dressed, calling him "the beekeeper"— but in this instance there was actually some advance publicity. In the spring of 1978 *Down Beat* reported that "veteran saxmaster Warne Marsh has signed a reportedly lucrative deal with ABC, at the suggestion of Marsh-freaks Donald Fagen and Walter Becker (aka Steely Dan). Be prepared for some astonishing results."[27] As it turned out, the deal was indeed lucrative, probably by far the most financially rewarding of Marsh's career. Christlieb reported that Becker and Fagen were given a $50,000 budget to work with, and that he and Marsh split a $15,000 advance.

In a risky procedure for a saxophonist, Marsh played an unfamiliar mouthpiece for the session. Said Christlieb, Marsh wanted to "brighten up a bit" so as not to be overpowered by Christlieb's robust sound. Rummaging through his collection of mouthpieces, he came up with different, stronger-sounding Otto Link than the one he was playing and proceeded to record with it.

Apogee received mixed reviews. *Down Beat* loved it, giving it five stars: "Watch out when you slip this record out of its sleeve. It's hot enough to burn your fingers. . . . [B]oth [tenor players] are highly experienced but not terribly well known. Warne Marsh has been active since he played with Lennie Tristano in the '50s. Pete Christlieb is a busy session man who also plays in the *Tonight Show* band. . . . Christlieb has a driving, full-bore style and a tone as big as Texas. Marsh has a light sound that curls around the chords like smoke. And where there's smoke. . . . There's fire on every cut. Christlieb and Marsh seem to inspire each other, helped along by a good choice of material and Joe Roccisano's charts."[28] Leonard Feather also put in a good word for the record in a "Blindfold Test" interview with

Christlieb: "The release a few months ago of an album entitled *Apogee* . . . by Pete Christlieb and Warne Marsh, produced by Steely Dan, had the salutary effect of refocusing attention on two musicians whose talents . . . had too long been overlooked. . . ."[29]

In *Rolling Stone* Bob Blumenthal was more taken with the fact of Becker's and Fagen's involvement than with the music itself: "Unfortunately, the results aren't particularly stimulating. Pete Christlieb, best known to Dan fans as the tenor soloist in 'Deacon Blues,' is typical of the young breed of Hollywood studio saxists who can get hot with little ingenuity or originality. Warne Marsh, who's kept a low profile for thirty years and is finally beginning to gain recognition as one of jazz' most underrated improvisers, is another story. But Marsh doesn't sound inspired here and can be heard to better advantage on last year's *All Music*."[30]

Both Marsh and Christlieb were disappointed with the way the record finally came out. What they had in mind at first was the same two-tenor, bass, and drums format they had been using in their private sessions with Hughart and Ceroli. However, Becker and Fagen, who were allowed to produce the album by Warner Brothers as a reward for their own best-selling albums, insisted on adding piano (Lou Levy) and using arrangements (by Joe Roccisano). Marsh, like Christlieb and Hughart, always maintained that Becker and Fagen not only chose the wrong takes but destroyed the true sound of the band through their engineering techniques. He told jazz critic Kirk Silsbee, "They spoiled the master in such a way that you really lose the presence of the band. We have a master that's just spectacular. So we feel they just castrated the music. They didn't quite know what to do with us. Originally they wanted me alone but then I wanted Pete, because Pete can really play. There was no trouble with the band but the producers had something else in mind."[31]

In five days the group recorded a total of thirty-three takes of ten different tunes. Becker and Fagen rejected half a dozen tunes entirely, and even on tunes that they accepted, said Christlieb, they chose takes that the group didn't like. "Everything we had worked for was in jeopardy. They didn't want what we wanted." The band were particularly dismayed that Becker and Fagen rejected a "Body and Soul" that they all loved. "They looked at it with such disdain," said Christlieb, "that it wore a hole in our soul. That one tune alone, in place of their tune ['Rapunzel'], would have made a different album today." Christlieb felt so strongly about the way things were turning out that he appealed to Warner Brothers executives in an attempt to rein in Becker and Fagen. He was told that his problem was with the producers, not with them. Becker and Fagen made it clear that the album would be done their way or they would, in Christlieb's words, "shitcan the whole thing." After Marsh had already returned to New York, Christlieb and the rhythm section were called back to the studio, recording five different tunes, of which only one, a take of Christlieb's ballad feature, "I'm Old Fashioned," was issued on the LP. If Marsh was called for this final session—Christlieb said he wasn't—he declined.

It was not until 1991, when Criss Cross released the first volume of Christlieb's *Conversations with Warne,* consisting of material recorded by Jim Hughart before the *Apogee* sessions in 1978, that the original piano-less quartet was put before the public. Reviewing that record for *Cadence,* Carl Baugher wrote, "Marsh has never sounded more inspired. . . . [He] is spurred into some very active explorations by Christlieb's prodding. . . . Anyone who has ever been curious as to why a lion of the avant-garde like Anthony Braxton holds Warne Marsh in such high regard should find the answer on [this CD]."[32]

The tunes are all retitled standards without theme statements. Of the less obvious titles, "Lunch" is based on "Like Someone in Love," "Fishtale" on "On Green Dolphin Street," "Meat Balls" on "I Can't Give You Anything but Love," "Get Out" on "Get Happy," "India No Place" on "Indiana," and "You Drive" on "You're Driving Me Crazy."

"Weeping Willow," mistakenly identified by Baugher as "God Bless the Child"—it does include a quote from that tune—is "Willow Weep for Me." It is unique in Marsh's recorded output in that it contains what seems to be a metrical mistake but in all probability is a musically unfortunate and probably unauthorized job of editing by Criss Cross. After Marsh and Christlieb together play the first chorus of this thirty-two-bar, AABA tune, Christlieb solos on the first eight bars of the second chorus. Marsh then begins soloing on the second eight, but after four bars he is suddenly playing the last four bars of the bridge. He then continues with the last eight bars of that chorus and the first sixteen bars of the next chorus. Christlieb comes in at the bridge for his second eight-bar solo, after which he and Marsh play the last eight bars together. The upshot is that during Marsh's solo, eight bars are omitted, the last four of the second A part and the first four of the B part. It is conceivable, though just barely, that either Marsh or Hughart got lost, but to get lost in this particular way would be almost impossible, even for much less experienced musicians. Possibly the tape was damaged, or possibly the problem originated with the desire of an insensitive editor either to shorten the performance or to cut out mistakes or below-par material—though it is hard to imagine that Marsh could have played eight bars that would deserve to be edited out.

In my own review, I wrote: "The pairing [of Marsh] with the always swinging, more buoyant, more down home, but also more orthodox Christlieb is especially interesting. Where Christlieb skates and lifts, Marsh digs in, burrows. Where Christlieb outlines the beat, always telling you where the time is, Marsh deliberately plays across it, turns it around, comes out in funny places but always knows exactly where to dig in again. His phrases are determined by their own internal logic, and the tension between them and the harmonic meter of the original song is a primary feature of his aesthetic. He improvises sequentially, carrying rhythmic and melodic figures through extended passages, so that each segment of a solo seems to spring organically out of what went immediately before. Another aspect of comparison between Christlieb and Marsh is their approach to tone. Christlieb loves the sound of the tenor and will sometimes luxuriate in it for its own sake. Marsh never will. Sound is always secondary to notes. At the same time, this recording captures, as most others don't, the thickness and body of his later sound. Marsh is at his best on 'Lunch' and 'Fishtale.'"[33]

Both Christlieb and Hughart retain a deep admiration for Marsh. Said Christlieb, "I'll always be in awe of what he could do. He had a complex, completely new view, a new alternative for improvisation. He could take all this rhythmic and harmonic information and not be mechanical. I had the influence on him of making him work a little harder, play with a little more steam, and he made me think, helped me play more intelligently."[34] Hughart commented on a subtle difference between Marsh's earlier and later playing. In the 1950s, he said, the melodic line was more important to Marsh than the changes, but later, although the line was still there, the harmonic changes were more precisely delineated. "Miles [Davis] would kill to play like that," he said. "Very few people play so intelligently. He was one of the best that ever lived, I thought."

NOTES

1. Robert Ronzello, "Warne Marsh—A Conversation with Robert Ronzello," *Saxophone Journal* (Spring 1982): 17, 19.
2. Roland Baggenaes, "Warne Marsh Interview," *Coda* (December 1976): 5.
3. Jon Balleras, "Warne Marsh," *Down Beat*, June 16, 1977, 30.
4. Barry McRae, "Warne Marsh/Sal Mosca," *Jazz Journal* (January 1981): 37.
5. Ian Carr, Digby Fairweather, and Brian Priestley, *Jazz: The Essential Companion* (New York, London: Prentice Hall Press, 1987), 506.
6. Jack Sohmer, "Lew Tabackin and Warne Marsh," *Down Beat,* November 1980, 34.
7. Ibid.
8. Herb Wong, liner notes, *Tenor Gladness*, Inner City IC-6048.
9. Lew Tabackin, interview.
10. Wong, op. cit.

11. Sohmer, 34.

12. Ibid.

13. Chris Sheridan, "Warne Marsh and Lew Tabackin," *Jazz Journal* (March 1981): 27.

14. Litweiler, op. cit.

15. Jon Balleras, "The Bill Evans Trio with Lee Konitz and Warne Marsh," *Down Beat*, April 19, 1979, 20.

16. Ibid.

17. Gary Foster, interview.

18. Thomas Albright, "The Greatest Improvisors in Jazz," *San Francisco Chronicle*, 8 March 1977, 40.

19. Phil Ellwood, "Another Time, Another Jazz," *San Francisco Examiner*, 8 March 1977, 21.

20. Kellogg Wilson, "Konitz and Marsh," *Coda* (May/June 1977): 32–33.

21. Pete Welding, "Warne Marsh," *Down Beat*, December 21, 1978, 30.

22. Geraldyne Marsh, interview.

23. Welding, 30.

24. The title "Loco 47" was incorrectly given on the CD reissue (Discovery DSCD-945) as "Local 47." The pun is an example, said Hughart, of Nick Ceroli's sense of humor.

25. Steve Voce, "Warne Marsh," *Jazz Journal* (January 1980): 36–37.

26. Jim Hughart, interview.

27. "Potpourri," *Down Beat,* May 4, 1978, 9.

28. ___ Clark, "Pete Christlieb/Warne Marsh Quintet," *Down Beat*, January 11, 1979, 24, 26.

29. Leonard Feather, "Blindfold Test: Pete Christlieb," *Down Beat*, April 5, 1979, 34.

30. Bob Blumenthal, review, *Rolling Stone*, March 22, 1979, 64.

31. Kirk Silsbee, personal letter, May 31, 1996.

32. Carl Baugher, review, *Cadence* (November 1991): 23.

33. Safford Chamberlain, "Pete Christlieb/Warne Marsh," *L.A. Jazz Scene* (November 1991): 9.

34. Pete Christlieb, interview.

♫

One More Time

Having spent the previous thirteen years reestablishing himself on the Los Angeles jazz scene and, through the opportunities arising from his visibility with Supersax, reviving his recording career and his international reputation, Marsh now executed one of those curious left turns that Los Angeles bassist Putter Smith found so predictable. Shortly after appearing at Donte's with Gary Foster, Alan Broadbent, Monty Budwig, and Nick Ceroli in October 1977, he abruptly pulled up stakes in Los Angeles and returned again to New York.

"I was fifty-one," he told *Rolling Stone*'s Robert Palmer, "and when it came down to spending the rest of my life in L.A., I just couldn't see it. Jazz is a hobby there, even for the best players."[1] Having already quit Supersax, mainly on the advice, according to both Ted Brown and Gary Foster, of Lennie Tristano, he was under the impression that he could persuade Tristano, who was in ill health and had not performed in public for years, to form a working group with him. Now he sold the house in Pasadena (which his mother had bought for him) for a handsome profit of about $30,000, bought a near-new Chevrolet Malibu station wagon for $3,000, and with Geraldyne and his two sons—Casey, age nine, and Jason, age seven—drove back to New York. Geraldyne, whose desire for a settled suburban life was perfectly fulfilled by their situation in Pasadena, was not happy about the move, but accepted Marsh's decision.[2]

Their immediate destination was Ted Brown's home in Huntington, Long Island. Several of his students, including singer Judy Niemack, trumpeter Simon Wettenhall, and saxophonist Jeremy Kellock, aware of the impending move, had preceded him. Niemack and Wettenhall ended up sleeping on Brown's back porch.

Brown, a devoted family man, had been through a difficult period. He had found it impossible to make a living at jazz, and from 1967 to 1972 his day job at a textile mill in Andover, Massachusetts, left him no time even to practice. He was jolted back into practicing and some playing by the smell of marijuana smoke wafting through Boston Garden, where he had taken his daughter to a rock concert for her thirteenth birthday. When his old friend came to Boston with Supersax in the fall of 1973, for a concert at a local community college, Brown made a point of attending and came away duly impressed: "Warne was doing some unbelievable things with that band." In the summer of 1974, after steeply rising oil prices had caused the mill to cut back its operations, he visited Los Angeles in an unsuccessful search for another job, taking the opportunity to jam a couple of times with Marsh. When he returned to Andover, he was fired and was jobless for six months, supporting his family with unemployment compensation and food stamps before taking a job with CETA, a federal government jobs program. Having read that musicians often had an aptitude for computer programming, he took some computer courses and succeeded in landing a job in his new specialty with Polygram Records in New York. In 1976 he had done a few gigs and a record date with Lee Konitz. Now, in the fall of 1977, he was playing weekends at Gatsby's, a club near his new home in Huntington. Some of Tristano's students, including young saxophonists Jimmy Halperin and Victor Lesser, often came to the club to sit in and play the Tristano lines.

When Marsh and his family arrived at his doorstep, Brown found a motel room for Warne and Geraldyne and put the two boys up at his place. After perhaps a week of this arrangement, during which time Marsh several times visited Tristano, then living in the Jamaica section of Queens, the Marshes drove to Connecticut to visit Steve and Mickey Silverman. A day or two later, Marsh returned alone and said they'd decided to stay with the Silvermans, and without further elaboration picked up their luggage and drove off, leaving Brown puzzled by the abruptness of it all. He did not hear from Marsh again for months.

After staying as guests of the Silvermans for perhaps six months, in the summer of 1978 the Marshes found a place of their own in Ridgefield, Connecticut, and Marsh settled into the process of reestablishing himself in and around New York, despite the inconvenient distance from Manhattan. His idea of doing this was to renew his ties with Tristano and his circle. In February he had participated in recording sessions in Manhattan for Judy Niemack's and Simon Wettenhall's first LP, *By Heart*, produced by Toshiya Taenaka for Sea Breeze Records. With Eddie Gomez on bass and Skip Scott, stepson of Tristano drummer Dick Scott, on drums, the record included two tracks with Marsh. It was released late in 1978 and attracted no notice whatsoever. His old colleague Sal Mosca, who was also a friend of the Silvermans, was within driving distance in Mt. Vernon, New York, and the two played together once or twice a week at Mosca's studio. Mosca taped everything, and the four duo tracks on *How Deep, How High* were from similar sessions later in the following year. At one point, said Mosca, "some friends were interested in buying a club where Warne and I could work," and Mosca checked out some fifty pianos for the proposed club, "but it never came to pass."[3]

Sometime after settling in Ridgefield, in late summer or early fall, Marsh agreed to a lengthy series of interviews with Marcel Clemens, a French journalist. Having recently moved to New York from Paris, where she had had success writing for slick magazines of general interest, Clemens was anxious to establish herself in the United States and saw in Marsh a promising subject. He was to prove, finally, a totally frustrating one.

"I couldn't really get through to him, to the core," said Clemens. "I felt I didn't really understand who he was. . . . He was very very nice, and very polite—he was sort of sweet, really. He was trying to be open, I think it was interesting for him to talk to me—and yet it was just about impossible to corner him in a substantial way. . . . He admitted very little. . . . He was a surface that things bounced off of."

Linked to the "fugitive, aloof, very evanescent" quality that made it so difficult to get through to him, she thought, was the fact that "he was stoned a lot." Once she smoked some of his marijuana with him: "It was the strongest marijuana I had ever had. I was literally stupefied. . . . I couldn't believe he functioned at all on this stuff, even allowing for the fact that he had it all the time."

"The highlight of our conversations," she said, "and maybe of his life, was his Central Avenue period [1945–46 and 1947–48]. He made it sound incredibly colorful and vivid, and he remembered the names of every single person. For a long time he went down there just to listen. . . . There was also one player in particular that he was influenced by. . . . Maybe it was Wardell Gray." At the time she bought some Wardell Gray records and thought it must have been as a result of Marsh's talking about him.

Other than Central Avenue, said Clemens, the only things Marsh talked about with some vehemence were "his feeling that Americans didn't value jazz as one of *their* art forms, and that jazz in general was neglected and undervalued; secondly that . . . when the world at large decided to notice, usually in some frozen way, it was usually black musicians, and that white jazz musicians were really brutally discriminated against. . . . And then he would talk about Lennie Tristano, who he felt was one of the very great artists of the century, who was really unjustifiably obscure, and had been discriminated against by people outside and inside of jazz. . . . He spoke of Tristano with *incredible* veneration. That was astounding."

At one point Clemens asked about the "long dry period" of the 1960s: "I said, 'I don't understand what happened to you,' and he said, 'I don't either.' He did not understand his own life. . . . He had some understanding of the forces without . . . but [not] the forces in his family. . . . He was really trying . . . [but] it's as if he was lost to himself. . . . I found him really heartbreaking and I wished that I could help him. That's the feeling he gave me."

During the course of his interviews with Clemens, Marsh attended one of Lennie Tristano's frequent recitals for his students, this one featuring saxophonist Lenny Popkin with Stan Fortuna on bass and Peter Scattaretico, a former rock drummer who had been studying jazz with Tristano for the past year, on drums. According to Scattaretico, Marsh had told Tristano that he was looking for a rhythm section, and Tristano was eager for him to hear Scattaretico and Fortuna. After the performance Tristano told them that Marsh had loved their playing and had said, "I've been looking for a rhythm section like this for fifteen years." Sure enough, Marsh called them a few days later, and after a few rehearsals Tristano announced his plan to feature the new Warne Marsh trio at his next recital.

Without denigrating the talents of Scattaretico and Fortuna, which were undoubtedly considerable, it is hard not to see in Marsh's enthusiasm for their playing the influence of Tristano. An older student of Tristano's, bassist Joe Solomon, saw in Marsh the same "incredible veneration" of Tristano that Clemens observed. He felt that Marsh "suspended his whole independent mind around Lennie." Solomon recalled an occasion in the early or middle 1970s when Marsh made an appearance in New York for the first time in many years, probably with Supersax. The visit was eagerly anticipated by Tristano's students, who looked on Marsh as a conquering hero, an early student who had become a major player. Expecting someone with a bearing commensurate with his reputation, Solomon was "taken aback at how deferential Warne was to Lennie. When Lennie was around, he was like me, like a student. Whatever Lennie said, Warne would agree with it." When Marsh came to New York again for his 1975 concert with Connie Crothers, Roger Mancuso, and Solomon, there was talk after the concert of the same group possibly playing at a club on Long Island. When Crothers declined, because the club's piano was in terrible shape, Solomon and Mancuso suggested a pianist friend they had been playing with. Marsh, said Solomon, was agreeable until Tristano proposed one of his favorite students, guitarist Larry Meyer. "Lennie said one word, pushing Larry, and Warne immediately stopped listening to anything we were saying, with the attitude of 'Whatever Lennie says goes.'" Given the condition of the piano, Marsh's attitude made sense, but to Solomon it was evidence of Marsh's subservience to Tristano.

Clemens, who had interviewed Tristano as part of her project with Marsh—he greeted her unshaven, in a blue bathrobe and slippers—had been invited to the scheduled performance of the Marsh-Fortuna-Scattaretico trio. On the day of the concert, November 18, 1978, she received a phone call from Marsh. Tristano, he told her, was dead.

Tristano had been in poor health for years. He had constant itching and pain in his eyes and had been advised by several doctors to have his eyeballs removed, but had decided against it. In 1974 he had had walking pneumonia. Forced at that time to give up smoking, he took up drinking and became grossly overweight. He also suffered from emphysema. Knowing all this, and aware that Tristano had not performed in public since 1969, Marsh had nevertheless envisioned playing once again with his mentor. Yet according to Geraldyne, he had hardly done so, if at all, in the year since he had returned to New York, just as he had seldom gotten together for private sessions with Tristano in 1964 when he and Geraldyne were living in Tristano's house.

Marsh, said Geraldyne, was devastated but, as when his real father died, showed little emotion. "He was not a demonstrative man." Probably the closest he came to expressing what he must have felt was at a gathering a week later at bassist and Tristano compatriot Sonny Dallas's home on Long Island. A reporter for *Jazz* magazine wrote: "The occasion was a private party and a jam, not a wake for Lenny Tristano, but the music inevitably became the medium for memorial. *You'd Be So Nice to Come Home To, Subconsciously* [sic] . . . *What's New, Pennies from Heaven*—with the minor changes [of 'Lennie's Pennies']. At one point, calling the next tune, Marsh said it for everybody: '*I Remember You*. That's the mood I'm in.'"[4] Dallas reported that Marsh, private man that he was, was annoyed that Dallas had invited a reporter to the gathering.

Clemens, her interviews with Marsh interrupted by Tristano's sudden death—"that whole little world of 'Tristanoland' was thrown into an uproar"—abandoned the project, not only because of its intrinsic difficulty but because she had been unable to market it.[5]

The Lennie Tristano Memorial Concert took place January 28, 1979, at New York's Town Hall. It was a marathon four- or five-hour affair of performances by Tristano students and associates, past and present, among them, besides Marsh, Sal Mosca, Lloyd Lifton, Connie Crothers, Lenny Popkin, Harold Danko, Sheila Jordan, Cameron Brown, Larry Meyer, Lynn Anderson, Virg Dzurinko, Nomi Rosen, Fran Canisius, Stan Fortuna, and

Liz Gorrill. About half of the performances were solo, the rest being duos, trios, or quartets.

Among Tristano associates who did not play at the concert were Ted Brown, Sonny Dallas, and Lee Konitz. Popkin asked Brown to play, and Brown agreed at first, but was surprised to receive by mail, without accompanying explanation, a legal document that offered him the choice of being paid union scale or donating his pay to Tristano's children, and of being included or not on a recording of the event. Although willing to donate his pay to the family, he put the document aside pending further discussion. Eventually he received a phone call from Popkin, who told him he was scheduled to play with Popkin's own rhythm section, Peter Scattaretico and Stan Fortuna, and indicated that they needed to use Tristano-associated musicians as much as possible. Brown had other rhythm players in mind: "I was working a lot with Lee [Konitz] and Dave Shapiro [bass] and Jo Jones, Jr. [drums]."[6] He particularly liked working with Jones. "I wasn't locked in on that, but I didn't want them going down a list and saying, 'This is your rhythm section.'" Negotiations broke down over this conflict between Popkin's desire to use Tristano-associated personnel and Brown's desire to play with a rhythm section he felt comfortable with.

Dallas, despite his many years as Tristano's regular bassist, was not asked to perform at the memorial concert. According to Crothers, this was because Dallas had not been close to Tristano for almost ten years, and he had not called the house after Tristano died. Also he had abandoned acoustic bass for electric bass, which Tristano disliked.[7] Although it was true that Dallas had not been in close contact with Tristano for many years, he said that he had talked to Tristano by phone not long before his death.

As for Konitz, he and Tristano had had little contact since 1965, when the shortlived reunion band had broken up. In January of 1972 Mosca, who was playing with Konitz at the Top of the Gate, had invited Tristano to the club, having in the back of his mind the thought of effecting a reconciliation. As Mosca told the story, Tristano attended in the company of Connie Crothers and Lenny Popkin. When Konitz approached and said casually, "Hi, Lennie," the volatile Tristano exploded, hitting the table with his fist in exasperation. "Seven years, and all he says is 'Hi Lennie'! There's no history in it!" Konitz excused himself and walked away. Crothers remembered it slightly differently: "Lee came up to the table, and what he said was, and I'm quoting exactly, he said, 'I just thought I'd say hello.' Lennie just didn't know how to relate to that, and what he said to Lee was 'Thank you.' Lee was hurt by that, and walked away. After Lee walked away, Lennie did say what Sal said." She did not remember Tristano's hitting the table.

Mosca thought there had been no further contact between Konitz and his former mentor up to Tristano's death. But Crothers told this story: "Nine or ten months before Lennie died, I was sitting with him in his studio and the phone rang. At this time Lennie was extremely ill. He had emphysema and it just about robbed him of all his energy, and he was in pain all the time. He walked over to the phone, and all of a sudden I saw his face light up like a Christmas tree. It was hard to believe, he was laughing and talking in this amazingly animated way. . . . For those few moments he looked like a kid, just all lit up. Then he put down the phone, and he turned to me with this great big smile, and he said 'Can you imagine that? Lee Konitz called me from London!'"

No overt alienation ever clouded Tristano's relations with Marsh, who shared with Mosca and pianist Lloyd Lifton the distinction of being the most loyal of Tristano's early followers. For his part in the memorial concert, Marsh was accompanied by Eddie Gomez on bass and Scattaretico on drums. Scattaretico was a last-minute replacement for Max Roach, who, like Roy Eldridge, had to cancel because of injuries in an auto accident.

Marsh's trio played three numbers, "I Love You," "Trilogy" ("I'll Remember April"), and "I Should Care." These were included in an expensive five-LP set of recordings, produced by George Crothers and Russell Rockman, and probably few outside the inner circle of Tristano devotees ever heard them. Both Marsh and Gomez play with virtuosity and great energy, especially on "Trilogy," but the sound is echoey, and the pairing of the two seems less happy than Marsh's efforts with Niels-Henning Orsted-Pedersen in 1975 and Red Mitchell in the 1980s. Gomez seems to bring out the more austere, pricklier side of Marsh, as opposed to the Prez-like warmth and lyricism of his playing with the latter two.

Jon Balleras, noting in his review of the records the negative criticisms of Tristano as "a cult figure, a witch doctor, a father confessor," diplomatically sidestepped the issue: "Perhaps Tristano purposely exploited his posture as a mythic blind prophet; perhaps the force of his music alone inspired his followers' admiration. Whatever the reason, his music and personality were intense, innovative and charismatic enough to attract a hearty grouping of students, followers and fellow musicians (plus a noisy, indiscriminate audience) to pay Town Hall tribute to his memory and carry on, in some sense, his musical directions." The climax of the concert, and the record set, "comes when Warne Marsh, a bona fide, first-rate disciple and musical companion of Tristano, takes—almost seizes—the stand." He found the high point of Marsh's set to be "Trilogy": "Opening a cappella in a crystalline, altoish tone, Marsh roams through the full range of his instrument, playing off Gomez' taut, walking background. Tristano would have been pleased."[8]

NOTES

1. Robert Palmer, "Warne Marsh: The Return of a Radical," *Rolling Stone,* March 20, 1980, 34.

2. Gary Foster, interview.

3. Sal Mosca, personal letter to Marcus Cornelius, February 12, 1989.

4. Jan Sturdevant, "Tristano Tributes," *Jazz* (c. January 1979): 10.

5. When I talked to Clemens, she still had the "many, many hours" of tapes she had made with Marsh but could not put her hands on them. She was in the process of selling her Manhattan home, and the tapes were buried somewhere in her basement. Presumably she still has them.

6. Ted Brown, interview.

7. Connie Crothers, interview.

8. Jon Balleras, "Tristano's Disciples," *Down Beat,* April 1981, 38–39.

After Lennie

After Tristano's death Marsh maintained his residence in the New York area for the next seven years. Mostly he drifted along in the Tristano orbit, playing not only with Sal Mosca and Connie Crothers but with many of their and his own students. He seems to have viewed this practice as part of his legacy from Tristano, whose recordings and performances after 1948, when not solo, were almost entirely with his own best students.

In April 1979 Marsh, Mosca, Peter Scattaretico, and Eddie Gomez played an engagement at Lulu White's in Boston, with Mosca playing solo opposite Marsh's trio and then joining them. That summer Marsh, Mosca, and Gomez performed with Lee Konitz and drummer Eliot Zigmund at Storyville in New York as part of the Kool Jazz Festival.[1] Throughout the year Marsh and Mosca met once or twice a week at Mosca's studio in Mt. Vernon to play duos, four of which were included in the *How Deep, How High* album.

On August 28 Marsh and Mosca began the first of several weeklong engagements at the Village Vanguard with Frank Canino, a student of Mosca's who had been playing upright bass for only a year and a half, and young Tim Pleasant on drums.[2] John S. Wilson keyed his review on the Tristano connection: "Two disciples of the late Lennie Tristano, the pianist who led a group at the Village Vanguard 30 years ago, are themselves leading a quartet in that same room through tomorrow. [They combine] to recreate the light, running lines with billowing rises and falls that were characteristic of Mr. Tristano's playing. Their solos, however, move into more distinctive personal territory. . . . Mr. Marsh's variations on such

208

ballads as 'Gone With the Wind' and 'Body and Soul' have a mulling, brooding quality, with passages in which he seems to be chewing reflectively on his phrases. There's a feeling of tension, of fullness in his lines, whereas Mr. Mosca's solo approach is more open, more relaxed and yet with a similar sense of probing." Wilson was appreciative of the fact that the solos did not go on ad infinitum, as many had done in the intervening thirty years: "[T]he quartet stands out from the common run of jazz groups today in its realization that enough is enough—when you have said what you have to say on a tune, it is time to stop."³

It was at this engagement that the drummer Jo Jones, who had been in the audience and acting rather strangely, perhaps drunk, jumped on the stage to play drums during a Mosca solo set. It gradually became clear that Mosca was annoyed, and after *Night in Tunisia* and another number he rose from the piano to prematurely terminate the set.⁴

Following their initial experience together at the Vanguard, Canino called Marsh for a few casuals, such as afternoon teas at the New York University Law School, and his association with Marsh lasted several years. He found Marsh usually "grumpy" and "frustrated." There was always, he said, "that racial thing," a certain feeling about his lack of recognition in comparison to that accorded black players. But recognition, Canino saw, "won't just come to you. You gotta *work* it, and that's the side of it that he just refused to do, didn't have the ability to do. He had something to be bitter about, but he just didn't *do* anything about it."

Another Vanguard gig a few months later, January 1–6, 1980, was with Connie Crothers, along with Scattaretico and Eddie Gomez. Critic Robert Palmer, who had written the liner notes for *Apogee,* took the occasion to write a feature story on Marsh in *Rolling Stone.* Capitalizing on the Steely Dan connection, Palmer wrote, "Marsh's music has a lot in common with the music of [Donald] Fagen and [Walter] Becker, who idolize him. It's intellectually rigorous, harmonically challenging—the work of an iconoclast and a perfectionist." Summarizing Marsh's background, he noted that "after a number of lean years . . . he hooked up with Supersax, providing most of the band's best moments. That affiliation, and the liberalizing of jazz listeners' tastes during the Seventies, led to renewed opportunities. He made some brilliant new recordings, including *All Music . . .* , *Warne Out . . .* , and *Tenor Gladness.*" Palmer concluded by "wondering whether people were still calling Warne Marsh's music cool and unemotional, as they had in the Fifties. For me, and for a growing number of fans, it packs plenty of emotional wallop in addition to its intricate craftsmanship."⁵

Around this same time, early 1980, Marsh and some of his and Mosca's students began playing Thursday nights and Sunday brunches at Peachtree's, normally a disco club in New Rochelle, on Long Island Sound a few

miles from Mosca's home in Mt.Vernon. The owner had been persuaded
by Dan Fiore and Joseph Squillante, friends of Mosca, Marsh, and Steve
Silverman, to adopt a twice-a-week jazz policy.[6] For the first year Fiore
booked the jazz groups, with Squillante taking over for another year or
so. Marsh played there frequently. Joining him on the bandstand at various times were Judy Niemack and Simon Wettenhall, both of whom had
studied with Marsh in California; Frank Canino; tenor saxophonist Jimmy
Halperin, who had learned Marsh solos while studying with Tristano and
Mosca; pianist Tardo Hammer, another of Mosca's students; guitarists
Mark Diorio and Fiore; drummers Taro Okamoto and Skip Scott; and bassists Murray Wall and John Ray.[7] When Skip Scott's mother, Betty Scott,
herself a former Tristano student, sang there, appearing for the first time
in public in twenty years, Marsh sat in, saying to Fiore, "I'm just here to
help Betty with her life." The psychiatrist Steve Silverman, who had studied with Tristano, Mosca, and Marsh, sometimes played piano.

Among those who came to hear them and visit with Marsh during
1980–82 was Ted Brown. Since he had last seen Marsh, Brown had been
hospitalized with an irregular heartbeat. When he told Marsh of his ill-
ness, Marsh said, in his usual cryptic way, "That ought to tell you something. That's one of the symptoms." Marsh was always coming up with
some mysterious pronouncement, said Brown. He was not sure what this
one meant. He half-understood it to mean that he had brought his heart
problem on himself by the way he was living, but he let it pass.

It was not until several years later, in a visit to Marsh at his studio in
Bretton Hall, after Brown had been hospitalized a second time, that he
learned more specifically what Marsh had meant. "I was very depressed
because I was not playing, I'd just had this heart thing, I didn't like what
I was doing for my day gig, my whole life was just not where I wanted it
to go. And I figured he'd understand that more than anybody else. And
then you know what he told me? He even put me down more because I
was in the hospital a second time. That was really proof that I wasn't living the life I should be living, and he was preaching this shit to me, he's
telling me what you have to do is, if you're going to be an artist, you have
to be an artist twenty-four hours a day, you have to devote your whole
life to it, otherwise you just can't do it. I said, 'What the fuck you telling
me, man? I'm fifty-five years old. You expect me to give up my job and
my family and everybody and everything, just to play?' I said, 'That's not
why I'm here, I'm not going to do that, but that doesn't mean I don't want
to play. I want to play as bad as you do.' That really pissed me off. Five
minutes later, the doorbell rang. He said, 'Well, my next student is here.'
He had timed me into his teaching schedule!"

Just before Peachtree's became a regular haunt for Marsh, his old friend
Red Mitchell had shown up in New York. The renewal of their relation-

ship was to produce some of Marsh's finest work of the 1980s. Since recording *Music for Prancing* in 1957, the two had gone their separate ways, Mitchell moving to Stockholm in 1966 and playing in Europe for ten years. According to Torgrim Sollid, the Norwegian trumpeter who helped arrange Marsh's visits to Norway from 1980 on, Mitchell and Marsh toured Scandinavia in 1978–79. Now, in 1980, after a few rehearsals, Marsh, Mitchell, and Peter Scattaretico played a concert at Alice Tully Hall on January 26, 1980. Although the concert was sponsored by the Lennie Tristano Jazz Foundation, Mitchell was in no sense a Tristanoite. Besides having played with every kind of musician, from Billie Holiday, Red Norvo, and Woody Herman to Dizzy Gillespie, Phil Woods, and even Ornette Coleman, he had never agreed with Tristano's conception of the rhythm section and had developed a lyrical solo style that made him the equal of any horn player.

No tapes or records have surfaced of this concert, though it would be surprising if none existed. One reviewer admired the way in which Marsh "took initially simple lines to the limits of their structural and melodic implications" to create a Lester Young-influenced music that was "airy, full of sunshine, yet densely complex." However, the overall effect he found "austere." Mitchell, he wrote, "both in ensemble and solo, came close to dominating the recital's two hours. His deep, resonant tone and sure pulse played both foundation and foil for Marsh. His solos shone with simplicity and lyric imagery. In their directness, they achieved a poignancy hard to perceive in the swoops and dives and skyrockets of Marsh's work."[8]

Mitchell's visit to New York apparently led to a quickly arranged Scandinavian tour for Marsh. April 8–9, 1980, found him and Mitchell both in Oslo, where they recorded with the Norwegian singer Karin Krog. The resultant LP, *I Remember You*, was issued some twenty months later on Spotlight, an English label that probably received limited distribution in the United States. Marsh sounds relaxed behind the understated, lightly swinging Krog. His solo on the title tune is unusually oblique, but on "Speak Low" and "That Old Feeling" he plays with the simple, unforced lyricism of his recorded duos with Mosca.

On April 17 Marsh and Mitchell participated in a concert in Stockholm, and the next two days, April 18–19, they played as a duo at Stockholm's Fasching Club, an engagement that resulted in one of Marsh's most engaging records of the period. His tone is beautifully controlled and full of nuance, and his linear explorations are completely coherent harmonically even when Mitchell lays out. Mitchell's warmth, sprightly lyricism, and immense good humor are a perfect complement. There are times when the two are able to suggest a whole big band, as on the out-chorus of "Tea for Two," where Marsh initiates a Basie-type riff to which Mitchell spontaneously provides the rhythmic counterpoint.

Unfortunately, the release of this record, *The Marsh-Mitchell Big Two: Hot House*, Storyville LP-4092, occurred not twenty months but seven years later. When it was finally issued, in the spring of 1987, it was to high praise. Jon Balleras wrote, "The quality of communication between these men is absolute. Call it intuition, confluence, or whatever, however we describe it, these players are operating on a highly intuitive level, and their intuitions are unerringly fortuitous."[9] The repertoire, as Balleras noted, was mainstream standards like "Tea for Two," with an out-chorus by Al Cohn; "Lover Man"; and "Gone with the Wind," plus a couple of Charlie Parker variations on standards, "Hot House" and "Ornithology." In his later career Marsh had focused so compulsively on lines by Tristano or his students that it is refreshing to hear him do an entire program without one. Balleras's summary evaluation is apt: "What results is . . . seemingly layer upon layer of paraphrase, and not a measure of wasted improvisational energy."[10]

Still another highly listenable, relaxed record to emerge from the same Scandinavian tour, not released, deplorably, until about 1988, was made from a radio broadcast April 21, 1980, in Copenhagen. Here Marsh was the guest of the Kenny Drew Trio, consisting of Drew, piano; Bo Stief, bass; and Aage Tangaard, drums. Marsh acquired a tape of the performance and sold it to Toshiya Taenaka of Interplay records. Taenaka leased it to Art Union in Japan, who subleased it to Venus Records, who finally released it after Marsh's death. Taenaka, however, never bothered to obtain legal rights to the music from Danish Radio. These were eventually acquired by Karl Knudsen of Storyville Records, which issued the same material in 1999, plus one additional track, on a CD titled *Warne Marsh and Kenny Drew Trio: "I Got a Good One for You,"* STCD 8277. Because it was made from the broadcast master, the fidelity of this release is markedly superior to the Venus issue. It is one of the few records to capture the extraordinary sound of Marsh's later playing, making one realize how much is lost in the many low-fidelity recordings.

Again the repertoire included songs that Marsh never played on records and seldom on club dates, "Sophisticated Lady," "Softly as in a Morning Sunrise," and "On Green Dolphin Street," and the feeling is loose and free-wheeling. Marsh expressed to Taenaka his satisfaction with Drew's trio. The exuberant, extroverted rhythm section seems to free Marsh from any vestiges of introspective constraint he may have retained from his early years with Tristano, even on such a Tristano favorite as "It's You or No One" (here retitled "I Got a Good One for You". His solo on "Body and Soul" is sheer melodic genius, a solo so logical and seemingly natural that one wonders why no one ever thought of this approach before.

A final important result of Marsh's renewed relationship in 1980 with Red Mitchell was another duo engagement, this time at Sweet Basil in New York. On June 5 the pair were recorded live at the club, and in 1995 a CD, *Warne Marsh-Red Mitchell Duo*, was issued on Fresh Sound.[11] Happily, critic Art Lange of *Down Beat* was on hand for the live performance. Comparing Lee Konitz's recorded duos with Mitchell (on SteepleChase and Inner City) with the live Marsh-Mitchell collaboration, Lange wrote, "[W]here Konitz is playful, angular and probing, Marsh is intense, linear and probing; and Mitchell is Mitchell, effervescent, elastic and intelligent in any context."[12] At intermission, Lange noted, Mitchell introduced Marsh by saying, "'I'd like to take this opportunity to introduce the orchestra' . . . —tongue in cheek, but true, too, because of the effortlessness and variety of Marsh's never-ending flow of ideas, constantly suggesting, discarding, stretching, invoking new directions with an elaborate, alchemistic chromatic variation, walking through a maze into uncharted, unexplored territory, seemingly into harmonic dead ends . . . only to tie it all together in a series of canny calisthenics and appear unscathed at the other end of the tune." Lange's conclusion: "Red Mitchell and Warne Marsh: an extraordinarily felicitous experience."[13]

For much of the rest of 1980 and 1981 Marsh was back in the Tristano orbit. Along with his teaching and appearances with students and other little known players at out-of-the-way places like Peachtree's, there were occasional gigs at major venues. The week of June 10–16, 1980, he played the Village Vanguard with Mosca, Eddie Gomez, and a drummer, perhaps Scattaretico. Probably the most remunerative performance of 1980 was at the Berlin Jazz Festival on October 30, with Mosca, Gomez, and the great drummer Kenny Clarke. Marsh had probably not played with Clarke for twenty-five years, since their 1955 record with Konitz, as Clarke had taken up permanent residence in Paris in 1956. At least part of the concert was broadcast in Germany, and a recording was issued on Interplay in the early 1990s. Both Marsh and Mosca seem uninspired, though Clarke's drumming sounds as good as ever. An unissued videotape of the group shows Marsh, not "chewing" on the mouthpiece "bubblegum-style," as some described him in the early days, but in almost equally unorthodox fashion moving the whole horn back and forth, causing the mouthpiece to be at different positions in his mouth. This is in total violation of standard saxophone pedagogy, which holds that the embouchure should remain firm and stresses that the saxophone is played with the fingers and the breath, not the mouth.

In the spring of 1981 he found time to record three numbers for Pete Christlieb's self-produced album, *Pete Christlieb: Self Portrait* (Bosco 1), presumably visiting Los Angeles for the occasion. Though the record probably received limited distribution, it nevertheless garnered a favorable review in *High Fidelity/Musical America:* "Marsh joins [Christlieb] in a masterly, half-unaccompanied duet [on the changes of 'What's New'], Marsh's cool, Getz-ish tone and long, flowing passages floating beneath Christlieb's alternately bluesy and boppish runs; their superbly sensitive interplay suggests a deep musical friendship."[14] Back in New York, on July 5, 1981, Marsh joined Lenny Popkin, Scattaretico, and bassist Michael Moore for a Kool Jazz Festival concert in Purchase. The concert was apparently never reviewed. Although *Down Beat* writers Lee Jeske and Art Lange covered the New York City venues of the festival extensively, heavy rains discouraged them from traveling to Purchase.

In November 1981 Marsh and Mosca did another week at the Village Vanguard, with Mosca's student Frank Canino again on bass and Skip Scott on drums. Mosca recorded the entire week's proceedings on his "boom box," and in 1992, probably with financial help from producers Steve and Mickey Silverman and from Dan Fiore of Zinnia Records, released two CDs of remastered material on Fiore's obscure Zinnia label.

Marsh plays with controlled tone and great fluency and has some fine solos. Nevertheless, these records have a monochromatic, sterile quality to them. No doubt this is partly due to the recording equipment used, though the sound, while lacking in presence, is otherwise not glaringly deficient. But the problem seems mainly due to the journeyman playing of Canino and Scott and the meandering, often humorous, intellectuality of Mosca, who, inventive and virtuosic as he is, gives an impression of cleverness and ingenuity rather than passion.

On Volume One Marsh has excellent, fleet-fingered solos on "Silver Man" ("All the Things You Are") and "Digi-Doll" ("Softly as in a Morning Sunrise"). Mosca's comping on both is more or less conventional, though on the beginning of "Silver Man" he echoes the rhythmic pattern and intervallic shape, though not the notes, of Marsh's line in an ingenious way that to another player might have been disconcerting. Both tracks begin abruptly with Marsh's solo and fade out after it, an idiosyncracy of Tristanoite recording that tellingly reveals Tristano's radical emphasis on improvisation at the expense of overall form and presentation. On "Under-Bach," a blues that similarly isolates only Marsh's solo, Mosca lays out, and Marsh seems to relish the freedom from chordal accompaniment. "Confirmation," with its aura of Charlie Parker, swings harder than any of the other pieces, especially in the opening theme statement and Marsh's solo over Mosca's more traditional comping. "Shakin' Out" ("Body and Soul") begins in the middle of the bridge with Marsh responding to dissonant, impressionistic, belllike comping by Mosca that continues through the last eight bars of the chorus. Then Mosca drops out as Marsh begins another, characteristically fluent chorus with only bass and drums, after which the track fades out again. Some of Mosca's best playing is on the up-tempo "Dick's Favorite" ("Cherokee").

Volume Two provides similar experiences. Marsh's playing is uniformly admirable, yet something is missing. On "Testament" ("Foolin' Myself") Mosca improvises harmonically behind Marsh, who adapts responsively, but the track has a cold, intellectual feel to it. There is above-average Marsh on "Pulsafer" ("Autumn in New York"), "Marionette" ("September in the Rain"), "Thermology" (another truncated track with only Marsh's solo), "Subconscious-Lee," and "Featherbed." "Way in There" ("You Go to My Head") commands interest for the interplay between Marsh and Mosca.

Over and beyond the ordinariness of the rhythm section, especially Scott's mechanical drumming, one is tempted to attribute the emotional deficiency to a kind of Tristanoite inbreeding. Scott, the son of Tristano's close friend Betty Scott and stepson of Tristano drummer Dick Scott, could be said to have been born a Tristanoite, and Mosca was even more of a Tristano disciple than Marsh. Accepting Tristano's dogmas unquestioningly, he was proud of the fact that in the eight years he studied with the master he missed only three lessons, and he recounted how Tristano had told him that one way to achieve one's individuality was to submerge one's ego and submit absolutely to one's teacher. In the matter of repertoire, Mosca saw no problem with restricting oneself to the same body of material year after year. The idea of mastering a tune by repeated study, he maintained, came originally from Charlie Parker. Actually the practice was typical of older musicians. In any case, Mosca felt that to achieve total freedom, one needs to know a tune on the deepest level. "Everybody's repertoire . . . is limited to the tunes they really think a lot of."[15]

Most jazz musicians would undoubtedly agree, up to a point. But players like Phil Woods and Sonny Rollins are constantly in search of fresh new material, and Lee Konitz, who has probably played "Body and Soul" every day of his life for over fifty years, has not limited himself either to the Tristano repertoire or to Tristano-schooled partners. In the case of Marsh and Mosca, it may be that what was lacking was the stimulus of difference, the kind of stimulus that resulted in such congenial music on the record with The Kenny Drew Trio.

In 1981–82 Marsh's life began to center less on his home and family in Ridgefield than on his studio at Bretton Hall, the hotel at West 85th and Broadway where he taught, jammed, and hung out with students and other musician-tenants of the place. Among his newer students were singers Carla White and Janet Lawson, violinist and singer Linda Fennimore, guitarists Josh Breakstone and John Klopotowski, and saxophonists David Frank and Victor Lesser. Another Bretton Hall resident, guitarist Bob Ward, introduced him to bassist Steve LaSpina, who participated in sessions at both Ward's studio and Marsh's home in Ridgefield "morning, noon, and night." According to Ward, Marsh loved to play with LaSpina.

Marsh would always have a chess game going, playing at session breaks with an electronic partner or live opponents such as Mark Diorio. Like others, including Ward, Diorio saw a similarity between Marsh's fondness for chess and other games, such as scrabble, bridge, and the Japanese game Go, and his approach to jazz. Said Diorio, "We were about even in chess, but I couldn't get lax with him. If I got an early advantage and got lazy, he would kick my ass. That says something about him as a musician. He always looked at each situation freshly and was never mechanical."

Besides Peachtree's, there were occasional gigs at Eddie Condon's in Manhattan, Gulliver's in West Paterson, the Far and Away in Cliffside Park, just across the George Washington bridge, and once or twice a year at the Village Vanguard. As a rule his colleagues were either students or younger, still-developing players. His longtime student Judy Niemack found in him an "incredible resignation" to obscurity, saying he had no concept of seeking out well-known, established players to perform or record with.

He never kept any group together for very long. Frank Canino recalled hearing him at the Vanguard with Niemack, pianist Tardo Hammer, drummer Taro Okamoto, and bassist John Ray. "I thought they sounded great, but at the end of the week Warne was sick of it." Possibly the rhythm section wasn't as good as Canino thought. Still, Marsh made no real effort to work with more experienced players on his own level.

He could be amazingly casual about his rhythm sections. Before their Vanguard gig in 1980, he had never worked with Earl Sauls. He told the young bassist to write down one hundred tunes he knew, and when Sauls later handed him the list, slightly padded with blues lines, Marsh said, "Okay, thanks," put it in his pocket, and never referred to it again. After one forty-minute rehearsal they went into the Vanguard and played his usual Tristano-school tunes: "Out of Nowhere," "It's You or No One," "All the Things You Are," "Subconscious-Lee," "Victory Ball," "Lennie's Pennies," plus a few standards like "Body and Soul," "Lover Man," and "Cherokee."

From time to time he would conceive projects, pursue them for a brief period, then drop them. At one point he envisioned doing a duet album with Diorio. At another he briefly rehearsed a two-tenor band with Jimmy Halperin, Hammer, Scott, and Ray. Neither project came to anything. He had a perennial dream of recreating the classic Tristano band, talking about forming one as late as the fall of 1987, two months before his death. Earlier he talked to John Klopotowsi about putting together a band including Klopotowski, Okamoto, altoist Gary Foster, bassist George Mraz, and perhaps a piano player. The band would play not only the normal Tristano repertoire but some free jazz along the lines of what Tristano had done in 1949. It never happened.

Marsh's professional passivity was attributed by Murray Wall to his marijuana habit. Wall had first been introduced to Marsh's playing in his native Australia, where a friend had a number of hard-to-get records by Tristano and his associates. He met Marsh in Pasadena in 1975 and became, along with Simon Wettenhall and Jeremy Kellock, a key member of the "Australian connection," introducing other immigrant Australian musicians to Marsh. Daily use of marijuana, he felt, resulted in Marsh's "decision-making processes" being "impaired." "This guy couldn't make up his mind about anything. He'd like a drummer one day, then couldn't stand him the next. You smoke that much reefer for that long. . . ."

Others interpreted the drifting, directionless quality of Marsh's life as commitment to improvisation as a guiding principle, in life as in music. He insisted to pianist Susan Chen, who first met him in 1974 and maintained a close relationship with him as student, friend, and colleague until his death, that improvisation was note to note, and in similar fashion, she thought, he lived his life from day to day. He was committed, she said, to spontaneity. At the recording session for *Posthumous,* later issued on LP as *Newly Warne,* she recalled that George Mraz asked, "So, Warne, what are we playing?" He answered, "I don't know." He disliked arrangements, worked-out introductions and endings, and even the process of establishing an order of solos.

He had what struck some, including his wife, Geraldyne, as a "cruel streak." Skip Scott recalled an interchange between Marsh and Lee Konitz's son Josh. Josh had studied bass and displayed talent, but had experienced personal problems and quit playing. When he said this to Marsh, Marsh responded dismissively, "Well, you know, some people just save it up forever," meaning presumably that Josh should just forget about his personal problems and get on with playing. Scott himself was still smarting from two painful experiences with Marsh. On one occasion, he had carried his drum set up to Marsh's room in Bretton Hall for a rehearsal only to hear Marsh say, in front of Scott's friends, "I'm going to stick with Taro [Okamoto]." Another time Scott rode on the train with Marsh to and from a gig in Washington, D.C. Scott, the product of a broken home, expressed to Marsh some of his feelings about growing up without a real father. Later he learned that Marsh had told mutual acquaintances that "he didn't want to work with me anymore because I had a father image of him." Marsh told Gary Foster that he didn't like it when students or younger players deferred too much to him.

In the spring of 1982 the *Saxophone Journal* published an interview with Marsh in which he expressed feelings about the racial division in jazz which do not appear with such clarity in any other interviews. Asked to comment on the influence of Miles Davis, Marsh said, "He always had the best band available. But then, so did Lennie. And that was different.

He was our own . . . it was just self-expression, as it still is. But the Black-White thing [relationship] is not what it used to be."

Whether the ellipsis after "he was our own" is Marsh's or the interviewer's or editor's cannot be determined, but it seems that Marsh is pointing out that Tristano was white and suggesting that the self-expression of whites and blacks is different. Or perhaps he meant that Tristano was as good as Davis but did not receive the appropriate recognition because he was white.

Pursuing "the Black-White thing," the interviewer asks if it is better or worse than it used to be. Marsh replies, "It is no longer any kind of marriage." The interviewer persists: "Are you the recipient of flack from some of the more politically-minded black fellows?" "No," says Marsh, "our paths just don't cross. They are somewhere else. I have to believe that they are capitalizing on their own history, without even understanding it. I don't like it. . . . I can't concern myself with it because I never did. It's not what brought me into music in the first place. It certainly wasn't for political or social reasons. It was for musical ones." To the interviewer's question, "But you now find that it plays a greater role in the scheme of things?" Marsh answers, "It does in their thinking."

This exchange indicates quite clearly that in this period Marsh felt himself, as Marcel Clemens and later Frank Canino observed, a victim of antiwhite bias in jazz. And his remark that Tristano was "our own" reinforces what Lee Konitz has suggested, that Tristano was consciously pursuing a line of development in jazz that he saw as "white," that is, as significantly influenced by European music from Bach to Stravinsky, Bartók, and Hindemith.

NOTES

1. This engagement was never listed or reviewed in *Down Beat*, apparently because the magazine was undergoing personnel changes. No listings of any kind for New York clubs were published between March 8 and September 6, 1979.

2. Mark Diorio, a student of Mosca's and Marsh's, thought that their first engagement at the Vanguard had Earl Sauls on bass and Skip Scott on drums, and that Canino and Pleasant played with them the second time. But Sauls said that the one time he played the Vanguard with Marsh and Mosca was in July or August of 1980, not 1979.

3. John S. Wilson, "Jazz: Quartet Revives Spirit of Tristano," *New York Times*, 1 September 1979, 10.

4. Source of this story is Lewis Porter, who was present.

5. Robert Palmer, "Warne Marsh: The Return of a Radical," *Rolling Stone*, March 20, 1980, 34.

6. Ted Brown, interview.

7. Elaine Russell, "Jazzing Up Area Music Scene," *Gannett Westchester Weekend*, 7 March 1980, 7. Also interviews with Mark Diorio, Judy Niemack, Jimmy Halperin, Tardo Hammer, Murray Wall, Dan Fiore, and Skip Scott.

8. Richard M. Sudhalter, "Warne Marsh Brings Sunshine to Tully," *New York Post*, 29 January 1980, 39.

9. Jon Balleras, "Warne Marsh," *Down Beat,* June 1987, 42–43.

10. Ibid.

11. The recording may have been broadcast over National Public Radio, and it may have been done by Michael Cuscuna, now of Mosaic Records.

12. Art Lange, "Caught!" *Down Beat,* November 1980, 54–55.

13. Ibid.

14. Crispin Cioe, review of "Pete Christlieb: Self Portrait," *High Fidelity/Musical America* (January 1982): 92–93.

15. Sal Mosca, interview.

Warne Marsh solo on "Of Love and Things" (based on the chords of "Body and Soul"),
recorded April 21, 1980, WARNE MARSH AND KENNY DREW TRIO, Storyville
STCD 8277 (also released as ORNITHOLOGY, Venus (J) TKCZ 79037), transcribed for
tenor saxophone by Safford Chamberlain and Gary Foster.

Analysis

ANALYSIS OF WARNE MARSH SOLO ON "OF LOVE AND THINGS" ("BODY AND SOUL") RECORDED WITH THE KENNY DREW TRIO, APRIL 21, 1980, *ORNITHOLOGY* (VENUS (J) TKCZ 79037), BY SAFFORD CHAMBERLAIN

From the beautifully simple sequence of rising scales in the first four bars, to the climactic 32nd note passages in bars 53–58, to the stately, triplet-slowed descent to the final cadenza, this improvised solo, relentless in its pursuit of fresh melody and selfless in its avoidance of mere technical display, is a masterful instance of jazz balladry.

One way of approaching it is to notice where Marsh takes his breaths. In sixty-four slow-tempo bars, complete with a ritard and cadenza at the end, he takes only twenty-four breaths. About half of these come after phrases of three or more bars, the two longest being four-and-one-half bars. His breath control in these long phrases is remarkable. It is not easy to think as melodically as he does if you are running out of breath.

The number of breaths he takes might seem a minor detail, but in fact it is a guide to his phrasal thinking. For example, his first breath comes after beat 1 of the 3rd bar, ending a phrase of three parallel scalar figures. After the breath another rising scalar figure leads to a sequence of triplet figures (bars 5–7). The next phrase begins with a transitional turnaround to bar 9, where a new sequence of paired 16th and dotted 8th notes emerges, carrying, with a phrase-ending variation, to the end of bar 10. There he takes another breath and begins a long four-and-a-half-bar phrase ending in another motivic sequence (bars 14–15).

It is interesting to note that in his later years Marsh voiced to a student, Paul Altman, his disagreement with what had become Tristanoite dogma, the contention that improvisation is note-to-note, not phrase-by-phrase. Doubtless the truth is that it is both, to varying degrees. But Marsh told Altman that the proof that it was phrase-by-phrase was in the breath: when you take a breath, he maintained, you take just enough to finish the phrase, which you must therefore have had in mind, or at least in the back of it. It could be argued equally well that one takes a breath simply because one needs it, and ends the phrase of necessity when the breath runs out. But whatever the logic of his argument, Marsh seems to have thought in phrases and taken his breaths accordingly. I do not think this means he knew every note he was going to play in a phrase in advance, but he may well have had an idea of its shape and length.

With a wind-instrument player, breaths and phrases are usually, but not necessarily, marked by rests. In this instance Marsh's first breath, marking the end of his first phrase, comes at the eighth-note rest in bar 4. But his second breath comes in the middle of beat 3 in bar 7, separating the triplet-centered phrase preceding it from the transition into bar 9, where without a breath he initiates a new motivic sequence.

To pursue this kind of analysis of breath-phrases through the entire solo would surfeit the reader in a mass of detail. But the interested reader can do it for himself or herself, by listening and reading the transcription, which includes breath marks. Such analytic listening can only deepen one's appreciation of Marsh's ability spontaneously to create at the same time fresh melody and original structure.

A caveat should perhaps be offered here for the reader who has the record at hand and is comparing it to the transcription. Written music is a kind of shorthand or code for what is actually played, and this is especially true of jazz. In particular, there are times here when Marsh plays so far behind the beat that it is difficult to hear where the downbeats fall. No attempt has been made to notate this "lag-along" characteristic on the page.

Criss Cross

Among Marsh admirers whose active interest compensated for Marsh's own career passivity in the 1980s, none was more important than Gerry Teekens. Of the twenty-some records featuring Marsh that eventually came out of that period, the four that Teekens produced for his Criss Cross label were among the only ones made for immediate release, and they were the only ones that received something like adequate distribution during Marsh's lifetime. The first two, especially, were major additions to the Marsh canon, and all four presented Marsh in refreshingly non-Tristanoite company.

The first came about in August of 1982 when Marsh visited Amsterdam to perform at the NOS Jazz Festival with Sal Mosca, Frank Canino, and Taro Okamoto. Teekens had just recently launched Criss Cross and was anxious to record Marsh, but he felt strongly that Marsh habitually surrounded himself with the wrong people, Mosca being one of them. Marsh himself, according to Teekens, was not eager to record again with Mosca. He had apparently begun to tire of Mosca's work at their last engagement at the Village Vanguard, remarking to Frank Canino, "Sal's playing that weird shit again," and telling Mosca that he had trouble following a Mosca solo on "All the Things You Are." He still, however, expressed a desire to record with some of his own students. Teekens diplomatically pointed out that while his students might be very fine players, their names would not help sell his records. As the Hank Jones Trio was also appearing at the festival, Teekens suggested, "How about using Hank?" Marsh's response, said Teekens, was, "Let me check him out."

Jones, universally recognized as a master of his craft, was nine years older than Marsh and had been active in bebop circles in New York in the mid-1940s when Marsh was still playing in youth bands in Hollywood, so that one would assume that Marsh knew his work. On the other hand, Jones was emphatically mainstream, far from the Tristano orbit, and it is entirely possible that Marsh, in his Tristano-influenced seclusion, was relatively unfamiliar with him. More likely, he had never seriously contemplated playing with him and merely wanted to listen to Jones with that in mind. Jones, for his part, was quite ignorant of Marsh's work except for his early records with Konitz and Tristano. When contacted for purposes of this book, he had little to say. Marsh did "check him out" at the festival, and the ultimate result was the *Star Highs* record with Jones on piano, George Mraz on bass, and Mel Lewis on drums. With the possible exception of Supersax, with whom he never recorded a solo, not since 1958 had Marsh recorded with so highly regarded a rhythm section, and only once before, for a record not then issued, had he recorded in a quartet setting with a black pianist, Kenny Drew.

They went into Teekens' studio on Saturday, August 14, two days after the Marsh-Mosca Quartet and Hank Jones Trio performed separately at the festival. With no rehearsal, the entire session required only four and a half hours, enough time for two takes of all seven titles except "Hank's Tune," a bluesy piece based on "Ja-Da" that required only one take. Marsh told Teekens it was "the best record I've made in the last twenty years." Jones, said Teekens, "was really crazy about Warne," asking where he had been all these years. And indeed the two seem a perfect match, both thinking melodically and lyrically, neither given to indulging in technical display for its own sake. Marsh was right in considering the record one of his best.

Contemporary reviews were sparse but laudatory. A. T. Tolley wrote in *Coda* that Marsh was "one of the finest white tenor saxophonists playing today. . . . With his warm, but slightly strangled tone, and his unusual intervals, Marsh reminds one of Stan Getz on 'Sweet Rain' (Verve). Lean and lyrical, he plays excitingly on every track. . . . This may be one of my records of the year. . . ."[1]

In a review for a Dutch publication, Wim Van Eyle praised the record as "fabulous." On "Hank's Tune" he finds Marsh "playing more down to earth than I ever heard him before. Tone and ideas are remarkable to hear for anyone who knows Marsh as a player out of the intellectualistic Tristano school."[2] Another Dutch writer, reviewing a Marsh-Lou Levy concert in 1983, felt that both the concert and the *Star Highs* album "confirmed the impression that the tenor saxophonist has switched from a rather academic approach of improvising towards a more emotional interpretation. . . ."[3] In 1985 a French reviewer wrote that Marsh, a "superb musician" who was among the most "valiant" of Tristano's followers, appeared in this session "completely at ease, maturing and affirming the design [style] that he had begun constructing with Konitz and Tristano—but the continuity is here the sign of authenticity."[4]

Mike Shera reviewed the CD reissue in *Jazz Journal* in 1990: "This is the CD version of an album that was never reviewed in its LP form. . . . [Hank] Jones has always been a fine accompanist, and he rises to the challenge of a more demanding soloist than he often works with these days. George Mraz and Mel Lewis are quite magnificent in the rhythm section. Marsh uses a variety of different sounds on this CD, from his familiar thin alto-like upper register, to a full-bodied sound that if not quite like Dexter Gordon, is a lot closer than anything I've heard previously from Marsh. This, together with his ceaselessly inventive imagination, never taking the obvious approach, makes for a highly enjoyable listening experience. . . . One for the 1990 top ten, I think."[5]

Eight months later, on April 7, 1983, while touring France, Holland, and England with pianist Lou Levy, Marsh made his second record for Criss Cross, *A Ballad Album*, with the fine European bassist Jesper Lundgaard and a little known drummer, James Martin. Lundgaard and Martin, recruited by Teekens for the Continental part of the tour, proved to be excellent choices for this exceptional record.

Reviewing the record for *Coda*, John Norris took the unusual approach of questioning the value of Tristano's influence. Although Tristano was almost always mentioned by critics, no one had ever explicitly voiced the opinion that his influence on Marsh may have been in some respects harmful. Norris does, focusing on Tristano's inclination to take an "art-for-art's sake" stance at the expense of audience appeal: "Warne Marsh's link with Lennie Tristano seems to have hindered rather than helped his career. Tristano's intellectual examination of jazz music's fundamentals often diminished his communication with an audience. . . . [In *A Ballad Album*] the delicate balance between sophisticated harmonic progressions and melodic statement is intertwined in such a manner that both musician and ordinary listener can respond to Marsh's interpretations of these outstanding standards. . . . Lou Levy's piano playing is completely in tune with Marsh's sensibilities and they have made, between them, one of the great ballad records of our time. This record deserves a place alongside similar projects by John Coltrane and Art Tatum/Ben Webster."[6]

A French reviewer, Jacques Reda, mentioning that he has heard the group on their tour at the New Morning club in Paris, praised the record as "perhaps the best disc by Warne Marsh in recent years. . . . It seems to me that there are some masterpieces here, among them How High the Moon, . . . by one of the greatest jazz musicians remaining to us."[7]

When the CD reissue came out in 1989, two years after Marsh's death, it was again highly praised. Mike Shera, long a Marsh admirer, wrote: "This music must rank with Marsh's finest achievements on record. Whilst he may lack the emotional and dynamic range of a Stan Getz, he plays these beautiful songs with great tenderness and sensitivity. . . . He has simplified his approach . . . without losing his uniquely oblique lines and sound."[8] Another reviewer found Marsh "no less creative . . . than he was [in his early days]. He still effortlessly twists phrases that would sound forced coming from other players. . . . Marsh plays these ballad selections as unhurriedly as if he had all the time in the world while each new phrase is pure spontaneous improvisation."[9] Jean-Pierre Moussaron praised the "perfect musical integrity" of the record, which contains "some of the most beautiful ballads in the jazz repertoire interpreted by a genius of the tenor saxophone, to whom justice has never been fully rendered. . . ."[10]

A Ballad Album is fully deserving of these accolades. As John Norris pointed out, it is far removed from Tristano-like intellectuality. Its melodic logic communicating directly to sophisticated and unsophisticated listeners alike, it is an elegant distillation of Marsh's profound harmonic understanding. The comparison with Getz is apt, not only in melodic directness but in a gentle, unironic approach to tone that is unique in Marsh's work. And pianist Levy, bassist Lundgaard, and even the little-known Martin complement Marsh beautifully, both in solo and ensemble. It is an inspired piece of work all around.

While in Holland, Marsh took a week to teach a master class at the Royal Conservatory in The Hague that Teekens says musicians there still rave about. From Holland, Marsh's itinerary took him to London for duo appearances with Levy at Pizza on the Park and Pizza Express.

The London duo performances received laudatory reviews, as was usual with English critics. In the *Times* Richard Williams wrote that on a Monday night at Pizza on the Park Marsh and Levy "redrew the parameters of an audience's attention with duets of such sensitive detail that even the brief rasp of a cigarette lighter or the gentle gurgle of liquor into a glass seemed barbaric intrusions. . . . Marsh's playing has scarcely changed at all in 30 years. His sound is unique: light, pale, pressureless, his astonishingly complex phrases extruded with a minimum of apparent effort. His lines are shaped with exotic unpredictability, yet their logic is so implacable that one gasps and grins as they unfold."[11]

About the performance the following night at Pizza Express another critic, Dave Gelly, wrote, "It's not seductive music; in fact it's quite hard going if you're intent on following everything, but the interplay of tenor saxophonist Warne Marsh and pianist Lou Levy rewards the persistent listener. The material upon which they build their improvisations has been common currency in jazz for decades—venerable old songs such as 'You

Stepped Out Of a Dream' and 'Limehouse Blues'—but the harmonies that underlie the tunes are sliding and treacherous, and it is in exploring them that Marsh and Levy demonstrate their mastery. Their performance at the Pizza On the Park on Tuesday night took the form of a dialogue, a conversation between two equally subtle intelligences. A phrase from one would send the other off on a new, complementary tack, a pattern of bewildering chromatic intricacy. But there was no sense of strain, because they seemed to read each other's minds." Gelly noted that "Marsh has always been an aloof, rather marginal figure. . . . He has cultivated a style that has never had much popular appeal, working mainly with a small coterie of like-minded players and sometimes dropping out of professional music-making altogether." On the rapport between Marsh and Levy, Gelly wrote, "The partnership showed itself at its peak in a performance of a number called 'Subconscious Lee,' a fiendishly intricate line based on the chords of 'What Is This Thing Called Love?' Without bass and drums to hold down the rhythms the whole thing threatened to collapse at any moment, but the players kept it aloft like a couple of master jugglers. If you managed to stay with them there was a gratifying sense of achievement at one remove."[12]

Marsh's next record for Criss Cross, *Blues for a Reason*, was made a year and a half later, September 30, 1984, when Marsh was in Holland for the Heinekens Jazz Festival in Rotterdam. For the festival Marsh's quartet consisted of Frank Canino, Tim Pleasant, and Susan Chen. For the recording, as on the *Star Highs* album, Teekens again separated Marsh from his usual cohorts and paired him with a big-name player, Chet Baker, along with Hod O'Brien on piano and black artists Cecil McBee, bass, and Eddie Gladden, drums.

Marsh himself was not happy with the session, grumbling about the way in which he, Baker, and the rhythm section were placed in separate rooms, wearing earphones but unable to see each other. Yet, while the record as a whole is not on the level of *Star Highs* and *A Ballad Album*, both Baker and Marsh are in fine form. On "Well Spoken" ("Speak Low") Baker combines strategically held long tones with crisp eighth-note passages to great effect in both the jointly improvised opening chorus and his own solo. Marsh begins his solo by echoing Baker's last phrase and proceeds in his customary fashion, developing motif after motif, seemingly stimulated by the lively backing of Gladden and McBee. On "We Know It's Love" ("What Is This Thing Called Love") Marsh discovers in his first chorus a rising six-note figure at the end of the bridge that he repeats or echoes four more times at different places in the song, providing a spontaneous unity to his solo. On the title tune the contrast between Marsh's and Baker's approach to the blues is striking. Baker sounds at home and at ease, feeling himself part of the tradition. Marsh's sound, note selection, and phrasing, however, seem alien to the blues; there is something jagged, prickly, introspective, that does not fit the idiom. Otherwise both horn players play well throughout, and the excellent improvised counterpoint on several tunes reveals Baker's affinity for this important aspect of the Tristano esthetic, one shared by the Gerry Mulligan group in which Baker got his start.

The few reviewers who gave the record their attention found much to praise. Mike Shera was especially taken by "the superb playing of Baker—the best record by him I have come across since *Once Upon A Summertime*." He found Marsh "not quite up to his very best form—but that's still better than most tenor players today."[13] John Norris also was impressed by Baker's playing—"his solos are among the most fluent he has recorded in recent years"—but the record as a whole, although containing rewarding moments, "doesn't hold together in the same kind of way that the *Ballad [Album]* date [did] . . . and it doesn't match Marsh's collaboration with Pete Christlieb a few years back."[14]

A reviewer for *Cadence*, noting that this was the first time that Marsh had recorded with a trumpet player as his sole front line partner in "an orthodox bop quintet," commended the way in which "the very tensions inherent in Baker's brittle melodic invention are released through Marsh's floating rhythmicity.[15] Thus, this is both beautiful and healing music."[16] A French reviewer praised Marsh as "an improviser who always surprises with his art of eschewing cliches." Baker and Marsh, he wrote, were similar in "their fondness for the pleasing and the well made, their sensitivity in counterpoint, [and] their taste for harmonically demanding standards," and though Marsh tended to intellectualize his emotions, he was, like Baker, "a remarkable communicator."[17]

Marsh was to make one more record, *Back Home*, for Criss Cross. Unlike the first three, it was a lackluster affair, in part because of his insistence on using one of his favorite students (Jimmy Halperin). But it was mainly Gerry Teekens, through the Criss Cross releases, who kept the Warne Marsh of the 1980s in view of the record-buying public.

NOTES

1. A. T. Tolley, review, *Coda*, No. 194 (February 1, 1984): 36–37.

2. Wim Van Eyle, "De LP Starhighs," *Jazz Freak* (n.d.): 143. Photocopies of this and the following review by Gjus Tra and a partial translation by an unknown person were among Marsh's papers.

3. Gjus Tra, "Geinspireerde solo's by Warne Marsh Kwartet," *NRC/Handelsblad*, March 3, 1983, n.p.

4. "Warne Marsh," *Jazz Magazine* (Paris), No. 341, July-August 1985, 50. My translation.

5. Mike Shera, "Warne Marsh: Star Highs," *Jazz Journal* (July 1990): 33–34.

6. John Norris, "The Tenor Sax," *Coda*, October 1, 1985, 12–13.

7. Jacques Reda, "Warne Marsh," *Jazz Magazine* (Paris), No. 339, May 1985, 45. My translation.

8. Mike Shera, "Warne Marsh," *Jazz Journal* (October 1989): 33.

9. Paul Matthews, review of *A Ballad Album*, *Cadence* (October 1989): 23.

10. Jean-Pierre Moussaron, *Jazz Magazine* (Paris), No. 383, July-August 1989, 46. My translation.

11. Richard Williams, "Relaxed Intensity," the *Times*, 13 April 1983, n.p.

12. Dave Gelly, "Fine Focus," publication unknown, c. 12 April 1983, 31.

13. Mike Shera, review of *Blues for a Reason, Jazz Journal* (January 1986): 21.

14. John Norris, "The Tenor Saxophone," *Coda,* October 1, 1985, 12–13.

15. However, Marsh reportedly recorded in a quintet setting with trumpeter Rolf Erickson in an as yet unreleased record for Mode in 1957.

16. Anon., review of *Blues for a Reason*, *Cadence* (October 1985): 69–70.

17. Jean-Louis Genibre, "Les Disques du Mois," *Jazz Magazine* (Paris), No. 347, February 1986, 21. My translation.

Singing Love Songs

For Marsh the years 1982–87 were a rollercoaster of highs and lows, both artistically and personally. The highs were a series of European tours, the first three Criss Cross records, two high-profile engagements with Hank Jones at the Village Vanguard, laudatory articles by two of the most eminent jazz critics in America, and his love affair with Susan Chen. The lows were cocaine addiction, the breakup of his marriage, and, from an artistic standpoint, his love affair with Susan Chen.

Marsh had long been a user of cocaine, as he confessed to a doctor shortly before his death in 1987. By the fall of 1982, perhaps long before, recreational use had apparently passed over into addiction. Around September 5, having just returned from Europe and the *Star Highs* session of August 14, he arrived in Chicago for the Kool Jazz Festival looking ravaged and emaciated. "I was stunned when I saw him," said Harriet Choice, "because I thought he was dying of cancer." She learned that the cause was coke, not cancer. When she told him, after the concert, how awful he looked, he said, "But how do I sound?" "Fantastic," she told him. Lawrence Kart said as much in his review for the *Chicago Tribune*, describing Marsh's playing as "simply sublime. . . . [He] repeatedly surpassed himself, producing a solo on 'I'm Old Fashioned' of such musing grace that one could scarcely believe it had been improvised."[1]

Marsh's domestic relations had already begun to disintegrate. In March 1982 he had begun spending the entire week, from Monday through Friday, at his Bretton Hall studio in Manhattan, going home to Geraldyne and his two young sons in Ridgefield, Connecticut, only on weekends. Geraldyne had begun to suspect the presence of other women in Marsh's

234

life. She particularly suspected a liaison with a singer and student of his who frequented Bretton Hall. She found phone calls to this singer on their telephone bill, and once, in the summer of 1982, she found in his studio an unsigned note of thanks for a "wonderful time." Marsh told her he had loaned the room to someone else and that the note was the other person's. "It's all in your head," he insisted. With Marsh spending most of his time at Bretton Hall and increasingly remote when he did come home, she began drinking, and one night, apparently after Marsh's return from the Chicago festival, ended up in the psychiatric ward of the local hospital following what looked like, but she insisted wasn't, an attempted suicide.

"I felt so isolated, so alone," she said. "He let me know I couldn't talk to him, it was not his problem. There were always drugs around, pills. I was drinking vodka and I took some Valium and I don't remember what happened. I called Mickey [Silverman] and I was crying, maybe I passed out when she was talking to me. I didn't set out to do that, I just kept doing it so I wouldn't feel anything, but I didn't say, 'I want to kill myself.' I don't remember anything till the hospital. They pumped my stomach, they said I was very close to death."

The Silvermans had called the police, who had come to the house and found Geraldyne unconscious. Shortly after she got out of the hospital, Marsh took her to a club in Manhattan to hear the singer whom she suspected, telling Geri she couldn't drink because "you can't handle it." The whole experience, she felt, was "a slap in the face."

By October of 1982 Marsh had decided they should live separately. As Geraldyne recounted, "He just said, 'I want us to separate for while. I want you and the boys to go the California. I'm going to stay here in New York and try to get some work together and get enough money so we can have a home and all be together again as a family.' It was all bullshit, he was just crazy, very cruel." In October the family, Marsh included, flew to Los Angeles and from there three hundred miles north to Santa Cruz in order to relocate Geraldyne and their two sons, Casey and Jason, with Geraldyne's mother and stepfather there.

On Marsh's return to Los Angeles, another of the fortuitous coincidences that governed much of his professional life occurred. He was contacted by Toshiko Akiyoshi to do a record with Gary Foster for Eastwind, a Japanese company. Akiyoshi had originally intended to record Lee Konitz with Foster, who was a regular member of her and husband Lew Tabackin's Los Angeles-based big band, but she could not fit Konitz's fee into her budget. When Foster told her that Marsh happened to be in town and suggested him as a substitute, Akiyoshi, long a Marsh admirer, quickly agreed. At first she suggested some of the early Marsh-Konitz repertoire, such as "Wow" and "Sax of a Kind," but Foster, who acknowledges Konitz as a major influence, felt that there was no point in recreating something that was "so perfectly recorded before." In the end he and Marsh did three lesser-known Tristano lines not associated with Konitz: "Ablution" ("All the Things You Are"), "Victory Ball" ("S'Wonderful"), and "All about You" ("How about You"), plus the Miles Davis blues "Sippin' at Bell's," Clifford Brown's "Joy Spring," Tadd Dameron's "If You Could See Me Now" (which they retitled "You Should See Me"), and "'D' Pending" ("How Deep Is the Ocean").

The rhythm section was Foster's working group at the time: Alan Broadbent, piano; Peter Donald, drums; and Pat "Putter" Smith, bass. Smith recalled that during the recording session, while the others were listening to a playback, Marsh asked him, "Are you going to play with me?" It was the only personal contact he and Marsh, who had been close in earlier years, had at the session, and Smith interpreted it as an invitation to play more spontaneously. "I was dealing with my own problems as a bass player. I wasn't having a great day. When you play it safe you're sort of on the outside of things, and my assumption was he understood that and he was inviting me to come in." Smith got the impression that Marsh did not particularly care for Donald's drumming.

The album, recorded October 12 and 14, 1982, and released as *Warne Marsh Meets Gary Foster*, garnered few reviews. It was, nevertheless, a thoroughly professional effort, even if it does not have the élan of the records with Kenny Drew and Hank Jones. Marsh and Foster expertly handle the three intricate Tristano lines, and beginnings and endings reflect Akiyoshi's concern for presentation values. Marsh's strikingly individual phrasing, note selection, and unique sound are in sharp contrast with Foster's and Broadbent's more orthodox styles, but all have their moments. Foster is especially spirited and swinging on "Victory Ball," while Broadbent stands out on "Joy Spring" and "'D' Pending." Marsh is at his eccentric best on "Victory Ball," 'D' Pending," and "All about You," where his solo includes a quote from Lester Young's "Jumpin' with Symphony Sid."

After the recording session Marsh returned to New York and his teaching schedule. David Frank, a clarinetist and alto saxophonist who had been studying with Marsh while completing medical school to become a psychiatrist, remembered that Marsh looked depressed after returning from California, and that there was one lesson when a red-eyed Marsh appeared to have been crying. He returned to California briefly to visit his family in Santa Cruz at Christmas.

Among those present at the Eastwind session had been Susan Chen, then living in Los Angeles. Shortly afterward she moved back to New York, where she and Marsh entered into a love affair that was to have manifold consequences for his career.

The consequences at first appear to have been happy ones. Although it is pure speculation, the temptation to attribute the tender lyricism of *A Ballad Album*, recorded April 7, 1983, to his feelings for Chen is well nigh irresistible. This is so not only because it coincides with the beginning of their affair, or even because the album is so atypical in Marsh's recorded output, but also because it coincides with a new emphasis in Marsh's teaching on the importance of learning to sing the lyrics of a song.

One of the first of Marsh's instrumental students to receive this emphasis was the accomplished young guitarist John Klopotowski. A graduate student at the State University of New York at Stonybrook, Long Island, Klopotowski had studied and played with Thad Jones before apprenticing himself to Sonny Dallas. Dallas introduced him to the music of Lennie Tristano and his circle, and Klopotowski became an instant convert. He first heard Marsh live, with Sal Mosca, at the Village Vanguard in November 1981, and he described the performance as "one of the greatest hunks of music I ever heard." He spoke to Dallas of possibly studying with Marsh, whom Dallas considered "the greatest living improviser." After continuing with Dallas for several months, at his last lesson he sang Tristano's solo on "Line Up" for him. "You're ready," said Dallas.

Klopotowski's first lesson with Marsh was in March 1982, at his studio in Bretton Hall. It was the first week, he learned, that Marsh had begun spending the whole week, Monday through Friday, at Bretton Hall, instead of just three days a week as before. "Sonny still playing Fender [electric bass]?" asked Marsh. "He'd never play that thing with Lennie." After hearing Klopotowski play "You Stepped out of a Dream" and sing "Line Up," Marsh told him, "You're good, you don't have to study, but if you do there's a place for you to go. The only thing is, if you go there, you can't come back. That's what you have to think about for your next lesson."

Klopotowski had been fascinated by the rhythmic displacement he heard in the music of Marsh, Mosca, and Tristano, and for the next eight months Marsh systematically took him through the polyrhythmic exercises he had imbibed from Tristano. Marsh told him he had never taught this material to anyone else, not even Susan Chen. When they had worked through it, Marsh said, "You got it?" Klopotowski nodded. "Never play it again," said Marsh. The idea was to have the material available on a spontaneous basis but not to use it as something preprogramed.

Shortly after appearing with Klopotowski, Dallas, and Skip Scott at a concert February 7, 1983, at State University of New York at Stonybrook, Marsh dismissed Klopotowski as a student, feeling he had nothing else to teach him. "Now it's up to you," he said. "You can do whatever you want now. You're finished." But six months later, after touring Europe and

recording *A Ballad Album*, when Klopotowski inquired about studying
with him again, Marsh told him, "There's only one thing left to do: sing
love songs. Come in next week able to sing a standard, with the words."
"Have you done this?" Klopotowski asked. "It's the final piece of work,"
said Marsh. "It's the most recent work I've done."

He had been living with Chen when not on tour, and "singing love
songs" seems a perfect metaphorical description of his playing on *A Ballad Album*. But he was being literal, not simply metaphorical, in his advice to Klopotowski, who spent the next six months learning the words
to the standards in his repertoire, listening to Marsh-approved vocalists
like Frank Sinatra, and making tapes of himself singing. On the benefits
of the approach, he said, "I learned how to play the melody, and I learned
that there's a meaning to this stuff that's beyond the notes, beyond technique. I learned there's some kind of message, and it's basically about
love." One week he became aware of the problem of audience: "All week
I was saying to myself, 'Who am I singing to? Me, my wife, my mother?'"
When he went for his lesson, Marsh, with eerie perceptivity, remarked,
"You have to think who you're singing *to*, man."

According to Chen, Marsh himself actually knew the words to only a
few songs. After singing "A Foggy Day" and "The Song Is You" for her,
he had confessed, "You've exhausted my repertoire." Together they rehearsed Dave Frishberg's "Wheelers and Dealers," planning that Marsh
would sing it at the New Morning club in Paris during their upcoming
European tour in the spring of 1984.

In the summer and fall of 1983, at about the same time he launched
Klopotowski on his course of singing love songs, Marsh, prodded by Chen
out of his usual reluctance to approach others not in the Tristano orbit,
renewed his association with Hank Jones. The pair played at the Village
Vanguard in July with George Mraz on bass and Bobby Durham on drums
and again in October, with Tim Horner replacing Durham.

The October performance elicited an important review by *Village Voice*
critic Stanley Crouch. Crouch titled his piece, rather pejoratively, "The
Swan and the Odd Duck," Jones being the elegant swan and Marsh the
odd duck. But despite the headline, Crouch was warmly appreciative of
Marsh's work. Marsh's association with Tristano, he wrote, "led to his
being pigeonholed as a coldhearted and unswinging oddball. But even
those highly critical of the Tristano school often commend Konitz and
Marsh as white saxophone players with original ideas." Among players
influenced by Marsh, he stated, were Wayne Shorter and "the many
younger saxophonists taken by [Shorter's] work with Miles Davis from
the 1965 *Live at the Plugged Nickel. . . .*" Referring to Marsh's work on *The
Art of Improvising* (Revelation 22), Crouch wrote that on that record "the
Marsh of 1959 can be heard messing with areas Shorter would later per-

sonalize in his own pursuit of fresh harmonies and phrasing." Crouch preferred Marsh's playing at the earlier Vanguard appearance in July, with Bobby Durham on drums, feeling that Marsh was then "at his elusive best." But although in the October appearance "Marsh didn't play with his usual oblique unpredictability, . . . his accommodations to conventional bar-lines hardly lacked conviction. The swing of his playing has never been more directly stated and the linear plasticity of his motific variations glowed. At heart, Marsh's music is one of subtle joy and noble concerns that are most clearly aristocratic as he shifts from fervor to elevation by working retards into double-timed passages. On an Ellington song, Marsh did a dazzling chromatic reconstruction of the melody's opening phrases and even worked through 'Sonnymoon for Two' with a startling affection for the sidewalk." Crouch ended his piece by noting that "Marsh has spoken of using Billy Higgins someday [on drums]. If that happens, another band thick with originality and experience will loom on the scene."[2]

Crouch's suggestion that Marsh was an influence on Wayne Shorter is intriguing. Shorter, contacted for purposes of this book, acknowledged that Marsh was one of his favorite saxophonists but declined to elaborate, saying only, "That's all I'm going to say." As for Billy Higgins, Marsh clearly admired him and had spoken of using him before, but as before, it never happened.

A few days before the October Vanguard gig, Marsh had sent to Geraldyne in Santa Cruz two notarized documents that are evidence of a deep sense of marital responsibility, paradoxical because a year earlier he had basically abandoned his family and was now living with Susan Chen. Even before the separation Marsh, who had left the rearing of his children and often the procuring of a living to Geraldyne, had often been, in spirit if not in fact, a husband and father in absentia—stoned on his daily intake of pot, spending his time practicing in his studio or jamming with students and friends, devoting himself always to his music first.

But on October 14, 1983, he wrote to Geraldyne: "Dear Geri, Here are two documents meant to insure that you receive half of my fathers' [*sic*] trust whether I am living or not. You remember the trust says that if I am deceased the money goes to my children, but I want you to have a legal claim to half of it." The document giving Geraldyne "title and full rights to one half of my fathers' [*sic*] trust money" is "binding whatever our marital status." The other document, addressed "To the Court, or Trust Officer, or whomever it may concern," directs Geraldyne to present the document to the Trust Officer "for the purpose of overriding the abhorent [*sic*] condition whereby my sons receive every thing, and she nothing." It continues: "I direct the trust officer to either redistribute my inheritance himself—one half to my wife, one quarter to each of the two boys—or to assist my wife in any court action she may have to take to secure what I feel is rightfully hers; If my brother's and sister's influence is necessary I implore them to use it."

This letter was never to serve a legal function, as Marsh's mother, who had steadfastly refused to relinquish control of his father's trust, outlived him by three years, dying in 1990. The letter remains in Geraldyne's possession.

Early in 1984 Marsh and Chen embarked for Europe, his Dutch friend, record-producer Gerry Teekens, having arranged a short tour with Frank Canino and Tim Pleasant.[3] The tour began with two nights at the New Morning club in Paris, where Marsh had planned to make his vocal debut singing Dave Frischberg's "Wheelers and Dealers." Whether out of stage fright or, as he claimed, because of a sore throat, he did not sing, but Chen said she taped him playing clarinet, an almost equally rare occurrence. After Paris the group presumably also played venues in the Netherlands where Teekens had contacts. Marsh and Chen continued to Norway, where Torgrim Sollid and his friends had arranged bookings (discussed in the next chapter).

After Marsh and Chen returned to the states in the spring of 1984, Marsh played the weekend of May 18 at the West End Café. He had begun playing there the latter part of 1983. His different quartets included Klopotowski and another talented youngster, Randy Johnston, on guitar, the Russian trumpeter Valerie Ponomarev, Nat Reeves and Steve LaSpina on bass, and Earl Williams, Tim Horner, and Curtis Boyd on drums. On four occasions at the West End, half-hour sets were broadcast over WKCR-FM, emceed by Phil Schaap.[4]

The West End was near his Bretton Hall studio, and he enjoyed hanging out there with Schaap. An extremely knowledgeable jazz disc jockey for WKCR who also booked the West End, Schaap grew up as a neighbor of Lennie Tristano's on Palo Alto Street in Hollis. At one point he introduced Marsh to some recently reissued Chu Berry records. Berry had never made it onto Tristano's short list of preferred masters, but Marsh, said Schaap, was appreciative of what he heard.

During a taxicab ride to the West End with Torgrim Sollid, in New York for a visit, Marsh suddenly and without any introduction said that he had a student who was a psychiatrist and that this student had suggested that he might profit from some psychotherapy. "What do you think?" he asked. Sollid, who had a background in psychology and special education and had worked with psychiatric patients for many years, responded as a trained clinician, stressing that the decision was Marsh's and should be independent of the views of others. Recalled Sollid, "After a long pause Warne said, as if to himself, 'Maybe it's all connected with dope.'"

Marsh's romantic relationship with Chen had begun to encounter difficulties. On their arrival in Norway earlier that year, Chen had told Sollid that it was over. Still, said Sollid, despite what Chen had told him, "It was very touching to see them together, I mean 'the magic light' around people in love." After their tour they had asked him "to arrange for both of them to live in Norway for a while, to play and teach." If their love affair was over, their friendship was not.

However, they apparently had a falling out shortly after returning from Norway, when Marsh abruptly left New York for Los Angeles after playing at the West End. But two or three months later he returned to New York, and in the late summer of 1984 Chen again accompanied him, Canino, and Tim Pleasant to Europe to play the New Morning club and the Heinekens Festival. At the New Morning they received word of drummer Shelly Manne's death on September 26. The news, said Chen, moved Marsh to tears. Staying at the home of Francois Poudras, the benefactor of Bud Powell, Marsh was told by Poudras that Bill Evans considered him his favorite saxophonist.

While in Rotterdam for the festival, Marsh made the record with Chet Baker for Criss Cross, *Blues for a Reason.* After the festival he and Chen proceeded to Oslo, where Sollid had arranged for four concert appearances with himself, Ole Jacob Hansen on drums, and Olaf Kamfjord on bass.

Back in New York by mid-October 1984, Marsh conferred with his friend Toshiya Taenaka about future albums on Taenaka's Interplay label. A typed memo among his papers titled "Future Album Project," probably drawn up by Taenaka, lists proposed personnel for various projects. A quartet album was to be recorded "around January 1985 in L.A." with drummer Billy Higgins, bassist Charlie Haden, and pianist Mike Wofford. Taenaka's idea was to do a tribute to Lester Young, but Marsh was hesitant and suggested simply a collection of standards. A trio date with Higgins and bassist George Mraz was tentatively scheduled for "May (in New York) 1985," and a duo date with either Higgins, Mraz, Hank Jones, Lou Levy, or an unnamed guitarist for "May or Aug 1985." Also mentioned was a solo saxophone album.

Though Taenaka or Marsh may have briefly mentioned these possibilities to Haden, Higgins, and Wofford, no serious discussions ever took place with them, and only one of the players mentioned, George Mraz, appeared on any of the six albums Marsh made in 1985–87. He did record some unissued solo tapes for Interplay.

Since May, Torgim Sollid had proceeded with the arrangements for Marsh and Chen to live and work in Norway. "Warne and I set up a contract concerning renting my studio on a part-time basis. We made all the needed agreements with the Norwegian Musicians Union and the State Foreign Department. The possibilities for Warne to have a more or less stable post as a teacher in different conservatories were examined, and the results were promising. It was obvious that he really wanted to do this, and he put quite a lot of work in this effort. We also made contact with some booking people to arrange for various kinds of work throughout Scandinavia. Suddenly, in the beginning of March 1985, he called me and told me to halt the whole process. At that point we had started the final talks with the immigration authorities, and a couple of flats had been inspected for renting. He gave me no reason for his decision."

Marsh's unexplained decision may or may not have reflected a new stage of his and Chen's relationship. Their close friendship, however, continued as before, along with Marsh's sponsorship of her career. She made her recorded debut on Marsh's next album for Interplay, recorded March 15, 1985, at Vanguard Studio in New York City. Others on the date were Mraz and the rising young drummer Akira Tana. The record was not issued until 1989, over a year after Marsh's death in December 1987, and there were two different versions. Taenaka, who earlier had produced the *How Deep, How High* and *Warne Out* albums, released it under the title *Posthumous* on Interplay, and it also appeared as *Newly Warne* on Storyville. This unusual occurrence was the result of some confused dealings between Taenaka, the Art Union Group in Japan, and Storyville, which, according to Taenaka, acquired the material from Art Union. The first eight tracks on both CDs are the same, except that "What Is This?" is titled "Things Called Love" on *Posthumous*. The ninth track on *Newly Warne* is "On a Slow Boat to China," which does not appear on *Posthumous*. Instead the latter includes two alternate takes.

Marsh's playing continues the radically simplified, emotionally direct, lyrical mode he had perfected on *A Ballad Album*. There are none of the patterns on scales or chords so common in the work of other players over the previous thirty years, and none of the unfeeling intellectuality for which he and others of the Tristano school had often been criticized in the early years. His understanding of his material is so complete that he is free to think purely melodically, and his originality is such that each version of a tune sounds completely new. *Posthumous* contains two versions of "My Romance" and three of "Stella by Starlight," under different titles. The original melody is never stated, and the improvised melodies that Marsh superimposes on the chord structure are so different and so fresh that one hardly realizes they are variations of the same song.

Chen displays some of the promise that Marsh must have heard, playing with singing tone, precise articulation, and occasional grace, especially on "Inside Out," one of the versions of "My Romance." On her blues line, "Emperor's Old Clothes," she handles the idiom with competence. However, here and elsewhere she plays with more than a hint of the classically trained, even-eighth-note stiffness that dogged some Tristano disciples and that would unfortunately be more evident on her duo records with Marsh.

Some of the generally laudatory reviews are tinged with an elegiac impulse to speak well of the dead, as with Alan Bargebuhr's review of the *Posthumous* LP for *Cadence:* "The word that serves as title for this LP clangs with boreal ferocity in the heart. We know the Jazz life exacts its toll and may only blink when a Warne Marsh 'crashes' out at age 60. . . . And the past is summoned by this lovely, but slightly ruptured, program of varied Marshland tracks. The very near perfect jostles the puzzlingly incomplete. What really happened at this session? Had Marsh not departed, would all or any of it have emerged from his gloomy vault? . . . What if Interplay had not been reactivated?. . . But even though these final tracks ["Beautiful Love Fades Out" and "Turn Out the Night"] quit without warning, the disc contains quite enough evidence of the imperishable achievement of one of the music's most thoughtfully resolute improvisers."[5]

A similar elegiac tone colors reviews by Chuck Berg and David Liebman. Marsh, says Berg, was a "singular talent whose sophisticated linear and harmonic twists, however complex, were always delivered with an aura embodying the quintessence of integrity in pursuit of artistic truth." The performance is "superbly interactive," the music "imbued with great passion and warmth, and the indelible signature sound of the singular Warne Marsh."[6] Liebman, himself a top-level jazz saxophonist, notes that "the influence of Lester Young, and by association, Stan Getz, are . . . clearly evident. . . . Marsh literally weaves in and out of the changes, rarely stating the normal eighth-note lines commonly associated with bebop time. Somehow, the two soloists defy the law of gravity, and . . . still manage to keep the music alive rhythmically. . . . This is an important document, tracing an important saxophonist who was one of the main representatives of a very unique approach to jazz improvisation."[7]

Barry McRae was warmly appreciative of Chen, "an imaginative soloist who never takes the easy option and her oblique examination of Things Called Love will please all listeners." Still, "it is the stunning playing of Marsh that really matters."[8]

A lone dissenter with regard to Marsh's performance was Mike Shera, an attentive and usually highly commendatory listener who, though unimpressed by Marsh, had high praise for Chen: "I would not put [the album] in the same class [as *Star Highs* and *A Ballad Album*]. The lines do not flow so effortlessly, and from time to time they are mundane. Listen to [Marsh's] opening solo on Parisian Thoroughfare, for example. . . . Most of the good things on this album come from the talented hands of Susan Chen on piano, and the rhythm section. . . . She has little trouble outshining her somewhat lacklustre leader."[9]

In April 1985 Marsh made one of his frequent visits to Los Angeles, booked by veteran promoter and record producer Ozzie Cadena at the Silver Screen Room of the Sunset Hyatt Hotel with fellow Los Angeles saxophonist Harold Land and a rhythm section of Art Hillery, piano; Albert "Tootie" Heath, drums; and Bob Maize, bass. The performance elicited an unusually sympathetic review from Leonard Feather in the *Los Angeles Times*: "The two had never worked together before, yet an immediate rapport was established. . . . Common ground was established through such war horses as 'I Love You' and 'Star Eyes,' with Land's full-throated, probing lines squaring off effectively against Marsh's less resonant sound and subtle phrasing. . . . Both saxophonists shone on the closing 'Oleo' at a challenging tempo. The tenor solos were gems, so well constructed that one wished Jon Hendricks could have been on hand to set lyrics to them. In general, the interaction between these two strongly personal stylists worked out to their mutual benefit. Sweet are the uses of maturity."[10]

Marsh and Chen's musical relationship climaxed on June 17 and December 24, 1985, when they recorded their first duo efforts at Music Box Recording Studio in Los Angeles, and January 14, 1986, when a third session took place at Classic Sound Productions Studio in New York. Their first duo album, *Warne Marsh/Susan Chen,* drew entirely on the New York date except for one track, "Skylark," which came from the June session in Los Angeles. Issued by Taenaka's Interplay in early 1986, the album was a radical departure not only from standard bebop procedures but also from Marsh's earlier duo recordings with Sal Mosca.

With Mosca, on the album *How Deep, How High,* although there were passages of joint improvisation in which the two interacted contrapuntally, each soloist had his own solo space in which the other played a secondary role. With Chen the dominant conception on most tracks is one of radical equality, with each player as much in the lead as the other, both in effect soloing simultaneously.

Chen does not come off well in this situation, in my opinion. Her time is stiff and mechanical, and her phrasing lacks variety. She does not know how to use space, sometimes pounding out chords on every beat. The most successful tracks are the more conventional ones, where she and Marsh trade off the lead while the other either accompanies or lays out. A prime example is "Skylark," where Chen plays a lovely rubato first chorus and Marsh enters as the lead voice for most of the second chorus. Other examples are "It's You," where Chen plays a single-note line as counterpoint to Marsh's lead, "Always," "Another You," and "This Be Love." One of the problems, perhaps, is the brevity of all the tracks, none being more than four minutes and many less than three. Combined with the rhythmic monotony of Chen's conception, the short tracks make for a heavy dose of sameness when one listens to the album as a whole. One might find a single track refreshingly different from the usual bebop fare, but fifteen tracks in a row become tiresome.

The problem is more pronounced on the second album, *Ballad for You*, which consists of originally rejected outtakes from the two Los Angeles sessions on June 17 and December 24, 1985. This album was the result of discussions between Marsh and Taenaka concerning the considerable amount of money the latter had lost on earlier releases and his present financial straits. According to Taenaka, in late 1987 Marsh listened again to the outtakes, chose the tunes to be included, and gave permission for release of *Ballad for You*, which was issued early in 1988. Because Art Union was in poor financial condition and undergoing bankruptcy proceedings, only about five hundred records were made and distributed.

The critics took a surprisingly (to me) favorable view of the *Warne Marsh/Susan Chen* album. Victor Schonfield, usually one of Marsh's most perceptive British admirers, had no reservations, appreciating both the unusual conception and the execution: "Nobody ever made an LP like this, dedicated to two-part contrapuntal improvisation on standards by a duo of piano and tenor. . . . [Marsh plays with] a floating simplicity and freshness hitherto found only in the best Lester Young. . . . Parts of *Summer Morning, Summer Evening* and *Marvelous Words* are among the most inspired things this great improviser has ever done. . . ." As to Chen, Schonfield comments that "Tristano-influenced pianists these days normally adopt the harshness of his late period, but Chen's cheerful temperament reflects the younger Lennie and his own influences, Art Tatum and I suppose J. S. Bach. Her most impressive achievement is a spirited chorus on *This Be Love* that pierces right to the heart of vintage Tatum, but though elsewhere she is more diffuse, she certainly keeps the session alive and helps make it one of the most notable of Marsh's career."[11]

Alan Bargebuhr was even more rhapsodic: the album is "billowingly melodic, as piano and tenor soar and glide on currents of their own design. . . . The music flows naturally. The music is full-hearted and warming. The music seems to cleanse the air it occupies and bring the surrounding world into sharper focus. The inspiration and delight of creation is communicated. . . . [On "Skylark"] Chen's serenely unequivocal touch summons Hoagy's fabled bird of singing flight, and when, after her fervent invocation, Marsh enters, you know he is that bird."[12]

Similarly, Jon Balleras's brief mention in *Downbeat* contained only praise: the album is "a rigorous exploration of the seemingly endless permutations of one fixed idea. . . . 14 [actually 15, one title being omitted from the liner notes] short, gem-like tracks. . . . Marsh's tone is dry, with long, smooth breathsweeps sliding through these elaborate games in which the dancers do indeed become the dance."[13]

A significant feature of this album is that Marsh, for the first time in his career, wrote the liner notes. He begins with what, as a player, he would usually avoid like the plague, a cliche, and an embarrassingly corny one at that: "Some people 'play Jazz.' Personally, I let jazz play me." By way of elaboration, he credits his major influences: "I abandon myself to influences whose love of music and generosity of spirit—Lester Young, Charlie Parker, Lennie Tristano and a few others—lead me throughout my career." He disavows "any need to impose technical prowess or vast stores of information, or"—in an allusion to the black cultural nationalism of the 1960s and 1970s and the lingering antiwhite bias in jazz—"social (or political) sentiments on music. I've felt caught in a welter of attitudes and I've been missing the clean pure spirit of the musicians who drew me into jazz in the first place."

There follows a statement of the universality of music, its ability to bring people together, and a dismissal of those who would place their individual egos above universality: "There's a force in music that unites people and draws them into the musical experience, a total willingness to be in time and in harmony with another mortal; and how simple it really is; and it amuses me to watch people struggle to maintain their precious personal identity and in so doing lose the very quality that draws the listener to jazz in the first place, that feeling of a shared experience." But although the ego is to be submerged in the universal, one can find one's personal way into the universal without egotistical clamoring for attention: "There is such a thing as a universal sense of time—the musical sense. The imitative mind has to assume someone else's sense of time, and in so doing avoids that primary musical responsibility of discovering its own way through melody and structure." In other words, the problem of jazz improvisation is to express one's individuality in terms that are universal without being caught up in either imitation or egoistic display. Marsh also seems to see one's sense of time, perhaps in both musical and metaphysical senses, as central to the project of bringing together the individual and the universal.

That Marsh believed Chen, "my fellow musician in these duets, has divined that unique sense of time that allows for sharing, and that we call musical," is probably attributable to his personal relationship with her. Although Marsh told John Klopotowski that Chen was the finest jazz pianist since Tristano, reviewers of her albums with him, her only albums so far, generally tended to express encouragement for her continuing development rather than hail her in superlative terms.

Marsh's loyalty to Chen as a musician was steadfast. From 1985 through 1987 he appeared several times at the Silver Screen Room at the Sunset Hyatt Hotel in Hollywood, where Ozzie Cadena booked him with groups including Harold Land, Tal Farlow, and, at least once, Chen. Bob Maize was the bassist for one night of an engagement with Chen. But at an intermission, when a friend of Marsh's asked Maize what he thought of Chen's playing, he remarked that she was making a lot of mistakes, sometimes losing her place. The next day Marsh, fiercely supportive of Chen, called and fired him.

NOTES

1. Lawrence Kart, "Jazz Festival Rises to the Pitch of Excellence," *Chicago Tribune*, 6 September 1982, 20.

2. Stanley Crouch, "The Swan and the Odd Duck," *Village Voice*, 8 November 1983, 61.

3. Frank Canino thought that this tour and a subsequent one that took them to the Heinekens Festival in Rotterdam were in 1983, but Chen and Teekens said 1984, and I believe this to be correct, as it fits better with known facts and other reports of Marsh's movements in those two years.

4. The broadcasts were on September 23 and December 2, 1983, and January 25 and May 18, 1984.

5. Alan Bargebuhr, review, *Cadence,* February 1990, 71–72.

6. Chuck Berg, review, *Jazz Times,* November 1990, 40.

7. Dave Liebman, review, *Saxophone Journal* (January-February 1991): 33.

8. Barry McRae, review, *Jazz Journal* (February 1990): 42.

9. Mike Shera, review, *Jazz Journal* (October 1990): 39.

10. Leonard Feather, "Land and Marsh: Rapport on Sax," *Los Angeles Times*, 12 April 1985, 10 (6).

11. Victor Schonfeld, review, *Jazz Journal* (February 1988): 30–31.

12. Alan Bargebuhr, review, *Cadence,* May 1987, 69.

13. Jon Balleras, review, *Downbeat,* June 1987, 42–43.

♫

Norwegian Cool

Since touring in Scandinavia with Red Mitchell in 1978–79 and recording in Oslo with Karin Krog and Mitchell in 1980, Marsh had developed strong ties to the Norwegian jazz community, making almost yearly trips to Norway to teach and play. The central figure in this relationship was trumpeter Torgrim Sollid. He and Marsh had met in 1980, when Marsh was engaged, on the recommendation of Krog, as the saxophone and ensemble teacher at the Norwegian Jazz Federation's summer school. Marsh was in fact taking the place of the celebrated Norwegian saxophonist Jan Garbarek, who had to cancel because of other commitments. Sollid, with his training in psychology, described himself and Marsh as "very different personalities," but they established a friendship and collaboration that lasted until Marsh's death in 1987.

Together with his colleagues John Paal Inderberg, Erling Aksdal, and Espen Rud, Sollid arranged tours, seminars, and living accommodations and introduced Marsh to a circle of musicians respectful of Tristano but in no way idolatrous. Most of the Norwegians who played with Marsh, said Sollid, knew more about him than about Tristano. By his account, Norway became for Marsh a refuge from the stresses of the American jazz scene—its competitiveness, its racial tensions, its cliques, and its ignorant or indifferent audiences.

Speaking of the shift toward lyrical simplicity in Marsh's style, Sollid thought it began with the recordings with Krog and Mitchell and accelerated as a result of his experience in Norway over the next seven years. It was partly, he felt, because of "the very deep emotional effort the Norwegian musicians put into the collaboration with Warne. He did not have

248

to represent anything but himself, and he did not have to defend himself musically either. We respected and loved him as he was, and we were not timid about making critical remarks about the Lennie-cult. From time to time Warne went very deep into his Tristano thing. This was strange for some of us to listen to. This kind of 'religious' behavior is not that common in Norway. We had the usual Charlie Parker cult as late as the 1960s, but that mostly disappeared during the 1970s."

Sollid's wife, Marianne, once said to Marsh that Tristano was "one of the most monochromatic and stereotyped piano players" she had ever heard, and that she considered Marsh's playing much more interesting musically and "utterly human." Marsh, said Sollid, "responded calmly and wanted to know all the reasons for a remark like that. We discussed the Tristano cult for several hours after that, a quite objective discussion, without any firm conclusions. We were very polite, and Warne was very patient." Marsh, said Sollid, gradually "changed from a dark, no-compromise, Lennie-talking musician to a friendly, laughable guy with a lot of fresh ideas. It was like a burden slowly went off him. . . . From time to time I was wondering if this man had had any friends at all before in his life, I mean people he could relate to socially and emotionally outside the music."

The first tour that Sollid and drummer Espen Rud arranged was in January and February of 1981 and included engagements at twenty-one different venues and a broadcast over Norwegian national radio (NRK). Besides Sollid, Rud, and Marsh, the musicians included John Pal Inderberg, baritone saxophone; Erling Aksdal, piano; and Terje Venaas, bass. The tour took the band to almost every jazz club in Norway. The audiences were invariably enthusiastic. In the town of Aalesund a member of the audience came up after the second set and asked Marsh if they could clear the room of tables and chairs and have a dance. Marsh unhesitatingly said yes. In the next set he played his usual standards and lines, without compromise. Afterward he explained that his first gig with Charlie Parker had been playing for dancers, in 1948 or 1949. "It was for the American Communist Party, their annual meeting," he said. "So why can't I do the same thing in Aalesund? I'm sure we had some communists in this audience!"

To his Norwegian colleagues on this tour Marsh revealed significant aspects of his later esthetic. After a few performances one of the musicians suggested that Marsh should give himself more numbers featuring himself. Marsh responded, "But why? I'm just one-sixth of the band. What really interests me is not your or my solos, but what we can do when improvising together." Later, said Sollid, "he explained his deep-rooted, almost fanatic interest in collective improvisation, and the reason why he sometimes called for other tunes than those the band had rehearsed, or took the same tunes fast one time and slow the next. He wanted to surprise the band as well as himself, and he argued that the 'mistakes' that might be made in such situations could lead to more creative solutions. The point was of course also to make the musicians forget about themselves and their egos. He envisioned a modern version of New Orleans-style collective improvisation, which he called 'my updated Dixieland.' Ideally, sometime in the future, he would have a band that improvised everything—form, rhythm, melody, harmony, dynamics—whose music would be as rewarding as good written compositions. Such a band, he acknowledged, would require a near-perfect blend of knowledge and intuition, together with the open-minded and direct, noncompetitive friendship of an ideal musical situation."

About ego and individualism in jazz, Marsh told his Norwegian colleagues: "Your personal emotions are of no interest to any audience. A good picture, taken from a certain distance, of the same feelings could be." And again: "The improvised solo coming out of one musician, with others supporting him, is a dead end. It has all been done. In front of us we have many years of the collective improvised effort, the intuitive and adult collaboration between peers."

In July of 1981 Marsh was back in Norway teaching at the Norwegian Jazz Federation summer school again and playing at the Club Cavalero in Trondheim with the English singer Norma Winstone. In April of 1982 he participated in concerts for the Jazz Alive series, and on July 30–31 of the same year he played with his Norwegian colleagues at the Molde International Jazz Festival. The band included Sollid, Inderberg, pianist Terje Bjoerklund, bassist Bjoern Kjellemyr, and drummer Frank Jakobsen. After the festival, Marsh and Sollid played three concerts in the Jazz Alive club with a different rhythm section.

Describing his playing at Molde, Sollid said, "He was very relaxed, and played with great strength in an almost simple, noncomplicated way. Of course his playing was from time to time utterly complicated, if we talk about linearity and rhythm, but everything in his playing was executed with ease, it just poured out of him. We could also hear a natural simplicity that was new to us. His little out-of-tune tendency was gone, and this event showed some of his absolute best, maybe in a way better than the playing from his heyday in the 1950s. That could partly be due to the better interaction from the Norwegian band, compared to the more indifferent support you hear in a large part of his so-called heyday recordings."

What Sollid termed "Warne's endless ability to improvise variations" was occasionally a problem for his fellow musicians. "When his playing was at its best," said Sollid, "he could leave many who played with him in despair about their own playing, but mostly he managed to keep this matter on a positive level, and thus to create situations that were helpful in his fellow musicians' development. If he heard some genuine talent, he was extremely patient, but if you did not do anything with that talent he could be very harsh."

In the winter and spring of 1982–83 he was the subject of a documentary produced by Jan Horne for Norwegian television (NKR-TV) titled *Logical Lines*, and also was a principal interviewee for *Manhattan Studio*, Horne's documentary on Lennie Tristano. On May 22, 1983, he did a broadcast for Norwegian radio with a slightly modified version of his Norwegian unit. In addition to Sollid on trumpet and John Pal Inderberg on baritone, the group included Terje Bjoerklund, his favorite Norwegian piano player, bassist Bjorn Kjellemyr, and drummer Carl Waadeland. This group also made a record, *Warne Marsh in Norway: Sax of a Kind* (Hot Club HCR-7).

On the record Sollid displays a Chet Baker influence, Inderberg contributes brightly flowing solos, and the ensemble feel is pleasantly relaxed. The material includes Tristano's "All about You" and "Leave Me"; Ted Brown's "Featherbed"; Marsh's "Sax of a Kind"; and "My Romance" and "Time on My Hands" from the *Ballad Album* repertoire. Marsh's solos again have the unstrained, melodic quality evident on that slightly earlier recording.

A French reviewer called the record "dreamy and poetic. . . . Marsh is one of the most inventive soloists of the last thirty years: his solos . . . are full of unexpected and renewing subtlety; a superb melodist, Warne is never short of ideas." The Norwegian quintet he found "excellent, dynamic and supple, in perfect accord with Warne."[1]

When Sollid and his wife, Marianne, visited Marsh in New York in the summer of 1983, Marsh's sometimes impish sense of humor as well as his disdain for convention were exhibited when they attended an all-Gershwin program by the New York City Ballet at Lincoln Center. "Imagine," Sollid recalled, "2,497 tuxedos and blue-haired ladies, then Warne in his overcoat bought in Norway for the winter tour in 1981, *very* dirty, Marianne in a typical Norwegian overcoat, called an 'anorakk,' and me in an overcoat bought in a second-hand shop, also a little on the rough side." In the bar at intermission the room fell silent at the sight of them, as if it had been invaded by bums. Afterward, "as the tuxedos and the blue-haired had their discussions in the lobby, I saw a certain look on Warne's and Marianne's faces. They nodded and started a crazy 'pas de deux' in the lobby, with pirouettes and jumps, all the difficult stuff. After some time I found my role as the Director, with comment and advice. It all came to its conclusion when I set the rotary door in a fast spin. Warne and Marianne pirouetted out the door, I made a deep bow to the totally motionless (frozen in despair) audience, and we left for some ice cream sodas."

In October 1984, after the Heinekens Festival and Marsh's recording session with Chet Baker, Marsh and Susan Chen proceeded to Oslo for the four concert appearances in the Oslo area arranged by Sollid. At the close of the first concert Chen precipitated a minor crisis, telling the band, "If you are going to continue that silly men's competition on this stage I am not going to play with you tomorrow." The Norwegian players, she felt, were only interested in their own solos, their own licks and tricks. As she stomped off Marsh said, "This is serious. We have to talk." The ensuing discussion focused on interacting collectively—in Sollid's summation, "what to do together, doing too much or too little, the art of guessing what was going to happen in the next bar, intuition, the dynamics in a certain kind of solo, balancing the tempos, agreeing on chords and sequences," and the like. The concert the next night, said Sollid, was "more cooperative."

At one of these concerts Marsh finally made his vocal debut, singing "You'd Be So Nice to Come Home To." Sollid and Chen also contributed vocals, he scat-singing on "Confirmation" and she on "All God's Chillun Got Rhythm." Marsh had instigated a bet on who would be the first to sing. Chen won the prize, a bottle of champagne, because nobody knew she had prepared that number. According to Sollid, both audience and band "fell out laughing" several times during this concert.

Marsh's schedule also included a seminar for music therapy students and another for students and teachers of composition at the Norwegian State Academy of Music. For the music therapists Marsh was to discuss the teaching of improvisation. Among the students, Marsh discovered, were one or two good players, and the seminar turned into a two-hour jam session, with Marsh as leader. After the session Marsh was called to a meeting with faculty members, some of whom were scandalized that Marsh had merely played, not taught. Marsh cagily defended himself by stressing the importance of nonverbal training, maintaining that the session had actually incorporated all the ingredients of improvisation he could think of. The only thing not done, he said, was to verbally name the scales, chords, and rhythms and write them on the blackboard. Otherwise the session had evolved along the same lines as a lecture would have. Students taking part in the discussion enthusiastically agreed with Marsh, asserting that they had indeed understood his point in the playing process, and the "scandal" of Marsh's noncompliance with contractual obligations dissipated amidst hearty laughs.

Afterwards Marsh proceeded to the Norwegian Broadcasting Company radio station in Oslo to record with the Norwegian Radio Big Band. He had brought with him some challenging arrangements by Clare Fischer, Bill Holman, Alf Clausen, and others, provided by Gary Foster. The producer had dispensed with the services of a conductor, assuming that

Marsh would conduct, but Marsh, who had no experience as conductor, flatly refused. He was the soloist, he said, and his sole duty was to improvise. He handed the parts to a saxophonist, Bjoern Johansen, told him to rehearse the band, and retired to the control booth for a chess game with Chen, much to the dismay of the producer. The recording went well despite the conflict. Sollid thought it showed both Marsh and the band at their best. With Marsh's favorites Bjoern Kjellemyr on bass and Frank Jakobsen on drums playing in a contrapuntal, post-bebop style, Marsh was spurred to what Sollid thought was his finest performance in Norway since the Molde concerts of 1982.

The next day, in a rehearsal with a Supersax-type group named Fast Fingers, Marsh gave vent, for perhaps the first time in his life, to negative feelings about Lennie Tristano. From an unreleased 1964 tape Sollid had transcribed a chorus of a Tristano solo on "All the Things You Are" and had arranged it for the Fast Fingers group. When he heard the arrangement, said Sollid, "Warne turned white." Complimenting Sollid, saying he had come about as close as one could to Tristano's chordal thinking, he asked to hear the arrangement again. After the second hearing he said, "I can't play a solo on that." When Chen asked him why not, he shouted, in a departure from his normal cool reserve, "Because it reminds me so much of a time I'm desperately trying to get away from!" After a long moment of silence, said Sollid, "Warne provided himself with the solution, almost talking to himself: 'I play a rubato solo on the changes with Susan, and then the head.' The result was a beautiful solo and a slightly ragged head."

At Marsh's other academic seminar for the Composition Department at the state academy, which prided itself on its modernity, Marsh gained the enmity of many in the audience when a student asked his opinion of Arnold Schoenberg. After a motionless interval of ten seconds, he said, "Schoenberg was probably the worst crock of them all, because he was the first composer that managed to write music to death."

Another student asked, "Mr. Marsh, what do you think about improvisation on quarter-tones?" Quarter tones can be played on stringed or wind instruments, but not on a piano, which is limited to the half-tones of the chromatic scale. To answer the question, Marsh walked to the grand piano in the room, played middle C, and asked the student to sing a C major triad (C-E-G). The student did so, but with imperfect pitch. "If you can't do that," said Marsh, "why bother with quarter-tones?"

To his friend Sollid, Marsh in Norway was like "a musician on vacation from it all. You have to think of the difference between Norway and almost any other European country with regard to jazz. Norway is the least stylized of them all. In a strange way we have no respect for anything, and the real American influence that is so active in all the European countries disappeared here mostly during the last part of the 1970s, partly because of an interest among jazz musicians for that very strong folk music we have here. Norwegians do their own things! They could even be friendly as usual with a visiting celebrity, treating him like a neighbor or a man they met in a bar. What a relief for this, in my opinion, deeply disappointed and somewhat confused musician, so musically and personally soft, honest, and emotional in that crazy extreme man-versus-man world of competition called jazz in America!"

NOTES

1. Jean-Louis Ginibre, "Warne Marsh," *Jazz Magazine* (Paris), June 1986, 50.

Out Chorus

Sometime in the latter half of 1982 the critic Francis Davis interviewed Marsh at his Bretton Hall studio, and his extended profile of Marsh appeared in the January 1983 issue of *Down Beat.* It was the first that the magazine had ever published.

At the time of the interview Marsh was approximately fifty-five, an age by which many have found it possible to shed youthful insecurities. But Davis found in Marsh a striking duality: "The first impression a stranger might get from Marsh is that he is guarded and rather distant. But it soon becomes apparent that he is painfully shy, almost jittery, as he paces around the small disordered room, lighting cigarettes he lets burn out, pouring coffee he doesn't finish, repeatedly adjusting the mouthpiece on the tenor saxophone that stands idle next to a drum set in the center of the floor."[1] Musically he was "a perfectionist in the Tristano mold, both arrogant and insecure about his own abilities."[2]

Davis noted that Marsh, "who has remained secluded in the folds of the Tristano legend to a great extent, ironically achieving a high level of visibility only when he reunited with Tristano or Konitz,"[3] was known by younger jazz fans, if at all, "by reputation or by the well-received two-tenor records he made in the late '70s with Lew Tabackin (*Tenor Gladness*) and Peter Christlieb (*Apogee*)—records that Marsh himself . . . does not particularly care for."[4]

The comments Davis elicited from Marsh about Tristano are revealing: "Lenny always knew me at least two years better than I knew myself. I mean, he could sit and listen and tell me what was original and what was derivative. I doubt my personal education would have ever gotten to

255

where it has without him, because he presented it all so clearly to me when I was 20 that I've never really been at a loss for ideas since, and if I want more ideas, I know from him exactly where to look—to 20th century classical thinking, which is best heard in Bartok. . . . Lenny really knew music. My life would be a lot different if I had never met him. For one thing, I probably would never have taught."[5]

Quoting Lee Konitz on what he perceived as Marsh's early "fear of breaking loose," of expressing himself emotionally, Davis asks, "What character armor did Marsh have to shed before he could get in touch with his feeling and create to his full capacity?" Marsh's answer was, "*Fear*. . . . Fear of really expressing myself. It's not exactly encouraged in American life. It leaves you exposed, but that can be your strength too. I got over it once and for all around 1963 or '64. I just felt like playing all the time." He had not, he admitted, felt that way before.[6]

Davis's only negative comment, aside from a suggestion that Marsh was too intellectual for the average listener, concerned his tone: "[T]he *idea* of melody is something he bears proudly and carefully aloft, as though it were a sacred chalice from which he were determined not to spill one precious drop. If he is a melodic player, however, he is not really a lyrical one in the conventional sense—his tone is one of the palest and brittlest in jazz."[7]

Overall, Davis praised Marsh in terms that had never before been used by a major American critic: "Laboring in relative obscurity, . . . Marsh has matured into one of the most stimulating improvisers in all of jazz. . . . He has a knack for rhythmic displacement, and he uses silence and space almost as tellingly, if not as mischievously, as did Thelonious Monk. . . . But because he is not a virile, breast-beating swinger, many of his rhythmic niceties are lost on all but his most attentive and most sophisticated audiences. Above all else, there is an inner-directed quality to Marsh's best solos, a feeling of rigorous soul-searching as riveting as that which one hears in Coltrane, but quite different in character. There is nothing purgative, nothing Promethean or sheerly physical about Marsh's solos. Instead, one hears in them what critic Harvey Pekar has described as 'the kind of intense concentration a scientist must feel when deeply involved in his work.' It is this quality of passionate intellectual involvement, no doubt, which draws some listeners to Marsh at the same time it keeps larger numbers—seeking simpler, more immediate pleasures from jazz—away."[8]

Davis's conclusion: "He hasn't always been able to call his own tune. . . . But he has always faced the music—he has accepted the responsibility of his own melody—and that melody is an eternal and individual one that has thrilled and enlightened everyone who has listened closely enough to hear it."[9]

Later in 1983, in November, the appreciative review by Stanley Crouch appeared in the *Village Voice*, and in mid-1985, at about the time Marsh and Susan Chen were recording their first duo tracks, Marsh was interviewed at his Bretton Hall studio for a *New Yorker* profile by Whitney Balliett, perhaps America's most eminent writer on jazz. The resulting profile, even more than Francis Davis's article, gave Marsh the kind of recognition that had eluded him most of his life.

After a brief overview of jazz, ending with the "disquieting" impact of Ornette Coleman and free jazz, Balliett announces that "there is a savior on the horizon—a fifty-seven-year-old tenor saxophonist named Warne Marsh."[10] Although Balliett dutifully presents Marsh's history, much of it in Marsh's own words, there is an odd sense of his having only recently loomed into Balliett's view as a major figure: "During his most recent stay in New York, two things became clear about Marsh: he is one of the most original and daring jazz improvisers alive, and he is perfecting a kind of improvisation that draws on all jazz."[11]

Some of Marsh's remarks to Balliett clearly pertain to what he was attempting to do with Chen: "I want to get away from bebop music, and what I mean is the really stifling form of starting a number by playing a melody, then going into a string of long solos, then restating the melody. I want to structure everything in terms of polyphony and polyrhythms— the kind of counterpoint that we did with Lennie Tristano thirty years ago and that has been done all too rarely since."[12]

Balliett is a master of nontechnical metaphor in describing music, and his description of Marsh's playing is typically provocative: "Marsh makes his listeners work. His long, multiplying melodic lines seem to flee, disappearing around corner after corner, moving at a constant speed—all the while drawing us on hypnotically. In the early days of jazz improvisation, the listener could hang on to the bar lines; they fenced the soloist in and preserved the shape of the melody. Marsh ignores such frameworks, allowing his melodic lines to pour until he runs out of either breath or (rarely) ideas. Marsh's tone does not make him any easier to listen to. It is makeshift, and even abrupt; it surrounds his notes, as his clothes surround him. . . . Marsh's solos move in a snakelike fashion—shooting forward and up, down and to one side, up and to the other side, precipitously down, then straight up. He also doubles back on himself, tumbles through double-time passages, restrains the time. He likes to move the beat back and forth and just off center. He plays hob with harmony. He moves along just at the edge of the key he is working in, and sometimes he steps outside it. These rhythmic and harmonic liberties give his melodic flow a great spaciousness. . . . Marsh's emotions are filtered through his mind. What is moving about him is the logic and order of his phrasing, his little, almost sighing connective notes, the sheen and flow of his ideas, his density and prolificacy and urgency."[13]

Although for a quarter of a century critics had been quick to recognize the worth of Marsh's major contemporaries— Konitz, Getz, Rollins, Coltrane—seldom, till the appearance of these two articles, had influential critical recognition been extended to Marsh. At this late date, the results were inconsequential. The stampede of major record companies offering contracts, which might have followed thirty years earlier, was conspicuous by its absence.

What moved Balliett and Davis was only sparingly in evidence on Marsh's next album, *Back Home,* his fourth for Gerry Teekens's Criss Cross label, recorded on March 31, 1986, at Rudy Van Gelder's studio in Englewood Cliffs, New Jersey. As on the album with Chet Baker, Teekens provided a black rhythm section including a pianist, Barry Harris, with some name recognition but with whom Marsh had seldom played, if at all. He was more familiar with the bassist, David Williams, with whom he toured Trinidad in 1983 with Carla White and trumpeter Manny Duran. The drummer was Tootie Heath, whom Marsh had played with in Los Angeles a year earlier. Marsh, living in Los Angeles again since the fall of 1985, had contacted Heath, and the two had flown together to New York for the date. Marsh had previously discussed with Teekens the possibility of recording with young Jimmy Halperin, whom he regarded as the most talented saxophone student he had ever had, and on this occasion he brought Halperin along and insisted he be included on the album.

It was not a good decision. Halperin had also studied with Tristano, and in unison with Marsh he played the three difficult Tristano lines on the album more or less acceptably. His nervous-sounding solos, however, are journeyman at best, melodically ordinary and rhythmically punchy and disconnected. At this stage in his career Halperin was not quite ready for this kind of challenge. As one reviewer put it, he "shows more promise than achievement."[14]

Halperin's rhythmic jerkiness even seems to have influenced Marsh on their three tracks together. The rest of the album, however, is on a higher level. Williams is solid on bass, Harris contributes tasteful bebop professionalism, and Heath is superb, especially on "Two Not One." Though Marsh's solo on "Big Leaps for Lester," an "I Got Rhythm" tune in F rather than the usual B♭, is not particularly notable for ideas, it is nevertheless one of his most fluent and swinging up-tempo performances. On "See Me Now, If You Could" his sound is appealingly light and gentle, even wistful, but the solo is rhythmically eccentric, the insistently off-beat attacks giving the whole a tense, angular feel. His most satisfying playing is on the other ballad, "Heads Up" ("You Go to My Head"). Trading solos with Harris, he maintains his lyrical sound and combines it with a more flowing rhythmic conception. *Down Beat* reviewer Jim Roberts wrote, "Today, Marsh's solos are deeper and more intricate than ever, and his tightly controlled style is refreshing in an era of post-Coltrane exhibitionism."[15]

Marsh later told Tosh Taenaka that he had wanted to do at least one duo track with Harris, but that Harris demurred.

It would be a year before Marsh made another record. He returned to Los Angeles in the fall of 1985, living for a time in a trailer in the front yard of Fred and Carol Waters's home in North Hollywood. While there he practiced endlessly, read novels by writers as diverse as Anne Tyler, William Styron, Doris Lessing, and Louis L'Amour, watched television, and played bridge or endless games of chess, usually with Fred. Occasionally he would play chess with Carol, but she had always felt he didn't like to play with women. He had what she called "a pat-on-the-head attitude" towards women, as if he felt they were not intellectually equal to men. Throughout October, November, and December he played with drummer Chiz Harris's group on Saturday evenings at the Studio Café in Balboa. Other members of the group were pianist Joe Lettieri and bassist Ken Filiano.

By early 1986 he had moved into a house his mother bought for him at 14226 Runnymede in Van Nuys. Although Elizabeth Marsh provided the money for the house, she kept the title in her name, remembering when in 1977 Marsh had sold the house she had bought for him in Pasadena and used the money to move back to New York.

In February 1986, a month after Marsh and Susan Chen had recorded most of their first duo album in New York, Marsh had received a visit at his new home in Van Nuys from his friend and student John Klopotowski. It is of some interest because their sessions together followed the same format as the duos with Chen. Marsh wanted no solos, just contrapuntal improvising, three or four choruses on each tune. Klopotowski found it exhilarating. "Each tune got better, we were so together. I've never been able to do that with anyone else." Before he returned to New York there was a session that included another student, altoist Jon Whinnery. It turned out to be the last time Klopotowski and Marsh played together. He would visit again in February 1987 but, to Marsh's great displeasure, had left his guitar at home because the airline would not allow him to carry it on.

In May of 1986 Gary Foster invited Marsh to perform as guest soloist with the Pasadena City College studio big band, of which Foster was the director. Marsh, in top form, played seven numbers, of which the highlights were "Round Midnight," "Body and Soul," and, with Foster joining him on alto, "Lennie's Pennies." Marsh's melodic inventiveness and structural ability were striking on all seven numbers, and "Lennie's Pennies" included some stunning triplet passages. The concert was memorable not only for Marsh's playing but for the standing ovation he received from an audience packed with fellow musicians.

I was studying with Marsh at the time and had attended the concert. Knowing that Foster habitually tape-recorded his concerts, I mentioned at my lesson the following week that I would love to hear the tape. Marsh, who had been visibly touched by the audience's response, had already suppressed all vestiges of sentimentality. "You know," he growled, referring to the taping, "that's completely illegal."

Illegal or not, from the standpoints of both sound quality and performance the tape is one of the best private recordings of Marsh extant. It has only one flaw: someone apparently disconnected the power cord in the middle of Marsh's solo on "'Round Midnight," resulting in a gap before the power was restored.

In addition to appearing at various clubs in the Los Angeles area, such as Donte's and Alphonse's, Marsh built up his teaching practice again and hung out with old friends Fred and Carol Waters, Lou Levy, Lou Ciotti, Dick Forrest, Jim Krutcher, and students like Rhonda Dameron, Jon Whinnery, and George Khouri.

Pianist Khouri, a friend and fellow graduate student of John Klopotowski's at SUNY Stonybrook, had moved to San Francisco in 1983, and when he learned that Marsh had returned to Los Angeles, he arranged to study with him, commuting from San Francisco for perhaps ten weekly lessons. After the four hundred-mile commute became impractical, Khouri remained in frequent contact with Marsh by phone through 1986–87, and he and his wife, Mary Fleming, a classical pianist, occasionally visited Marsh, staying at the house on Runnymede. Marsh loved hearing Mary play Debussy, and he enjoyed the couple's Near Eastern cooking.

Another of Marsh's new friends in this period was Rhonda Dameron, an attractive young aspiring jazz pianist. Dameron shared, on a platonic basis, a small house in an industrial district of Van Nuys with Marsh's old friend, bassist Jim Krutcher. Because of the area, music could be played there at any hour of the day or night, and in the fall of 1985, soon after he had returned from New York, Marsh began coming over for sessions. To Dameron, he was the first horn player she had heard in whose improvising, no matter how complex, she could clearly hear all the changes. She was taking a class in rhythm, but he convinced her to drop it and to begin studying with him. At first Marsh expressed a sexual interest in her, but she already had a boyfriend, drummer John Nolan, and she and Marsh became strictly platonic "hanging buddies" in an exceptionally close student–teacher relationship.

As a teacher, she said, Marsh was adamant about fundamentals. He told her he did not have perfect pitch but that he had developed his sense of relative pitch to such a point that it was virtually perfect, and he believed anyone with an adequate ear could do the same. To this end he drilled her in singing different intervals and recognizing chords. He would tape a passage on piano and assign her to take it home, transcribe it, and identify the chords. On a few occasions Marsh invited Dameron to sit in at Donte's.

He also tried to convince her that despite her experience of playing badly whenever she smoked marijuana, she could learn to do it well. It was, as he told another student, a matter of "training."

Among the older friends who lived nearby were Lou Ciotti and trumpeter Dick Forrest. Besides their regular bridge games, the three would exercise together. In earlier days they had played tennis, but now their activity was walking in a park near Van Nuys Boulevard and Magnolia, which had a half-mile track. Ciotti and Forrest were serious about exercise, for health reasons. Marsh was not. He might stroll around a bit, but generally, while his pals walked their serious mile or two around the track, he would sit on a bench and wait.

At the same time as he was omitting healthful exercise, he was consuming cocaine on a regular basis. A friend and admirer from his teenage years, at one time a physics teacher at a local university who had long ago fallen into cocaine addiction, was his supplier. This friend, who prefers not to be named, was also a dealer, and for a certain period he was staying with Marsh and dealing cocaine out of the house on Runnymede. Marsh later told a doctor that he had been using cocaine for the last twenty years, and it is probable that his old friend had been one of his main suppliers in California.

In the spring of 1987 Marsh apparently toured briefly in Europe, but details are lacking. On his return he began informal sessions with veteran drummer Larence Marable, the young guitarist Larry Koonse, the fine Swiss bassist-trombonist Isla Eckinger, and, on occasion, the brilliant young bassist Eric Von Essen.

Koonse, the son of guitarist Dave Koonse, had first met Marsh when he was six years old and his father and Marsh were both teaching at the Berry and Grasmueck music store in Pasadena. His father, who had played with the George Shearing Quartet, had told him, "Respect that man." When Marsh called him, around April 1987, to rehearse with the quartet and later as a duo, he was thrilled and somewhat anxious, wondering if he could keep up—"Warne's ears were so sharp, and he was so spontaneous, all the time, that you really had to learn to let go and play with him. He was always playing over the bar lines, never did anything tried and true. But he was never lost, no matter how free he got with the changes and the bar lines. Even playing duo, if I kept my place in the form,

it always came out." Playing with Marsh, said Koonse, was a lot like playing Baroque music. "The melody was the key, not the vertical harmony.
It was linear and melodic, very Bachlike."

In May and June the new quartet, with either Von Essen or Eckinger
on bass, played a few jobs at Donte's; one at Carmelo's on Van Nuys Boulevard; and, on May 27, one at Hop Singh's, a new club in Marina del Rey
operated by Rudy Onderweiser, the former business manager of Shelly's
Manne Hole.

On June 4–5 Marsh went into John Morrell's Backroom Recording Studio in Sherman Oaks, very near Marsh's home, for another recording for
Interplay, *Two Days in the Life of. . . .* Marsh had personally chosen Morrell's
studio, with Tosh Taenaka's acquiescence. The personnel included Marsh's
old compatriot Jim Hughart on bass, Ron Eschete on guitar, and Sherman
Ferguson on drums. Eschete, as a student at Loyola University in New
Orleans in the late 1960s, had admired Marsh's early playing with Tristano
and Konitz, and he had frequently played with Marsh at Donte's and other
local clubs around 1972–74. Their relationship had been renewed, since
Marsh's return to the area, in sessions at Marsh's house and occasional
gigs. Ferguson, on the other hand, had never played with Marsh and in
fact had only recently met him, although he had played with both Hughart
and Eschete on separate occasions. Marsh had undoubtedly heard him
play at Donte's prior to calling him for the recording.

The energy level of the record is well above that of *Back Home,* and it is
a stronger performance than *Posthumous.* Ferguson plays with taste and
vibrant swing, and he, Hughart, and Eschete mesh well. Hughart's solos
are unfailingly melodic and economical, and his full, deep sound provides
a springy cushion for the others. Eschete's eighth notes are a bit uneven
on "All God's Chillun Got Rhythm," as if he were uncomfortable with the
fast tempo, but his harmonic innovations on his composition "Blues
Warne-ing" and "Asterix" ("These Foolish Things") give those pieces a
fresh edge. Eschete, who considered the record one of the highlights of
his career, composed "Blues Warne-ing" the night of June 4, after Marsh
had expressed a desire to include an original.

Marsh's playing, while not astonishing in the manner of his finest work,
and perhaps not quite at the level of *Star Highs,* is representative of his
work in the 1980s. His solo on "Geraldyne's Arrangement" ("Darn That
Dream") has a gentleness and lyricism reminiscent of *A Ballad Album.*
Reviewing the record in *Cadence,* Kevin Whitehead observed, "The bittersweet quality in Marsh's ballad playing . . . isn't marred by self-pity,"
adding that "For many Tristanoites, weeding out the bad they absorbed
along with the good became a lifelong project. Marsh showed how to retain the master's clarity while regaining ensemble heat."[16]

As usual, the tunes are almost all improvisations on standards, retitled and with the original melody omitted. Ferguson recalled that when the band listened to the first-day playbacks, Marsh remarked that they would have to redo one of the retitled tunes because he had played "too much of the melody," which meant that he could not claim composer credit.

A month after the *Two Days* sessions, on July 8, Marsh experienced chest pains. He took some aspirin but did not bother to see a doctor. A week later, on July 14, on his way to Donte's, he was picked up by police for driving erratically. Realizing that he was suffering from something other than drink or drugs, the police arranged for him to be taken to the emergency room of Valley Hospital, where he was diagnosed as suffering a heart attack. After a short stay at Valley he was transferred to County General. He remained there for three or four days, then signed himself out. His student Jon Whinnery was one of those who visited him at Valley Hospital. Afterwards Marsh carried on with his teaching, at least in Whinnery's case, for Whinnery came for lessons on July 26, less than two weeks after the attack, and again on August 5. At the latter lesson Marsh sheepishly informed him that he was raising his fee from $30 to $35.

In the next few months Marsh saw several doctors: Dr. Maurice Dicterow in Sherman Oaks, who saw Marsh perhaps twice and who, because he was also a violinist, was probably recommended to Marsh by another musician; possibly Dr. Gary Sugarman in Beverly Hills, recommended to Marsh by altoist Joe Lopes, though Dr. Sugarman did not remember treating him; and a Dr. El Newhi in Van Nuys, who wrote him a prescription for Cardizen.

On August 11 he first saw his mother's personal physician, Dr. Arthur Feinfield. Marsh had no health insurance, and the visit was perhaps insisted on, and undoubtedly paid for, by his mother. On August 15 he was admitted, at Dr. Feinfield's behest, to St. Joseph's Hospital to undergo a coronary angiogram. The angiogram showed that he had indeed suffered a severe heart attack in July. It also showed that there was no point in performing heart bypass surgery: "Interestingly," said Dr. Feinfield, "his coronary arteries looked pretty good." The heart attack, in other words, was not caused by clogged arteries but by something else, probably cocaine. On the questionnaire the doctor had him fill out, Marsh wrote that in addition to a pack of cigarettes a day, he had been smoking marijuana all his adult life. And it was to Dr. Feinfield that he revealed that he had used cocaine with some regularity for the last twenty years.

Dr. Feinfield found Marsh intelligent, well read, and all in all "a charming man," philosophical rather than bitter about the course of his career. Marsh's psychological questionnaire indicated he was "pretty normal," none of his answers suggesting depression. Cardizen had previously been

prescribed for him, and Dr. Feinfield prescribed various other medica-
tions—Basotech, Diltiazem, aspirin, and the sleeping pill Halcyon, a relative of Valium—and counseled Marsh to avoid cocaine, alcohol, and cigarettes. He did not, as at least one previous doctor had done, tell him he
must quit playing the saxophone.

Marsh did abstain from playing any instrument for two or three weeks.
According to Carol Waters, he lay on his couch watching television, ignored phone calls, and would not answer the door. Then he began playing his flute. His doctor had given approval, he told Rhonda Dameron,
and they played Bach together. Later he started practicing his tenor, again
telling Dameron his doctor said it was okay, which she doubted. He tried
to quit cigarettes, but found it impossible, sneaking smokes behind
Rhonda's back. She talked with him daily, some days two or three times,
and often cooked for him, wondering why Geraldyne did not come down
from Santa Cruz. But Geraldyne had been told, she said by Marsh's
mother, that there was no need for her and the children to come, as the
heart attack had not been serious. She had not been able to talk to Marsh
by phone when he was in the hospital, either because he was in intensive
care or because, though they were still legally married, her name was not
placed on the list of immediate kin.

With the help of Torgrim Sollid, Marsh had made arrangements in the
spring for another round of concerts and clinics in Norway in the fall.
Now, in September, barely two months after his heart attack, he was determined to fulfill his commitments. It was agreed that several concerts
would be canceled to make the schedule less strenuous. When Sollid and
his wife, Marianne, met Marsh at the airport in Oslo on September 17, they
were shocked at his condition. He could hardly walk to their car. They had
arranged for him to stay at Sollid's studio, a pleasant place that Marsh was
fond of, but now, worried about leaving him there alone, they took him
home. Despite his physical weakness, the scheduled events went as
planned, without mishap. After a rehearsal September 18, he played his
first concert at the DOELA Jazz Festival in Lillehammer with Sollid on
trumpet; John Pal Inderberg, alto and baritone saxophones; Erling Aksdal,
piano; Bjorn Alterhaug, bass; and Ole Jacob Hansen, drums. The next day
he met with a group of students, among them bassist Thomas Winther
Andersen and guitarist Haakon Storm Mathisen.[17]

The next three days, September 21–23, were devoted to recording what
would be Marsh's last record, *For the Time Being* (Hot Club HRCD 44), with
the Lillehammer band. The sessions were difficult for him. At times, said
Sollid, he cut his solos short because he was in danger of fainting. The final
takes were all done the last day. On three tunes, "No Splice" ("You'd Be
So Nice to Come Home To"), "Everything You Could Be" ("All the Things

You Are"), and "This Thing" ("What Is This Thing Called Love") he does not solo, playing only in collectively improvised passages. His sound is noticeably gentler than usual, and he plays particularly moving, lyrical solos on "Here's That Rainy Day" and "So Ro," both ballads. One can hear the inner softness that Sollid spoke of, as if a hard outer shell had dropped away. One perhaps hears also, as Sollid thought, "the voice of a man knowing that his time is limited." All of his solos are representative of the period, flowing and full of ideas, and Inderberg, Sollid, Aksdal, and his other Norwegian colleagues are more than adequate, playing un-pretentiously with skill, spirit, and individuality.

According to Sollid, "very little was arranged or rehearsed. Most of the collective passages came right out of the air, amongst them some quite striking endings. We from time to time had a feeling of playing in a strange kind of symphonic orchestra with that well known conductor, the honor-able Mr. Warne Marsh."

Wrote *Down Beat* reviewer Art Lange: "The ringer in an unobrusive sex-tet of Norwegians, Marsh provides characteristically serpentine solos. The tunes are thinly veiled standards in the best Tristano tradition, and the arrangements are suitably underwrought, with an occasional maze of counterpoint."[18] The Norwegian critic, Roald Helgheim, who had done interviews with Marsh for several Norwegian newspapers, wrote, "The best parts of this recording give you a feeling of this special collective world of improvisation that Marsh had as his lifelong goal."[19]

Marsh, said Sollid, never heard the actual recording, just a couple of premixed tracks. Anticipating Marsh's return for a scheduled European tour in February 1988, Marsh's Norwegian colleagues decided to leave the final mixing until then. Only a thousand pressings were eventually made.

On the 24th Marsh conducted a workshop at Troendelag Music Con-servatory in Trondheim, and on the 25th he played his last Norwegian concert there. Sollid described the concert as "fantastic": "He was like a demon all evening, played almost one extra set, and left the audience breathless. For the first and last time we got an impression of what it had been like in his heydays. After the last tune the audience waited for him to pack up (it took some time), and when he was ready to go they all rose and applauded him out of the room. Then for the first time I saw a tear in his eye. He was very happy. Next morning he was like a tower of en-ergy. We drove to the airport, said goodbye, and I think that we both knew that it was for the last time."

Back home, Marsh uncharacteristically went out of his way to seek out playing situations. Always before, others had come to him. Now it was the other way around. He saw Dr. Feinfield again on October 9, telling him he felt good, had given up cocaine and cut back on alcohol, had experienced no more chest pains, and was working regularly. Dr. Feinfield advised him to try again to give up cigarettes and to come again in six weeks.

George and Mary Khouri visited him from San Francisco. In the process of making him some hummus and tabouli, they were appalled to find in his kitchen a coffee can of bacon grease near the stove. Marsh liked bacon, and saved the grease to fry things in. He told them how one of his doctors had advised against playing the saxophone: "Can you believe it, telling *me* to quit playing?"

He had been in touch with Geraldyne, and they had talked of reconciliation. He had also argued with his mother, both about the old bone of contention, his father's trust, and about putting the house in his name. He wanted this, he told Geraldyne, so that if he died, she and their sons would get the house. But he said the only way his mother would sign over the house was if he were divorced. Geraldyne responded that a divorce decree was only a piece of paper; they could still get back together if they wanted to. Later Marsh told Rhonda that if he got a divorce in order to gain title to the house, he would marry Geraldyne again, for the sake of the boys.

Avant-garde saxophonist Anthony Braxton, an enthusiastic admirer, had engaged Marsh and Larry Koonse to play a duo concert at Mills College in Oakland, where Braxton was teaching. Early in October Marsh flew to San Jose, where Geraldyne met him, and the two drove to Oakland. Near the end of the concert Marsh asked Braxton to play a number with them, which he did. After a post-concert party at Braxton's on-campus home, the Marshes drove across the bay to San Francisco, where George and Mary Khouri put them up. Commenting on the concert, Marsh expressed appreciation for Braxton's warmth and enthusiasm but wondered if he really understood his music. He spoke about forming a quintet modeled on the Tristano-Marsh-Konitz groups of the early years. Before returning to Los Angeles he taught a master class in improvisation at Sonoma State University. Arrangements had been made by Khouri, who had attended Sonoma State as an undergraduate. On the way back from the college the conversation turned to saxophonist Joe Henderson, and they stopped in San Francisco to buy two of Henderson's records. On listening to them in Khouri's apartment, Marsh asked Khouri, "Do you understand this music?" Khouri replied that he wasn't sure, but that clearly it was serious and worth listening to. Marsh grunted agreement but made no further comment. The next day he and Geraldyne drove to the San Jose airport, where she was struck by Marsh's manner. Ordinarily, she said, his leave-takings were as abrupt and laconic as his conversation. This time he stood facing her, arms dangling, as if he did not want to get on the plane.

On October 18, two weeks after the Mills College concert, Marsh and Koonse were again in the Bay Area, this time for a performance in a loft for an organization called Jazz in Flight in San Francisco. They used local musicians Jim Zimmerman on drums and Seward McCain on bass. Again Marsh stayed with the Khouris. Lee Konitz was also in San Francisco that evening, but his own performance was scheduled so close to Marsh's that it would have been inconvenient to stop by to hear him. Konitz later expressed regret at not having made the effort to see Marsh on this and an earlier occasion in that year.

On November 29 Marsh attended Fred Waters's birthday party. For the first time in their long friendship, he brought his horn and played in a casual, haphazard session that included Lou Ciotti, pianist Dick Shreve, and Fred and Carol's grandson, Jamie Trotter. Carol thought Marsh was "driven," wanting to be around people he cared about.

He did not keep his suggested six-week return appointment with Dr. Feinfield. In telephone conversations with his former student in New York, the young psychiatrist David Frank, he seemed to be in denial. When Frank had earlier raised the question of heart bypass surgery, Marsh had responded that he would never let anyone "cut" him. Now, after the angiogram had ruled out the need for surgery, he simply evaded questions about his health, saying he was "playing better than ever and enjoying it more than ever."

Possibly as a result of the clinic arranged earlier by George Khouri at Sonoma State, he had begun thinking about a regular teaching job at some California college, and with the help of Rhonda and Carol Waters he drew up a resume listing people he had studied and played with and most of the records he had made. In phone conversations with Torgrim Sollid he planned a European tour that would begin in Oslo in February. He also received confirmation and an itinerary for another tour April 14–May 5 with guitarist Joe Pass, Niels-Henning Orsted-Pedersen, and Louis Stewart. The tour, arranged by an Italian producer named Filippo Bianchi, would include Edinburgh, Scotland, half-a-dozen cities in Italy, and Geneva, Switzerland.

In December he got a call to sub for trumpeter Conte Candoli at Donte's, as he had done on other occasions. Rhonda called him the afternoon of the 17th, the day of the gig, and was surprised to hear him say he had been sleeping. He explained that he had gone to a music store in Hollywood, a favorite hangout for hip jazz musicians, and they had all gotten "real high," and when he got home he had taken a nap to sleep it off. At the time she had got the impression, though he did not specify the drug, that it was marijuana, but somebody later told her it was cocaine. She called him again, just before he was to leave for Donte's, to tell him she wanted to practice and would come by the club later, around 10:30. After practicing, she was on her way out the door, but suddenly decided not to go after all. Later she wondered if she had had some kind of extrasensory premonition.

The audience at Donte's was depressingly sparse. Among the patrons was Gene Lesner, an amateur alto player and regular frequenter of the valley clubs. He had first heard Marsh at Alphonse's, where a glitzy poster in the entrance had advertised the appearance of "Warner Marsh." He had turned the sign over and made a handwritten sign with the correct spelling. While he was replacing it Marsh had come in and commented that the sign didn't look so good, whereon Lesner had turned it over to show the misspelled original. Said Marsh, "Oh yeah, they do that all the time." In fact, mistakes about his first name were so common that his friend Gary Foster habitually made a joke of addressing him as "Wayne." Lesner thought he could hear a lifetime of critical neglect in his voice, as if saying, "If they can't even learn my name, they're obviously not listening to my music."

On this night the band at Donte's included Ross Tomkins, who normally worked the Thursday night gig with Candoli, on piano, Buddy Clark on bass, and Larence Marable on drums. They played a set and drifted off the stand. After a time Lesner and veteran jazz radio personality Chuck Niles left their seats at the bar to mingle with the musicians: "We went to that table on the south side where the hotshots used to sit," said Lesner, "and Warne was just so *up* and cheery! I thought, godalmighty, he's almost like a Guy Lombardo employee. He wandered off and we went back to the corner of the bar, and he came up and slapped us both on the back, said 'Hey, what's going on?' He wasn't a backslapper, it was completely out of character."

For the first number of the second set Marsh called an old favorite, "Out of Nowhere." He finished his solo, sat on his stool, then abruptly stepped off it, and, as Lesner saw it, staggered, "gently laid his horn on the floor, and lay down on his side. The first to notice was Marable. Larence kind of leaned forward and stood up. He said something like, 'What the fuck you doing, Warne, what's going on?' Tomkins looked around with his usual quizzical look on his face. It was so slick, so smooth, the way he went down. Everyone of course knew that he'd had that heart attack. Marable yelled, 'For Christ's sake somebody call an ambulance!' and the place just stopped cold. It seemed like a month before the paramedics got there. It was probably only ten minutes. The lights went on, and my god, you were not only in the maelstrom of reacting to the horror, but suddenly here's this dump Donte's in all its grime and crumbiness. There was a little bit of vomit on the floor by Warne's mouth."

Somebody covered Marsh with a coat or blanket. When the paramedics arrived and attempted to revive Marsh, Clark asked Lesner to put

Marsh's horn in its case. Recalled Lesner, "It was just a mess. The corks were all frazzled, the mechanism was worn down beyond belief. It was amazing that he got a sound out of it."

The paramedics wheeled him away. The few customers milled around in the unaccustomed light and gradually drifted out. The band packed up. According to Clark, they never got paid. They didn't finish the gig.

NOTES

1. Francis Davis, "Warne Marsh's Inner Melody," *Down Beat*, January 1983, 27.
2. Ibid.
3. Ibid., 26.
4. Ibid., 27.
5. Ibid.
6. Ibid., 28.
7. Ibid.
8. Ibid., 27.
9. Ibid., 28.
10. Whitney Balliett, "A True Improviser," *New Yorker*, October 14, 1985, 110.
11. Ibid.
12. Ibid., 117.
13. Ibid., 116.
14. Victor Schonfield, "Warne Marsh," *Jazz Journal* (April 1987): 25–26.
15. Jim Roberts, [review of *Back Home* and Lee Konitz's *Ideal Scene*], *Down Beat*, December 1987, 35.
16. Kevin Whitehead, [review], *Cadence*, October 1988, 84.
17. In later years, after Marsh's death, Andersen and Mathisen toured Norway with Sollid, drummer John Engels, and Marsh's former student Jimmy Halperin as members of a band called Line Up.
18. Art Lange, "Tenor Tales," *Down Beat*, April 1990, 49.
19. Quoted by Torgrim Sollid in E-mail correspondence, October 2, 1997.

Coda

That Marsh was still barely alive when the ambulance took him from Donte's is suggested by his death certificate, which gives the place of death as St. Joseph's Medical Center in Burbank. He died, according to the certificate, at 12:25 a.m., December 18, 1987. His ethnicity is given as "White/Russian," with "Dutch" immediately over "Russian," which seems to mean that he was a white man of Dutch and Russian ancestry. He was sixty years old, and according to the certificate, he had been a musician all those sixty years: thus did either a hospital clerk or a member of the family, most likely Owen or Gloria, contribute the stuff of myth, as if Marsh had sprung from his mother's womb fully formed, tenor saxophone in hand.

There are other curious features of this document. The cause of death is given as "arteriosclerotic cardiovascular disease," but no physician's signature appears—the whole "physician's certification" section is blank. The only signatures are those of a deputy coroner and the county registrar, both dated December 24, 1987, six days after Marsh's death. Apparently it was customary, if a deceased person had been under treatment by a doctor in the previous six months, to call that doctor by phone and waive the requirement of his signature. Presumably the hospital called one of the several doctors Marsh had been seeing.

There was no autopsy. Had there been, it would almost certainly have revealed that the immediate cause of Marsh's death was cocaine, which constricts the arteries at the same time as it speeds up the heartbeat and thus can cause a heart attack in a person with reasonably normal arteries, as the angiogram that Marsh took in August had shown his to be.

Rumors abound that Marsh took cocaine during the break at Donte's. His doing so would account for his uncharacteristically jovial, backslapping mood before going on again, and it would account for his sudden death.

News of his death traveled fast. Buddy Clark called Fred Waters, who had just arrived home from his own gig. After calling Geraldyne in Santa Cruz, Waters rushed to St. Joseph's. Geraldyne called Owen and Gloria, Marsh's brother and sister, who informed Elizabeth, his mother. Cary Leverette, the owner of Donte's, called pianist Lou Levy. Somebody, probably Chuck Niles, called KLON-FM, the local jazz station.

Among the first to hear the news was Jim Amaresco, a friend and former student who had first met Marsh in the early 1970s. He had contributed the cover art for the first duo record with Susan Chen and had frequently discussed with Marsh his dream of opening his own club, with financial backing from Amaresco. In a 1986 interview with San Francisco disc jockey Jerry Dean, Marsh had spoken as if such a club were an imminent reality. Asked what it would be called, he replied, "Amaresco's—one of the investors." Amaresco was in possession of a key to Marsh's house, which he said Marsh had given him after the first heart attack, along with instructions to look after things in the event of another attack. After consulting by phone with Fred Waters and Lou Ciotti, Amaresco determined that he should go to the house on Runnymede to take calls and safeguard Marsh's belongings. Around 2 a.m. he called Jon Whinnery, whom he had known since high school, and the two met shortly afterward at Marsh's. Whinnery stayed until daybreak, taking with him, when he left, two or three LPs, by Clifford Brown and others, that he had loaned Marsh. Amaresco remained, fielding calls from as far away as New York.

At about 2 p.m. Rhonda Dameron and Jim Krutcher arrived. Rhonda, who felt that she had been providentially spared the sight of Marsh's collapse at Donte's, wanted to retrieve her music for flute and piano that she had played with Marsh. Amaresco, who said he had been instructed not to part with anything in the house unless a family member was present, nevertheless let her take the piano parts, but she could not find the flute parts. Owen and Gloria came by, Gloria confiding to Amaresco that she was glad he was there.

Within a day or two Geraldyne arrived, accompanied by Carol Waters. Amaresco admitted them. In addition to numerous empty vials of cocaine, Geraldyne found unsigned life insurance forms, as well as final divorce papers, also unsigned. There were a few cassettes as well as three seven-and-a-half-inch reel-to-reel tapes from October 1957 of Marsh playing at the Galleon Room in Dana Point with Joe Albany, Von (Bob) Whitlock, and an unidentified drummer. Among the missing items, for which Geraldyne arbitrarily held Amaresco responsible, were Marsh's personal phone and contact book and a publicity photo of Charlie Parker, which, along with a picture of Lester Young and Roy Eldridge, had adorned one wall. The Parker photo had been inscribed, "To Warne—Till we meet again." The inscription was not genuine. Geraldyne assumed that Marsh had inscribed the photo himself, but according to Amaresco it was the product of Hollywood jazz community humor. Lou Levy possessed the original plate of a Parker publicity photo, and Maury Stein, pianist and proprietor of Stein on Vine, a music store across from the musician's union on Vine Street, had had a stack of prints made. He and Levy liked to inscribe and hand them out as a joke to friends who frequented the "Party Room" at the store.

While Marsh's body was still at St. Joseph's Hospital, Geraldyne sat with it for thirty or forty minutes before it was removed for cremation.

The funeral, held at Forest Lawn in Glendale on December 23, was attended by some fifty to seventy-five people. The day was clear, windy, and cold enough that Jon Whinnery wore gloves. Some, like Putter Smith and Clare Fischer, had been given faulty directions that led them to the Hollywood Hills Forest Lawn instead of the correct one in Glendale. Even after reaching the right cemetery, Smith had trouble getting clear directions to the graveside service from an attendant in the information booth who spoke broken English. He arrived just in time to hear Chuck Niles's eulogy, which he described as eloquent and appropriate. Fischer, who Smith said was "fuming and raging" because he had gone through the same misdirection adventures as Smith, arrived a few minutes later, just before trumpet player Clora Bryant's tribute.

Reminiscing about her friendship with Marsh, which began when they both played and hung out on Central Avenue in the late 1940s, Bryant sang some, played the trumpet some, and, as Smith heard it, clearly implied in her extemporaneous remarks that she and Marsh had "made it"—had a sexual relationship—over a period of years. She then recited a two-page rhymed poem she had composed for the occasion, a chronological overview and commentary on Marsh's musical life. It began this way:

> Warne Marion Marsh was born right here in the city of L.A.,
> That's why I have chosen these few words to say today.

It ended as follows:

> To Warne's mother and all of his family, I'd like to remind
> each one of you
> That I know you'll miss his physical being and you know we
> will too.
> But don't forget he came a long way and played a lot of jazz,

> And I'll bet he's still doing his thing out there and that's no
> razz a ma tazz!
> But to all of his pals and peers gathered here today we won't
> say goodbye,
> Ole musician friendships like ole soldiers, fade away,
> they never die.
> Now Warne will play the second ending and he'll tacit for
> about 32 bars,
> Then he'll take it from the top one more time with Shelly
> Manne, Pepper Adams, Buddy Rich all joining in somewhere . . .
> out there . . . among the stars.[1]

After Bryant, the next self-appointed eulogist was a union hanger-on and saxophonist who had never had more than a nodding acquaintance with Marsh. Not a good musician, he was in the habit of claiming friendship with first-rate players who had no reason to associate with him. He would sometimes hire them, only to commit such gaffes as playing pick-up notes as part of the first bar of a song. Clare Fischer told of a time when this musician, beginning "Body and Soul," was so sharp that the famously pitch-sensitive Fischer, playing behind him, angrily raised the key a half step.

Seeing Fred Waters's mother standing beside her son, this speaker assumed that she was Marsh's mother, who did not attend the service. As Smith recounted, "He starts talking to her personally—he's addressing the company at large, but he's talking to her, and he's telling her about Warne and how much he did for us all musically, how when you thought he'd go up, he'd go down, and vice versa, and how his fingerings were so special, how he gave us such wonderful fingerings. His fingerings! He wanted to thank her for all that stuff and thought he was talking to Warne's mother, who wasn't even there."

"The whole thing," reflected Smith, "was awful, so unsatisfactory. It seemed like a metaphor for the whole Warne Marsh trip. As a musician and improvisor, he was the greatest, but he could have done so much more with his career. There was always this not-quite-there feeling. His playing was incredible, but he could have done what Stan Getz did, he could have done what all sorts of guys did who couldn't carry his horn."

After the service Cary Leverette invited everyone to Donte's, normally closed at that hour of the afternoon, for an impromptu wake, and the crowd filled the place as it rarely had to hear his music. On Tuesday, February 5, a variety of groups—Supersax; a quartet featuring fluegelhornist Stacy Rowles, pianist Frank Strazzeri, and guitarist Doug MacDonald; Clora Bryant, who again read her poem; and Gary Foster—played at a memorial concert at Donte's. Don Heckman's review suggests the flavor of it:

> If the music occasionally had the feeling of Valley jazz—crisp, clean, controlled and very smooth around the edges—well, that was OK. That was, after all, the kind of environment in which Marsh spent most of his life.
>
> Yet Marsh, in his unobtrusive way, usually managed to take chances, to stretch his music and his abilities, no matter what or where he was playing.
>
> As loving and caring as the evening was, one couldn't help wondering how much more appropriate the tribute might have been if more of the music performed in his memory had taken the kinds of risks that were so intrinsic to Marsh's musical identity.[2]

Marsh left very little in the way of an estate. The house on Runnymede was still in his mother's name, and his mother's refusal to relinquish control of his father's trust fund had been a perennial source of conflict. When his mother died a few years later, in 1990, the trust fund of some $50,000 passed to his two sons, Casey and Jason. Although the legal document he had drawn up in 1983 was now moot, because it had assumed that his mother's death would precede his own, Casey and Jason nevertheless carried out their father's wishes, giving half of the fund to Geraldyne and splitting the other $25,000 between them. When the boys reach thirty years of age, they will inherit additional money from their grandmother, Elizabeth, whose estate was substantial, probably in the millions.

From Marsh, who died intestate, Geraldyne inherited his Musician's Union pension of $30 per month, around $1,200 cash in his bank account, his Selmer Mark VI tenor saxophone, a student model Armstrong flute given him by Lou Ciotti, and his piano. Ciotti bought his tenor for $1,500, a better-than-fair-market price at the time for a Mark VI in its below-average condition. Ciotti stipulated that Geraldyne could buy it back at the same price any time in the future. The flute was of minimal value, perhaps $75. As for the piano, it was generally understood that Marsh wanted twelve-year-old Jamison Trotter, grandson of Fred and Carol Waters, to have it. Jamie was so gifted that before his first heart attack Marsh had planned to take him to Norway and to have him open his concerts playing solo.[3] Now Shelly Trotter, his mother, had the piano moved to her house, some months later paying Geraldyne $1,600 for it.

Geraldyne, of course, inherited copyright and royalty rights to Marsh's records and compositions (almost all of which were improvisations on the chords of unstated standards). However, many of his accounts with such record companies as were still in existence were actually debits, and he had been such an indifferent businessman that he had never followed through on claiming most of the royalties legally due him for his improvisatory compositions.

Obituaries appeared all over the jazz world. *Down Beat* accorded him
its usual minimal attention, about two hundred words.[4] The French critic
Francois Billard waxed poetic and obscure:

> 'Disciple' of Tristano, he became so by denial. Not by denial of allegiance
> (the comfort of revolutionaries), but by disgust for comfort. As a disciple,
> he preserved the discipline, the absolute sense of perspective, the icy eye and
> the weary glance (and do not talk to me about 'intellectual coldness': pas-
> sion must not love that which makes one lovable).[5]

Carolyn See, whose main experience of Marsh's music was in the peak
years of 1956–57 in Los Angeles, wrote of how she and her hero-worship-
ping friends once took the bus to Marsh's address in North Hollywood
to deliver birthday presents:

> Wind chimes for listening, Japanese prints for seeing, scraps of silk for touch-
> ing, all in a bed of jellybeans. But your address turned out to be a regular
> house! A regular woman, your *Mom*, answered the doorbell. . . . You lived
> in an ordinary house, with an ordinary mom, but you, and those few like
> you, showed us another world, somewhere between the wretched strivings
> of suburban house/car/kids and the equally wretched world of New York
> art/art/*art*. In Southern California you slid the perfect notes of 'Topsy' into
> 'Everything Happens to Me.' You gave us glimpses of an elusive, heavenly
> art where it really is just one soul singing, some soul listening.[6]

Perhaps the most judicious and satisfying pieces appeared in the English *Jazz Journal*. Mike Hennessey, quoting Revelation Records's John
William Hardy's description of Marsh as "a giant, and the equal in stature of Parker, Coltrane, Gillespie, Armstrong, and Lester Young," declared
that Marsh "had nothing like the same influence and he was positively
not an innovator to anything like the same degree. But if you restrict the
comparison to that essential element in jazz which is extemporisation over
a given chord pattern, then Marsh was certainly on a comparable level.
He had one of the quickest harmonic minds in jazz and a marvelous assurance. His technical facility was informed by a flawless sense of structure as he built solos into ingenious, elliptical compositions, starting and
ending phrases with scant regard for bar lines, spinning off neat and
nimble phrases which he pursued through the changes. . . . His playing
was totally free of cliches. . . . and he had a remarkable continuity of
invention. . . . Jazz has lost one of its most distinctive and brilliantly gifted
improvisers."[7]

John O'Neill struck a more personal note. He first heard Marsh in concert with Lee Konitz at the Shaw Theatre in March 1976. Up to that time
he was an aspiring saxophonist "very much under the spell of Coltrane,"

but at that London concert "Warne had shown me that there was another way to play the saxophone. What had impressed me more than anything else was the speed at which he could be melodically inventive." He tells of taking two lessons from Marsh, who gave him "a lifetime's work," and spending the next ten years trying "to persuade other musicians and fans that Warne was the greatest living improviser on the tenor saxophone." O'Neill recalled that when Marsh and Lou Levy spent a week in 1983 as a duo at Pizza on the Park and Pizza Express, musicians of the stature of Cedar Walton and Bob Berg "were frequent visitors. . . . Stan Getz also made an appearance. Perhaps he remembered the occasion when, in Peter Ind's words, Warne had 'run circles' around him at a 1950s jam session." He ended with a point that Marsh frequently made, that "jazz is essentially a live music. Warne was closer than any I knew to this magic spirit of a music that is here for the moment and then 'gone in the air.' . . ."[8]

NOTES

1. Clora Bryant, "A Portrait of Warne Marion Marsh." A condensed version was published in the "Final Notes" section of the publication of the American Federation of Musicians Local 47, *Overture*, February 1988, 8.

2. Don Heckman, "Friends Offer Tribute to Warne Marsh at Donte's," *Los Angeles Times*, 5 February 1988, 19, (6), Calendar section.

3. In 1997, Jamison Trotter was playing as a professional and attending California State University at Northridge as a music major.

4. "Final Bar," *Down Beat,* March 1988, 13.

5. Francois Billard, "Blues Marsh," *Jazz Magazine* (Paris), No. 368, February 1988, 13. My translation.

6. Carolyn See, "One Soul Sings, Some Listen," *Los Angeles Times,* 9 January 1988, 8, (II).

7. Mike Hennessey, "Obituaries," *Jazz Journal* (February 1988): 22.

8. John O'Neill, "Warne Marsh, A Personal Recollection," *Jazz Journal* (August 1988): 10–11.

Evaluations

How good, really, was Warne Marsh? What is his place in jazz history? Many of Warne Marsh's earliest admirers, both fans and musicians, must have had an experience like that of tenor saxophonist Joe Henderson. Henderson, born in 1937, was around fourteen when he first heard Marsh with Lee Konitz and Lennie Tristano on their earliest records. Those records, said Henderson, "just opened my ears. . . . That was a very magical kind of sound that they had. . . . I had heard Flip Phillips and Lester Young, Coleman Hawkins, and a lot of people that were associated with Jazz at the Philharmonic—and then somewhere in there Warne Marsh and Lee Konitz showed on the scene. . . . There's a vital part of whatever it is I'm about today, I'm sure came from that zone, from hearing players [like Marsh and Konitz] who had some technical mastery over the instrument as well as great feeling, I mean in terms of what they came up with as creative people. . . ."

Henderson, however, never heard the 1955 Atlantic record with Konitz, Oscar Pettiford, and Kenny Clarke, or any other of Marsh's subsequent recordings, and spent the next thirty-five years wondering whatever happened to Warne Marsh. "I was forever asking . . . and most people didn't know who I was talking about. . . . He was never really in my sight, only through those records that I had early on. . . . So I never really got a chance to know him, [except] through those records, which I treasured. I mean, I could have had a hundred other records and they wouldn't have meant as much to me as that one album" [the 1955 reissue of the 1949 titles "Marshmallow," "Fishin' Around," "Tautology," and "Sound-Lee"].

Henderson was unaware that Marsh had been a member of Supersax,

277

though he had heard the group's records, until he finally met him in 1987, shortly before Marsh's death. On that occasion, Henderson, playing in Los Angeles with the George Gruntz Concert Jazz Band, had been informed by Lee Konitz, also with the Gruntz band, that Marsh was appearing at Donte's. The next night he went out to see him. "I was really impressed with meeting him, but I was even doubly impressed by the way he was playing, . . . with the way he explored the saxophone, and the way his imagination was working. . . . He was just full of a lot of great surprises, like, 'Wow! Do it again!'"

About a month after their first meeting, Marsh came to hear Henderson at Catalina's in Hollywood. Henderson, chatting with record producer Orrin Keepnews, was thrilled to see Marsh, but Marsh had to introduce himself to Keepnews, who hadn't seen him in years.

Latter-day disciples of Lennie Tristano such as Connie Crothers and Lenny Popkin are adamant in their belief that Marsh was one of the all-time greats, the equal of Charlie Parker and Lester Young and at least as important, in terms of intrinsic value, as such widely influential players as Sonny Rollins or John Coltrane.

Crothers views Marsh as one of the few real innovators in jazz and considers it a "deep tragedy," not just for Marsh but for "the art form as a whole . . . that Warne Marsh's great innovations have not been acknowledged, and studied." She cites as among his innovations his sound: "How do you describe a sound where every note has a different quality? Warne carried inflection in that sense to a different level. It goes way beyond dynamic inflection, or variation in articulation, or even timing. . . . It's a level of insight, musical insight, and because it has not been acknowledged by the world of jazz as a whole, there is this great void there." Also, she says, Marsh "has to be credited with innovation in lines. . . . If you listen to his great solos, one of the things that you will discover is his entirely different and completely innovative conception of phrasing." In *The Art of Improvising* records "his phrasing is so intrinsic that you might not be able to know what tune he's playing . . . [or] where the bar line is going to go. . . ." It was not just the notes but the spaces between them. It was "completely unique to him, his concept of phrasing, space, and form."

Another way he was an innovator, Crothers felt, was in "harmonic improvisation in melodic lines. . . . It went way beyond the conception that we have generalized now in the jazz world of harmonic substitution, which Warne was thoroughly acquainted with, . . . [to] a conception which is less generally known, of harmonic alteration, which changes the *function* of a chord so that it resolves in a different way, maybe beats later, and hence alters the harmonic flow. . . . Warne Marsh did not play changes. What he did was create melody." And Marsh, she adds, was also an innovator in a technical sense, as a saxophonist, especially in his perfectly melodic, unstrained use of the altissimo register, previously used only in a screeching, exhibitionistic way.

To Crothers, as well as to Popkin, Liz Gorrill, and other second-generation adherents of the Tristano school, as well as first-generation students like Peter Ind, the recognition of Marsh as one of the major innovators is merely a matter of time. "There's no way," says Crothers, "that that will be excluded from people's awareness. It's going to happen. We don't know when, but it's inevitable that that will happen."

One of Marsh's most articulate champions is the avant-garde saxophonist, theorist, and composer Anthony Braxton. Braxton, born in 1945, describes how as a precocious twelve year old studying at the Chicago College of Music, already familiar in 1957 with the likes of Jackie MacLean, Ornette Coleman, Miles Davis, John Coltrane, and Paul Desmond, he first heard "Marionette" and "Sax of a Kind" with Marsh, Konitz, and Tristano. "Immediately I was aware of a very different kind of fragile beauty, a music that was for me a very positive and hopeful kind of music, even a wistful kind of music." Unlike Henderson, he made a point of following Marsh's career. The 1955 Atlantic record with Konitz, Oscar Pettiford, and Kenny Clarke, "was a very special record for me," and Marsh's solo on "The Song Is You" on the *Lee Konitz Meets Jimmy Giuffre* album "represented one of the points of definition in my whole life. It struck me so profoundly. I have bought the record four times now, and I *still* play it."

"I have followed his work," said Braxton, "and tried to keep up with every record. His music has influenced me on every level. I think he is one of the great instrumentalists. I refer to him in my classes as a profound . . . stylistic master. He did not, as a composer, have an involvement that would have allowed him to build a restructural music in the way that, for instance, John Coltrane, through composition, developed in the 'Giant Steps' period, changed the harmonic dynamics of the music, and from that point began to move out. Warne would be a stylist who would accept the laws of bebop, but inside of those laws, his work would for me fulfill tendencies of the European mystic dynamic. . . . I consider his work to be the personification of invention and creativity, and for me that's what it's all about."

Marsh's lack of recognition, Braxton believes—and here he is in agreement with Crothers and Popkin—is in large part a matter of race: "Warne's music was not respected by the white or the black community. I have listened all my life, from high school on, to Europeans and African Americans laugh at this guy, not understand this man, talk of his music as if it was cerebral, without feeling, without commitment—incredible, incredible! . . . [I]n America, if you're an African American man, you're perceived as having all this great rhythm and natural talent, but you have no intellectual dynamic that's respected. While the white improviser, an improviser like Warne, is continually challenged about the depth of his feelings and his emotional involvement in the music, and whether or not he can be involved in the music as pure[ly] as an African [American], rather than just trying to rip off the music to get ahead and make a living. . . . [Warne] wasn't believed by the young white *or* African [American] musicians. . . . [W]hen I was in high school I'd be talking with guys and saying, 'I love John Coltrane too, but you can still love Warne.' I mean, it's big enough for everybody, there are many different ways to go forward, but Warne was always—'Well, it doesn't swing,' [they'd say]. . . . You couldn't have both Coltrane and Warne Marsh. . . ."

In fact, says Braxton, "Warne's music, for me swung like hell, it was just different, in the same way that Charlie Parker was different, a different kind of swing." The difference was largely attributable to the influence of Lennie Tristano. "Tristano's understanding of chromaticism would respect what he learned from Bud Powell and Charlie Parker, as well as Arnold Schoenberg, and the French reaction to the Germans, *and* Johann Sebastian Bach at the same time. Warne would come out of that, from that school, and [in] every period in his documented history he always spoke with respect for the African [Americans] *and* the Europeans. But in fact there was no room for a white man with a universal perspective. . . . [O]ur country has a very difficult time in looking at each other separate from preconceived notions about race."

Despite his admiration of Marsh—"There is no stage of his music that doesn't fascinate me"—Braxton does not rank him as highly as Coltrane and Charles Mingus. "By the time John Coltrane died, his music was not just a post-Charlie Parker music. When Charlie Mingus died, he had created a body of music that transcended even his work as an instrumentalist." He sees Marsh as "a master stylist" whose focus on improvisation within the post-Parker mode prevented him from expanding the music as he believes Coltrane and Mingus did. "I wish," he says, "Warne had composed more."

The person with the longest and deepest perspective on Marsh is undoubtedly Lee Konitz. Musically, said Konitz, speaking of the earliest days with Tristano, "There were times when he really felt like a brother, for moments, mainly because we had this mutual affinity with Lennie." Their musical rapport he described as a kind of "magic," a "mysterious" something that "was really special. . . . On a one-to-one basis I can't think of, offhand, any horn player that I've ever had that kind of affinity with. . . . He was an inspiration, to play on the same bandstand with. . . . You had to play at your highest level, or else fall by the wayside, because he was in there doing these ingenious things with the music."

Their personal relationship, however, was a different matter: "I always felt uncomfortable about, around Warne, most all the time." He perceived Marsh as intensely shy and related this character trait to both his use of drugs and his ineptitude in career matters: "I don't think Warne really wanted that much to go out in public. He was a very shy man, and he was involved with drugs, and I think he had a problem, at times, confronting his audience. . . . I frequently thought that the main effect [of his use of drugs and alcohol] is that it would enable someone who doesn't like maybe to come into public as much to come out into public. . . . I can't understand otherwise why he wouldn't have pursued a playing career, because when one spends his life developing to that extent, it seems like he'd want to get approval and use it as much as possible, to do the communicating thing that is supposed to be the name of that game."

Concerning Marsh's willingness to play with journeyman rhythm sections, often students, Konitz commented, "It's the same with Tristano; it's a way of getting off the hook, I always thought. . . . I mean, training people and everything is the ideal way, in some sense—but there are some very well-established rhythm players, and certainly one of my favorite records of Warne's is the one with Paul Chambers and Paul Motian. . . . And I can't forget for a minute, as I'm doing it all the time, that the rhythm section is doing most of the creating of the atmosphere, and if they're just mediocre, as far as you can excel, it still doesn't get beyond what you can do. But when the rhythm section is really contributing an equal share, you get some special music."

Asked what younger players can learn from the example of Warne Marsh, Konitz drew both positive and negative lessons: "Well, they certainly, first of all, can learn a very true dedication to the development of the music. I think that his music came full flower, musically. Sometimes the actual expression of it was not, possibly, full blown, but the actual construction of the music was an indication of a scholarly approach to developing the music. So they can certainly learn that. And again, as with Bird and Prez and all the other really special people who could not handle, in some way, their private and public lives, and had to use substances to get them through the day, we see that that doesn't work. Warne lived longer than most of them did, but still, that's the reason he died, finally. Maybe [without drugs] he would still be living. So that's always an object lesson, I'm afraid a negative one. And also, to make a choice of whether you really want to go out and make a career of communicating whatever it is you're able to do, or just sit back and develop the music for yourself, primarily, is the choice that has to be made, and he was a perfect example of that."

Despite his reservations about Marsh's career and personal life, Konitz had little but praise for his music: "He gave great thought to the lines that he played, and through analysis they stand up, all the time." Speaking of the richness of "surprise" in Marsh's music, Konitz compared him to Joe Henderson: "I heard Joe Henderson last night do incredible technical things, and musical things, he's a great saxophone player, and a very, very creative musician, but—I don't know how to compare that, really—I think Joe has similar qualities, but Warne more so."

Like Braxton, Konitz found it "regrettable" that Marsh did not develop his talent for composition. What value composition—Braxton's "restructural innovation"—has in jazz in relation to improvisational inventiveness—Konitz's and Henderson's "surprise"—is a tricky issue. One might argue, like Connie Crothers, that they are two different things, that jazz is an improvisational art, and that Braxton and others confuse matters by introducing composition into their evaluations. Yet a musician who is primarily a composer can profoundly influence the music, as Duke Ellington and Thelonious Monk have shown. Ultimately the line between composer and improviser is artificial: the perfect jazz artist would improvise solos that have the lasting value and "restructural" power of great compositions.

Finally, given Marsh's consistent use of drugs, mainly marijuana, methamphetamine, and, in the last twenty years of his life, cocaine, it is necessary to ask what effect drugs may have had, not just on his life but also on his music. It seems clear, to begin with, that he was a person of enormous energy. Otherwise he would not have been able to support the simultaneous drain on his system of both the drugs and the high level of musical creativity on which he operated.

Pondering the question on the basis of his association with Marsh throughout the 1980s, Torgrim Sollid said:

> Warne was almost always brilliant in some kind of way, but some times mediocre. It could change from set to set, from tune to tune. When he played the Molde festival [in 1982] he was very relaxed, and played with great strength in an almost simple, noncomplicated way. . . . Same when he was here with Susan [Chen] in 1984. . . . But it is also clear that his bad relationships with drugs from time to time made playing quite difficult for him. You know, we all knew that he smoked [marijuana] a lot. His pot smoking was like his daily coffee, and after awhile we did not even notice it. But the cocaine he kept in deep secret to us in Norway. I don't think he used cocaine that much in Norway anyhow, but more than once his fellow musicians and other friends in Norway observed the devil that haunted him. He could be downright hilarious one second, harsh and unfriendly the next, and then suddenly the most charming and observant friend. Especially business matters could be extremely difficult to handle, with Warne giving out signals of being the exploited musician surrounded by gangsters and devils, in situ-

ations that absolutely nobody with common sense intact could be suspicious. Mostly, all this was clearly related to pot. If it was available, everything was more or less OK; if not, anything could happen. When he saw certain weaknesses in others that he might possess himself, he could lose all his natural empathy and turn into an insensitive and fanatic authority who could come up with long and almost surrealistic speeches reflecting the usual jazz competitiveness, almost always ending with examples from his time with Tristano. The same picture surrounded his playing, but with an absolute difference. With pot his playing was mostly consistent, sometimes brilliant, but it also could vary a lot during the same concert. On such nights he would have trouble controlling his tone, his attack, and even his impeccable time and structural sense. It was like his consciousness was drifting and he had basic trouble in being awake and alert. He just showed all the symptoms common to everybody using cannabis regularly for a very long time, jazz musicians or not. From time to time he made desperate efforts to quit, that would last for a week at the most. A couple of times these short periods happened to be in playing situations, and then he regained all his abilities like magic and played the best possible music, but with a frightened face, like he was being filled up with despair and anxiety. The difference in his music in these two situations really shocked some of his musicians, and they slowly had to realize his very difficult personal situation and adjust to that. As I said, he mostly stayed away from cocaine in Norway. But the day before the start of the recording session for *Sax of a Kind* he came to me in the middle of the night with serious burns on his hands, and on my direct question he told a little bit about his relationship with cocaine. He was very honest, and explained that from time to time it was the only way that he knew that could make him 'reasonably comfortable' and save him from the 'unbearable.' He refused to explain what 'the unbearable' was.

OK, his mental stability could vary, and from time to time he could have problems (very little) with time, timbre, etc. that *could* be related to drugs. I said could be—we will never know. But the fact is that he compensated for his 'lack of the highest level of technical ability' with the greatest emotional power, and this is the focus I miss in his 'heyday' playing from the 1950s. What was really like lightning that evening in Trondheim [in September 1987] was the strong and sudden combination of those ingredients, the sad emotions, the fantastic musical architectonic ability. . . . The music he played in the 1950s was maybe his 'best,' objectively speaking, summing up all musical ingredients, and his playing in the 1980s was different and of mostly very mixed quality. That I blame on the drugs, but not all. Let me say it simply: When he was happy he played good, sometimes fantastic. When he was sad and unhappy, . . . he could even miss a beat or two. And the music he played on his last concert in Norway reminded me so much of the best from 'The Art of Improvisation' and 'Lee Konitz Live at the Half Note.' There it is in a nutshell, what really made him stand out: His one-and-only ability to dare to be intimate in an almost shocking way, at least through his music.

Personally, in listening to Marsh's music of the 1970s and 1980s, I often feel that he is playing his defenses, his hard, tough-guy outer shell, rather than expressing his vulnerable inner self. The conflict between the two was, I think, his central creative battle. Some musicians who worked with Marsh maintain that his greatest playing never got on record, and given his commitment to improvisation and his dislike of formal recording situations, this is entirely possible. However that may be, Marsh's finest recordings—especially from the peak 1949–60 period but also including such later work as *Warne Out*, *A Ballad Album*, his solos with the Clare Fischer big band and on the Elek Bacsik record, his duos with Sal Mosca and Red Mitchell, his trio and quartet work with Niels-Henning Orsted-Pedersen—reveal him as an improviser who could rise to a level that only the greatest jazz artists have reached.

Warne Marsh solo on "Black Jack" ("Blue Lou," aka "Casino"), recorded October 24, 1956, A MODERN JAZZ GALLERY, Kapp KXL5001, transcribed for tenor saxophone by Ted Brown.

Analysis

ANALYSIS OF WARNE MARSH'S SOLO ON "BLACK JACK"
("BLUE LOU," AKA "CASINO"), RECORDED OCTOBER 24, 1956,
A MODERN JAZZ GALLERY, KAPP KXL5001, BY TED BROWN

Many people talk about Warne's harmonic sense, which was certainly formidable. Others talk about his long lines and choice of intervals, which were also remarkable. But I think the essence of Warne's playing was in his ability to improvise great, singing, melodic figures that seem to just soar effortlessly over the whole tune.

There is also a very subtle shifting of time figures back and forth against the underlying 4/4 beat that really starts to generate a sense of forward motion, kicking the time along. In other words, it swings!

This solo on the changes of "Blue Lou" has always interested me because it feels so relaxed and flowing while really moving along at a pretty fast clip.

Melodically it is just great. The chord structure in the first four bars of each section (except the bridge) is moving back and forth chromatically, one bar each: / A♭7 / G7 / A♭7 / G7 / (in the tenor key). This sequence is fun to piay, but is a challenge to improvise on from a horizontal, melodic standpoint, because you constantly have to deal with that chromatic undercurrent, without falling back on devices that will automatically handle that problem. Warne just flows through this stuff like butter. Absolutely brilliant.

290

Rhythmically there is a lot going on underneath the surface that a person may not pick up on when they first hear Warne's solos. They know something is going on, but they are not sure what.

For example: Right from the very first note, he is setting up a series of accents on the down beat, as though he wants to make sure the train is running smoothly down that track before he starts shifting things around on it. At the same time there is also a simple descending melodic line developing by accenting the first beat of each bar, for the first four bars. By the sixth bar, the accents start to move around and continue shifting in groups that emphasize the up beats and down beats in very unpredictable ways.

Throughout jazz history, the great players have always had a way of pushing or bending notes to make their individual sounds, more expressive. Coleman Hawkins, Ben Webster, Lester Young, and Charlie Parker each had his own way of doing it, which is how you knew right away who was playing.

Warne certainly assimilated all of these influences as well as that of Lennie Tristano. And you can sometimes see little segments of these various influences by observing where the accents fall in the solo. To me, Coleman Hawkins and Ben Webster had a feeling of accenting mainly on the down beat. Lester Young had such a beautiful way of floating over everything in that hip, relaxed manner of his—and with that sound! He truly was a swing player with a great, inventive, melodic line.

Charlie Parker changed everybody around. He was swinging so hard, playing great melodic and rhythmic figures that he made stronger by pushing on certain notes, that he just picked up the whole band, especially with the interplay between him and Max Roach on drums. Sometimes Bird would accent a series of eighth notes only on the up beats. Sometimes he would use figures where he was accenting in groups of three eighth notes instead of the usual groups of two or four.

Lennie Tristano picked up Bird's feeling of phrasing in groups of three eighth notes and began to experiment with it to generate a 3/8 feeling over the 4/4 of the rhythm section. He pushed this further by developing figures that were five eighth notes long, seven eighth notes long . . . and so on. He expanded that into a feeling for various odd times (3/8, 5/8, 7/8, or 3/4, 5/4, 7/4) that were superimposed over the basic 4/4 time. Then he started combining eighth-note phrases of different odd lengths to create some very swinging rhythmic figures.

For example: A figure made up of four eighth notes followed by three eighth notes, when repeated, created a 7/8 feeling. A figure of three eighth notes followed by two eighth notes, when repeated, generated a 5/8 feeling. The best combination of all was what Lennie wrote in the last sixteen bars of his line on "I Remember April," using eighth notes in groups of 3–2–3–3 to create an 11/8 figure, which he repeated three times!

You can hear all of these influences in Warne's playing. After doing it for so long it just became a part of him. Lennie told me he was joking around with Warne one time and bet him that he couldn't play a C-scale straight, with no inflections—and Warne supposedly tried and couldn't do it! But those feelings had become so ingrained in him that it just became the way he pushed the air through his horn.

In this solo, for example:

- *Take a look at bar six*, where he uses eighth notes in groups of three and five. Here the accents fall on the first two down beats of the bar, then on the up beat of beat two to finish the bar with the 5/8 group, which emphasizes the fact that the first phrase was a 3/8 and starts that feeling of bouncing off the time like Bird did. In this case those 3/8–5/8 groups are played twice, through bar seven.
- Sometimes he uses this same grouping (3/8–5/8) but does not repeat it, so it is just a one bar figure, where only the *first down beat* of the bar is accented, while the *up beat of beat two* is accented as above and gets that same type of 3/8 push. (See bars 15, 28, 65, 107.)
- *Look at bar twenty-four*—this is the same 3/8–5/8 grouping, *with the whole phrase shifted back a 1/2 beat so it starts on the upbeat of one* in this bar and finishes on the first note of bar twenty-five.
- *Starting on bar seventy-one*, he uses groupings that make up one bar of 3/8–4/8–1/8. But that last 1/8 is the *up beat of beat four*, and that is where he starts a long phrase using only 3/8 accents, played eleven times, through bar seventy-five.

Sometimes on the last note of a phrase, Warne would give a little extra push of air and perhaps *one* wave of vibrato, which would keep pushing the time forward to the next beat while he was taking a breath. You can see some examples of this in bars 17, 26, 31, 44, 53, 61, 69, 106, 110, 113, 123.

Even though Warne was heavily involved with incorporating all of these accents and inflections into his playing, he still maintained that overall continuity of feeling that Lester Young had, that loose, laid back, flowing, legato feeling, in spite of the fact that some of those tempos were really flying.

In this solo, take a look at some of the great melodic ideas that just seem to come pouring out of him:

- The bridge on the second chorus (bars 49–53) creates such a good uplifting feeling.

- The phrase just before the bridge on the fourth chorus (bars 111–113) is weaving such an interesting line . . . but is still pushing those accents at the same time.
- The bridge itself on the fourth chorus (bars 115–120) generates such a happy feeling . . . and the way the phrase ends (on bar 121) is just perfect. [Editor's note: bars 115–117 seem to have reference to the second eight bars of Lester Young's solo on "Jive at Five," a favorite of the Lennie Tristano school. A more direct reference occurs to Marsh's solo on "Broadway," q.v.]

I have also spent a lot of time listening to this solo at half speed. I enjoy it very much because everything is so much more relaxed. You can really hear the subtleties of his phrasing and breath control.

Of course, putting it down on paper slows everything way down, so you can examine it at your own pace and see how it all comes together as a great improvisation. And that is a very important point to remember. It is a pleasure to study Warne's solo on paper. But this whole thing was *improvised* in about *two minutes*. And here we are, still looking at it forty years later. Amazing!

Warne Marsh solo on "Body & Soul," recorded Fall 1957, JOE ALBANY: THE RIGHT COMBINATION, Riverside RLP 12-270, doubletime section only, transcribed for tenor saxophone by Safford Chamberlain.

♫

Analysis

ANALYSIS OF WARNE MARSH SOLO ON "BODY AND SOUL,"
DOUBLE-TIME SECTION, RECORDED FALL 1957, *JOE ALBANY:
THE RIGHT COMBINATION*, RIVERSIDE RLP 12270,
BY RON HOOPES

To talk only about Warne's choice of notes, i.e., use of 3rds, 5ths, 9ths, 13ths, rhythmic figures, nonchord tones, and other musical details, although formidable, would miss the heart of his creativity. What makes the difference between solos by Bach or Charlie Parker and their less-valued contemporaries? In both cases basically the same rhythms and harmonic content are being used. Therefore the essence goes deeper than these surface contents. First, the solos of Bach and Parker are born of emotion rather than mental processes. And that emotion stems from an artistic approach rather the egotistical expression of a personality. Personality is a shell that must be set aside in order for true creative expression to be brought forward.

Warne aptly enlarges on this in the liner notes of his Atlantic 1291 album with Paul Chambers. The goal, he said, was "not to have the music distorted by any elements of your personality that might tend to take away from it as music. That's the difference between an artistic approach and the approach of a personality. The artistic approach doesn't mean you yield self-expression, but it does mean that emphasis is placed on talent rather than personality. . . . [I]t's a matter of how one's ability, one's talent is used—either with complete integrity and artistically or primarily as a means of maintaining a 'personality'. . . . [I]t's the essence of your

298

personality that is transmuted into music; the 'I' is no longer italicized."
He further states that after Charlie Parker's great improvisations, many
absorbed his ideas and level of playing but "very few people are continuing to grow as improvisers." I believe Warne was one of these few.

Even Warne's beautifully rich and unique tone is not sought after as an
end in itself, but is a result or by-product of emotional/artistic expression.

Joe Albany, who joins forces with Warne here, was a highly creative
player. Here he pushes and inspires Warne, at times with an almost an-
tagonistic interplay. If not "the right combination," it's a unique combination. The bass and drums seem to just hold on.

Improvisation and composition are related to each other the way "step
time" and "real time" entries are related in a computer music-notation
program. The same information can be entered with both methods. The
main difference is the time factor. In step time, notes are entered one by
one, with as much time for reflection as may be desired. In real time notes
are entered by playing the piece as in a performance, with much need for
accuracy and spontaneous input, void of reflection.

Warne is a real-time master. His sense of time is demanding and authoritative. A good example of his driving rhythm might be measures 49–56.
The stronger the rhythm section, the more authoritative control Warne
takes. His lyrical beauty is penetrating, as in measures 9, 25, and 43–44,
where the original melody is singing its way through the improvisation.
Another example of his lyrical flow is in measures 33–35, where the
eighth-note phrase beginning on beat 4 of measure 32 is further developed
in a second eighth-note phrase beginning on beat 4 of measure 34 and
continuing through measure 35.

I have a Charlie Parker recording on which Bird or someone in the band
calls out to the pianist taking a solo, "Hear yourself!"—i.e., the pianist
probably was into some cliches, or "finger licks," however nice they might
have been. When the musician and the creation are in harmony, as with
Warne, he truly "hears himself."

Some details observed:

- Measure 9 is a masterful embellishment of the original melody, the phrase
  ending an octave higher.
- Measure 16—Beat 2 anticipates the modulation, which actually begins on
  beat 3, from the D♭ of the first 16 bars to the D Major of the bridge.
- Measures 20–21—Hang on! With the shift in beat 4 of measure 20 from
  sixteenth notes to a triplet figure that is repeated throughout measure 21,
  Warne displaces the time. By the end of measure 21 the listener (mistakenly) feels that beat 1 is on the "and" of beat 4. The sixteenth notes starting in beat 2 of measure 22 bring the time-feel back in line.
- Measures 13–14, 25, 32–33, 34–35, and 43—Dramatic lyrical use of eighth
  notes (as opposed to sixteenth notes) from time to time as the solo builds.

Measure 43 is a rhythmically displaced quote of the original melody, leading to the quarter-note quote of measure 44, a major high point of the solo.
(Measure 63 is another fine use of quarter notes.)

- Measures 11, 16, 53, 54—Warne starts these phrases with a nonchord tone
  that perfectly illustrates their classic use, i.e., accented passing tones and
  appoggiaturas. Notice how the rest in measures 11 and 53 suggests the
  chord tone.
- Measures 32–35—Beautiful dramatic use of a motive treated sequentially:
  the eighth-note figure on beat 4 of measure 32 and beat 1 of measure 33
  is repeated from beat 4 of measure 34 through beat 1 of measure 35, but
  separated by a wonderful lead into the sequenced motive.
- Measures 59–60—sixteenth-note pattern, with the strong beat alternating
  falling on each note of the pattern.

Warne's solo has great form, with a wonderful forward motion, and like
a good story it reaches a peak about two-thirds of the way through. This
is usually true with most literary and musical compositions. The solo really starts to build in measure 25, the last 8 bars of the first chorus, and
continues to build in intensity to a climax around measure 44, with a secondary emotional flurry in measures 49–52. Measures 53–56 probe the
chord structure in depth, and the solo tapers off with a little light-hearted
feel in measures 57–60. Measures 61–62 add some final driving thoughts
in this masterful solo.

Warne Marsh solo on "It Could Happen to You," recorded April 18-19, 1980, THE MITCHELL-MARSH BIG TWO: HOT HOUSE, Storyville LP-4092, transcribed for tenor saxophone by Gary Foster.

Analysis

ANALYSIS OF WARNE MARSH SOLO ON "IT COULD HAPPEN TO
YOU," RECORDED APRIL 18–19, 1980, *THE MITCHELL-MARSH BIG
TWO: HOT HOUSE*, STORYVILLE LP-4092, BY GARY FOSTER

Performed as a duo with bassist Red Mitchell before an enthusiastic live
audience in Stockholm, Sweden, this solo demonstrates how perfectly
an often-played standard can be raised to the level of great art. Virtually
a symphonic performance is implied by the single-line voices of two of
jazz's masters.

Warne's stream-of-thought improvising is here, as in virtually all of his
work, full of surprise. Measures 14–16, 39–44, and 56 contain examples
of extraordinarily Warne-like moments.

Looking at these few measures first:

Measures 14, 15, and 16: Over these three 4/4 measures Warne accents the
equivalent of four measures of 3/4 as four groups of six eighth notes. The
first group of six derives from a simple G7. The next two groups imply
the altered dominant scale on the G7, and the final six-note group implies
the altered dominant scale on C7.

Measures 39 through 44: Beginning on the third beat of measure 39 and continuing through the first two beats of measure 44, Warne plays a long phrase
with subtle shifting accents that creates a moment of remarkable tension. The
integrity of this line obviates the actual changes, and the brilliance of its
construction justifies the way it evolves. He resolves this chromatic moment
by returning to a diatonic choice of tones in the following two measures. Red
holds his own beautifully through all of this.

Measure 56: Over D7 harmony, Warne outlines the tri-tone (A Flat) with diatonic tones of the A Flat scale. Another lovely surprise for the ear.

Other points of interest:

Measure A: These pick-up notes to his first chorus, uncharacteristically for Warne, invoke the sound of a simple blues scale.
    Measures 31 and 32: At the same place in the form as measure A, here bridging from his first to second chorus, Warne again uses the blues scale sound over the tonic and turn-around chords.
    Measures 5–6, 21–22, 37–38, and 53–54: These measure occur in each A section of the song. Warne treats them quite diatonically as the basic sheet music changes: F Major 7 and B Flat Major 7. These measures are often played B Flat minor 7-E Flat 7 / A Flat minor 7-D Flat 7. Warne avoids any substitute harmony or chromaticism here.
    Measures 58 through 65: From the fourth beat of measure 58 to the end of the solo, Warne plays only tones of the F Major scale. It is as if he reminds us that, for all the rhythmic and harmonic subtlety of his musical language, Lester Young is still his inspiration. The solo ends with a very "Prez-like" wind-up.

All of the above comes with apologies to Warne. He most sought spontaneity and concentration on finding the new when improvising. I believe Warne respected those qualities above almost everything else in life. Except for using the ear to study and internalize a solo, Warne would probably have thought this after-the-fact written critical analysis unimportant.

Persons Interviewed

1. Alexander, Claude
2. Altman, Paul
3. Amaresco, Jim
4. Anthony, Ron
5. Aplanalp, Peter
6. Arms, Brewster
7. Aronoff, Darwin
8. Bank, Dick
9. Bannister, John
10. Bauer, Billy
11. Block, Jack
12. Boyd, Curtis
13. Braxton, Anthony
14. Breckow, John
15. Broadbent, Alan
16. Brown, Ted
17. Bryant, Clora
18. Bunker, Larry
19. Byers, Billy
20. Cadena, Ozzie
21. Candoli, Conte
22. Canino, Frank
23. Canterino, Mike
24. Cantor, Mark
25. Chech, John
26. Chen, Susan
27. Choice, Harriet
28. Christlieb, Pete
29. Ciotti, Louis
30. Clark, Buddy
31. Clemens, Marcel
32. Coffman, Charles
33. Coleman, George
34. Cornelius, Mursalin M.
35. Crothers, Connie
36. Crouch, Stanley
37. Cuscuna, Michael
38. Dallas, Sonny
39. Davidson, Don
40. Diorio, Mark
41. Drasnin, Robert
42. Drewes, Billy
43. Easton, Jon
44. Eckinger, Isla
45. Eschete, Ron
46. Everett, Tom
47. Fagen, Donald
48. Falkner, Chuck
49. Feinfield, Arthur
50. Ferguson, Sherman

51. Fiore, Daniel
52. Fischer, Clare
53. Fiskin, Arnold
54. Flory, Med
55. Fontana, Carl
56. Forrest, Dick
57. Foster, Gary
58. Frank, David
59. Garretson, Ralph
60. Gerheim, Jake
61. Gianelli, Rhonda Dameron
62. Gilbert, Judy Moore Tristano
63. Gitler, Ira
64. Giuffre, Jimmy
65. Gold, Bob
66. Gold, Mike
67. Goldings, Larry
68. Goldman, Albert
69. Golia, Vinny
70. Gorrill, Liz
71. Grant, Hal (Harold Granowsky)
72. Gregorio, Guillermo
73. Gruber, Freddie
74. Haden, Charlie
75. Halperin, Jimmy
76. Hammer, Tardo
77. Hanna, Jake
78. Hardaway, Bob
79. Hardy, John William
80. Heath, Albert "Tootie"
81. Heath, Jimmy
82. Heggeland, Norm
83. Henderson, Joe
84. Hentoff, Nat
85. Heymann, Jim
86. Higson, James
87. Hoopes, Ron
88. Hughart, Jim
89. Immel, Earl
90. Ind, Peter
91. Ingram, Cliff
92. Jacobson, Peter
93. Johnston, Randy
94. Jones, Hank
95. Jones, Rick
96. Kart, Lawrence
97. Keepnews, Orin
98. Kellock, Jeremy
99. Khouri, George
100. Kiffe, Karl
101. Klopotowski, John
102. Konitz, Lee
103. Koonse, Larry
104. Kreiswirth, Gabe
105. Krutcher, Jim
106. Lang, Ronnie
107. LaPorta, John
108. LaSpina, Steve
109. Lathower, Mauri
110. Lawson, Janet
111. Leonard, Anita
112. Lesser, Victor
113. Lester, James
114. Levitt, Alan
115. Levy, Lou
116. Liebman, David
117. Lifton, Lloyd
118. Litweiler, John
119. Lopes, Joe
120. Lynn, Bobbi
121. Mancuso, Roger
122. Mandel, Johnny
123. Manning, Chuck
124. Manning, Don
125. Marable, Larance
126. Markowitz, Richard (Dick Allen)
127. Marsalis, Branford
128. Marsh, Casey
129. Marsh, Elizabeth Marion
130. Marsh, Geraldyne
131. Marsh, Jason
132. Marsh, Owen
133. Martin, Terry
134. Mayer, Frances

135. McComb, Beverly Carpenter
136. McKay, Dave
137. McKenna, Dan
138. McKinney, John F. "Jack"
139. McKusick, Hal
140. Migliori, Jay
141. Miner, Bill
142. Mitchell, Dick
143. Mitchell, Keith "Red"
144. Montrose, Jack
145. Morgan, Alun
146. Morgan, Lanny
147. Mosca, Sal
148. Motian, Paul
149. Mraz, George
150. Nearhoff, Betty Churchill
151. Nelson, Don
152. Nessa, Chuck
153. Niemack, Judy
154. Nimitz, Jack
155. Okamoto, Taro
156. Overberg, Don
157. Oxford, Gloria Marsh
158. Pekar, Harvey
159. Perkins, Bill
160. Ponomarev, Valery
161. Popkin, Lenny
162. Richmond, Kim
163. Roach, Max
164. Rockman, Russell
165. Rumsey, Howard
166. Runyan, Thomas
167. Sauls, Earl
168. Scattaretico, Peter
169. Schaap, Phil
170. Schlitten, Don
171. Schwartz, Anton
172. Scott, Betty
173. Scott, Skip
174. See, Carolyn
175. Sewing, Harold
176. Shain, Roy
177. Shorter, Wayne
178. Shostac, David
179. Silsbee, Kirk
180. Silverman, Mickey
181. Silverman, Steve
182. Smith, Carson
183. Smith, Pat "Putter"
184. Sollid, Torgrim
185. Solomon, Joe
186. Specht, Donald
187. Squillante, Joseph
188. Stambaugh, Richard
189. Stewart, Robert
190. Stone, Butch
191. Strazzeri, Frank
192. Stubblefield, John
193. Sunkel, Suzanne
194. Swofford, Meri
195. Tabackin, Lew
196. Taenaka, Toshiya
197. Talbert, Thomas
198. Tana, Akira
199. Teekens, Gerry
200. Tirabasso, John
201. Tristano, Carol
202. Trujillo, Bill
203. Ulanov, Barry
204. Velasco, Art
205. Vinnegar, Leroy
206. Von Essen, Eric
207. Walter, Donald
208. Ward, Bob
209. Waters, Carol
210. Weber, Mark
211. Westbrook, Forrest
212. Wettenhall, Simon
213. Whinnery, Jon
214. Whitlock, Von "Bob"
215. Williams, Earl
216. Williams, Keith
217. Windo, Gary
218. Wofford, Mike
219. Woods, Phil
220. Ziskind, George

Warne Marsh's Recorded Legacy

This listing follows formal discographical procedure in some respects but departs from it in others. For issued records and broadcasts I have used the standard format, with titles of tunes in columns. I have attempted to include all known issues as of mid-1998. For the many private tapes, however, I have simply listed tunes linearly in italics. An advantage of this practice is that one can tell at a glance whether an entry is a private tape or an issued record or broadcast. I have also elected to classify by issued recordings rather than by date. Thus, although the listing is on the whole chronological, there are times when different recording sessions for the same record result in violations of chronology.

Previously the most complete listing was that of Dr. Michael Frohne of Germany, published under the title *Warne Marsh Discography* on the internet. The internet address is http://www.uni-duisburg.de/AVMZ/frohne/marsh/disco.htm. Frohne's e-mail address in April 1998 was michael-frohne@t-online.de. I am heavily indebted to Dr. Frohne for information on reissues and private tapes from performances in Europe. Where I have used information found only in his discography I have so indicated. I have also drawn on Jack Goodwin's discography for his additions to Frohne's.

Alun Morgan first apprised me of the Storyville recordings of December 1975 with Nels Orsted Henning-Pederson, and Emil Knudsen of Storyville was kind enough to send me complete information on those sessions from the Storyville files. Mark Cantor, Betty Churchill Nearhoff, and James Higson have contributed information on films.

For private tapes other than those listed by Frohne and Goodwin I have drawn on information from Claude Alexander, John Breckow, John Burton, Mursalin Cornelius, Tom Everett, Jeremy Kellock, Bill Miner, Alun Morgan, Lewis Porter, Harold Sewing, and George Ziskind.

I have also consulted the following standard print discographies:

Bruyninckx, W. *Modern Jazz: Be-Bop, Hard Bop, West Coast*, [Alt. title: *Modern Discography*] *1942–1985*. 6 vols. Copy Express, c/o Projekt, Schuttersvest 44, 2800 Mechelen, Belgium. 1985.

Bruyninckx, W. *Progressive Jazz: Free, Third Stream, Fusion* [Alt. title: *Progressive Discography*], *1942–1985*. 5 vols. Copy Express, c/o Projekt, Schuttersvest 44, 2800 Mechelen, Belgium. 1985.

Jepson, Jorgen Grunnett. *Jazz Records 1942–1962*. J. G. Jepson, Nillavey 14, Hasseris-Aalborg, Denmark, 1963.

Warne Marsh–Karl Kiffe–André Previn. Marsh, ts; Kiffe, d; Previn, p. (Los Angeles, c. 1942–43, private, 1 tune.) *How High the Moon.*

Hollywood Canteen Kids: *Junior Jive Bombers*. Exact personnel unknown. In June 1943 known personnel included Warne Marsh, Morton Friedman, Bill Cushman, ts; Betty Churchill, Dick Selix, as; Don Walter, as, bs; Johnny Chech, Chuck Falkner, Harry Matthews, Don Cowan, Neil Cunningham, tpt; Scott McKenna, Dave Wells, Chris Martin, Bob Hall, tb; Bob Clarke, p; Harold Jacobs, guit; Ronnie Steelman, b; Karl Kiffe, d. Later personnel included Billy Byers, tb; Don Davies, tpt; Ronnie Lang, as; Bob Hardaway, ts. Marsh plays in the ensemble on the sound track but does not appear on screen. (Short film, Warner Brothers, Los Angeles, 1944.)

Drumboogie (features Karl Kiffe, w/Marsh solo)
Mutiny in the Nursery (w/unknown female vocalist)
Unknown titles

Hollywood Canteen Kids: *Song of the Open Road*. Full-length movie, Republic/United Artists, starring Jane Powell, with Edgar Bergen/ Charlie McCarthy, Bonita Granville, W. C. Fields, Sammy Kaye band. Personnel: See *Junior Jive Bombers*, above. Marsh both plays on sound track and appears on screen. (Los Angeles, prob. Republic Studios sound stage, Jan.–Feb. 1944.)

The Teen-Agers. Known personnel in 1945–46 included Jimmy Higson, leader; Warne Marsh, Harold Kuhn, ts; Robert Drasnin, Earl Siskind (sp?), Ronnie Lang, as, cl, fl; Gordon Reeder, bs; Ralph Clark, Don Davies, Ollie Mitchell, Hank Geis, tpt; Norman Barker, Billy Byers, Robert Butler, tb; Al Terry, g; André Previn, p; Chick Parnell, b; Phil Ramacher, d. (Radio broadcast, NBC, *The Hoagy Carmichael Show*, Los Angeles, c. Nov. 1945-April 1946, private.)

Apple Honey   NBC radio broadcast

Hollywood Canteen Kids with Kay Thompson and the Williams Brothers: Title Unknown. Kay Thompson, Andy Williams, Richard Williams, Robert Williams, Donald Williams, v; for Canteen Kids band, see *Junior Jive Bombers*, above. (Movie short, MGM? Los Angeles, c. 1946.)

Hollywood Canteen Kids: *Double Rhythm.* Jimmy Higson, leader, p; Warne Marsh, ts; Ronald Langer (Ronnie Lang), as; Gordon Reeder, bs; Ralph Clark, Henry (Hank) Geis, Don Davies, Robert Fowler, Richard Yates, tpt; George Faye, Norman Barker, Robert Butler, tb; Albert Terry, g; Ray Turner, Jack Golden, p; Charles (Chick) Parnell, b; Richard Rolf, Ralph Lee, George Wideler, Richard Hazard, unknown instrs. One tune on sound track has tenor sax solo that probably is by Marsh, who does not appear on screen. (Short film, Paramount Studios, Los Angeles, sound track recording session Jan. 11, 1946.)

Second Group Special Services Band, U.S. Army, Camp Lee, Virginia. Known personnel included Phil Vincent, leader; Warne Marsh, ts; Fred Waters, as; Gaynor Maxwell, bs; Herb Patnoe, Bill West, tpt; Jim Lester, tb, arr; Don McCrady, tb; Dick Mitkowski, p; Jimmy Joyner, d; Four Jacks and a WAC, v; others unknown. (Camp Lee, Va., 1946, private, 28 tunes. Asterisk [*] identifies tunes with tenor solos, probably by Marsh.) *Just You, Just Me, *Exactly Like You, *Just the Way You Look Tonight,*Oodles of Needles, *Opus 3, *How High the Moon, *Dinah, *This Is Our Waltz, untitled, *Jeannie with the Light Brown Hair, Adios, Prisoner of Love, When Your Lover Has Gone, untitled theme, My Heart Stood Still, *Prelude to a Kiss, I Don't Know Why, *Where or When, Ghost of a Chance, I've Got You Under My Skin, *Cherokee, *Somewhere in the Night, untitled, *I'm Thrilled, *Hopeless Opus, The Very Thought of You, Night and Day, untitled theme. (*Marsh arranged half of "Jeannie with the Light Brown Hair.")

Buddy Rich: *The Legendary '47–'48 Orchestra*.*Tommy Allison, Charlie Walp, Frank LoPinto, tp; John Mandel, btp; Rob Swope, Mario Daone, Jack Carmen, tb; Hal McKusick, cl, as; *Warne Marsh, Ben Lary, *Martin "Mickey" Rich, ts; Harvey Levine, bs; Jerry Schwartz, p; Terry Gibbs, vb; Charlie Leeds, b; Stan Kay, Buddy Rich, d. (*Liner notes for the record cited below list "Eddie Sands," alto sax, in place of Martin Rich, tenor. But according to Hal McKusick, Marsh, playing tenor, took Nick [not Eddie] Sands's place in the band, playing Sands's alto book. Also, Allison is said by John Mandel to have played lead trumpet on this band, not Dale Pearce as listed in the liner notes.) (Hollywood, Calif., Hollywood Palladium, July 20, 1948.)

Fine and Dandy	Hep CD 12
I May Be Wrong	————

Same personnel (Hollywood, Calif., July 27, 1948.)

Little White Lies	————
You Go to My Head	————
Queer Street	————
Robbin's Nest	————

Same personnel, except Doug Mettome, tp, for Lo Pinto; Bob Ascher, tb, for Carmen; Jimmy Giuffre, ts, for M. Rich (New York, October 28, 1948.)

I've Got News for You	————
A Man Could Be a	
Wonderful Thing	————
Good Bait	————
Four Rich Brothers	————
The Carioca	————

(Marsh does not appear on other tracks on this record. The tenor solos on "Fine and Dandy," "Queer Street," "Four Rich Brothers," and "The Carioca" may be by Marsh, but could be by Ben Lary, who played most of the tenor solos on this band.)

Lennie Tristano Group. Lennie Tristano, p; Lee Konitz, as; Warne Marsh, ts; John LaPorta, as and/or cl; others unknown. (Probably Tristano's studio, New York City, 1948, private, 2 long cuts.) *Unknown titles.*

Lennie Tristano Sextet. Lee Konitz, as; Warne Marsh, ts; Lennie Tristano, p; Billy Bauer, g; Arnold Fishkin, b; Harold Granowsky, d. (New York City, Capitol Recording Studio, Mar. 4, 1949.)

3413 Wow	Capitol 57-60003; H/T 371; M11060; STBO-1970; HCdV(A)1013
3414 Crosscurrent	————; unissued; ————; unissued; unissued

Same personnel except Denzil Best, d, replaces Granowsky. (New York City, May 16, 1949.)

3784 Marionette	Capitol 57-60013;	H/T371;	M11060
3785 Sax of a Kind	———;	EAP1-491;	M11060
3786 Intuition	Capitol 1224;	EAP1-491;	M11060
3787 Digression (Intuition II)	unissued;	———;	———

(The above six tracks were originally issued on 78-rpm discs, and Capitol Records has destroyed written files concerning old 78s. All six tracks were reissued on LP on *CAPITOL JAZZ CLASSICS*, Vol. 14, M11060, and later on LENNIE TRISTANO/TADD DAMERON: *CROSSCURRENTS*, Affinity (GB) AFF-149. Frohne lists the following additional reissues of all six titles:

VIP (A) LP17; Cap (NL) 5CO52-80853; Capitol (J) CR8084 entitled *JAZZ MASTERS OF THE 40's: HOT VS. COOL*; Capitol (J) ECJ-50076 entitled *COOL & QUIET*/LENNIE TRISTANO-BUDDY DEFRANCO. Additionally he lists "Crosscurrents" as reissued on Capitol EAP1-491, Capitol (D) K-41549, and Telefunken (D) 80177; "Marionette" on Franklin Mint FMJAZZ061; "Sax of a Kind" on Telefunken (D) K-1549; "Intuition" on Telefunken (D) C80263, Capitol 1224, Capitol (GB) CL13456, Capitol (GB) T20578, HCdV (A) 1013 entitled *JAZZ PERSPECTIVE—LENNIE TRISTANO*, Capitol T796 and Capitol (E) IJ060-80156M entitled *HISTORY OF JAZZ*, Vol. 4, *ENTER THE COOL*, and Franklin Mint FMJAZZ061 entitled *COOL JAZZ, 3RD STREAM*.)

Lee Konitz Quintet. Lee Konitz, as; Warne Marsh, ts; Sal Mosca, p; Arnold Fishkin, b; Denzil Best, d. (New York City, June 28, 1949.)

JRC28 untitled	unissued
JRC29 & JRC30-G Marshmallow	New Jazz 807; Prestige 7004 & 24081
JRC30 & JRC31-D Fishin' Around	———; ———& ———

JRC31 untitled* unissued

(*Bruyninckx assigns matrix number JRC29, not JRC31, to this cut and adds, "It is generally accepted that JRC28 and JRC29 are the rejected versions of 'Tautology' and 'Sound-Lee' which [i.e., the issued versions] were recorded in September." Prestige 7004 is titled *LEE KONITZ WITH TRISTANO, MARSH & BAUER*; Prestige 24081 is titled *FIRST SESSIONS 1949/50*. Frohne lists the following additional reissues for "Marshmallow" and "Fishin' Around": Prestige EP1314, LP101, 7250; Prestige/Fantasy OM-2008, OJC-1861/2; MIDsc (GB) 1111; Esq (GB)

EP15, 32-027; Xtra (GB) 5049; Gazelle (S) 2003; Metronome (S) MEP-44: *LEE KONITZ QUINTET WITH WARNE MARSH*; Barclay (F) 4014, BLP84062; HMV (F) FELP100008; VSM (I) FELP10013; Prestige (J) SMJ-6522.)

Same personnel except Jeff Morton, d, replaces Best. (New York City, Sept. 27, 1949.)

JRC39 F Tautology	New Jazz 813; Prestige 813, 7004 & 24081
JRC40-B Sound-Lee	————; ————, ———— & ————

(Reissues: Same as for "Marshmallow" and "Fishin' Around." Additionally, "Sound-Lee" appears on *LEE KONITZ: PALO ALTO*, Giants of Jazz CD 53182 and, says Frohne, MusicaJazz (I) 2MJP-1018 (*I MAESTRI DEL SAX-ALTO*).

Lennie Tristano Group. Lennie Tristano, p; Lee Konitz, as; Warne Marsh, ts; others unknown. (Soldier Meyer's, Chicago or New York City, 1949, private, 1 tune.) *Fishin' Around.*

Lennie Tristano Quintet: *Live at Birdland, 1949*. Warne Marsh, ts; Lennie Tristano, p; Billy Bauer, g; Arnold Fishkin, b; Jeff Morton, d. (New York, Dec. 15–31, 1949.)

Remember	Jazz Records JR1-CD
Pennies	————
Foolish Things	————
Indiana	————
I'm No Good without You	————

Lennie Tristano Sextet: *Stars of Modern Jazz Concert*. Lee Konitz, as; Warne Marsh, ts; Lennie Tristano, p; Billy Bauer, g; Joe Shulman, b; Jeff Morton, d. (*Voice of America* overseas radio broadcast, "Jazz Club USA" series, Carnegie Hall, New York City, Dec. 25, 1949.)

You Go to My Head	VOA ET J65; IAJRC-20
Sax of a Kind*	————; ————; VOA ET JC21

(*Lewis Porter says "Sax of a Kind" is identified erroneously by an announcer as "Crosscurrent," indicating the possibility of another extant VOA title. Additional reissues listed by Frohne: VOA (GB) CP2; Dan (J) VC-5013; Braba (I) BB-01: *LENNIE TRISTANO, BLUES OF A KIND*; Jass Records J-CD-16:*CARNEGIE HALL XMAS '49*.)

Lennie Tristano Sextet: *Wow.* Lennie Tristano, p; Warne Marsh, ts; Lee
Konitz, as; Billy Bauer, g; unknown, b and d. (New York City, c. 1950.)

Wow	Jazz Records JR-9 CD
Remembrance	————
April Fool	————
Subconscious-Lee	————
Fugue in D Minor, BWV 899	————
Chord Interlude	————
Sound-Lee	————
Do the Things You Do	————
No Figs	————

Hadda Brooks. Lee Konitz, as; Warne Marsh, ts; Hadda Brooks, p and vc;
unknown, b and d. (New York City, c. Mar. 1950.)

DLGF 50286 Hadda's Boogie	London (E) 30116 (45 rpm)
DLGF 50287 I Hadn't Anyone	
Till You (v)	————

Warne Marsh-Lloyd Lifton Duo. Warne Marsh, ts; Lloyd Lifton, p. (Unknown location, probably New York City, private, 1 tune.) *Somebody
Loves Me*.

Kai Winding Group. Kai Winding, tb; Warne Marsh, ts; Billy Taylor, p;
Jack Lesberg, b; Charlie Perry, d; Melvin Moore (1), vc. (New York, Apr.
27, 1951.)

L8050 Deep Purple (1)	Cosmopolitan 300; IAJRC-15;
	Xanadu 172
L8051 You're Blase (1)	unissued; unissued ; ————
L8052 I'm Shooting High	Cosmopolitan 300; IAJRC-15; ————
L8053 The Moonshower	unissued; unissued; ————

(Xanadu 172 is titled *BE-BOP REVISITED*, Vol. 3. Marsh solos only on
"I'm Shooting High" and "The Moonshower." Frohne lists reissue on
IAJRC (Can) 15: *BATTLE OF TENOR SAXES*.)

Lennie Tristano Quintet: *Live in Toronto, 1952*. Lee Konitz, as; Warne
Marsh, ts; Lennie Tristano, p; Peter Ind, b; Alan Levitt, d. (UJPO Hall,
Toronto, Canada, Jul. 17, 1952.)

Lennie's Pennies	Jazz Records JR5; Jazz Records JR5-CD
317 East 32nd Street	————; ————

content

You Go to My Head	———; ———
April	———; ———
Sound-Lee	———; ———
Back Home	———; ———

Warne Marsh: *Live in Hollywood.* Warne Marsh, ts; Hampton Hawes, p; Joe Mondragon, b; Shelly Manne, d. (The Haig, Los Angeles, Dec. 23, 1952.)

Fine and Dandy	Xanadu 151
You Go to My Head	———
I Can't Believe that You're in Love with Me	———
Buzzy	———
All the Things You Are	———
I'll Remember April	———
I Got Rhythm	———

Metronome All Stars. Roy Eldridge, tp; Kai Winding, tb; John LaPorta, cl; Lester Young, Warne Marsh, ts; Terry Gibbs, vb; Teddy Wilson, p; Billy Bauer, g; Eddie Safranski, b; Max Roach, d; Billy Eckstine, v. (New York City, Jul. 9, 1953.)

53S507 How High the Moon, Part I	MGM X1078 & (GB) 2353071)
53S508 How High the Moon, Part II (Eckstine out)	——— & ———
53S509 St. Louis Blues, Part I	——— & ———
53S510 St. Louis Blues, Part II (Eckstine out)	——— & ———

(Marsh solos only on "How High," Part II. MGM 2353071 is titled *BILLY ECKSTINE'S GREATEST HITS.* Reissues listed by Frohne: "How High," Part II, on MGM (GB) EP574; MGM (J) EMG3; MCM (J) MM2095; MCM (J) 109. "St. Louis Blues," Parts I and II, on Radio Television Belgrad (YU) RBT 4329; all on MGM E-31: *BILLY ECKSTINE, MISTER B WITH A BEAT*; Swingtime (DK, I) ST-1015: *BILLY ECKSTINE, BLOWING THE BLUES.*)

Lee Konitz with Warne Marsh. Lee Konitz, as; Warne Marsh, ts; Sal Mosca, p; Billy Bauer, g; Oscar Pettiford, b; Kenny Clarke, d. (New York City, June 14, 1955.)

| 1573 Two Not One | Atlantic LP1217 |

1574 There Will Never Be
   Another You   ————
1575 Donna Lee   ————
1576 Don't Squawk   ————
1577 Topsy (Mosca out)   ————
1578 I Can't Get Started
   (Mosca out)   ————
1579 Background Music   ————

(All titles reissued on Mosaic MD6-174, *THE COMPLETE ATLANTIC RECORDINGS OF LENNY TRISTANO, LEE KONITZ & WARNE MARSH*; "Topsy" also appears on Atlantic R2-71726: *ATLANTIC JAZZ SAXOPHONES*, Vol. 2; Metronome MEP 252; GdJ (I) 43: *I GRANDI DEL JAZZ, LEE KONITZ*; "I Can't Get Started" also appears on *POST BOP*, Atl 81705; Metronome MEP 253; GdJ (I) 43; Frohne lists the following additional issues: "Two Not One" on Atl EP552; Metronome MEP253; Franklin Mint FMJAZZ061: *COOL JAZZ, 3RD STREAM MUSIC*; "Another You" on GdJ (I) 43: *I GRANDI DEL JAZZ, LEE KONITZ*; "Donna Lee" and on Metronome MEP 252; New World NW242: *NICA'S DREAM*; "Don't Squawk" on GdJ (I) 43; all on Atl (J) P6071 & P4549A; Atl (Eu) 900501; Atl (GB) 590020: *ABSTRACTIONS*; Atl (Eu) 50298: *THAT'S JAZZ, Vol. 21, LEE KONITZ & WARNE MARSH*. Lon (GB LTZ-K15025); Mus (I) LPM-2007.)

Same personnel, but Ronnie Ball, p, replaces Mosca. (New York City, June 21, 1955.)

1580 All the Things You Are   unissued
1581 I Saw You Last Night   unissued
1582 Ronnie's Line   Atlantic EP552 & LP1217

("Ronnie's Line" reissued on Mosaic MD6-174, *THE COMPLETE ATLANTIC RECORDINGS OF LENNIE TRISTANO, LEE KONITZ & WARNE MARSH*; Frohne lists the following additional issues: Atl (J) 6071 and P4549A; Atl (Eu) 90050; Atl (GB) 509920; Atl (Eu) 50298; Lon (GB) LTZ-K15025; Mus (I) LPM-2007; Metronome MEP 253.)

Lee Konitz: *From Newport to Nice*. Lee Konitz, as; Warne Marsh, ts; Russ Freeman, p; Bob Carter, b; Buzzy Drootin, d. (Broadcast, *Voice of America*, Newport Jazz Festival, Freebody Park, Newport, R.I., July 16, 1955.)

Two Not One   Philology W-65-2 (CD)
Sweet and Lovely   unissued, incomplete on VOA
                        broadcast

(Frohne notes that "Two Not One" was titled "Colorous" on the VOA broadcast.)

Warne Marsh Quintet. Warne Marsh, ts; Don Overberg, g; Ronnie Ball, p; Ben Tucker, b; Jeff Morton, d. (Whisling's Hawaii or The Haig, Los Angeles, summer 1956, private, recorded by Ronnie Ball, tape owned by Peter Ind, 16 tunes.) *On a Slow Boat to China, My Old Flame, Smog Eyes, If I Had You, Ronnie's Line, Three Little Words, Don't Blame Me, Crazy She Calls Me, Featherbed, Sweet and Lovely, Two Not One, Smog Eyes (alt. take), Three Little Words (alt. take), Don't Blame Me, Ear Conditioning, Ghost of a Chance.* (This material was scheduled to be issued in 1998 by Robert Sunenblick on his *Uptown* label. Some tunes may duplicate tunes in the following entry.)

Warne Marsh Quintet/Sextet. Warne Marsh, Ted Brown, ts; Ronnie Ball, p; Ben Tucker, b; Jeff Morton, d; Don Overberg, g (1). (Probably The Haig or Whisling's Hawaii, Los Angeles, Summer-Fall 1956, private, 8 tunes.) *Limehouse Blues (1), Three Little Words (1), Don't Blame Me, Crazy She Calls Me (1), Featherbed (1), Sweet and Lovely, Back Home (1), On a Slow Boat to China (1, inc.).*

Rick Jones Quartet. Warne Marsh, ts; Ronnie Ball, p; Ben Tucker, b; Rick Jones, d; Gwenn Johnson (1), v, with Bob Moody vocal group (1). (Los Angeles, Summer-Fall 1956.)

Now Hear This (1)	Arjay RJ-103; PIV-1004 (both 45 rpm)
Swingin'	————; ————

Warne Marsh Quintet: *Jazz of Two Cities*. Warne Marsh, Ted Brown, ts; Ronnie Ball, p; Ben Tucker, b; Jeff Morton, d. (Los Angeles, Oct. 3 & 11, 1956.)

Smog Eyes	Imperial LP9027; LP12013; Capitol CDP7243-8-52771-2-2
Ear Conditioning	————; unissued; ————
Ear Conditioning (alt. take)	unissued; ————; ————
Lover Man	————; unissued; ————
Lover Man (alt. take)	unissued; ————; ————
Quintessence	————; ————; ————
Jazz of Two Cities (alt. take)	————; unissued; ————
Jazz of Two Cities (orig. take)	unissued; ————; ————
Dixie's Dilemma	————; ————; ————
Tchaikovsky's Opus 42, 3rd Mvmt .	————; ————; ————

| I Never Knew (alt. take) | ————; unissued; ———— |
| I Never Knew (orig. take) | unissued; ————; ———— |

(Imperial LP9027, *JAZZ OF TWO CITIES*, is monaural. Imperial LP12013, titled *WINDS OF MARSH*, is stereophonic. On it, Marsh's solo on "Ear Conditioning" is spliced in, as is Ball's solo on "Lover Man." Frohne notes the following reissues of Imperial LP9027: Liberty (J) LR-8055; Blue Note (F) BNP-25106; London (GB) P-15080.)

Warne Marsh Quintet: *A Modern Jazz Gallery*. Warne Marsh, Ted Brown, ts; Ronnie Ball, p; Ben Tucker, b; Jeff Morton, d. (Radio Recorders Studio, Los Angeles, CA, Oct. 24, 1956.)

Ben Blew	Kapp KXL5001, Vol. 1; unissued
Time's Up	————
Earful	————
Black Jack	————

("Time's Up," "Earful," and "Black Jack" were retitled "Up Tempo," "Decisions," and "Casino," respectively and reissued on Discovery DSCD-945, WARNE MARSH GROUPS: NOTEWORTHY. Frohne lists the following reissues: London (GB) LTZ-R-15083 for "Ben Blew" & "Time's Up," & 15084 for "Earful" & "Black Jack"; Fresh Sound (E) KXL-5001-252282-1-Kapp: *MODERN JAZZ GALLERY*.)

Warne Marsh Quintet. Warne Marsh, Ted Brown, ts; Ronnie Ball, p; Ben Tucker, b; Jeff Morton, d. (Los Angeles, probably The Haig or Whisling's Hawaii, 1956–57, private, 13 tunes.) *Oops (All the Things You Are/Dixie's Dilemma), The Best Thing for You, Au Privave, Pop Goes the Weasel, Featherbed, line on Lover Come Back to Me, Easy to Love, Limehouse Blues, Memories of You, Smog Eyes, Out of Nowhere, Donna Lee, I'll See You in My Dreams.*

Ted Brown Sextet: *Free Wheeling*. Ted Brown, Marsh, ts; Art Pepper, as; Ronnie Ball, p; Ben Tucker, b; Jeff Morton, d. (Hollywood, Dec. 21, 1956*.)

Aretha	Vanguard VRS 8515; Vanguard (F) 662089CD
Arrival	————; ————
Avalon	————; ————
Broadway	————; ————
Crazy She Calls Me	————; ————
Foolin' Myself	————; ————
Long Gone	————; ————

On a Slow Boat to China
   (Marsh out) ———; ———
Once We Were Young ———; ———

(*The date given here was supplied by Ted Brown. Wim van Eyle gives Nov. 26, 1956, which is the same date as for ART PEPPER: *THE WAY IT WAS*. Brown's date is preferred here, as it is highly unlikely that the two groups, which were almost identical, would do two lengthy recording sessions on the same day, for two different labels. Reissues, Frohne: SR(m)3136, (J) LAX-3075.)

Art Pepper: *The Way It Was*. Art Pepper, as; Warne Marsh, ts; Ronnie Ball, p; Ben Tucker, b; Gary Frommer, d. (Contemporary Studios, Los Angeles, Nov. 26, 1956.)

I Can't Believe that You're in
   Love with Me   Contemporary S-7630; OJCCD-389-2
I Can't Believe that You're in
   Love with Me (alt. take) ———; unissued
All the Things You Are   ———; ———
All the Things You Are (alt. take) unissued; ———
What's New (Marsh out)   ———; ———
Tickle Toe   ———; ———

(Frohne lists the following additional issues: Contemporary M7630, (J) LAX-3131, (J) GXC-3155; Contemporary/Fantasy OJC-389, OJC-5389; Contemporary/Victor (J) VDJ-1577(CD); Contemporary/JVC (J) VICJ-23640 (CD).)

Art Pepper with Warne Marsh. Art Pepper, as; Warne Marsh, ts; Ronnie Ball, p; Ben Tucker, b; Gary Frommer, d. (Los Angeles, Nov. 26, 1956.) Same titles as *The Way It Was*, plus:

Avalon   Contemporary (J) S-9001 & Contem/
                     Victor (J) VDJ-1577 (CD)
Warnin'   ——— & ———
Warnin' (alt. take)   ——— & ———
Stompin' at the Savoy
   (Marsh out)   ——— & ———

(Additional issues, Frohne: Contemporary/JVC (J) VICJ-23640; Contemporary/Fantasy OJCCD-389-2 (CD).)

Warne Marsh Quintet. Broadcast, *Stars of Jazz* television series, hosted by
Bobby Troup. Marsh, Ted Brown, ts; Ronnie Ball, p; Ben Tucker, b; Jeff
Morton, d; Ann Richards, vc (1). (ABC Television studios, Los Angeles,
Jan. 1957, private, 6 tunes.)

Au Privave	ABC Television
Ad Libido*	————
These Are the Things I Love	————
You Took Advantage of Me	
(1, Marsh, Brown out)	————
Softly (1, Marsh, Brown out)	————
Background Music	————

(*Not the same "Ad Libido" as on *Music for Prancing* LP.)

Warne Marsh Quartet: *Music for Prancing*. Warne Marsh, ts; Ronnie Ball,
p; Red Mitchell, b; Stan Levey, d. (Los Angeles, c. Sept. 19, 1957.)

You Are Too Beautiful	Mode LP 125; Tofrec (J) CD TFCL
	88910
Autumn in New York	————; ————
Playa del Rey	————; ————
Ad Libido	————; ————
Everything Happens to Me	————; ————
It's All Right with Me	————; ————

(Reissues, Frohne: Criss Cross (NL) 1004-x; VSOP CD No. 8.)

Joe Albany: *The Right Combination*. Warne Marsh, ts; Joe Albany, p; Von
(Bob) Whitlock, b; Ralph Garretson, brushes. (Long Beach, Calif., Fall
1957.)

Daahoud	Riverside RLP 12-270
Angel Eyes	————
I Love You	————
Body and Soul	————
It's You or No One	————
All the Things You Are	————
The Nearness of You	
(Marsh out)	————

(Reissues, Frohne: Riverside RS-3023, (J) SMJ-6071; Riverside/Fantasy
OJC-1749.)

Warne Marsh-Joe Albany. Warne Marsh, ts; Joe Albany, p; Von (Bob)
Whitlock, b; unknown, d. (Galleon Room, Dana Point, Calif., Oct. 6,

1957, private, 18 tunes. Selections from this tape are scheduled to be issued by VSOP/Mode Records.) *These Are the Things I Love, Daahoud, Now's the Time, Billie's Bounce, Body and Soul, Limehouse Blues, Our Love Is Here to Stay, I've Got You under My Skin, Once in a While, Night and Day, My Little Suede Shoes, Darn that Dream, After You've Gone (inc.), Easy to love, S'Wonderful, Tea for Two, The Song Is You, The Way You Look Tonight.*

Warne Marsh-Ted Brown. Warne Marsh, Ted Brown, ts; Ronnie Ball, p; unknown, b; Jeff Morton or Paul Motian, d. (Opera House, Chicago, Ill., Oct. 19, 1957, private, unknown number of tunes, information from Tom Everett.) *Unknown titles.*

Warne Marsh. Warne Marsh, ts; Ronnie Ball, p; Paul Chambers, b; Philly Joe Jones, d. (Atlantic Studios, New York City, Dec. 12, 1957.)

2869 Will You Still Be Mine	unissued
2870 The Best Thing for You	unissued
2871 Too Close for Comfort	Atlantic LP-1291
2872 It's All Right with Me	————
2873 Tune Up	unissued

Warne Marsh, ts; Paul Chambers, b; Paul Motian, d. (Atlantic Studios, New York, Jan. 16, 1958.)

2908 Yardbird Suite	Atlantic LP-1291
2909 My Melancholy Baby	————
2910 Excerpt	————
2911 Just Squeeze Me	————
2912 Untitled	unissued

(All titles reissued on Mosaic MD6-174, *THE COMPLETE ATLANTIC RECORDINGS OF LENNIE TRISTANO, LEE KONITZ AND WARNE MARSH.* Reissues, Frohne: Atlantic SD-1291, (J) P4573, (J) P6136A.)

The Subject Is Jazz. Lee Konitz, as; Warne Marsh, ts; Don Elliott, tpt, mellophone, vib; Billy Taylor, p; Mundell Lowe, g; Eddie Safranski, b; Ed Thigpen, d. NBC Television broadcast, hosted by Gilbert Seldes. (NBC Television broadcast, New York City, May 14, 1958.)

Move, under announcer (inc.)	US TV Education Films; NBC-TV
"Cool Jazz," spoken definition by Gilbert Seldes	————; ————
Godchild	————; ————
"Cool Jazz," conversation between Seldes & Konitz, with recorded examples	————; ————

Lady Bird/Half Nelson	————; ————
Ever so Easy	————; ————
Subconscious-Lee (Elliott out)	————; ————
Move	————; ————
Theme	————; ————

(Reissues, Frohne: broadcast at a later date by National Educational Television.)

Lee Konitz Group. Lee Konitz, as; Warne Marsh, ts; others unknown. (30 minute radio broadcast, including Five Commuters vocal group, Bandstand USA #46, probably New York City, c. 1958, perhaps 3 tunes, private.) *Titles unknown.*

Lee Konitz-Warne Marsh Quartet. Lee Konitz, as; Warne Marsh, ts; Knobby Totah, b; Paul Motian, d. (Frohne lists four separate radio broadcasts over unknown U.S. station from The Half Note, New York City, Jul. 1958, specific dates unknown, private.)

Yardbird Suite	U.S. radio broadcast, station unknown
Topsy	————
'Round Midnight	————
Background Music	————
317 E. 32nd Street	————
Billie's Bounce	————
I Can't Get Started	————
Two not One	————
Billie's Bounce	————
Will You Still Be Mine (Marsh out)	————
Cheek to Cheek (Konitz out)	————
April	————

Lennie Tristano. Warne Marsh, ts; Lennie Tristano, p; Henry Grimes, b; Paul Motian, d. (Radio broadcast over unknown U.S. station from The Half Note, New York City, Aug. 9, 1958.*)

I'll Remember April	Bombasi 11:235; Jazz Records JR6 & JR6CD
She's Funny That Way	————; ———— & ————
My Melancholy Baby	————; ———— & ————
Everything Happens to Me (inc.)	unissued

(*Frohne gives this date and says date of Oct. 1958, given on JR-6, is incorrect. Tristano began at the Half Note on a weekend "early in August" according to *Down Beat*, Sept. 18, 1958. On Jazz Records JR6 & JR6CD, *LENNIE TRISTANO: CONTINUITY*, "I'll Remember April" is called "Continuity" and "My Melancholy Baby" is called "My Baby.")

WARNE MARSH AND OTHERS. Warne Marsh, Zoot Smis, ts; Gerry Mulligan, bs; Bob Brookmeyer, vtb; Dave McKenna, p; Nobby Totah, Bill Crow, b. Garry Hawkins, d. (Loft session at 821 Sixth Ave., New York City, Dec. 22, 1958, private, 6 tunes.) *I Got Rhythm, After You've Gone, spoken dialogue, The Way You Look Tonight, slow blues in F, Moten Swing (inc.)*

Lee Konitz Live at the Half Note. Lee Konitz, as; Warne Marsh, ts; Bill Evans, p; Jimmy Garrison, b; Paul Motian, d. (The Half Note, New York City, Feb. 24 and possibly Mar. 3, 1959.)

Palo Alto	Verve 314 521 659-2 (CD)
How About You?	———
My Melancholy Baby	———
Scrapple from the Apple	———
You Stepped out of a Dream	———
317 E. 32nd	———
April	———
It's You or No One	———
Just Friends	———
Baby, Baby All the Time	———
Lennie-Bird	———
Subconscious-Lee	———

(These are complete versions of 12 of the tunes included on *The Art of Improvising*, Vols. 1 & 2, Revelation 22 & 27, below, which contain only Marsh's solos with rhythm section.)

Warne Marsh: *The Art of Improvising*, **Vol. 1**. Warne Marsh, ts; Lee Konitz, as*; Bill Evans, p; Paul Motian, d; Jimmy Garrison, b. *(The Half Note, New York City, 1959. *All tunes edited to contain only Marsh solos with rhythm section.)

Strike up the Band	Revelation 22
It's You or No One (1)	———
Subconscious-Lee	———
You Stepped out of a Dream (1)	———
Scrapple from the Apple (1)	———
I'll Remember April	———
Indiana (1)	———
Lunar Elevation	———

A Song for You	————
How about You?	————
Scrapple from the Apple (2)	————
Blues	————
I Can't Believe That You're in Love with Me	————
It's You or No One (2)	————
Indian Summer	————
It's You or No One (3)	————
You Stepped out of a Dream (2)	————
April, I'll Remember	————
Indiana (2)	————
Half Nelson	————

(*Frohne gives date as May-August '59. Originally recorded by Peter Ind for Verve. On some tracks one hears a few notes from Lee Konitz. *Marsh's solos were excerpted from the original tapes by Connie Crothers and Lennie Tristano. Complete versions, with solos by Konitz, Marsh, Evans, et al., exist on private tapes which include everything on *The Art of Improvising,* Vols. 1 & 2, as well as six tracks not on either *Art of Improvising* or *Lee Konitz Live at the Half Note,* Verve 314-521-659-2, above. Originally it was thought that Peter Ind was the bassist, then Henry Grimes. But the Verve issue identifies Garrison as the bassist on the twelve tunes it includes.)

Warne Marsh: *The Art of Improvising,* **Vol. 2.** Warne Marsh, ts; Bill Evans, p; Paul Motian, d; Jimmy Garrison, b. (The Half Note, New York City, 1959. All tunes edited to contain only Marsh solos with rhythm section. See note to Vol. 1.)

Sweet Georgia Brown	Revelation 27
Out of Nowhere	————
Fishin' Around	————
Tangerine	————
Lennie's Pennies	————
Yardbird Suite	————
Will You Still Be Mine	————
What Is This Thing Called Love	————
Out of Nowhere	————
You Stepped out of a Dream	————
untitled (All of Me)	————
untitled (Yardbird Suite)	————
Lennie's Pennies	————
untitled (Pennies in Minor)	————

Lee Konitz Meets Jimmy Giuffre. Lee Konitz, Hal McKusick, as; Warne Marsh, Ted Brown, ts; Jimmy Guiffre, bs, arr; Bill Evans, p; Buddy Clark, b; Ronnie Free, d. (New York City, May 12–13, 1959.)

22829 Moonlight in Vermont	Verve MGV 8355
22830 The Song Is You	————
22831 Somp'n Outa Nothin'	————
22832 Uncharted	————
22833 Someone to Watch over Me	————
22834 Palo Alto	————
22835 When Your Lover Has Gone	————
22836 Cork 'n Bib	————
22837 Darn That Dream	————

(All titles reissued on Verve CD 314 527 780-2, *LEE KONITZ MEETS JIMMY GIUFFRE*; "The Song Is You" also appears on LEE KONITZ: *PALO ALTO*, Giants of Jazz CD 53182. Reissues, Frohne: Verve MGMS-6073 (stereo), V6-8335 (stereo), (F) 230481, (J) 23MJ-3172; "Uncharted" and "Palo Alto" on Jazzbox (S) JLEP-136; "Somp'n Outa Nothin,'" "Someone to Watch over Me," "Palo Alto," "Darn That Dream" on HMW (GB) 7EG-136.)

Warne Marsh: *Release Record, Send Tape*. Warne Marsh, ts; Ronnie Ball, p; Peter Ind, b; Dick Scott, d. (New York City, Dec. 19, 1959.)

Sweet Georgia Brown	Wave (GB) LP-6
Coolhouse	————
It's You or No One	————
I Remember You	————

Same personnel (New York City, Feb. 22, 1960.)

You Stepped out of a Dream	————

Same personnel, except Scott replaced by unknown, possibly Bob Minnicucci, playing brushes on telephone directory. (New York City, Sept. 8, 1960. Most tunes incomplete, containing Marsh solos only.)

Alone Together	————
A New Kind of Blues (Ball out)	————
Foreground Music	————
Happening	————
Marshlight	————
Commentary	————

Warne Marsh: *Jazz from the East Village*. Warne Marsh, ts; Ronnie Ball, p; Eddie de Haas, Peter Ind (1), b; Bob Minnicucci, brushes on telephone directory. (New York City, Aug. 9, 1960. All tunes incomplete, mainly Marsh solos with rhythm section.)

Summer Session	Wave LP-10
Easy Beat	————
Sunshine	————
East Side Swing	————
223 East 2nd St.	————
August in New York	————
Change Around (1)	————
Get Together (1)	————
Tracery	————

("Tracery" is not mentioned on LP cover but is on label.)

Warne Marsh: *Live in Las Vegas, 1962*. Warne Marsh, ts; Don Overberg, g; Carson Smith, b; Frank Severino, d. (Las Vegas, Nev., Feb. 28, 1962.)

317 E. 32nd	Naked City Records CD 007
Joy Spring	————
You Stepped out of a Dream	————
Hello Young Lovers	————
Kary's Trance	————
Subconscious-Lee	————
The Best Thing for You	————
People Will Say We're in Love	————
The Best Things in Life	————
Feather Bed	————

Warne Marsh. Warne Marsh, ts; Marvin Coral, fl (1); unknown as, possibly Coral (2); Don Overberg, g; Roy Shain, b; Santos Savino, d. (Home of Don Overberg, Las Vegas, c.1962, private, 12 tunes.) *It's You or No One* (no d), *It's You or No One* (no d), *Avalon, Fascinating Rhythm (1), Subconscious-Lee (2), Sweet and Lovely (2), unidentified fragments, Yardbird Suite, unknown title, Donna Lee, You'd Be So Nice to Come Home To (2), Makin' Whoopee* (inc.).

Warne Marsh. Warne Marsh, ts; unknown, as (1); Jimmy Malador, fl (2); Don Overberg, g; Roy Shain, b; Santos Savino, d. (Home of Don Overberg, Las Vegas, c. 1962, private, 8 tunes.) *Tangerine (1), Sweet and Lovely (1, 2), Hello Young Lovers (1, 2), Tangerine, Sweet and Lovely, I'll Remember April* (inc.), *I've Got You under My Skin, I Want to Be Happy.*

Warne Marsh. Warne Marsh, ts; Don Overberg, g; Roy Shain, b; probably
Santos Savino, d; (Home of Don Overberg, Las Vegas, c. 1962–63, pri-
vate, 15 tunes.) *The Best Thing for You Would Be Me, People Will Say We're
in Love, The Best Things in Life Are Free, Featherbed, Joy Spring, Kary's
Trance, Stella by Starlight, Woodyn' You, Without a Song, Fascinatin' Rhythm,
You Stepped out of a Dream, Kary's Trance, Hello Young Lovers, 317 E. 32nd
Street, Subconscious-Lee.*

Kim Novak Documentary. Reportedly, a video documentary of the film
actress was made c. summer or fall of 1963 at or near Novak's home in
the Carmel-Big Sur area and broadcast in the United Kingdom and
Australia. The sound track and possibly the video is said to include
Warne Marsh, ts; Lee Konitz, as; Al Shackman, g; Peter Ind, b; and Larry
Bunder, d. I have not been able to obtain confirmation of this.

Lennie Tristano Quintet. Lee Konitz, as; Warne Marsh, ts; Lennie Tristano,
p; unknown b, d. (The Half Note, New York City, c. 1964, private, 2
tunes.) *What Is This Thing Called Love, 317 E. 32nd Street.*

Lennie Tristano: *Continuity*. Lee Konitz, as; Warne Marsh, ts; Lennie
Tristano, p; Sonny Dallas, b; Nick Stabulas, d. (Television broadcast
titled "Look Up and Live," recorded at The Half Note, New York City,
June 6, 1964, and broadcast Aug. 9, 1964, over CBS.)

Subconscious-Lee (a)	Jazz Records JR-6; Richelieu AX-120*; CBS Television
317 E. 32nd Street (b)	————; ————; ————
Background Music (inc.) (c)	————; ————; ————

(*On Richelieu AX-120, *THE AMERICAN JAZZMEN*, Vol. 5, (a) is titled
"What Is This Thing Called Love-Subconscious-Lee," (b) is "32nd Street
East!-Out of Nowhere," and (c) is "Musical Background-All of Me."

Modern Jazz Composition. Warne Marsh (under pseudonym Rawen
Shram), ts; others unknown. (Place unknown, Feb. 1966*)

unknown title(s)   GM LP-001

(*Information from Marcus Cornelius. Frohne lists a *MODERN JAZZ
COMPOSITIONS FROM HAITI* with the date of 1975, location Haiti.
In addition to Marsh he lists Gerald Merceron, p, and the title
"Ouagadougou Blues" issued on GM Records LP-001.)

Clare Fischer: *Duality*. Conte Candoli, John Audino, Jimmy Zito, Larry McGuire, tp; Roy Main, Ron Smith, Gil Falco, Phil Teele, tb; Gary Foster, Bud Shank, as; Lou Ciotti, *Warne Marsh, ts; Bill Perkins, John Lowe, bs; Clare Fischer, p, org; Bobby West, b; Larry Bunker, d. (KNX/CBS Studios, Sunset Blvd., Hollywood, Jan. 1967.)

Thiers', Tears	Trend/Discovery DS-807
This Is Always	————
Come Sunday	————
The Greek	————
Dancing on the Ceiling	unissued

(*Thiers*, which rhymes with *tears*, refers to Walter Thiers, a South American concert producer. Liner notes also incorrectly list David O'Rourke instead of Marsh. According to Gary Foster, O'Rourke played on side one of this LP—not listed here, recorded June 20, 1966—but was replaced by Marsh for the second recording session in January 1967. The date of 1969 in the liner notes is wrong. The album was originally recorded by Albert Marx for Columbia, but was not issued until Marx bought it back from Columbia and issued it c. 1980 on Trend/Discovery. Discovery, now owned by First Media, Santa Monica, Calif., reports that it no longer has a copy in its archives. Information from Albert Marx is unavailable, as he died several years ago. Marsh does not solo on any of the tracks.)

Warne Marsh. Warne Marsh, ts; Gary Foster, as; Clare Fischer, p; George Willliams, b (1). (Los Angeles, Apr. 16, 1967, private, 6 tunes. Frohne says information comes from Revelation Records files.) *April (1), unknown title (1), Out of Nowhere (1), You'd Be So Nice to Come Home To, All the Things You Are, Love Me or Leave Me.*

Clare Fischer: *Thesaurus*. Larry McGuire, Buddy Childers (1), John Audino (2), Conte Candoli, Steve Huffsteter, Stewart Fischer, tp; Gil Falco, Charley Loper, David Sanchez, tb; Morris Repass, btb; Gary Foster, Kim Richmond, as; Louis Ciotti, Warne Marsh, ts; Bill Perkins, bs; John Lowe, bass-sax; Clare Fischer, p, ep, arr; Chuck Domanico, b; Larry Bunker, d; Stweart Fischer, arr (3). (Los Angeles, TTG Studios, Aug. 26–27, 1968.)

15393 'Twas Only Yesterday (1)	Atlantic SD 1520; Discovery DS-798
15394 Bitter Leaf (2)	————; ————
15395 Upper Manhattan Medical Group (2)	————; ————

15396 In Memorium JFK and
   RFK (1)   ————; ————
15397 The Duke (1)   ————; ————
15398 Miles Behind (1)   ————; ————
15399 Calamus (2, 3)   ————; ————
15400 Lennie's Pennies (1) ————; ————

(Discovery DS-798 is titled *'TWAS ONLY YESTERDAY*. Marsh solos on "Miles Behind" and "Lennie's Pennies.")

Warne Marsh: *Ne Plus Ultra*. Warne Marsh, ts; Gary Foster, as; Dave Parlato, b; John Tirabasso, d. (Herrick Chapel Lounge, Occidental College, Los Angeles, Sept. 14, 1969 (1) and Oct. 25, 1969 (2))

You Stepped out of a Dream (1) (take 1)	unissued; unissued
You Stepped out of a Dream (1) (take 2)	Revelation 12; Hat Art CD 6063
You Stepped out of a Dream (2) (take 3)	unissued; unissued
How about You (1)	unissued; unissued
Lennie's Pennies (2)	————; ————
317 East 32nd Street (2)	————; ————
Subconscious-Lee (2)	————; ————
Touch and Go (2)	————; ————
Smog Eyes (2)	unissued; unissued
Featherbed (1?)	unissued; unissued
Bach Two-Part Invention #13	unissued; ————
Bach Two-Part Invention #13 (alt. take)	unissued; unissued
Bach Two-Part Invention #13 (alt. take)	unissued; unissued
Bach Two-Part Invention #13 (alt. take)	unissued; ————

(Frohne does not list "Featherbed," which may be confused with "Smog Eyes." He says it is unknown which take of "Bach Two-Part Invention #13" was used. Beginning of "Lennie's Pennies" was edited, according to liner notes for Rev. 12. Additional reissue, Frohne: Crown (J) BRJ-4111 (CD).)

Warne Marsh Quartet. Warne Marsh, ts; Gary Foster, as, sop s; Dave Parlato, b; John Tirabasso, d. (The Ice House, Pasadena, Calif., Jan. 11, 1971.)

317 East 32nd	Revelation, unissued

Two Not One	————
Fuzz Blues	————
Kary's Trance	————
If You Could See Me Now	————
Subconscious-Lee	————
Bach 2 Part Invention	————
Featherbed	————
How about You	————
Confusion in Dallas	————
Background Music	————

Warne Marsh Quintet. Warne Marsh, ts; Gary Foster, as, sop s; probably Dave Koonse, g; unknown, b; probably John Tirabasso, d. (The Ice House, Pasadena, Calif., 1971, private, 7 tunes. Probably duplicated on WARNE MARSH-GARY FOSTER, below, except for "Lennie's Pennies.") *You'd Be So Nice/Featherbed, If You Could See Me Now, 'Round Midnight, Fuzz Blues, Subconscious-Lee, All about You, Lennie's Pennies* (inc.).

Warne Marsh Quartet. Warne Marsh, ts; Gary Foster, as; Dave Parlato, b; John Tirabasso, d. (The Ice House, Pasadena, Calif., Mar. 29, 1971, private, recorded by Ron Hoopes, 14 tunes.) *You Stepped out of a Dream, Featherbed, Body and Soul, Two Not One, Background Music, Fuzz Blues, All the Things You Are, Bach Two-Part Invention, Two Not One, If You Could See Me Now, Confusion in Dallas, How about You, Lennie's Pennies, 317 E. 32nd Street* (inc.).

Warne Marsh-Gary Foster. Warne Marsh, ts; Gary Foster, as; others unknown. (California Institute of Technology, Pasadena, Calif., Apr. 28, 1971, private, unknown number of tunes, information from Tom Everett.) *Unknown titles.*

Warne Marsh-Gary Foster. Warne Marsh, ts; Gary Foster, as, sop s; Dave Koonse, g; Frank De La Rosa, b; John Tirabasso, d. (The Ice House, Pasadena, Calif., Aug. 8, 1971.)

You'd Be So Nice to Come Home To	Revelation, unissued
If You Could See Me Now	————
Round Midnight	————
Fuzz Blues	————
Subconscious-Lee	————
How about You	————
Confusion in Dallas	————

(Frohne says "entry according to Revelation files." Extant on private tape.)

Warne Marsh Quartet. Warne Marsh, ts; probably Ron Hoopes, p; Paul Ruhland, b; John Tirabasso, d; unknown female, v, possibly Judy Niemack (1). (Probably The Gilded Cage, Arcadia, Calif., Aug. 22, 1971, Frohne, private, 9 tunes.) *Unknown title, Autumn Leaves, Have You Met Miss Jones, Theme, You Stepped out of a Dream, Watch What Happens (1), Mountain Greenery (1), Mountain Greenery, Misty (Marsh out), Stompin' at the Savoy.*

Warne Marsh Quartet. *A Giant Passes*. Warne Marsh, ts; Ron Hoopes, p; John Tirabasso, d; probably Paul Ruhland, b. (The Gilded Cage, Arcadia, Calif., Aug. 22 and/or 26, 1971.)

Lullaby of the Leaves (a, b)	Revelation, unissued
It's You or No One (b)	————
Day by Day (a, b)	————
I Love You (a, b)	————
Sonnymoon for Two sign-off	————

Clare Fischer, p, org, replaces Hoopes. (Los Angeles area, possibly Clare Fischer's home, June 1972.)

Strike up the Band (a)	Revelation, unissued
The Best Thing for You (a)	————
After You've Gone (Fischer plays org.) (a)	————
That Old Feeling	————
Indian Summer	————
The More I See You	————
Nardis	————
This Can't Be Love (inc.)	————

(Tunes labeled (a) were projected by John William Hardy and Revelation to be issued after Marsh's death under the title *A Giant Passes*. Tunes labeled (b) were projected as part of an album titled *At the Gilded Cage*. Frohne says his information is "according to Revelation files.")

Warne Marsh. Warne Marsh, ts; Anthony Braxton, Gary Foster, as; probably Ron Hoopes, p; Paul Ruhland, b; John Tirabasso, d. (Place unknown, possibly The Gilded Cage, Arcadia, Calif., Aug. 28, 1971, private, Frohne, 4 tunes.) *What Is This Thing Called Love/Subconscious-Lee, You Stepped out of a Dream (inc.), 317 E. 32nd Street, Donna Lee/Indiana.*

Report of the 1st Annual Symposium on Relaxed Improvisation. Gary Foster, as; Warne Marsh, ts; Clare Fischer, p; Paul Ruhland, b; John Tirabasso, d. (Clare Fischer's home, Van Nuys, Calif., May 9, 1972.)

It Could Happen to You	
(Foster out)	Revelation 17
Bluesy Rouge	————
In a Mellotone	————
Yesterdays	————
Just Friends	unissued
I Got It Bad and That Ain't	
Good	unissued
Untitled	unissued
Kary's Trance	unissued
Stella by Starlight	unissued
There Will Never Be Another	
You	unissued
In a Sentimental Mood	unissued
Cherokee (Fischer plays org.)	unissued
You've Changed (Fischer plays	
org.)	unissued
Watch What Happens	
(Marsh out)	unissued

(Frohne says "according to Revelation files." "Just Friends" and "I Got It Bad" are extant on private tape.)

Warne Marsh-Clare Fischer. Warne Marsh, ts; Clare Fischer, p; Paul Ruhland or Dave Parlato, b; John Tirabasso, d. (Los Angeles area, early 1970s, private, 3 tunes.) *Strike Up the Band, The Best Thing for You Would Be Me, After You've Gone.*

Warne Marsh-Clare Fischer. Warne Marsh, ts; Clare Fischer, p; Paul Ruhland or Dave Parlato, b; John Tirabasso, d. (Los Angeles area, early 1970s, private, Frohne, 8 tunes. Those marked with asterix probably duplicates of previous entry.) *That Old Feeling, *Strike Up the Band, Indian Summer, The More I See You, Israel, *The Best Thing for You Would Be Me, *After You've Gone, This Can't Be Love.*

Warne Marsh Quartet. Warne Marsh, ts; Gary Foster, as; Dave Parlato, b; John Tirabasso, d. (The Ice House, Pasadena, Calif., May 27, 1972, private, 9 tunes.) *Kary's Trance, Lennie's Pennies, 317 E. 32nd Street, You Stepped out of a Dream, Featherbed, Body and Soul* (Marsh out), *Fuzz Blues, Background Music, Star Eyes* (inc.).

Warne Marsh-Gary Foster. Warne Marsh, ts; Gary Foster, as; Frank DeLaRosa, b; John Tirabasso, d. (Ice House, Pasadena, Calif., May 29, 1972.)

Kary's Trance*	Revelation, unissued
Lennie's Pennies*	————
317 E. 32nd Street*	————
You Stepped out of a Dream*	————
Featherbed*	————
Body and Soul*	————
Two Not One	————
All the Things You Are	————
Bach Two Part Invention No. 13 (Marsh, Foster only)	————
Two Not One	————
If You Could See Me Now (Foster out)	————
Confusion in Dallas	————
How about You	————
Fuzz Blues*	————
Background Music*	————

(Frohne says "according to William Hardy" of Revelation Records. Title marked with * probably duplicate of previous entry.)

Warne Marsh. Warne Marsh, ts; prob. Lou Levy, p; unknown, b, g, and d. (Hollywood, probably early 1970s, private, 5 tunes.) *Little Willie Leaps, Tune Up, untitled blues, Subconscious-Lee, All the Things You Are.*

Supersax Plays Bird, **Vol. 1**. Conte Candoli, tp; Med Flory, Joe Lopes, as; Warne Marsh, Jay Migliori, ts; Jack Nimitz, bs; Ronnell Bright, p; Buddy Clark, b; Jake Hanna, d; Med Flory, Buddy Clark, arr. (Capitol Records Studios, Los Angeles, Calif., Feb. 1, 1973; released May 15, 1973.)

Be-Bop	Capitol ST-11177
Oh, Lady Be Good	————
Hot House	————

Same personnel, Feb. 4, 1973:

KoKo	————
Parker's Mood	————
Star Eyes	————
Night in Tunisia	————
Just Friends	————
Moose the Mooche	————

Add Ray Triscari, Larry Mcguire, Ralph Osborn, tp; Charley Loper, Mike Barone, Ernie Tack, tb:

Just Friends   _____
Moose the Mooche   _____
Repetition   _____

(No Marsh solos on this or any other Supersax studio recording. Reissues, Frohne: Capitol (J) IGJ- 50042, C-96264(cd); Mobile Fidelity Sound Lab 1511.)

Supersax. Prob. Med Flory, Joe Lopes, as; Warne Marsh, Jay Migliori,ts; Jack Nimitz, bs; Conte Candoli, tp; Ronnell Bright or Walter Bishop, p; Buddy Clark, b; Jake Hanna, d. (Prob. Jimmy's, New York City, Oct. 18, 1973, private, 1 tune, recorded by Harold Sewing, prob. Marsh solo only.) *KoKo.*

Supersax. Prob. Med Flory, Joe Lopes, as; Warne Marsh, Jay Migliori, ts; Conte Candoli, tp; Ronnell Bright or Walter Bishop, p; Buddy Clark, b; Jake Hanna, d. (Prob. Jimmy's, New York City, Oct. 20, 1973, private, 4 tunes, recorded by Harold Sewing, prob. Marsh solos only.) *Salt Peanuts, Groovin' High, KoKo, The Bird.*

Supersax. Prob. Med Flory, Joe Lopes, as; Warne Marsh, Jay Migliori, ts; Jack Nimitz, bs; Conte Candoli, tp; Ronnell Bright or Walter Bishop, p; Buddy Clark, b; Jake Hanna, d. (Prob. Jimmy's, New York City, Oct. 22, 1973, private, 7 tunes, recorded by Harold Sewing, prob. Marsh solos only.) *Scrapple from the Apple, Parker's Mood, Just Friends, Groovin' High, Salt Peanuts, Confirmation, KoKo.*

Supersax. Prob. Med Flory, Joe Lopes, as; Warne Marsh, Jay Migliori, ts; Jack Nimitz, bs; Conte Candoli, tp; Ronnell Bright or Walter Bishop, p; Buddy Clark, b; Jake Hanna, d. (Prob. Jimmy's, New York City, Oct. 23, 1973, private, 10 tunes, recorded by Harold Sewing, prob. Marsh solos only.) *Just Friends, Salt Peanuts, Lover Man, Confirmation, KoKo, The Bird, Night in Tunisia, Moose the Mooche, Embraceable You, My Old Flame.*

Supersax. Prob. Med Flory, Joe Lopes, as; Warne Marsh, Jay Migliori, ts; Jack Nimitz, bs; Conte Candoli, Dizzy Gillespie (1), tp; Ronnell Bright or Walter Bishop, p; Buddy Clark, b; Jake Hanna, d. (Jimmy's, New York City, Oct. 24, 1973, private, 9 tunes, recorded by Harold Sewing, prob. Marsh solos only, except Gillespie.) *Scrapple from the Apple, Groovin' High, Salt Peanuts (1), Confirmation, KoKo, The Bird, Lover Man, Moose the Mooche, Night in Tunisia.*

Supersax. Prob. Med Flory, Joe Lopes, as; Warne Marsh, Jay Migliori, ts; Jack Nimitz, bs; Conte Candoli, tp; Ronnell Bright or Walter Bishop, p;

Buddy Clark, b; Jake Hanna, d. (Jimmy's, New York City, Oct. 26, 1973, private, 5 tunes, recorded by Harold Sewing, prob. Marsh solos only.) *KoKo, The Bird, Groovin' High, Lover Man, Be-Bop.*

Supersax. Prob. Med Flory, Joe Lopes, as; Warne Marsh, Jay Migliori, ts; Jack Nimitz, bs; Conte Candoli, tp; Ronnell Bright or Walter Bishop, p; Buddy Clark, b; Jake Hanna, d. (Prob. Jimmy's, New York City, Oct. 27, 1973, private, 8 tunes, recorded by Harold Sewing, prob. Marsh solos only.) *Salt Peanuts, Confirmation, KoKo, The Bird, Embraceable You, Donna Lee, I Remember You, Be-Bop.*

Supersax. Prob. Med Flory, Joe Lopes, as; Warne Marsh, Jay Migliori, ts; Jack Nimitz, bs; Conte Candoli, tp; Ronnell Bright or Walter Bishop, p; Buddy Clark, b; Jake Hanna, d. (Unknown location, prob. Camden, N.J., Nov. 2, 1973, private, 8 tunes, recorded by Harold Sewing, prob. Marsh solos only.) *Scrapple from the Apple, Salt Peanuts, KoKo, The Bird, Groovin' High, Scrapple from the Apple,* Night in Tunisia, KoKo.** (*Sewing dated these two tunes Nov. 2, 1973, but it is unlikely that they were played twice in the same night.)

Supersax. Prob. Med Flory, Joe Lopes, as; Warne Marsh, Jay Migliori, ts; Jack Nimitz, bs; Conte Candoli, tp; Ronnell Bright or Walter Bishop, p; Buddy Clark, b; Jake Hanna, d. (Camden, N.J., Nov. 3, 1973, private, 12 tunes, recorded by Harold Sewing, prob. Marsh solos only.) *Scrapple from the Apple, KoKo, Salt Peanuts, The Bird, Moose the Mooche, Groovin' High, Be Bop, Hot House, How's the Time, Billie's Bounce, Star Eyes, Salt Peanuts.** (*Prob. not this date.)

Supersax. Prob. Med Flory, Joe Lopes, as; Warne Marsh, Jay Migliori, ts; Jack Nimitz, bs; Conte Candoli, tp; Ronnell Bright or Walter Bishop, p; Buddy Clark, b; Jake Hanna, d. (Prob. Camden, N.J., Nov. 4, 1973, private, 8 tunes, recorded by Harold Sewing, prob. Marsh solos only.) *Salt Peanuts, KoKo, The Bird, Now's the Time/Billie's Bounce, Groovin' High, Be Bop, Donna Lee, Salt Peanuts.*

Supersax. Prob. Conte Candoli, tpt; Med Flory, Joe Lopes, as; Warne Marsh, Jay Migliori, ts; Jack Nimitz, bs; Ronnell Bright or Walter Bishop, p; Buddy Clark, b; Jake Hanna, d. (Prob. New York City, c. 1973, private, 3 tunes.) *Donne Lee, KoKo, Hot House.*

***Supersax Plays Bird: Salt Peanuts*. Vol. 2**. Conte Candoli, tp; Carl Fontana, tb; Med Flory, Joe Lopes, as; Warne Marsh, Jay Migliori, ts; Jack Nimitz, bs; Ronnell Bright (1), Walter Bishop (2), Lou Levy (3), p; Buddy Clark, b; Jake Hanna, d; Med Flory, Buddy Clark, Warne Marsh, arr. (Capitol Records Studios, Los Angeles, Fall 1973; released Mar. 15, 1974.)

Yardbird Suite (3)	Capitol ST-11271
Groovin' High (2)	—————
Embraceable You (1)	—————
The Bird (3)	—————
Lover (3)	—————
Scrapple from the Apple (3)	—————
Confirmation (1)	—————
Lover Man (3)	—————
Salt Peanuts (2)	—————

(Marsh arranged "Salt Peanuts." Reissues, Frohne: Capitol (Eu) OC-062-81834; Pausa PR-9028, *SUPERSAX SALT PEANUTS*.)

Warne Marsh-Supersax. Warne Marsh, ts; Supersax rhythm section: prob. Lou Levy, p; Buddy Clark, b; Jake Hanna, d. (Just Jazz club, Philadelphia, 1974, private, unknown number of tunes, Marsh solos only, information from Jeremy Kellock.) *Unknown titles.*

Supersax. Carl Fontana, tb; Med Flory, Joe Lopes, as; Warne Marsh, Jay Migliori, ts; Jack Nimitz, bs; Lou Levy, p; Leroy Vinnegar, b; Jake Hanna, d. (Dirty Pierre's, city unknown, 1974, private, 13 tunes, information from Jeremy Kellock.) *Salt Peanuts, Ornithology, Blue 'n' Boogie, Ornithology, KoKo, The Bird, Dizzy Atmosphere, Salt Peanuts, KoKo, Ornithology, The Bird, untitled blues, Dizzy Atmosphere.*

Supersax. Prob. Med Flory, Joe Lopes, as; Warne Marsh, Jay Migliori, ts; Jack Nimitz, bs; Conte Candoli, tp; Lou Levy, p; Buddy Clark, b; Jake Hanna, d. (Rehearsal, prob. Med Flory's home, No. Hollywood, Calif., 1974, private, 1 tune, information from Jeremy Kellock.) *Ornithology.*

Warne Marsh Group. Warne Marsh, ts; others unknown. (The Times, Studio City, Calif., Jan. 18 & 22, 1974, private, unknown number of tunes, information from Harold Sewing.) *Unknown titles.*

Supersax. Frank Rosolino, tb; Med Flory, Joe Lopes,* as; Warne Marsh, ts; Jack Nimitz, bs; Lou Levy, p; Buddy Clark, b; Jake Hanna, d. (Recorded and broadcast by unidentified U.S. radio station, Baltimore, Md., Jul. 14, 1974.)

Scrapple from the Apple	U.S. radio broadcast
Salt Peanuts	—————
KoKo	—————

The Bird	————
Blue 'n' Boogie	————
Moose the Mooche	————
Parker's Mood	————
Now's the Time	————

(*Frohne lists Charlie Lopes, but Joe Lopes was the regular Supersax member.)

Supersax Plays Bird, with Strings. Vol. 3.; Conte Candoli, tp; Frank Rosolino, tb; Med Flory, Joe Lopes, as; Warne Marsh, Jay Migliori, ts; Jack Nimitz, bs; Lou Levy, p; Buddy Clark, b; Jake Hanna, d; Bobby Bruce, vi solo; Haim Shtrum, Wilbert Nuttycombe, John Santulis, Robert T. Jung, Bob Lido, Jesse Ehlich, Jerome Reisler, Robert Sushel, Gerald Vinci, Ambrose Russo, Frank Green, Leonard Selic, Evelyn R. Schuck, Raymond J. Kelley, Marilyn Baker, Frederick Seykora, James Getzoff, Spiro Stamos, strings; Med Flory, Buddy Clark, Roger Kellaway, Donald Specht, Warne Marsh, arr. (Capitol Records Studios, Los Angeles, Fall 1974, released Feb. 15, 1975.)

April in Paris	Capitol ST-11371
All the Things You Are	————
My Old Flame	————
Blue 'n' Boogie (strings out)	————
I Didn't Know What Time It Was (Candoli out)	————
If I Should Lose You	————
Ornithology (strings out) (arr. Marsh)	————
Cool Blues	————
Kim (strings out)	————
Country Gardens (sign-off) (strings out)	————

(Reissues, Frohne: Capitol (J) Toshiba 80029, (J) TOCJ-5324.)

Warne Marsh Group. Warne Marsh, ts; prob. Lou Levy, p; Jim Hughart, b; Frank Severino, d. (The Times, Studio City, Calif., Nov. 1974, private, unknown number of tunes.) *Unknown title(s).*

Warne Marsh. Warne Marsh, ts; other sax(es), b, dr, g, unidentified. (Marsh's home studio, Pasadena, Calif., c. Nov.-Dec. 1974. Marsh practicing, solo, with metronome, about 30 min., also instructional jam session with students, prob. at Nova Studioa, Pasadena, Calif., private, recorded by Jeremy Kellock.)

Warne Marsh Group. Warne Marsh, ts; probably Ron Eschete, g; Lou Levy, p; Buddy Clark, b; Dick Borden, d. (Hungry Joe's, Huntington Beach, Calif., Dec. 7, 1974, private, heads and Marsh solos only, 3 tunes.) *Untitled blues, Subconscious-Lee, All the Things You Are.*

Warne Marsh Quintet. Warne Marsh, ts; Ron Eschete, g; Lou Levy, p; Buddy Clark, b; Dick Borden, d. (Hungry Joe's, Huntington Beach, Calif., Dec. 8, 1974, private, heads and Marsh solos only, 10 tunes.) *April, Stella by Starlight, Dizzy Atmosphere, It's You or No One, Blue Lester, Little Willie Leaps, Tune Up, Sweet and Lovely, Subconscious-Lee, All the Things You Are.*

Warne Marsh Quartet. Warne Marsh, ts; Lou Levy, p; Jim Hughart, b; Frank Severino, d. (The Times, Studio City, Calif., Dec. 17, 1974, private, unknown number of tunes, information from Harold Sewing.) *Unknown titles.*

Warne Marsh Quartet. Warne Marsh, ts; Lou Levy, p; Jim Hughart, b; Frank Severino, d. (The Times, Studio City, Calif., Dec. 18, 1974, private, heads and Marsh solos only, 12 tunes.) *Subconscious-Lee, Blue Lester, See Me Now, Airegin, Strike up the Band, Stella by Starlight, 317 E. 32nd Street, Gee Baby, Ain't I Good to You, Kary's Trance, Come Rain or Come Shine, Indiana* (inc.)

Warne Marsh Quartet. Warne Marsh, ts; prob. Lou Levy, p; Jim Hughart, b; Frank Severino, d. (The Times, Studio City, Calif., Dec. 22, 1974, private, unknown number of tunes, information from Harold Sewing.) *Unknown titles.*

Supersax: *Live in '75: The Japanese Tour*. Med Flory, Joe Lopes, as; Warne Marsh, Jay Migliori, ts; Jack Nimitz, bs; Frank Rosolino, tb; Lou Levy, p; Buddy Clark, b; Jake Hanna, d; Med Flory, Buddy Clark, Warne Marsh, arr. (Sun Palace, Tokyo, Japan, c. Jan. 15, 1975.)

Scrapple from the Apple (arr. Flory)	Hindsight Records HCD-618
All the Things You Are (arr. Clark)	———
Salt Peanuts (arr. Marsh)	———
Parker's Mood (arr. Clark)	———
Just Friends (arr. Flory)	———
Ornithology (arr. Marsh)	———
Embraceable You (arr. Flory)	———
Moose the Mooche (arr. Flory)	———

(Marsh solos on "Salt Peanuts" and "Ornithology")

Warne Marsh Quartet. Warne Marsh, ts; prob. Lou Levy, p; Jim Hughart, b; Frank Severino, d. (Donte's, No. Hollywood, Calif., Jan. 21, 1975, private, Marsh solos only, unknown number of tunes, information from Harold Sewing.) *Unknown titles.*

Warne Marsh-Supersax. Warne Marsh, ts; Supersax rhythm section, probably Lou Levy, p; Buddy Clark, b; Jake Hanna, d. (Donte's, No. Hollywood, Calif., Jan. 24, 1975, private, 5 tunes, Marsh solos only, recorded by Harold Sewing.) *Salt Peanuts, KoKo, Ornithology, Cool Blues, Dizzy Atmosphere.*

Warne Marsh-Supersax. Warne Marsh, ts; Supersax rhythm section, prob. Lou Levy, p; Buddy Clark, b; Jake Hanna, d. (Donte's, No. Hollywood, Calif., Jan. 25, 1975, private, 5 tunes, Marsh solos only, recorded by Harold Sewing.) *Salt Peanuts, KoKo, Ornithology, Night in Tunisia, Cool Blues.*

Warne Marsh Quartet. Warne Marsh, ts; Lou Levy, p; Jim Hughart, b; Frank Severino, d; unknown, v. (1). (The Times, Studio City, Calif., Jan. 26, 1975, private, heads and Marsh solos only except for vocals, 18 tunes.) *Strike up the Band, If You Could See Me Now, Kary's Trance, Lady Be Good, 317 E. 32nd Street, My Old Flame, It's You or No One, Don't Blame Me (1), I Can't Give You Anything but Love (1), Stella by Starlight, Gee Baby Ain't I Good to You, Subconscious-Lee, Lester's Blues, Star Eyes, You'd Be So Nice to Come Home to, Will You Still Be Mine, Embraceable You, You Stepped out of a Dream* (inc).

Warne Marsh Quartet. Warne Marsh, ts; Lou Levy, p; Fred Atwood, b; Frank Severino, d. (Donte's, No. Hollywood, Calif., Jan. 28, 1975, private, unknown number of tunes, information from Harold Sewing.) *Unknown titles.*

Warne Marsh-Supersax. Warne Marsh, ts; Supersax rhythm section, prob. Lou Levy, p; Buddy Clark, b; Jake Hanna, d. (Donte's, No. Hollywood, Calif., Jan. 31, 1975, private, 5 tunes, Marsh solos only, recorded by Harold Sewing.) *Salt Peanuts, Ornithology, KoKo, Dizzy Atmosphere, The Bird.*

Warne Marsh-Supersax. Warne Marsh, ts; Supersax rhythm section, prob. Lou Levy, p; Buddy Clark, b; Jake Hanna, d. (Donte's, No. Hollywood, Calif., Feb. 1, 1975, private, 7 tunes, Marsh solos only, recorded by Harold Sewing.) *Scrapple from the Apple, Salt Peanuts, KoKo, Dizzy Atmosphere, Ornithology, Kim, Now's the Time.*

Warne Marsh Quartet. Warne Marsh, ts; Lou Levy, p; Jim Hughart, b; Frank Severino, d; unknown, v (1). (Donte's, North Hollywood, Calif., Feb. 4, 1975, private, heads and Marsh solos only, 15 tunes.) *Somebody Loves Me, April, It Might As Well Be Spring, It's You or No One, Will You Still Be Mine, Gee Baby Ain't I Good to You, Strike up the Band, Easy Living (1), Airegin, Autumn in New York, All the Things You Are, Stella by Starlight, This Can't Be Love, We'll Be Together Again, Featherbed.*

Warne Marsh Quartet. Warne Marsh, ts; probably Lou Levy, p; Jim Hughart or Fred Atwood, b; Frank Severino or Jake Hanna, d. (Unknown place, date, c. 1975, prob. Donte's, No. Hollywood, Calif., or The Times, Studio City, Calif., private, heads and Marsh solos only, 2 tunes.) *Easy Living, Kary's Trance.*

Warne Marsh-Sal Mosca. Warne Marsh, ts; Sal Mosca, p; unknown, as, tpt, b, d. (Sal Mosca's studio, Mt. Vernon, N.Y., Feb. 18, 1975, private, Ziskind, 4 tunes.) *Lullaby of the Leaves, Sweet Georgia Brown, Scrapple from the Apple, Two Not One.*

Warne Marsh Quartet. Warne Marsh, ts; Lou Levy, p; Jim Hughart, b; Frank Severino, d. (The Times, Studio City, Calif., Mar. 12, 1975, private, heads and Marsh solos only, 15 tunes.) *It's You or No One, You Stepped out of a Dream, Easy Living, Subconscious-Lee, This Can't Be Love, Squeeze Me* or *When Lights Are Low, When You're Smiling, Confirmation, If You Could See Me Now, I Didn't Know What Time It Was, April, Come Rain or Come Shine, 317 E. 32nd Street, Embraceable You, Alone Together* (inc.).

Warne Marsh Quartet. Warne Marsh, ts; Lou Levy, p; Jim Hughart, b; Frank Severino (1) and Dick Borden, d. (The Times, Studio City, Calif., Mar. 13, 1975, private, 14 tunes, complete. Another tape of same material exists which includes only heads and Marsh solos.) *317 E. 32nd Street (1), All the Things You Are (1), Indiana (1), Imagination (1), I Want to Be Happy (1), It's You or No One, Easy Living, Little Willie Leaps, If You Could See Me Now, You Stepped out of a Dream, The Way You Look Tonight, Stella by Starlight, Come Rain or Come Shine, Lover Come Back to Me.* (Note: Jack Goodwin has identified the tunes on which Severino and Borden play.)

Warne Marsh Quartet. Warne Marsh, ts; Lou Levy, p; Jim Hughart, b; Dick Borden, d; unknown, v. (The Times, Studio City, Calif., Apr. 12, 1975, private, heads and Marsh solos only, 12 tunes.) *Strike up the Band, God Bless the Child, Airegin, Sunday, Summertime (1), Walkin', There Will Never Be Another You, Godchild, I'll Take Romance, I Got Rhythm, Israel, Strike Up the Band* (inc.).

Warne Marsh Quartet. Warne Marsh, ts; Lou Levy, p; Jim Hughart, b; Dick Borden, d. (The Times, Studio City, Calif, Apr. 15, 1975, private, 9 tunes, prob. heads and Marsh solos only, information from Jeremy Kellock.) *The Best Thing for You, Someone to Watch over Me, Tune Up, You Stepped out of a Dream, Old Devil Moon, If You Could See Me Now, Little Willie Leaps, Kary's Trance, Every Time We Say Goodbye.*

Warne Marsh Quartet. Warne Marsh, ts; Lou Levy, p; Jim Hughart, b; Dick Borden, d. (The Times, Studio City, Calif., Apr. 16, 1975, private, 10 tunes.) *I Can't Give You Anything but Love, Come Rain or Come Shine, It's All Right with Me, Little Willie Leaps, Stella by Starlight, Tico Tico, Yesterdays, Featherbed, Israel, Strike up the Band* (inc.).

Warne Marsh Quartet. Warne Marsh, ts; Lou Levy, p; Jim Hughart, b; Dick Borden, d. (The Times, Studio City, Calif., Apr. 17, 1975, private, 7 known tunes but more recorded, information from Jeremy Kellock.) *Strike up the Band, unknown title, Subconscious-Lee, It's You or No One, All the Things You Are, My Old Flame, It's Only a Paper Moon.*

Warne Marsh-Art Pepper. Warne Marsh, ts; Art Pepper, as; Buddy Collette (1), cl; others unknown. (The Foxy Lady, Los Angeles, Apr. 20, 1975, private, 8 tunes, information from Jeremy Kellock.) *Sonnymoon for Two, Two-Chord Funk, Here's That Rainy Day, April, Broadway (1), Chameleon (1), All the Things You Are (1), Blues (1).*

Warne Marsh Quartet. Warne Marsh, ts; Lou Levy, p; Jim Hughart, b; Dick Borden, d. (California Institute of Technology, Pasadena, Calif., Apr. 29, 1975, private, 10 tunes.) *It's You or No One, All the Things You Are, Airegin, If You Could See Me Now, 317 E. 32ⁿᵈ Street, Israel, April, Stella by Starlight, untitled blues, Subconscious-Lee.*

Warne Marsh Quartet. Warne Marsh, ts; Lou Levy, p; Jim Hughart, b; Dick Borden, d. (The Times, Studio City, Calif., May 6, 1975, private, 11 tunes, information from Jeremy Kellock.) *It's You or No One, Israel, Strike Up the Band, Airegin (Levy out), I Can't Get Started (Levy out), Ornithology, I'll Remember You, Autumn Leaves, You Stepped out of a Dream, Everything Happens to Me, Little Willie Leaps* (inc.).

Warne Marsh Quartet. Warne Marsh, ts; Lou Levy, p: Jim Hughart, b; Dick Borden, d. (The Time, Studio City, Calif., May 6, 1975, private, 5 tunes, information from Jeremy Kellock.) *I Feel a Song Coming On (inc), Little Willie Leaps (inc.), Just the Way You Look Tonight,* All the Things You Are,* My Old Flame** (*heads and Marsh solos only).

Warne Marsh Quartet. Warne Marsh, ts; Lou Levy, p; Jim Hughart, b; Dick Borden, d. (The Times, Studio City, Calif, May 6–7, 1975, private, heads and Marsh solos only, 3 tunes.) *I Remember You, It's You or No One, Lennie's Pennies.*

Warne Marsh Quartet. Warne Marsh, ts; Lou Levy, p; Jim Hughart, b; Dick Borden, d. (The Times, Studio City, Calif., May 7, 1975, private, 7 tunes, information from Jeremy Kellock.) *Crosscurrent, All the Things You Are, Come Rain or Come Shine, Strike up the Band, The Night Has a Thousand Eyes, Play Fiddle Play/Kary's Trance, 'S Wonderful.*

Warne Marsh Quartet. Warne Marsh, ts; Lou Levy, p; Jim Hughart, b; Dick Borden, d. (The Times, Studio City, Calif., May 7, 1975, private, 5 tunes, information from Jeremy Kellock.) *God Bless the Child, Old Devil Moon, The Best Thing for You, Love Me or Leave Me, I Feel a Song Coming On.*

Warne Marsh-Blue Mitchell-Supersax. Warne Marsh, Jay Migliori, ts; Blue Mitchell, tpt; Supersax rhythm section: Jake Hanna, d; Lou Levy, p; prob. Buddy Clark or Fred Atwood, b. (Donte's, N. Hollywood, Calif., May 11 & prob. May 18 (1), 1975, private, solos only by Marsh, Migliori, Mitchell, 7 tunes.) *Cherokee, Ornithology, unknown, unknown, Ornithology (1), unknown (1), unknown (1).*

Warne Marsh-Supersax. Warne Marsh, ts; Supersax rhythm section, prob. Lou Levy, p; Fred Atwood, b; Jake Hanna, d; unknown, v (1), possibly Irene Kral. (Donte's, No. Hollywood, Calif., May 18, 1975, private, Marsh solos plus one vocal only, 3 tunes.) *Unknown, I Got Rhythm, Old Devil Moon (1).*

Warne Marsh Quartet. Warne Marsh, ts; Lou Levy, p; Jim Hughart or Fred Atwood, b; Dick Borden, d. (The Times, Studio City, Calif., June 4, 1975, private, heads and Marsh solos only, 2 tunes.) *I Feel a Song Coming On, Mean to Me.*

Warne Marsh Quartet. Warne Marsh, ts; Lou Levy, p; Fred Atwood, b; Dick Borden, d. (The Times, Studio City, Calif., prob. June 4, 1975, private, heads and Marsh solos only, 14 tunes, information from Jeremy Kellock.) *Unknown title, unknown title, Everything Happens to Me, I Feel a Song Coming On, All the Things You Are, Israel, If You Could See Me Now, April, You Stepped out of a Dream, Gee Baby Ain't I Good to You, The Night Has a Thousand Eyes, Confirmation, unknown title, Strike up the Band.*

Warne Marsh Quartet. Warne Marsh, ts; Dave McKay (1), Lou Levy, p; Fred Atwood, b; Dick Borden, d. (The Times, Studio City, Calif., June

5, 1975, private, heads and Marsh solos only, 12 tunes.) *Subconscious-Lee, Equinox, Little Willie Leaps, You Don't Know What Love Is, Strike up the Band, It's You or No One (1), All the Things You Are (1), April/I'll Remember April (1), You Go to My Head (1), Sippin' at Bell's (1), You Stepped out of a Dream, The More I See You.*

Warne Marsh Quartet. Warne Marsh, ts; Dave McKay,* p; Fred Atwood, b; Dick Borden, d. (The Times, Studio City, Calif., prob. June 5, 1975, private, heads and Marsh solos only, 9 tunes, prob. heads and Marsh solos only, information from Jeremy Kellock. *Six tunes appear to be duplicates of tunes on the preceding tape dated June 5, 1975, with McKay on piano, but Kellock has McKay on 5 additional tunes where the pianist may actually be Lou Levy.) *All the Things You Are, April/I'll Remember April, You Go to My Head, Sippin' at Bell's, You Stepped out of a Dream, The More I See You, The Trolley Song, Love Me or Leave Me, Giant Steps.*

Warne Marsh-Connie Crothers. Warne Marsh, ts; Connie Crothers, p; Joe Solomon, b; Skip Scott, d. (Prob. New York City, Jul. 1975, private, 4 tunes, information from Jeremy Kellock.) *Unknown titles.*

Warne Marsh Quartet. Warne Marsh, ts; Lou Levy, p; Fred Atwood, b; Dick Borden or Jake Hanna, d. (The Times, Studio City, Calif., Aug. 5–7, 1975, private, unknown number of tunes from three nights, recorded by Paul Hoffman, information from Jeremy Kellock.) *Unknown titles.*

Warne Marsh Quartet. Warne Marsh, ts; Lou Levy, p; Fred Atwood, b; Jake Hanna, d. (The Times, Studio City, Calif., Aug. 7, 1975, private, heads and Marsh solos only, 12 tunes.) *317 E. 32nd Street, It's You or No One, Giant Steps, The More I See You, Anthropology, Sippin' at Bell's, Subconscious-Lee, Embraceable You, You Stepped out of a Dream, Be-Bop, That Old Feeling, Strike up the Band.*

Elek Bacsik: *Bird and Dizzy, A Musical Tribute*. Elek Bacsik, ev, violectra; Med Flory, as; Warne Marsh, ts; Oscar Brashear, tp; Mike Wofford, p, ep, arp syn; Chuck Domanico, b; Shelly Manne, d. (Los Angeles; Frohne gives Sept. 4, 1975.)

| Night in Tunisia | Flying Dutchman BDL 1-1082 |
| Be-Bop | ——— |

Same, except Flory out and Buddy Clark, b, replaces Domanico:

Groovin' High	———
Moose the Mooche	———
Yardbird Suite	———

(Marsh solos on "Moose the Mooche" and "Groovin' High." He does not play on other tracks of album. Reissue, Frohne: RCA (J) RVP-6035.)

Warne Marsh Quartet. Warne Marsh, ts; Gary Foster, as; prob. Fred Atwood, b; prob. Dick Borden, d. (prob. The Times, Studio City, Calif., prob. Sept. 9, 1975, private, Marsh solos only, 3 tunes.) *It's You or No One* (Marsh solo only), *I Can't Get Started, Featherbed.*

Warne Marsh Quintet. Warne Marsh, ts; Gary Foster, as; Lou Levy, p; Monty Budwig, b; prob. Dick Borden, d. (Prob. The Times, Studio City, Calif., prob. Sept. 9, 1975, private, mainly Marsh solos only, some heads and ends, 5 tunes.) *You Stepped out of a Dream, Subconscious-Lee, Everything Happens to Me, 317 E. 32nd Street, I'll Remember April.*

Warne Marsh Quartet. Warne Marsh, ts; Gary Foster, as; prob. Fred Atwood, b; prob. Dick Borden, d. (The Times, Studio City, Calif., Sept. 10, 1975, private, 15 tunes.) *All About You* (inc.), *April, Lover Man, Kary's Trance, I'll See You in My Dreams, You Stepped out of a Dream, Two Not One, untitled blues, Lennie's Pennies, 317 E. 32nd Street, Kary's Trance, Here's That Rainy Day, Just Friends, Cherokee, Subconscious-Lee.*

Warne Marsh Quartet. Warne Marsh, ts; Gary Foster, as; Fred Atwood, b; Dick Borden, d. (The Times, Studio City, Calif., Sept. 11, 1975, private, 11 tunes.) *Just Friends, Lennie's Pennies, Walkin', 317 E. 32nd Street, Two Not One, How about You/All about You, Leave Me, Two Not One, Here's That Rainy Day, Background Music, Featherbed.*

Warne Marsh Quartet. Warne Marsh, ts; Gary Foster, as; Fred Atwood, b; Dick Borden, d. (The Times, Studio City, Calif., Sept. 11, 1975, private, 6 tunes, recorded by Teo Alexander, information from Jeremy Kellock.) *How about You, I'll Remember April, Lover Man, Kary's Trance, I'll See You in My Dreams* (inc.), *You Stepped out of a Dream.*

Warne Marsh-Connie Crothers Quartet. Warne Marsh, ts; Connie Crothers, p; Joe Solomon, b; Roger Mancuso, d. (Carnegie Recital Hall, New York City, Oct. 4, 1975, private, Frohne lists 15 tunes.) *Two Not One, My Old Flame, Background Music, 317 E. 32nd Street, unknown blues, Easy Living, unknown title, unknown title, You Stepped out of a Dream, unkown title, How Deep Is the Ocean, unknown title, April, Subconscious-Lee* (inc.), *It's You or No One.*

Warne Marsh and Friends: Warne Marsh, Ted Brown, ts; Lenny Popkin, ts; Bob Arthurs, tp; Billy Lester, p; Joe Solomon, b; Roger Mancuso, d; others unknown. (Someday Lounge, Long Island, N.Y., Oct. 5, 1975, private, unknown number of tunes, information from Harold Sewing.) *Unknown titles.*

Supersax. Prob. Med Flory, Joe Lopes, as; Warne Marsh, Jay Migliori, ts; Jack Nimitz, bs; Conte Candoli, tp; Lou Levy, p; Buddy Clark or Fred Atwood, b; Jake Hanna, d. (Unknown location, date, private, 5 tunes, information from Ted Brown.) *Billie's Bounce, If I Should Leave You, The Bird, 'Round Midnight, Night in Tunisia.*

Supersax. Prob. Med Flory, Joe Lopes, as; Warne Marsh, Jay Migliori, ts; Jack Ninitz, bs; Conte Candoli, tp; Lou Levy, p; Buddy Clark or Fred Atwood, b; Jake Hanna, d. (Prob. Donte's, No. Hollywood, Calif., Oct. 17, 1975, private, some tunes may have only Marsh solos with rhythm section, 12 tunes, information from Harold Sewing.) *Scrapple from the Apple, Parker's Mood, Just Friends, Salt Peanuts, Confirmation, Donna Lee, KoKo, Night in Tunisia, Lady Be Good, Moose the Mooche* (inc.)*, Star Eyes, Groovin' High.*

Supersax. Prob. Med Flory, Joe Lopes, as; Warne Marsh, Jay Migliori, ts; Jack Nimitz, bs; Conte Candoli, tp; Lou Levy, p; Buddy Clark or Fred Atwood, b. Jake Hanna, d. (Philadelphia, Pa., unknown club, Oct. 22, 1975, private, 9 tunes, except asterisk indicates tunes played but possibly not recorded, some tunes possibly with Marsh solos only, information from Harold Sewing.) *The Bird, Star Eyes, Night in Tunisia, Salt Peanuts,* Lover Man,* Ornithology,* Moose the Mooche, Yardbird Suite, KoKo.*

Supersax. Prob. Med Flory, Joe Lopes, as; Warne Marsh, Jay Migliori, ts; Jack Nimitz, bs; Conte Candoli, tp; Lou Levy, p; Buddy Clark or Fred Atwood, b; Jake Hanna, d. (Prob. Donte's, No. Hollywood, Calif., Oct. 25, 1975, private, 6 tunes, some tunes may have only Marsh solos, information from Harold Sewing.) *Salt Peanuts, KoKo, The Bird, Night in Tunisia, Be-Bop, Groovin' High.*

Supersax. Prob. Med Flory, Joe Lopes, as; Warne Marsh, Jay Migliori, ts; Jack Nimitz, bs; Conte Candoli, tp; Lou Levy, p; Buddy Clark or Fred Atwood, b; Jake Hanna, d. (Prob. Donte's, No. Hollywood, Calif., Oct. 26, 1975, private, 3 tunes, prob. Marsh solos only, information from Harold Sewing.) *Scrapple from the Apple, Salt Peanuts, Confirmation.*

Supersax. Prob. Med Flory, Joe Lopes, as; Warne Marsh, Jay Migliori, ts; Jack Nimitz, bs; Conte Candoli, tp; Lou Levy, p; Buddy Clark or Fred Atwood, b; Jake Hanna, d. (Camden, N.J., unknown club, Nov. 2, 1975, private, 8 tunes, prob. Marsh solos only, information from Harold

Sewing.) *Scrapple from the Apple, Salt Peanuts, KoKo, The Bird, Groovin' High, Scrapple from the Apple, Night in Tunisia, KoKo.*

Supersax. Prob. Med Flory, Joe Lopes, as; Warne Marsh, Jay Migliori, ts; Jack Nimitz, bs; Conte Candoli, tp; Lou Levy, p; Buddy Clark or Fred Atwood, b; Jake Hanna, d. (Prob. Camden, N.J., Nov. 3, 1975, private, 3 tunes, prob. Marsh solos only, information from Harold Sewing.) *Scrapple from the Apple, Star Eyes, KoKo.*

Warne Marsh-Supersax. Warne Marsh, ts; Supersax rhythm section: prob. Lou Levy, p; Buddy Clark or Fred Atwood, b; Jake Hanna, d. (Donte's, No. Hollywood, Calif., Nov. 1975, private, heads & Marsh solos only, 2 tunes.) *KoKo/Cherokee, Ornithology.*

Warne Marsh-Supersax. Warne Marsh, ts; Supersax rhythm section: Lou Levy, p; Fred Atwood, b; Jake Hanna, d. (Donte's, No. Hollywood, Calif., Nov. 1975, Marsh solos only, 8 tunes, information from Jeremy Kellock.) *Salt Peanuts, KoKo, Ornithology (with "Lunarcy" changes), rhythm changes, rhythm changes, Lover Man, blues, KoKo.*

Warne Marsh-Supersax. Warne Marsh, Jay Migliori, ts (1); Supersax rhythm section, prob. Lou Levy, p; Buddy Clark or Fred Atwood, b; Jake Hanna, d. (Donte's, No. Hollywood, Calif., Nov. 1975, private, Marsh solos only plus one by Migliori, 6 tunes.) *Ornithology, Salt Peanuts, unknown title, unknown title, unknown blues, KoKo/Cherokee (1, inc.).*

Warne Marsh-Supersax. Warne Marsh, ts; Blue Mitchell, tp (1); Supersax rhythm section, prob. Lou Levy, p; Buddy Clark or Fred Atwood, b; Jake Hanna, d. (Donte's, No. Hollywood, Calif., Nov. 1975, private, Marsh solos only plus one by Mitchell, 11 tunes.) *Scrapple from the Apple, KoKo, unknown minor tune, Donna Lee, I Remember You, KoKo, unknown title, unknown title, Salt Peanuts (1).* Same personnel plus Med Flory, Joe Lopes, as; Jay Migliori, ts; Jack Nimitz, bs. (Heads plus tenor solos) *KoKo* (solo may be by Migliori), *Ornithology.*

Warne Marsh Quintet. Warne Marsh, ts; Gary Foster, as; Ron Hoopes, p; Fred Atwood, b; Jake Hanna, d. (College of the Siskiyous, Mt. Shasta, Calif., Nov. 16, 1975, private, 6 tunes.) *You Stepped out of a Dream, Featherbed, All the Things You Are, Lover Man, Two Not One, All about You.*

Warne Marsh Quintet. Warne Marsh, ts; Jan Allan, tp; Robert Hamberg, p; Roman Dylag, b; Rune Carlsson, d. (Stockholm, Sweden, Nov. 1975, private, 8 tunes.) *317 E. 32nd Street, Little Willie Leaps, Darn That Dream,*

Lester Leaps In, All the Things You Are, Donna Lee, Walkin', Like Someone in Love.

Warne Marsh Quartet. Warne Marsh, ts; Ole Kock Hansen, p; Niels-Henning Orsted Pedersen, b; Alex Riel, d. (Frohne says broadcast by Danish Radio, Copenhagen, Nov. 1975, but "exact date and location unknown; probably more tunes recorded." Private.)

B♭ blues	Danish Radio broadcast
Tune Up	———
Little Willie Leaps	———

Warne Marsh-Lee Konitz Quintet. Lee Konitz, as; Warne Marsh, ts; Ole Kock Hansen, p; Niels-Henning Orsted Pedersen, b; Alex Riel, d. (Jazzhus Montmartre, Copenhagen, Dec. 2, 1975.)

Two Not One	Storyville, unissued
Walkin'	———
Sound Lee	———
Blues by Lester	———
Darn That Dream	———
Donna Lee	———
Ornithology	———
Subconscious-Lee	———
317 East 32nd Street	———
Little Willie Leaps	———

Warne Marsh Quintet, **Jazz Exchange, Vol. 1**. Lee Konitz, as; Warne Marsh, ts; Ole Kock Hansen, p; Niels-Henning Orsted Pedersen, b; Alex Riel (1), Svend Erik Norregard. (Cafe Montmartre, Copenhagen, Denmark., Dec. 2 (a), 3 (b), 4 (c), 5 (d), 1975. Information from Karl Knudsen of Storyville Records.)

April (b)	Storyville SLP4001; (GB)SLP1017; (S/DK)STCD8201
Blues by Lester (d)	———; ———; ———
Lennie-Bird (d)	———; ———; ———
You Stepped out of a Dream (d)	———; ———; ———
Kary's Trance (c)	———; ———; ———
Background Music (1) (b)	———; ———; ———
Subconscious-Lee (c)	unissued; unissued; ———
Sound-Lee (1) (b)	unissued; unissued; unissued
Wow (1) (b)	unissued; unissued; unissued
Little Willie Leaps (1) (b)	unissued; unissued; unissued
Blues by Lester (1) (b)	unissued; unissued; unissued
What's New (1) (b)	unissued; unissued; unissued

Ornithology (1) (b)	unissued; unissued; unissued
I Always Knew (1) (b)	unissued; unissued; unissued
Autumn Leaves (1) (b)	unissued; unissued; unissued
You or No One (1) (b)	unissued; unissued; unissued
I Remember April (1) (b)	unissued; unissued; unissued
Feather Bed (c)	unissued; unissued; unissued
Darn That Dream (c)	unissued; unissued; unissued
Little Willie Leaps (c)	unissued; unissued; unissued
Sound-Lee (c)	unissued; unissued; unissued
317 East 32nd Street (c)	unissued; unissued; unissued
I'll See You in My Dreams (c)	unissued; unissued; unissued
You Stepped out of a Dream (c)	unissued; unissued; unissued
Anthropology (c)	unissued; unissued; unissued
I'll See You in My Dreams (d)	unissued; unissued; unissued
Stella by Starlight (d)	unissued; unissued; unissued
Two Not One (d)	unissued; unissued; unissued
Tune Up (d)	unissued; unissued; unissued
I Always Knew (d)	unissued; unissued; unissued
Darn That Dream (d)	unissued; unissued; unissued
Feather Bed (d)	unissued; unissued; unissued
Donna Lee (d)	unissued; unissued; unissued

Lee Konitz, as; Warne Marsh, ts; Bo Stief, b; Svend Erik Norregard, d.

Star Eyes (c)	unissued; unissued; unissued

Warne Marsh-Lee Konitz, **Jazz Exchange, Vol. 3**. Lee Konitz, as; Warne Marsh, ts; Ole Kock Hansen, p; Niels-Henning Orsted Pedersen, b; Svend Erik Norregard, d. (Cafe Montmartre, Copenhagen, Denmark, Dec. 3 (a), 4 (b), 5 (c), 1975. Information from Karl Knudsen of Storyville Records.)

Just Friends (c)	Storyville SLP4096; STCD8203; (S/DK)STCD8203
You Don't Know What Love Is (a)	————; ————; ———
Back Home (b)	————; ————; unissued
Little Willie Leaps (a)	————; ————; ———
Old Folks (c)	————; ————; ———
Au Privave (c)	————; ————; ———
Wow (a)	unissued; ————; ———

Warne Marsh, ts; Lee Konitz, as; Dave Cliff, g; Peter Ind, b; Alan Levitt, d. (Café Montmartre, Copenhagen, Denmark, Dec. 27, 1975.)

Chi Chi	unissued; ————; ———

Lee Konitz-Warne Marsh Quintet. Lee Konitz, as; Warne Marsh, ts; Dave Cliff, g; Peter Ind, b; Alan Levitt, d. (Bim Huis, Amsterdam, Dec. 6, 1975, private, Frohne, 10 tunes. Frohne says "entry according to Al Levitt" and lists 5 additional tunes not on this tape.) *It's You or No One, Two Not One* (inc.), *Subconscious-Lee* (inc.), *Now's the Time* (inc.), *Background Music* (inc.), *317 E. 32nd Street* (inc.), *My Old Flame* (inc.), *Softly as in a Morning Sunrise* (inc.), *Cherokee* (inc.), *Wow* (inc).

Lee Konitz-Warne Marsh Quintet. Lee Konitz, as; Warne Marsh, ts; Dave Cliff, g; Peter Ind, b; Alan Levitt, d. (Pepijn, Den Haag, Holland, Dec. 7, 1975, private, Frohne, 12 tunes.) *Smog Eyes, Softly as in a Morning Sunrise, Background Music, Sound-Lee, Foolin' Myself, Wow, Two Not One, 317 E. 32nd Street, You'd Be So Nice to Come Home To, Subconscious-Lee, unknown title, April.*

Lee Konitz-Warne Marsh Quintet. Lee Konitz, as; Warne Marsh, ts; Dave Cliff, g; Peter Ind, b; Alan Levitt, d. (Recorded and broadcast over RTB Radio, Belgium, Heist-op-den-Berg, Belgium, Dec. 9, 1975, private, Frohne.)

Kary's Trance	RTB Radio, Belgium
Blues by Lester	————
April	————

(Frohne notes, "Prob. remaining titles of performance recorded as well.")

Warne Marsh Quartet. Warne Marsh, ts; Peter Ind, b; Alan Levitt, d; prob. Dave Cliff, g—Frohne labels group as quartet, but does not list Cliff. (Recorded and broadcast over Netherlands Radio from Laren, Holland, Dec. 11, 1975, private, Frohne.)

It's You or No One	Netherlands Radio broadcast
Get Happy	————
Easy Living	————
Softly as in a Morning Sunrise (inc.)	————

(Frohne notes, "Remaining titles of performance probably recorded as well.")

Lee Konitz-Warne Marsh Quintet. Lee Konitz, as; Warne Marsh, ts; Dave Cliff, g; Peter Ind, b; Alan levitt, d. (Amecitia, Franeker, Holland, Dec. 15, 1975, private, Frohne, 10 tunes. Frohn notes, "According to Rein deGraaf this concert took place on Dec. 18, 1975. Above date according to announcement during radio broadcast [tour schedule].") *Kary's*

Trance, Sound-Lee, Foolin' Myself, Background Music, You Don't Know What Love Is, Two Not One, It's You or No One, 317 E. 32ⁿᵈ Street, You Go to My Head, Little Willie Leaps.

Warne Marsh-Lee Konitz Quintet. Warne Marsh, ts; Lee Konitz, as; Dave Cliff, g; Peter Ind, b; Alan Levitt, d. (Seven Dials, London, England, Dec. 18, 1975, private, 13 tunes.) *Wow, Background Music, Softly as in a Morning Sunrise, You Go to My Head, 317 E. 32ⁿᵈ Street, It's You or No One, Subconscious-Lee, Bach 2-Part Invention, Kary's Trance, Just the Way You Look Tonight, Now's the Time, April (inc.), Darn That Dream (inc.).* (Note: Jack Goodwin adds *Donna Lee.*)

Warne Marsh Quartet Warne Marsh, ts; Dave Cliff, g; Peter In, b; Alan Levitt, d. (Stockport, Cheshire, England, Dec. 20, 1975, private, Goodwin, 14 tunes.) *It's You or No One, Motorway Blues, I Want to Be Happy, It's Only a Paper Moon, The Night Has a Thousand Eyes, Stella by Starlight, Dizzy Atmosphere, Crazy She Calls Me (inc.), I'm Getting Sentimental over You, They Can't Take That Away from Me, Now's the Time, Lennie's Pennies, God Bless the Child, Moose the Mooche.*

Warne Marsh Quartet. Warne Marsh, ts; Dave Cliff, g; Peter Ind, b; Alan Levitt, d. (Queen's Theatre, Sittingbourne, Kent, England, Dec. 21, 1975, private, 16 tunes.) *Easy to Love, Little Willie Leaps, God Bless the Child, You Stepped out of a Dream, Donna Lee, The Night Has a Thousand Eyes, Foolin' Myself, It's You or No One, All the Things You Are, Au Privave, Just the Way You Look Tonight, Body and Soul, Limehouse Blues, Darn That Dream, Softly as in a Morning Sunrise, Background Music.*

Warne Marsh-Lee Konitz Quintet. Warne Marsh, ts; Lee Konitz, as; Dave Cliff, g; Peter Ind, b; Alan Levitt, d. (Corner House Pub, Whitley Bay, Northumberland, England, Dec. 22, 1975, private, 12 tunes. Frohne gives place as "Whitley Bar, Grand Hotel, Newcastle.") *Wow, Subconscious-Lee, The Night Has a Thousand Eyes, Lover Man (Marsh out), Background Music, Sound-Lee, April, Star Eyes, God Bless the Child (Konitz out), Chi Chi, Two Not One, Kary's Trance.* (Note: Jack Goodwin omits *Kary's Trance* and adds *Back Home.*)

Warne Marsh-Lee Konitz Quintet: *Live at the Montmartre Club,* **Jazz Exchange, Vol. 2**. Lee Konitz, as; Warne Marsh, ts; Dave Cliff, g; Peter Ind, b; Alan Levitt, d. (Copenhagen, Denmark, Dec. 27, 1975. Information from Karl Knudsen of Storyville Records.)

Kary's Trance   Storyville SLP1020; SLP4026; STCD8202

Foolin' Myself	————; ————; ————
Sound-Lee	————; ————; ————
Two-Part Invention No. 1, Allegro	————; ————; ————
Two Not One	————; ————; ————
Darn That Dream	————; ————; ————
317 East 32nd Street	————; ————; ————
Two-Part Invention No. 13, Allegro Tranquillo	————; ————; ————
April	unissued; unissued; ————
Everything Happens to Me	unissued; unissued; ————
Little Willie Leaps	unissued; unissued; unissued
Background Music	unissued; unissued; unissued
You Stepped out of a Dream	unissued; unissued; unissued
The Night Has a Thousand Eyes	unissued; unissued; unissued
Yardbird Suite	unissued; unissued; unissued
The Way You Look Tonight	unissued; unissued; unissued
God Bless the Child	unissued; unissued; unissued
I'll See You in My Dreams	unissued; unissued; unissued
Ornithology	unissued; unissued; unissued
Now's the Time	unissued; unissued; unissued

(Reissue: Mobil Fidelity UDCD 707, Warne Marsh-Lee Konitz Quintet.)

Warne Marsh Quartet. Warne Marsh, ts; Dave Cliff, g; Niels-Henning ØrstedPedersen, b; Alan Levitt, d. (Ivar Rosenberg Studio, Copenhagen, Denmark, Dec. 28, 1975. Information from Karl Knudsen of Storyville Records.)

Blues in G Flat	unissued
Blues in G Flat	Storyville STCD8259
After You've Gone	————
God Bless the Child (1)	unissued
The Song Is You (1)	————
The Song Is You (2)	unissued
It's You or No One (1)	unissued
Lennie Bird (1)	unissued
Lennie Bird (Ornithology)(2)	————
It's You or No One (2)	————
The Way You Look Tonight (1)	————
The Way You Look Tonight (2) (inc).	unissued
The Way You Look Tonight (3)	unissued
Lennie Bird (3)	————
God Bless the Child (2)	————

God Bless the Child (3)	unissued
It Could Happen to You	unissued
Without a Song	———————
You Don't Know What Love Is	———————
Be My Love	———————

Warne Marsh Trio. Warne Marsh, ts; Niels-Henning Orsted Pedersen, b; Alan Levitt, d. (Ivar Rosenberg Studio, Copenhagen, Denmark, Dec. 29, 1975.)

Without a Song (1)	unissued
Without a Song (2) (inc.).	unissued
Without a Song (3)	Storyville STCD8278
Just One of Those Things (1)	unissued
I Should Care (1)	———————
I Should Care (2)	unissued
Just One of Those Things (2) (inc.).	unissued
Just One of Those Things (3) (inc.).	unissued
Just One of Those Things (4) (inc.).	unissued
Just One of Those Things (5)	unissued
Just One of Those Things (6) (inc.).	unissued
Just One of Those Things (7)	———————
The More I See You (1)	———————
Stella by Starlight, (inc.).	unissued
Confirmation (1)	unissued
Confirmation (2)	———————
When You're Smiling (1)	———————
When You're Smiling (2) (inc.).	unissued
When You're Smiling (3) (inc.).	unissued
When You're Smiling (?) (inc.).	unissued
Every Time We Say Goodbye, (inc.).	unissued
Every Time We Say Goodbye (2)	———————
I Can't Give You Anything But Love	———————
I Want to Be Happy	———————
All the Things You Are	———————
Taking a Chance on Love	———————
Little Willie Leaps	———————

Warne Marsh-Lee Konitz. Warne Marsh, ts; Lee Konitz, as; Martial Solal, p (solo on 3 tunes); Dave Cliff, g; Peter Ind, b; Alan Levitt, d. (Nantes, France, Dec. 30, 1975, private, 13 tunes. Frohne notes, "Completely [probably!] recorded and partly broadcasted by France Musique." Not known which tunes below were broadcast.)

Ah, Now	France Musique broadcast (?)
Wow	————
In a Sentimental Mood	————
Background Music	————
Darn That Dream	————
'Round Midnight	————
Chi Chi	————
Scrapple from the Apple	————
April	————
317 E. 32nd Street	————
Subconscious-Lee	————
Bach Invention	————
Anthropology	————

Warne Marsh. Warne Marsh, ts; others unknown, possibly Ben Aronov, p; Steve Gilmore, b; Bill Goodwin, d. (Place, date unknown, possibly 1976, private, 1 tune.) *Sax of a Kind.*

Warne Marsh-Zoot Sims-Supersax. Warne Marsh, Zoot Sims, ts; Supersax rhythm section, Lou Levy, p; Fred Atwood, b; Jake Hanna, d. (Ratso's, Chicago, Feb. 1976, private, 2 tunes.) *I'll Remember April, unknown blues* (inc.).

Warne Marsh-Supersax. Warne Marsh, ts; Supersax rhythm section, Lou Levy, p; Fred Atwood, b; Jake Hanna, d. (Ratso's, Chicago, Feb. 1976, private, Marsh solos only, 18 tunes.) *Scrapple from the Apple, KoKo, Ornithology, unknown blues, Salt Peanuts, KoKo, Ornithology, unknown title, unknown title, Salt Peanuts, KoKo, Ornithology, unknown blues, unknown title, Salt Peanuts, KoKo, Ornithology, unknown title.*

Warne Marsh: All Music. Warne Marsh, ts; Lou Levy, p; Fred Atwood, b; Jake Hanna, d. (Sound Studios, Carbide and Carbon Building, Chicago, Feb. 21, 1976. Unissued takes extant on private tape. Information from Chuck Nessa.)

I Have a Good One for You	Nessa N-7
It's You or No One (alt. take)	unissued
It's You or No One (alt. take)	unissued
A Time for Love	unissued
Background Music (alt. take)	unissued
Background Music	————
Blues	unissued
On Purpose (inc. take)	unissued
On Purpose	————

317 East 32nd (alt. take)	unissued
317 East 32nd	————
Lunarcy (alt. take)	unissued
Lunarcy (inc. take)	unissued
Lunarcy	————
Easy Living (inc. take)	unissued
Easy Living (alt. take)	unissued
Easy Living	————
Subconscious-Lee	————

Lee Konitz-Warne Marsh Quartet. Lee Konitz, as; Warne Marsh, ts; Peter Ind, b; Alan Levitt, d. (Middletone Hall, Hull, England, Mar. 9, 1976, private [?]), 11 tunes, Frohne, who notes, "Entry according to Edo Essed; not sure if a tape exists.") *Easy Living, It's Only a Paper Moon, You Go to My Head, Wow, Sound-Lee, Subconscious-Lee, 317 E. 32nd Street, Chi Chi, Donna Lee, Lady Be Good, Body and Soul.*

Lee Konitz-Warne Marsh Quartet. Lee Konitz, as; Warne Marsh, ts; Peter Ind, b; Alan Levitt, d. (Bergamo, Italy, Mar. 13, 1976, private, Frohne, 8 tunes. Frohne says, "Rest of performance probably recorded as well.") *Wow, Background Music, It's You or No One, My Old Flame, Subconscious-Lee, 317 E.32nd Street, Bach Invention, April.*

Lee Konitz-Warne Marsh Quartet. Lee Konitz, as; Warne Marsh, ts; Peter Ind, b; Alan Levitt, d. (Pescara, Italy, Mar. 14, 1976, private, Frohne, 13 tunes.) *Wow, Background Music, Chi Chi, Easy Living* (Konitz out), *Cherokee* (Marsh out), *Just the Way You Look Tonight, Body and Soul, Subconscious-Lee, April, Sound-Lee, Bach Invention, Kary's Trance, Two Not One.*

Lee Konitz-Warne Marsh: *London Concert*. Lee Konitz, as; Warne Marsh, ts; Peter Ind, b; Al Levitt, d. (Shaw Theatre, London, March 15, 1976. Frohne: Unissued tunes extant on private tape.)

Background Music	Wave (E) LP16
It's You or No One	————
Body and Soul	————
All the Things You Are	————
You Go to My Head (Marsh out)	————
Invention in A Minor	————
Easy Livin' (Konitz out)	————
Star Eyes	————
Wow	unissued
Cherokee	unissued
Subconscious-Lee	unissued

Fools Rush In   unissued
Sound-Lee (Ind only)   unissued
317 E. 32nd Street   unissued
The Night Has a Thousand Eyes
    (Konitz out)   unissued
Two Not One   unissued
Lady Be Good (Konitz out)   unissued

Supersax. Warne Marsh, Jay Migliori, ts; Med Flory, Lanny Morgan, as; Jack Nimitz, bs; Conte Candoli, tpt; Lou Levy, p; Fred Atwood, b; Jake Hanna, d. (Radio broadcast, KBCA, from Playboy Club, Century City, Beverly Hills, Calif., Apr. 5, 1976, private, 7 tunes, Marsh solo on "Salt Peanuts" and under announcer on "Koko.")

Scrapple from the Apple   KBCA Radio broadcast
Star Eyes   ————
Salt Peanuts   ————
April in Paris   ————
Moose the Mooche   ————
Just Friends   ————
Koko (inc.)   ————

Warne Marsh-Sal Mosca Quartet: *How Deep, How High*. Warne Marsh, ts; Sal Mosca, p; Sam Jones, b; Roy Haynes, d. (Concert, Sarah Lawrence College, Bronxville, N.Y. Date given on record jacket was Apr. 25, 1977, but this is incorrect according to the producer of the concert, Paul Altman. The probable date is Apr. 25, 1976.)

Background Music   Interplay IP7725; Discovery DS863 &
                                     DSCD-945
She's Funny That Way   ————; ———— & ————

Warne Marsh, ts; Sal Mosca, p. (Mt. Vernon, N.Y., May 2, 1979.)

The Hard Way   ————; ———— & ————
Noteworthy   ————; ———— & ————

Same personnel (Mt. Vernon, N.Y., Aug. 8, 1979.)

Finishing Touch   ————; ———— & ————
How Deep, How High   ————; ———— & ————

Warne Marsh-Sal Mosca Quartet. Warne Marsh, ts; Sal Mosca, p; Sam Jones, b; Roy Haynes, d. (Concert, Sarah Lawrence College, Bronxville, N.Y., Apr. 25, 1976, private, Ziskind, complete concert of 11 tunes, including those on IP7725, DS-863, & DSCD-945.) *It's You or No One,*

You Go to My Head, Sippin' at Bell's, I Love You, Cherokee, You Stepped out of a Dream, Background Music, She's Funny That Way, I'm Getting Sentimental Over You, Lover Come Back to Me, All the Things You Are.

Lee Konitz Meets Warne Marsh Again/**Warne Marsh Meets Lee Konitz Again** (PAUSA album cover uses both titles). Lee Konitz, as; Warne Marsh, ts; Peter Ind, b; Al Levitt, d. (Ronnie Scott's, London, May 24, 1976. Frohne: Unissued titles extant on private tape.)

Two Not One	PAUSA (E) PR7019; ProduttoriAssociati (It) PA/LP72
Star Eyes	————; ————
You Go to My Head	————; ————
All the Things You Are	————; ————
My Old Flame	————; ————
Sound-Lee	————; ————
Subconscious-Lee	unissued; unissued
Embraceable You (Konitz out)	unissued; unissued
Easy Living	unissued; unissued
Wow	unissued; unissued
Background Music	unissued; unissued
Just Friends	unissued; unissued

(Reissues: PAUSA 1977 and Epic (J) 25AP-897. PrAss (I) PA/LP72 gives date as May 21.)

Warne Marsh-Lee Konitz. Warne Marsh, ts; Lee Konitz, as; Peter Ind, b; Alan Levitt, d. (Ronnie Scott's, London, England, May 25, 1976, private, Frohne, 8 tunes.) *She's Funny That Way, Limehouse Blues, Chi Chi, Embraceable You, Background Music, Wow, All the Things You Are, Just Friends.* (Note: Jack Goodwin adds the following: *It's You or No One, Subconscious-Lee, Star Eyes, Two Not One, Kary's Trance, You Go to my Head, Easy Living, April.*)

Warne Marsh-Lee Konitz. Warne Marsh, ts; Lee Konitz, as; Peter Ind, b; Alan Levitt, d. (Ronnie Scott's, London, England, May 27, 1976, private, Frohne, 3 tunes.) *Limehouse Blues, Sound-Lee, Line On (?).* (Note: Jack Goodwin adds the following: *Chi Chi, Embraceable You, April, Wow, All the Things You Are, Just Friends.*)

Warne Marsh-Lee Konitz. Warne Marsh, ts; Lee Konitz, as; Peter Ind, b; Alan Levitt, d. (Ronnie Scott's, London England, June 1–2, 1976, private, Goodwin, 13 tunes.) *It's You or No One, Wow, You Go to My Head, Two Not One, Subconscious-Lee, Embraceable You, Chi Chi, Star Eyes, Sound-Lee,*

Background Music, Kary's Trance, All the Things You Are, She's Funny That Way.

Warne Marsh-Lee Konitz. Warne Marsh, ts; Lee Konitz, as; Sal Mosca, p; Eddie Gomez, b; Eliot Zigmund, d. (Storyville, New York City, July 1, 1976, private, 12 tunes. Frohne lists the last five of these in the same order, with a date of June 1976, which appears to be incorrect. Goodwin has the same five tunes with same date.) *You Stepped out of a Dream, Subconscious-Lee, Lover Man, Sound-Lee, Background Music, It's You or No One, Lennie's Pennies, Star Eyes, Wow, Taking a Chance on Love, I'll Remember April, Easy Living* (inc.).

Bill Evans Trio Featuring Lee Konitz & Warne Marsh. Bill Evans, p; Eddie Gomez, b; Elvin Jones or Eliot Zigmund, d; Lee Konitz, as; Warne Marsh, ts. (Radio broadcast by unknown station (VOA?), Radio City Music Hall, Newport in New York '76, NewYork City, July 2, 1976, private, Frohne: "remaining titles of performance probably recorded as well.")

Someday My Prince Will Come	U.S. radio broadcast
Unknown title	————
Subconscious-Lee (inc.)	————

Warne Marsh-Lee Konitz. Warne Marsh, ts; Lee Konitz, as; Roman Dylag, b; Rune Carlsson, d. (Kistiansand, Norway, July 10, 1976, private, Frohne, 11 tunes, some or all broadcast over Swedish radio.)

Subconscious-Lee	Swedish Radio broadcast (?)
All the Things You Are	————
Chi Chi	————
Body and Soul	————
Wow	————
Background Music	————
Donna Lee	————
Bach Invention (Konitz, Marsh only)	————
April	————
Lover Man	————
You Stepped out of a Dream	————

Lee Konitz-Warne Marsh Quartet. Lee Konitz, as; Warne Marsh, ts; Carl Schroeder, p; Peter Ind, b; Alan Levitt, d. (Verona, Italy, July 20, 1976, private, Frohne, 9 tunes.) *There Is No Greater Love* (Konitz only), *I'm*

Getting Sentimental over You (Konitz out), *Subconscious-Lee, 317 E. 32nd Street, What's New* (Marsh out), *April, I Didn't Know What Time It Was* (Konitz out), *Bach Invention, Chi Chi.*

Gary Foster. Gary Foster, as; Warne Marsh, ts; Fred Atwood, b; Peter Donald, d. (Pasadena City Hall, Pasadena, Calif., noon concert outdoors, July 28, 1976, private, 9 tunes, information from Jeremy Kellock.) *Just Friends, Subconscious-Lee, You'd Be So Nice to Come Home To, Gee Baby Ain't I Good to You, 317 E. 32nd Street, Background Music, Au Privave, If You Could See Me Now, Lennie's Pennies.*

Warne Marsh Quartet. Warne Marsh, ts; Dave McKay, p; Fred Atwood, b; Frank Severino, d. (Donte's, No. Hollywood, Calif., Sept. 1976, private, 16 tunes, information from Jeremy Kellock.) *It's You or No One, You Stepped out of a Dream, Subconscious-Lee, Every Time We Say Goodbye, April, unknown title, All the Things You Are, Hello Young Lovers, You Go to My Head, Speak Low, unknown title, What's New, The Night Has a Thousand Eyes, Strike up the 'Band, Stella by Starlight, If You Could See Me Now.*

Warne Marsh Quartet. Warne Marsh, ts; Alan Broadbent, p; Fred Atwood, b; Nick Ceroli, d. (Sand Dance Club, Long Beach, Calif., Oct. 3, 1976, private, 14 tunes.) *Speak Low, What's New, The Night Has a Thousand Eyes, Sippin' at Bell's, Subconscious-Lee, unknown title* (Marsh solo only), *unknown title* (Marsh solo only), *unknown title* (Marsh solo only), *All the Things You Are, Pent-Up House, Stella by Starlight, Night and Day, All the Things You Are, It's You or No One.*

Warne Marsh-Pete Christlieb Quintet. Warne Marsh, Pete Christlieb, ts; Lou Levy, p; prob. Fred Atwood, b; prob. Frank Severino, d. (Donte's, No. Hollywood, Calif., Oct. 6, 1976, private, unknown number of tunes, some complete but most with Marsh solos only, recorded by Harold Sewing.) *Unknown titles.*

Warne Marsh Group. Warne Marsh, ts; others unknown. (Donte's, No. Hollywood, Calif., Oct. 7, 1976, private, unknown number of tunes, Marsh solos only, recorded by Harold Sewing.) *Unknown titles.*

Warne Marsh Quartet. Warne Marsh, ts; Alan Broadbent, p; prob. Fred Atwood, b; prob. Nick Ceroli, d. (Donte's, No. Hollywood, Calif., Oct. 10, 1976, private, unknown number of tunes, mostly Marsh solos only, recorded by Harold Sewing.) *Unknown titles.*

Tenor Gladness. Lew Tabackin, Warne Marsh, ts; John Heard, b; Larry
  Bunker, d; Toshiko Akiyoshi, p (1). (Sound & Sage Studio, Hollywood,
  Oct. 13–14, 1976.)

Basic #2	Inner City IC6048; Discomate (J)
	DSP-5004
March of the Tadpoles	————; ————
Hangin' Loose	————; ————
Basic #1	————; ————
New-ance (Marsh out)	————; ————
Easy (Tabackin out) (1)	————; ————

Warne Marsh Quartet. Warne Marsh, ts; Lee Konitz, as; Peter Ind, b; Alan
  Levitt, d. (Ronnie Scott's, London, England, Dec. 1976, private. Frohne
  notes: "Not sure if date and location is correct. Maybe more tunes were
  recorded." Two tunes, he says, were recorded and broadcast by BBC.)

All the Things You Are	BBC Radio broadcast
I'll Remember April	————

Warne Marsh Quintet. Warne Marsh, ts; Gary Foster, as; Lou Levy, p; Fred
  Atwood, b; John Dentz, d. (Donte's, No. Hollywood, Calif., Feb. 13,
  1977, private, 4 tunes.) *You Stepped out of a Dream, Subconscious-Lee, All
  about You, Kary's Trance.*

Warne Marsh-Lee Konitz Quartet. Warne Marsh, ts; Lee Konitz, as; prob.
  Wilbur Campbell, d; prob. Eddie de Haas, b. (Jazz Showcase, Chicago,
  Ill., Feb. 23–27, 1977, private, unknown number of tunes, information
  from Harold Sewing.) *Unknown titles.*

Bill Evans Trio with Lee Konitz and Warne Marsh: *Crosscurrents*. Lee
  Konitz, as; Warne Marsh, ts; Bill Evans, p; Eddie Gomez, b; Eliot
  Zigmund, d. (Berkeley, Calif., Feb. 28 and Mar. 1–2, 1977.)

Eiderdown	Fantasy F-9568 & OJCCD-718-2
Pensativa	———— & ————
Speak Low	———— & ————
Night and Day	———— & ————
Ev'ry Time We Say Goodbye	
(Konitz out)	———— & ————
When I Fall in Love (Marsh out)	———— & ————

(Reissues, Frohne: Fantasy (I) HBS-6091, (F) 5951, (J) SMJ-6263, (J) VIJ-
4018, F-9568 (Cass), FCD 1012-2, DIDX 4306-4314, entitled *BILL EVANS,*

THE COMPLETE FANTASY RECORDINGS; Carrere (F) CA27-168523, entitled *BILL EVANS*; GdJ (I)-053, entitled *I GRANDE DEL JAZZ BILL EVANS*.)

Supersax: *Chasin' the Bird*. Med Flory, Joe Lopes, as; Warne Marsh, Jay Migliori, ts; Jack Nimitz, bs; Conte Candoli (1), Blue Mitchell (2), tp; Frank Rosolino (3), tb; Lou Levy, p; Fred Atwood, b; Jake Hanna (4), John Dentz (5), d. (Sound and Sage Studio, Los Angeles, 1977.)

Shaw Nuff (1, 4)	Verve 821867
'Round Midnight (1, 4)	————
Dizzy Atmosphere (1, 4)	————
Chasin' the Bird (2, 4)	————
The Song Is You (3, 4)	————
Now's the Time (3, 4)	————
Night in Tunisia (2, 5)	————
Driftin' on a Reed (3, 5)	————
Oop-Bop-Sh'Bam (1, 3, 4)	————

(Reissues, Frohne: MPS (D) 15491, 68160, (J) KUX-31, 821867-1/2 (lp/cd).)

Warne Marsh-Bill Evans Trio. Warne Marsh, ts; Bill Evans, p; Eddie Gomez, b; Eliot Zigmund, d. (Great American Music Hall, San Francisco, Calif., Mar. 5, 1977, private, Ziskind, 4 tunes.) *It's You or No One, Every Time We Say Goodbye, Speak Low, When I Fall in Love.*

Warne Marsh-Lee Konitz. Warne Marsh, ts; Lee Konitz, as; prob. George Cables or Art Lande, p; prob. James Leary or Harley White, b; prob. Eddie Marshall, d. (Keystone Corner, San Francisco, Calif., Mar. 6, 1977, private, Ziskind, 4 tunes.) *Night and Day, You'd Be So Nice to Come Home To, What's New* (Marsh out), *The Night Has a Thousand Eyes* (Konitz out).

Warne Marsh Quintet. Warne Marsh, ts; Gary Foster, as; Alan Broadbent, p; Jim Hughart, b; Nick Ceroli, d. (California Institute of Technology, Pasadena, Calif., Apr. 28, 1977, private, 4 tunes complete (*), 9 tunes, heads and Marsh solos only.) *Sippin' at Bell's, Featherbed, What's New, All about You, April, *Dixie's Dilemma, Lennie's Pennies, You Go to My Head, Bach Two-Part Invention #1, Bach Two-Part Invention #13, *You Stepped out of a Dream, *Subconscious-Lee, *317 E. 32nd Street.*

Warne Marsh: *Warne Out*. Warne Marsh, ts; Jim Hughart, b; Nick Ceroli, d. (Jim Hughart's Model A Studio, Granada Hills, Calif., May 14–15 and June 5, 1977.)

Loco 47*	Interplay 7709; Discovery DS-863 & DSCD-945
Liner Notes	————; ———— & ————
Warne Out	————; ———— & ————
Lennie's Pennies	————; ———— & ————
Duet	————; ———— & ————
Ballad	————; unissued; unissued
Warne Piece**	————; ————; ————
There Will Never Be Another You	unissued; unissued; unissued
It Might As Well Be Spring	unissued; unissued; unissued
This Can't Be Love	unissued; unissued; unissued
Pennies in Minor	unissued; unissued; unissued
Besame Mucho	unissued; unissued; unissued

(*Original title, later changed to "Local 47." **"Warne Piece" is mistakenly retitled "Ballad" on Discovery DS-863 and DSCD-945. On both "Duet" and "Warne Piece" Marsh is overdubbed. Reissue, Frohne: Trio (J) PAP-9092.)

Warne Marsh Quartet. Warne Marsh, ts; Gary Foster, as; Alan Broadbent, p; Monty Budwig, b. (Donte's, No. Hollywood, Calif., Sept. 1977, private, unknown number of tunes, information from Jeremy Kellock.) *Unknown titles.*

Warne Marsh-Pete Christlieb. Warne Marsh, Pete Christlieb, ts; Lou Levy, p; Fred Atwood, b; John Dentz, d. (Donte's, No. Hollywood, Calif., Sept. 27, 1977, private, 8 tunes, recorded by Claude Alexander, information from Jeremy Kellock.) *Woody'n You, Sippin' at Bell's, Airegin, You Stepped Out of a Dream, Joy Spring, Scrapple from the Apple, Night and Day, It's You or No One.*

Warne Marsh Quintet. Warne Marsh, ts; Gary Foster, as; Alan Broadbent, p; Monty Budwig, b; Nick Ceroli, d. (Donte's, No. Hollywood, Calif., Oct. 1977, private, 9 tunes.) *All the Things You Are, Just Friends, Subconscious-Lee, What's New, The Night Has a Thousand Eyes (inc.), Just Friends, On Green Dolphin Street, Willow Weep for Me, I'll Remember April.*

Warne Marsh. Warne Marsh, ts; Kenny Barron, p; Ron Carter, b; Ben Riley, d. (Marsh is heard playing with the Jamey Aebersold *All Bird* accompaniment record, JA 1215, Volume 6 in the series, which was recorded Feb. 6, 1976. Gary Foster remembers playing with Marsh and this record in late 1977, just before Marsh returned from California to New York. Though this tape could have been made any time after the original recording date before Marsh's death in 1987, a likely date might be circa 1976-77, when the novelty of Aebersold's accompaniment records was still fresh and Marsh was still in California, undistracted by resettling in New York. Private, 8 tracks.) *How High the Moon (1), How High the Moon (2), How High the Moon (3), Scrapple from the Apple (1), I Got Rhythm (1), How High the Moon (4), Scrapple from the Apple (2), I Got Rhythm (2).*

Warne Marsh. Interview with Jon Easton, "Jazz at One," WKCR-FM, c. late 1977.

Warne Marsh Trio. Warne Marsh, ts; Stan Fortuna, b; Peter Scattaretico. (Prob. home of Lennie Tristano, Jamaica, Queens, N.Y., late 1977 or 1978, private, 6 tunes.) *Local 47, It's You or No One, Body and Soul, All the Things You Are, The Sunny Side of the Street, I'll Remember April.*

Judy Niemack-Simon Wettenhall: *By Heart*. Judy Niemack, vc; Simon Wettenhall, tp; Warne Marsh, ts; Eddie Gomez, b; Skip Scott, d. (Downtown Sound Studio, New York City, Feb. 13, 16, 1978.)

Way Low	Sea Breeze SB-2001
I'll Remember April	————
I'll Remember April (alt. take)	unissued
Lover Man	unissued

(Marsh does not play on other eight tracks.)

Pete Christlieb-Warne Marsh Quintet: *Apogee*. Pete Christlieb, Warne Marsh, ts; Lou Levy, p; Jim Hughart, b; Nick Ceroli, d; Joe Roccisano, arr (1). (ABC Recording Studios, Los Angeles, May 17, 1978. Information from Steve Lang of Warner Brothers.)

317 E. 32nd (1, take 1)	unissued
I Never Told You (take 1)	unissued
Magna-tism (1, take 1)	unissued
Rapunzel (1, take 1)	unissued
Love Me (take 1)	unissued
Tenors of the Times (1, take 1)	unissued

Same personnel, May 18, 1978:

Magna-tism (1, take 2)	unissued
Magna-tism (1, take 3)	unissued
Lunarcy (take 1)	unissued
Lunarcy (take 2)	unissued
Lunarcy (take 3)	unissued
Love Me (take 2)	unissued

Love Me (take 3)	unissued
Rapunzel (1, take 2)	unissued
Rapunzel (1, take 3)	Warner Brothers BSK-3236

Same personnel, May 19, 1978:

317 E. 32nd Street (1, take 2)	unissued
Tenors of the Times (1, take 2)	————
I Never Told You (take 2)	unissued
Love Me (take 3)	unissued
Love Me (take 4)	unissued
Magna-tism (take 4)	————
Donna Lee	————
Body and Soul	unissued
I Never Told You (take 3)	unissued

Same personnel, May 20, 1978:

Lunarcy (take 4)	unissued
317 E. 32nd Street (1, take 3)	unissued
Lunarcy (take 5)	unissued
Lunarcy (take 6)	unissued
How about You	unissued
Love Me (take 5)	unissued

Same personnel, May 21, 1978:

Lunarcy (take 7)	unissued
317 E. 32nd Street (1, take 4)	unissued
317 E. 32nd Street (1, take 5)	————

Same personnel, but Marsh out, June 3, 1978:

I'm Old Fashioned (take 1)	unissued
I'm Old Fashioned (take 2)	unissued
How Was I to Know (take 1)	unissued
How Was I to Know (take 2)	unissued
I'm Old Fashioned (take 3)	————
Baby Ain't I Good to You	unissued
The Lamp Is Low	unissued
Just One of Those Things	unissued

Pete Christlieb Quartet Featuring Warne Marsh: *Conversations with Warne*, **Vol. 1**. Pete Christlieb, Warne Marsh, ts; Jim Hughart, b; Nick Ceroli, d. (Jim Hughart's studio, Granada Hills, Calif., Sept. 15, 1978.)

Lunch	Criss Cross (D) 1043CD
Fishtale	————

Meat Balls	———
Get Out!	———
Weeping Willow	———
India No Place	———
You Drive!	———
Woody and You	———

Pete Christlieb Quartet: *Conversations with Warne,* **Vol 2**. Pete Christlieb, Warne Marsh, ts; Jim Hughart, b; Nick Ceroli, d. (Jim Hughart's studio, Granada Hills, Calif., Sept. 15, 1978.)

No Tag	Criss Cross 1103CD
Fishtale	———
So What's Old	———
You Drive	———
Nate and Dave	———
Lunch	———
Woody and You	———
Bess You Is My Man	———
The April Samba	———

Lennie Tristano Memorial Concert. Warne Marsh, ts; Eddie Gomez, b; Peter Scattaretico, d. (Town Hall, New York City, Jan. 28, 1979.)

I Love You	Jazz Records JR-3
Trilogy	———
I Should Care	———

(Eleven other groups or soloists perform on this 5-disc set.)

Warne Marsh Trio/Quartet. Warne Marsh, ts; Sal Mosca, p; Eddie Gomez, b; Peter Scattaretico, d. (Lulu White's, Boston, Mass., Apr. 1, 1979, private, 23 tunes, Mosca solo on 5 & with Marsh trio on 12. Frohne gives Jan. 4, 1979, as date for all. Perhaps both dates valid for two groups of tunes?) *It's You or No One* (Mosca out), *You Stepped out of a Dream* (Mosca out), *untitled blues* (Mosca out), *Tangerine* (Mosca out), *I Should Care* (Mosca out), *I'll Remember April* (Mosca out), *Ghost of a Chance/Body and Soul* (Mosca only), *Foolin' Myself* (Mosca only), *Sweet Georgia Brown* (Mosca only), *Somebody Loves Me* (Mosca only), *Night in Tunisia* (Mosca only), *Featherbed, 317 E. 32nd Street, Cherokee* (inc.), *Body and Soul, Lennie's Pennies, Night and Day, Lover Man, All the Things You Are, The Best Thing for You, Lennie Bird, Back Home, Sunnymoon for Two.*

Karin Krog: *I Remember You*. Karin Krog, vc; Warne Marsh, ts; Keith "Red" Mitchell, b. (Oslo, Norway, Apr. 8–9, 1980.)

I Remember You	Spotlight (E) JLP-22
Trane	————
Lester's Happy	————
Moody's Mood for Love	————
It's You or No One	————
Lover Man	————
Speak Low	————
That Old Feeling	————

(Reissues: Swedisc (J) 27-5003; Meantime CD MR-08 (includes alt. takes of "It's You or No One," "Speak Low," and "That Old Feeling.")

Warne Marsh/Red Mitchell. Warne Marsh, ts; Red Mitchell, b. (Recorded by Johs Bergh in Studio 11, Norwegian Radio, Oslo, Norway, April 10, 1980, and probably broadcast on Jazzklubben program April 29, 1980.)

South American Way	Norwegian Radio broadcast
They Can't Take That Away from Me	
(take 1)	unissued
They Can't Take That Away from Me	
(take 2)	————
The Night Has a Thousand Eyes	————
Parisian Thoroughfare	————
Back Home	————
All About You (take 1)	unissued
All About You (take 2)	————
These Foolish Things	————
Interview conducted by Johs Bergh	————

Warne Marsh. Warne Marsh, ts; Jan Allan, Rolf Erickson, tp; Arne Domnerus, as; Rune Gustafson, g; Gerry Riedel, b; Egil Johansen, d; unknown voc (1). (Swedish radio broadcast, Estrad, Sodertalje, Sweden, Apr. 17, 1980, private, Frohne.)

Kurbitz (Marsh out?)	Swedish Radio broadcast
As You Are (1)	————
Blues for Bill	————
Trumpet Song	————
Suite for Trumpet, Tenor Sax,	
and Orchestra	————

Warne Marsh/Red Mitchell. Warne Marsh, ts; Red Mitchell, b, voc. (Reportedly recorded by Swedish Radio in Mitchell's apartment in Stockholm, Sweden, on unknown date, but possibly at the Fasching

Club, Apr. 18–19, 1980. Broadcast by Swedish Radio, on Program 3, Aug. 31, 1980. Information from Johs Bergh.)

It's You or No One	Swedish Radio broadcast
You Stepped Out of a Dream	————
Sorry, Son (Mitchell, p. & voc)	————
South American Way	————
The Night Has a Thousand Eyes	————
Embraceable You	————
Lester Leaps In	————
Walkin'	————

(Frohne lists a Swedish Radio broadcast, possibly the same one, giving a date of mid-April, 1980, which contains the same tunes minus "Sorry, Son" and plus "These Foolish Things," "La Carioca," and "Softly as in a Morning Sunrise.")

Hothouse: The Mitchell-Marsh Big Two. Warne Marsh, ts; Keith "Red" Mitchell, b. (Fasching Club, Oslo, Norway, Apr. 18–19, 1980.)

Hot House	Spotlight (E) LP-4092
Undertow	————
Lover Man	————
Tea for Two	————
Gone with the Wind	————
Ornithology	————
It Could Happen to You	————
Easy Living	————
I'm Getting Sentimental over You	————

These titles have also been issued on Storyville SLP4092 and STCD8257. Two additional titles appear on the latter:

Background Music	Storyville STCD8257
Scrapple from the Apple	————

Red Mitchell-Warne Marsh. Red Mitchell, b; Warne Marsh, ts. (Fasching Club, Stockholm, Sweden. Apr. 18–19, 1980.)

317 East 32nd St.	Storyville STCD8252
South American Way	————
Star Eyes	————
Lady Be Good	————
It's You or No One	————

These Foolish Things	————
In a Mellotone	————
Just You, Just Me	————
You Stepped out of a Dream	————
Embraceable You	————
Little Willie Leaps	————

Warne Marsh & Kenny Drew Trio: *I Got a Good One for You."* Warne Marsh, ts; Kenny Drew, p; Bo Stief, b; Aage Tangaard, d. (Broadcast by Danish Radio, Studio 11, Danish Broadcast Corp., Copenhagen, Denmark, April 21, 1980.)

I Got a Good One for You	Storyville STCD 8277
Sophisticated Lady	————
On Green Dolphin Street (1)	————
On Green Dolphin Street (2)	unissued
Sippin' at Bells	————
Ev'rytime We Say Goodbye	————
Little Willie Leaps	————
Easy to Love	————
Body and Soul	————
Ornithology	————
Star Eyes	————
Softly as in a Morning Sunrise (1)	————
Softly as in a Morning Sunrise (2)	unissued

(This material, except for "Little Willie Leaps," was also released on Venus/Interplay (J) TKCZ 79037, ORNITHOLOGY, where "I Got a Good One for You" is titled "This One's for Lester" and "Body and Soul" is titled "Of Love and Things.")

Warne Marsh-Sal Mosca. Warne Marsh, ts; Sal Mosca, p; unknown, b & d. (Place and date unknown, private, 3 tunes.) *Strike up the Band, The Trolley Song, The Trolley Song* (from different time, place).

Warne Marsh-Red Mitchell Duo. Warne Marsh, ts; Keith "Red" Mitchell, b. (Recorded and broadcast by WKCR and National Public Radio, Sweet Basil Club, New York City, June 5, 1980. Broadcast introduced by Billy Taylor and includes interview with Warne Marsh by Michael Cuscuna.)

It's You or No One	Fresh Sound FSCD-1038
Gone with the Wind	————
Everything Happens to Me	————
Cherokee	————
Sippin' at Bell's	————

Easy Living ———————
These Foolish Things ———————
Topsy ———————

(Frohne gives Oct. 1980 as date for last four tunes, but Fresh Sound CD gives June 5, 1980. Jack Goodwin adds the following tunes not on Fresh Sound CD: *It's You or No One* [alt. take], *You Stepped out of a Dream, These Foolish Things* [alt. take].)

Warne Marsh-Sal Mosca Quartet. Warne Marsh, ts; Sal Mosca, p; prob. Frank Canino, b; prob. Skip Scott, d. (Village Vanguard, New York City, June 10–15, 1980, private, Frohne, 6 tunes.) *Softly as in a Morning Sunrise, You Stepped out of a Dream, unknown title, unknown title, Donna Lee, unknown title.*

Warne Marsh Quartet. Warne Marsh, ts; Sal Mosca, p; unknown, probably Frank Canino, b; Skip Scott, d. (Village Vanguard, New York City, Jul. 1980, private, Goodwin, 6 tunes. Date is questionable; Marsh and Mosca played the Vanguard June 10–15, from which date this tape probably originates. The club has no record of a July engagement.) *You Stepped out of a Dream, These Foolish Things, On Green Dolphin Street, Cherokee, Yesterdays, Star Eyes.*

Warne Marsh/Red Mitchell. Warne Marsh, ts; Red Mitchell, b. (Radio broadcast, unknown location, Aug. 29, 1980. This date, either as recording date or broadcast date, is suspect. Best guess is that the material was recorded by Swedish Radion in min-April, 1980, either at the Fasching Club or Mitchell's apartment in Stockholm, Sweded, and later broadcast c. Aug. 29–31, 1980. See other entries of this time period.)

It's You or No One   Probably Swedish Radio
You Stepped Out of a Dream   ———————
These Foolish Things   ———————
Sorry Son (Mitchell only,   ———————
    p & voc)   ———————
South American Way   ———————
(Other titles probably recorded also.)

Warne Marsh Quartet: *Live in Berlin*. Warne Marsh, ts; Sal Mosca, p; Eddie Gomez, b; Kenny Clarke, d. (Broadcast by ARD Radio/TV, Berlln Jazz Festival, Berlin, Oct. 30, 1980. A videotape exists.)

Unknown title (inc.) (rehearsal)   ARD Radio Broadcast; Sender Freies
                                              Berlin b'cast
All of Me (rehearsal)   ———————; ———————

And There's Music	Interplay/Century CD CECC 00390; ARD TV/Radio
Like the Angeles [*sic*]	————; ————
Leave Me	————; ————
The Family Song	————; ————
Background Music	————; ————
April	————; ————

Warne Marsh-Connie Crothers. Warne Marsh, ts; Connie Crothers, p; others unknown. (Berlin Jazz Festival, Berlin, Germany, Nov. 1980, private, unknown number of tunes, information from Tom Everett.) *Unknown titles*.

Warne Marsh. Warne Marsh, ts; Tardo Hammer, p; John Ray, b; Taro Okamoto, d; Judy Niemack, v. (Village Vanguard, New York City, Jan. 9, 1981, private, unknown number of tunes, information from Tom Everett.) *Unknown titles*.

Warne Marsh Sextet. Warne Marsh, ts; John Pal Inderberg, bs; Torgrim Sollid, tpt; Erling Aksdal, p; Terje Venaas, b; Espen Rud, d. (Recorded at Norwegian Radio Studio 20, Oslo, Norway, Feb. 16, 1981. Asterisk (*) indicates titles probably broadcast Mar. 10, 1981. Double asterisk (**) indicates titles broadcast June 14, 1983.)

It's You or No One*	————
Dixie's Dilemma*	————
Body and Soul	————
Body and Soul (alt. take)*	————
317 E. 32nd Street**	————
Background Music**	————

Pete Christlieb: *Self-Portrait*. Pete Christlieb, Warne Marsh, ts; Jim Hughart, b; Nick Ceroli, d. (Los Angeles, c. April 1981.)

So What's Old	Bosco 1

Same personnel except Dick Berk, d, replaces Ceroli, and add Lou Levy, p:

Lunarcy	————
Close Enough for Love	————

(Marsh does not appear on the other four tracks of this LP.)

Alan Broadbent. Alan Broadbent, p; Warne Marsh, ts; Gary Foster, as; Nick Ceroli, d; others unknown. (Frohne says recorded and partly broadcast by unknown U.S. radio station, unknown location, possibly Nov. 1, 1981, private.)

Unknown title	U.S. radio broadcast (?)
Unknown title (inc.)	————

Sal Mosca-Warne Marsh Quartet, Vol. 1. Warne Marsh, ts; Sal Mosca, p; Frank Canino, b; Skip Scott, d. (Village Vanguard, New York City, Jan. 6–11 and/or Nov. 17–22, 1981. Recorded by Sal Mosca. Some tunes are edited.)

Sax of a Kind	Zinnia 103CD
Mickey Lynn	————
317 East 32nd	————
Silver Man	————
Digi-Doll	————
Under-Bach	————
Confirmation	————
Pub Bob (Marsh out)	————
Piano Juices	————
Under-Line (Marsh out)	————
Shakin' Out	————
Dick's Favorite	————

Warne Marsh-Sal Mosca Quartet, Vol. 2. Warne Marsh, ts; Sal Mosca, p; Frank Canino, b; Skip Scott, d. (Village Vanguard, New York City, Jan. 6–11 and/or Nov. 17–22, 1981. Recorded by Sal Mosca. Some tunes are edited.)

Pulsafer	Zinnia 104CD
Testament	————
Marionette	————
Thermology	————
Inner-Line (Marsh out)	————
Subconscious-Lee	————
Kitty B. (solo piano only)	————
Featherbed	————
Way in There	————
Steady as She Goes (Marsh out)	————
40 Steps	————

Warne Marsh-Sal Mosca Quartet. Warne Marsh, ts; Sal Mosca, p; Frank Canino, b; Skip Scott, d. (Village Vanguard, New York City, date unknown, possibly Jan. 6–11, 1981, private, 11 tunes, information from George Ziskind. Some tunes may also be on Zinnia 103CD and/or

104CD.) *All about You, Featherbed, Time on My Hands, Sax of a Kind, Too Marvelous for Words, Lennie's Pennies, Kary's Trance, Foolin' Myself, Leave Me, Wow, Back Home.*

Warne Marsh-Sal Mosca Quartet. Warne Marsh, ts; Sal Mosca, p; Frank Canino, b; Skip Scott, d. (Village Vanguard, New York City, prob. Nov. 17, 1981, private, 16 tunes, information from George Ziskind. Some tunes may also be on Zinnia 103CD and/or 104CD.) *Marionette, Featherbed, You Go to My Head, Fishin' Around, Imagination, Lover Come Back to Me, Lover Man* (Marsh-Mosca duet), *Lennie Bird, Two Not One, All the Things You Are, It's You or No One* (Marsh-Mosca duet), *Body and Soul, Dreams, Lennie's Pennies, Sophisticated Lady* (bass feature), *Background Music.*

Warne Marsh-Sal Mosca Quartet. Warne Marsh, ts; Sal Mosca, p; Frank Canino, b; Skip Scott, d. (Village Vanguard, New York City, prob. Nov. 18, 1981, private, 13 tunes, information from George Ziskind. Some tunes may also be on Zinnia 103CD and/or Zinnia 104CD.) *Sippin' at Bell's, Yesterdays, Goovin' High, Featherbed, You Go to My Head, Lennie Bird, Little Willie Leaps, I Love You, Autumn in New York, Leave Me, Confirmation, Body and Soul, Two Not One.*

Warne Marsh-Sal Mosca Quartet. Warne Marsh, ts; Sal Mosca, p; Frank Canino, b; Skip Scott, d. (Village Vanguard, New York City, prob. Nov. 19, 1981, private, 13 tunes, information from George Ziskind. Some tunes may also be on Zinnia 103CD and/or 104CD.) *You 'n' Me, The Best Thing for You, Gone with the Wind, Strike up the Band, I Can't Give You Anything but Love, The Song Is You, April, You Go to My Head, Wow, All the Things You Are, Background Music, Conception, Subconscious-Lee.*

Warne Marsh-Sal Mosca Quartet. Warne Marsh, ts; Sal Mosca, p; Frank Canino, b; Skip Scott, d. (Village Vanguard, New York City, prob. Nov. 20, 1981, private, 18 tunes, information from George Ziskind. Some tunes may also be on Zinnia 103CD and/or 104CD.) *Strike up the Band, Limehouse Blues, These Foolish Things, Lennie Bird, Lover Man* (Marsh-Mosca duet), *Leave Me, Sound-Lee, Cherokee, Sippin' at Bell's, Kary's Trance, The Man I Love, Embraceable You, Dreams, The Song Is You, Yesterdays* (Mosca solo), *All about You, Marionette, Little Willie Leaps.*

Warne Marsh-Sal Mosca Quartet. Warne Marsh, ts; Sal Mosca, p; Frank Canino, b; Skip Scott, d. (Village Vanguard, New York City, prob. Nov. 21, 1981, private, 12 tunes, information from George Ziskind. Some tunes may also be on Zinnia 103CD and/or 104CD.) *All the Things You*

Are, Featherbed, The Best Thing for You, Time on My Hands, Victory Ball, Leave Me, There Will Never Be Another You, Crosscurent, Body and Soul, Lennie's Pennies, April in Paris, Back Home.

Warne Marsh-Sal Mosca Quartet. Warne Marsh, ts; Sal Mosca, p; Frank Canino, b; Skip Scott, d. (Village Vanguard, New York City, prob. Nov. 22, 1981, private, 10 tunes, information from George Ziskind. Some tunes may also be on Zinnia 103CD and/or 104CD.) *Kary's Trance, She's Funny That Way, Fishin' Around, Sax of a Kind, Just Friends, Tangerine, Groovin' High, Ghost of a Chance, Background Music, untitled blues.*

Warne Marsh. Interview of Warne Marsh by Rick Petrone. (Stamford, Connecticut, WYRS radio studios, c. 1982.)

Warne Marsh Quartet. Warne Marsh, ts; Josh Breakstone, g; Earl Sauls, b; Taro Okamoto, d. (Far and Away club, Cliffside Park, NJ, Feb. 26–27, 1982, private, 6 tunes.) *Lester Leaps In, It's You or No One, Victory Ball, All About You, Two Not One, Body and Soul.*

Warne Marsh Quartet. Warne Marsh, ts; Manny Duran, tpt (1); Josh Breakstone, g; Earl Sauls, b; Roger Mancuso, d. (Eddie Condon's, New York City, May 23, 1982, private, 15 tunes.) *It's You or No One, All the Things You Are, 317 E. 32nd Street, Subconscious-Lee, On Green Dolphin Street, Lover Man, Strike up the Band, How about You, Kary's Trance, Yardbird Suite, These Foolish Things, Sippin' at Bell's, You Stepped out of a Dream (1), Star Eyes (1), April (1).*

Warne Marsh Quartet. Warne Marsh, ts; Josh Breakstone, g; Earl Sauls, b; Taro Okamoto, d. (Gulliver's, West Paterson, N.J., Jul. 24, 1982, private, 4 tunes.) *Victory Ball, Polka Dots and Moonbeams, April, Sippin' at Bell's.*

Warne Marsh Sextet. Warne Marsh, ts; John Pal Inderberg, bs; Torgrim Sollid, tpt; Terje Bjoerklund, p; Bjorn Kjellemyr, b; Frank Jakobsen, d. (Club Lucullus, Molde, Norway, Jul. 30–31, 1982, private, 8 tunes.) *Subconscious-Lee, Lover Man, Background Music, Lennie Bird, Lester Leaps In, How Deep Is the Ocean, Donna Lee, Topsy.*

Warne Marsh Quartet. Warne Marsh, ts; Sal Mosca, p; Frank Canino, b; Taro Okamoto, d. (Probably North Sea Jazz Festival, Meervart, Amsterdam, Holland, Aug. 12, 1982, private, Frohne, 11 tunes.) *Background Music, 317 E. 32nd Street, It's you or No One, These Foolish Things, Two Not One, All about You, Sax of a kind, Body and Soul, Leave Me, How Deep How High, Subconscious-Lee.*

Warne Marsh Quartet: *Star Highs*. Warne Marsh, ts; Hank Jones, p; George Mraz, b; Mel Lewis, d. (Studio 44, Monster, Holland, Aug. 14, 1982.)

Switchboard Joe	Criss Cross 1002 & 1002CD
Star Highs	———— & ————
Hank's Tune	———— & ————
Moose the Mooche	———— & ————
Victory Ball	———— & ————
Sometimes	———— & ————
One for the Band	———— & ————
Switchboard Joe (alt. take)	unissued & ————
Sometimes (alt. take)	unissued & ————
Star Highs (alt. take)	unissued & ————
Moose the Mooche (alt. take)	unissued & ————
Victory Ball (alt. take)	unissued & ————

(Frohne notes, "Informations about alternate [unissued] takes from producer Gerry Teekens.")

Warne Marsh Quartet. Warne Marsh, ts; Lou Levy, p; Jimmy Raney, g; John Whitfield, b; Dick Borden, d. (Chicago Jazz Festival, Grant Park, Chicago, Ill. Recorded and broadcast over unknown radio station, Sept. 5, 1982, private, Frohne, includes interview with Warne Marsh and Lou Levy.)

My Shining Hour (inc.)	U.S. radio broadcast
I'm Old Fashioned	————
213 W. 32nd Street*	————
Subconscious-Lee	————
Limehouse Blues	————
Lunarcy	————

(*Announced as such, but actually "317 E. 32nd Street.")

Warne Marsh Meets Gary Foster. Warne Marsh, ts; Gary Foster, as; Alan Broadbent, p; Pat "Putter" Smith, b; Peter Donald, d. (Hollywood, Oct. 12 & 14, 1982.)

Ablution	Eastwind (J) EWJ 90024
You Should See Me	————
Sippin' at Bell's	————
Victory Ball	————
"D" Pending	————
Joy Spring	————
All about You	

Warne Marsh Group. Warne Marsh, ts; Paul Altman, as; Joe Cohn, g; George Kay, b; Taro Okamoto, d. (Hasty Pudding Club, Cambridge, Mass., Nov. 1, 1982, private, various tunes.) *Unknown titles.*

Warne Marsh Quartet. Warne Marsh, ts; John Klopotowski, g; Geoge Mraz, b; Taro Okamoto, d; Judy Niemack, v (1). (Jazz Forum, Jan. 16, 1983, private, 14 tunes.) *It's You or No One, Victory Ball, Star Eyes, Background Music, This Is Always, Lennie's Pennies, Featherbed, Kary's Trance* (1, head and Marsh solo only), *You Stepped out of a Dream, Come Rain or Come Shine, The Best Thing for You, All about You, Bye Bye Blackbird, April.*

Warne Marsh Quartet. Warne Marsh, ts; John Klopotowski, g; Sonny Dallas, eb; Skip Scott, d. (State University of New York at Stonybrook, N.Y., Feb. 7, 1983, private, 7 tunes.) *You Stepped out of a Dream, You'd Be So Nice, Foolin' Myself, Lennie's Pennies, Embraceable You, Kary's Trance, Strike up the Band.*

Sonny Dallas: ***Sonny Dallas Plays and Sings***. Sonny Dallas, eb; Warne Marsh, ts; John Klopotowski, g; Skip Scott, d. (State University of New York at Stonybrook, N.Y., Feb. 7, 1983.)

Unbreakable Me	Sallad D-102731 (Cassette)
Kary's Trance	————

(Marsh does not appear on other tracks.)

The Skymasters Featuring Warne Marsh. Warne Marsh, ts; Piet Noordijk, as; others unknown; Kenny Naper (1), Clare Fischer, arr. (Recorded and broadcast by Netherlands Radio, Laren, Holland, Mar. 21, 1983, private, Frohne.)

Ellington Medley (1) (Marsh out)	Netherlands Radio
It's You or No One	————
Body and Soul	————
Lennie's Pennies	————
The Preacher	————

Warne Marsh Quartet. Warne Marsh, ts; Lou Levy, p; Jesper Lundgaard, b; James Martin, d. (Bim Huis, Amsterdam, Holland, Mar. 25, 1983, private, Goodwin, 10 tunes.) *Star Highs, I'm Old Fashioned, Background Music, My Old Flame, My Shining Hour, Speak Low, Limehouse Blues, All the Things You Are, Embraceable You, You Stepped out of a Dream.*

Warne Marsh Quartet. Warne Marsh, ts; Lou Levy, p; Jesper Lundgaard, b; James Martin, d. (New Morning Club, Paris, France, Mar. 27, 1983, private, Goodwin, 8 tunes.) *April, Star Eyes, Subconscious-Lee, Embraceable You, High on You, It's You or No One, Estate* (Marsh out), *3l7 E. 32nd Street.*

Warne Marsh Quartet. Warne Marsh, ts; Lou Levy, p; Jesper Lundgaard, b; James Martin, d. (New Morning Club, Paris, Mar. 28, 1983, private, 10 tunes.) *It's You or No One, Star Eyes, Kary's Trance, I'm Old Fashioned, The Night Has a Thousand Eyes, Subconscious-Lee, Easy Living, April, My Old Flame, Airegin.* (Note: Goodwin adds the following: *All the Things You Are, Lunarcy, High on You, All about You, Emily* [Marsh out].)

Warne Marsh Quartet. Warne Marsh, ts; Lou Levy, p; Jesper Lundgaard, b; James Martin, d. (New Morning Club, Paris, Mar. 29, 1983, private. Frohne notes, "Recorded and (partly?) broadcast" by France Musique.)

High on You	France Musique broadcast?
All about You	————
Easy Living	————
Switchboard Joe	————
Limehouse Blues	————
Lunarcy	————
I Can't Give You Anything but Love	————
Background Music	————
You Stepped out of a Dream	————
Star Eyes	————
Victory Ball	————
317 East 32nd Street	————
Lover Man	————

(Note: Goodwin adds *Spring Is Here* [Marsh out] and *The Night Has a Thousand Eyes.*)

Warne Marsh Quartet. Warne Marsh, ts; Lou Levy, p; Jesper Lundgaard, b; James Martin, d. (Recorded and broadcast by Netherlands Radio, Voorburg, Holland, Mar. 31, 1983, private, Frohne.)

Lunarcy	Netherlands Radio broadcast
All about You	————
If You Could See Me Now	————
Switchboard Joe	————
Emily (Marsh out)	————

Sax of a Kind   ————
317 E. 32nd Street   ————

(Frohne notes, "Remaining titles of this performance probably recorded as well." Goodwin adds the following: *Speak Low, Star Highs, I'm Old Fashioned, Easy Living, Devannah.*)

Warne Marsh Quartet. Warne Marsh, ts; Lou Levy, p; Jesper Lundgaard, b; James Martin, d. (Hnita Jazz Club, Helst op den Berg, Belgium, Apr. 2, 1983, private, 11 tunes.) *Background Music, Star Eyes, Kary's Trance, Embraceable You, High on You, Sax of a Kind, I'm Old Fashioned, Subconscious-Lee, Easy Living, Airegin, I Can't Give You Anything but Love.*

Warne Marsh Quartet. Warne Marsh, ts; Lou Levy, p; Jesper Lundgaard, b; James Martin, d. (Pepijn, Den Haag, Holland, Apr. 3, 1983, private, Frohn, 2 tunes. Frohne notes, "Probably remaining titles of this performance recorded as well.") *All about You* (inc.), *I Can't Give You Anything but Love* (inc.). (Note: Goodwin adds *High on You*.)

Warne Marsh Quartet. Warne Marsh, ts; Lou Levy, p; Jesper Lundgaard, b; James Martin, d. (Oosterpoort Cultural Center, Groningen, Holland, Apr. 6, 1983, private, 11 tunes.) *It's You or No One* (inc.), *I'll Remember April, Star Eyes, Sax of a Kind, I'm Old Fashioned, Easy Living, Lunarcy, The Night Has a Thousand Eyes, All God's Children, Kary's Trance, Lover Man.* (Note: Goodwin adds *What's New.*)

Warne Marsh Quartet: *A Ballad Album*. Warne Marsh, ts; Lou Levy, p; Jesper Lundgaard, b; James Martin, d. (Monster, Holland, Apr. 7, 1983.)

I Can't Give You Anything but Love, Baby	Criss Cross 1007 & 1007CD
The Nearness of You	———— & ————
How Deep Is the Ocean	———— & ————
Spring Is Here	———— & ————
How High the Moon	———— & ————
Time on My Hands	———— & ————
Emily	———— & ————
My Romance	———— & ————
How Deep Is the Ocean (alt. take)	unissued & ————
Time on My Hands (alt. take)	unissued & ————
The Nearness of You (alt. take)	unissued & ————
I Can't Give You Anything but Love, Baby (alt. take)	unissued; unissued
Spring Is Here (alt. take)	unissued; unissued

How High the Moon (alt. take)   unissued; unissued
Emily (alt. take)   unissued; unissued
My Romance (alt. take)   unissued; unissued

Warne Marsh Quartet. Warne Marsh, ts; Ack van Rooyen, flh; others unknown. (Vredenburg, Utrecht, Holland, Apr. 10, 1983, private, Frohne,
2 tunes.) *It's You or No One, All the Things You Are* (inc.).

Warne Marsh-Lou Levy Duo. Warne Marsh, ts; Lou Levy, p. (Pizza on the
Park, London, England, Apr. 11, 1983, private, 16 tunes, not listed in
order of performance.) *Speak Low, Emily, High on You, How High the Moon
Subconscious-Lee, I'm Old Fashioned, Lunarcy, April, I Can't Give You Anything but Love, Kary's Trance, My Old Flame, It's You or No One, Dance Only
with Me* (Levy solo), *Sax of a Kind, Limehouse Blues, Background Music.*

Warne Marsh-Lou Levy Duo. Warne Marsh, ts; Lou Levy, p. (Pizza on the
Park, London, England, Apr. 12, 1983, private, 15 tunes, not listed in or-
der of play.) *My Old Flame, Subconscious-Lee (1), Background Music, You
Stepped out of a Dream, 317 East 32ⁿᵈ Street, Limehouse Blues, I Can't Give
You Anything but Love, Star Eyes, I'm Old Fashioned (1), Lunarcy (1), April,
My Old Flame, High on You, It's You or No One, Airegin.* Frohne lists the
following additional tunes: *April (1), Kary's Trance, Sax of a Kind,
Limehouse Blues (1), Emily, I Can't Give You Anything but Love (1).* Tunes
marked (1), he says, "might be from a later date," but Goodwin says
this is incorrect and that "two sets from the same date were recorded.
But this does not explain the repetition of *April, Limehouse Blues,* and *I
Can't Give You Anything but Love* on the same night. Goodwin also adds
How High the Moon.

Warne Marsh-Lou Levy Duo/Quartet. Warne Marsh, ts; Lou Levy, p;
Kenny Baldock, b (1); Kenny Clare, d (1). (Pizza Express, London, England, Apr. 13, 1983, private, 12 tunes, not listed in order of performance.) *All about You (1), Star Eyes (1), All God's Children (1), Emily, It's
You or No One (1), Subconscious-Lee (1), April (1), All the Things You Are
(1), I'm Old Fashioned, Lunarcy, I Can't Give You Anything but Love, High
on You.* Frohne lists the following additional tunes: *My Old Flame,
Airegin.*

Warne Marsh-Lou Levy Quartet. Warne Marsh, ts; Lou Levy, p; Kenny
Baldock, b; Kenny Clare or Martin Drew (1), d. (Pizza Express, London,
England, Apr. 14, 1983, private, 12 tunes, not listed in order of perfor-
mance.) *Background Music, Speak Low, You Stepped out of a Dream, All the
Things You Are, I'm Old Fashioned* (Marsh-Levy duo), *How High the Moon,*

317 E. 32nd Street, Kary's Trance, Limehouse Blues, Sax of a Kind, Speak Low (1), How High the Moon (1). Frohne lists *High on You, I Can't Give You Anything but Love,* and *Lunarcy* as Marsh-Levy duos on April 14 and says that probably not all of the tunes in his list were actually recorded this date. Goodwin says the same after listing the following additional tunes: *Lover Man, Background Music, Star Eyes, Emily, It's You or No One, I Can't Give You Anything but Love, Lunarcy, Subconscious-Lee, I'm Old Fashioned, High on You,* and *317 E. 32nd Street.* Goodwin does not list Martin Drew for any tunes on this date.

Warne Marsh-Lou Levy Quartet. Warne Marsh, ts; Lou Levy, p; Kenny Baldock, b; Kenny Clare, d. (Pizza Express, London, England, Apr. 14–15, 1983, private, 13 tunes, prob. not listed in order of performance.) *How High the Moon* (Marsh-Levy duo), *317 East 32nd Street, Lover Man, Background Music, Kary's Trance, Star Eyes, Speak Low, Emily, It's You or No One, I Can't Give You Anything but Love, Lunarcy, Subconscious-Lee, High on You* (Marsh-Levy duo?). All but *How High the Moon, Kary's Trance,* and *Speak Low* are listed by Goodwin as definitely April 14.

Warne Marsh-Lou Levy Quartet. Warne Marsh, ts; Lou Levy, p; Kenny Baldock, b; Kenny Clare (1) or Martin Drew, d. (Pizza Express, London, England, Apr. 15, 1983, private, 19 tunes, not listed in order of performance.) *It's You or No One, Star Eyes, Subconscious-Lee, Emily, High on You, Spring Is Here, April, Background Music, You Stepped out of a Dream, High on You, My Old Flame* (Marsh-Levy duo), *Somebody Loves Me, Background Music, All about You, It's You or No One, Emily, Sax of a Kind, Limehouse Blues (1), Subconscious-Lee.* Goodwin additionally lists *Speak Low, Lennie's Pennies (1), How High the Moon* (Marsh-Levy duo), *How High the Moon* (quartet?), *Kary's Trance (1),* and *Limehouse Blues (1)* as on this date.

Warne Marsh-Lou Levy Quartet. Warne Marsh, ts; Lou Levy, p; Kenny Baldock, b; Martin Drew, d. (Pizza Express, London, England, Apr. 16, 1983, private, 8 tunes, not listed in order of performance.) *Lunarcy, Kary's Trance, Moonlight in Vermont, 317 E. 32nd Street, Airegin, I'm Old Fashioned, Dance Only with Me, Close Enough for Love* (inc.).

Warne Marsh-Lou Levy Quartet. Warne Marsh, ts; Lou Levy, p; Kenny Bullock (Baldock?), b; Kenny Clare, d. (Pizza Express, London, England, Apr. 16, 1983, private, Frohne, 2 tunes. Frohne says, "Tape not available so far. Entry according to John Craig." *How High the Moon, Background Music.*

Warne Marsh-Lou Levy Quartet. Warne Marsh, ts; Lou Levy, p; Kenny
Baldock, b; Martin Drew, d. (Pizza Express, London, England, April 17,
1983, private, Goodwin, 5 tunes.) *Kary's Trance, Moonlight in Vermont,
317 E. 32nd Street, Airegin, I'm Old Fashioned.* Date may actually be April
16, when most of the same tunes were listed in the same order. See
above.

Warne Marsh Quartet. Warne Marsh, ts; Bob Ward, g; George Kay, b; Taro
Okamoto, d. (West End Café, New York City, May 3, 1983, private, 13
tunes.) *Background Music, Gone with the Wind, Speak Low, My Romance,
April, Victory Ball, Emily, Sax of a Kind, The Nearness of You, You Stepped
out of a Dream, I Can't Give You Anything but Love, Subconscious-Lee, untitled blues.*

Warne Marsh Quartet. Warne Marsh, ts; Bob Ward, g; George Kay, b; Taro
Okamoto, d. (West End Café, New York City, May 9, 1983, private,
4 tunes.) *Star Eyes, You Stepped out of a Dream, Speak Low, My Romance*
(edited).

Warne Marsh Quartet. Warne Marsh, ts; Bob Ward, g; George Kay, b; Taro
Okamoto, d. (West End Café, New York City, May 10, 1983, private, 14
tunes.) *It's You or No One, All about You, Just Friends, Time on My Hands,
Victory Ball, Gone with the Wind, Airegin, Star Eyes* (inc.), *Emily, Sax of a
Kind, Kary's Trance, Speak Low, Background Music, untitled blues* (inc.).

Warne Marsh. Warne Marsh, ts; Torgrim Sollid, tpt; John Pal Inderberg,
bs; Terje Bjoerklund, p; Bjoern Kjellemyr, b; Carl Haakon Waadeland,
d. (Recorded by Oeystein Storm Johansen at a rehearsal in Studio 20,
Norwegian Radio, Oslo, Norway, May 18, 1983. Titles listed were used
in whole or in part for the *Logical Lines* television documentary, broadcast Nov. 25, 1984, q.v. below. A complete private tape also exists.)

317 E. 32nd St.	Norwegian Television
High on You	———
Easy Living	———

Warne Marsh Sextet. Warne Marsh, ts; John Pal Inderberg, bs; Torgrim
Sollid, tpt; Terje Bjoerklund, p; Bjoern Kjellemyr, b; Carl Haakon
Waadeland, d. (Recorded by Oeystein Storm Johnsen at the Jazz Alive
club, Oslo, Norway, May 19, 1983, private, 11 tunes. Asterix (*) indicates
titles recorded on video and audio; others are audio only. Double asterix
(**) indicates titles used in the *Logical Lines* video documentary, broadcast Nov. 25, 1984, q.v. below. All or some ot the titles may have been

broadcast by Norwegian Radio on May 22, 1983.) *Lennie's Pennies,* *Topsy,* 317 E. 32nd St.,** My Romance,* All About You,** Lester Leaps In, It's You or No One, Background Music, Kary's Trance, I'll Remember April, Topsy (alt. version).*

Sax of a Kind: Warne Marsh in Norway. Warne Marsh, ts; Torgrim Sollid, tp; John Pal Inderberg, bs; Terje Bjoerklund, p; Bjorn Kjellemyr, b; Carl E. Waadeland, d. (Roger Arnhoff Studio, Oslo, Norway, May 21–22, 1983.)

All about You	Hot Club (N) HCR-7
My Romance	————
How Deep Is the Ocean (Marsh out)	————
Sax of a Kind	————
Time on My Hands	————
Feather Bed	————
Easy Living (Marsh out)	————
Leave Me	————

Warne Marsh Sextet. Warne Marsh, ts; Jon Pal Inderberg, bs; Torgrim Tollid, tpt; Terje Bjoerklund, p; Bjoern Kjellmyr, b; Carl Waadeland, d. (Broadcast by Norwegian Radio, Oslo, Norway, May 22, 1983. Titles are unknown, but this is probably the material recorded at the Jazz Alive club on May 19, 1983, q.v.)

Warne Marsh and Students. Warne Marsh, ts; Oystein Trollsaas, ts; Stein Ine Solstad, g; Vigleik Storaas, p; Odd Magne Gridseth, b; Tor Haugerud, d. (Recorded by Oeystein Storm Johansen at the Troendelag Music Conservatory, Jazz Dept., May 23–27, 1983. All or part of the two tunes recorded were used in the TV documentary *Logical Lines*, broadcast by NKR-TV Nov. 25, 1984, q.v.)

I'll Remember April	Norwegian Television
What Is This Thing Called Love	————

Warne Marsh-Red Mitchell. Warne Marsh, ts; Red Mitchell, b, v. (Broadcast from Red Michell's apartment, Stockholm, Sweden, mid-1980s, private, 9 tunes.) *These Foolish Things, Sorry Son (v), Down South America Way, Embraceable You, Lester Leaps In, Walkin', Time on My Hands, It's You or No One, You Stepped out of a Dream.*

Warne Marsh Sextet. Warne Marsh, ts; Jon Pal Inderberg, bs; Torgrim Sollid, tp; Erling Aksdal, p; Terje Venaas, b; Espen Rud, d. (Recorded and broadcast by Norwegian Radio, Oslo, Norway, June 14, 1983, private, Frohne.)

317 E. 32ⁿᵈ Street   Norwegian Radio
Background Music   ———

Warne Marsh Quartet. Warne Marsh, ts; Hank Jones, p; George Mraz, b; Bobby Durham, d. (Village Vanguard, New York City, Jul. 26, 1983, private, 20 tunes.) *Strike up the Band, Star Eyes, Victory Ball, Come Rain or Come Shine, Slow Boat to China, What Is This Thing Called Love, All the Things You Are, I'll Remember April, Sweet Lorraine, Embraceable You, Love Me or Leave Me, Summertime, Moose the Mooche, Don't Get Around Much Any More, Out of Nowhere, Ow, This Is Always, Somebody Loves Me, Walkin', I Get a Kick out of You.*

Warne Marsh Quartet. Warne Marsh, ts; Hank Jones, p; George Mraz, b; Bobby Durham, d. (Village Vanguard, New York City, Jul. 27, 1983, private, 9 tunes.) *I'll Remember April* (inc.)*, Alone Together, Victory Ball, A Foggy Day, Yardbird Suite, Lover Man, Bluesette, The Nearness of You, Love for Sale.*

Warne Marsh Quartet. Warne Marsh, ts; Hank Jones, p; George Mraz, b; Bobby Durham, d. (Village Vanguard, New York City, Jul. 31, 1983, private, 14 tunes.) *Sonnymoon for Two, Woody 'n' You, Memories of You, There'll Never Be Another You, Hot House, But Beautiful, Blue Bossa, I'll Remember April, Star Eyes, On Green Dolphin Street, Emily, Don't Get Around Much Any More, Sax of a Kind, Embraceable You* (inc.).

Warne Marsh Quartet. Warne Marsh, ts; Randy Johnston, g; Steve LaSpina, b; Earl Williams, d. (West End Café, New York City, Sept. 22, 1983, private, 13 tunes.) *I Can't Give You Anything but Love, It's You or No One, Star Eyes, My Shining Hour, Time on My Hands, Almost Like Being in Love, Background Music, How about You, Subconscious-Lee, I'm Old Fashioned, Lover, Lover Man, The Night Has a Thousand Eyes.*

Warne Marsh Quartet. Warne Marsh, ts; John Klopotowski, g; Peck Morrison, b; Earl Williams, d. (Broadcast over WKCR from West End Café, Phil Schaap, ann., New York City, Sept. 23, 1983, private.)

Jumpin' with Symphony Sid   WKCR-FM broadcast
You Stepped out of a Dream   ———
These Foolish Things   ———
Anthropology   ———

Warne Marsh Quintet. Warne Marsh, ts; unknown p, g, b, d. (Date and location unknown, possibly West End Café, New York City, private, Frohne, 6 tunes.) *Unknown title, Three Little Words, Stompin' at the Savoy, Body and Soul, unknown title, Sweet and Lovely.*

Warne Marsh Quartet. Warne Marsh, ts; Bob Ward, g; Ed Howard, b; Earl Williams, d. (Far and Away Club, Cliffside Park, N.J., Oct. 21, 1983, private, heads and Marsh solos only, 5 tunes.) *It's You or No One, Star Eyes, Fine and Dandy, Come Rain or Come Shine, Speak Low.*

Warne Marsh Quartet. Warne Marsh, ts; Hank Jones, p; George Mraz, b; Tim Horner, d. (Village Vanguard, New York City, Oct. 26, 1983, private, 13 tunes.) *It's You or No One, Star Eyes, The Nearness of You, Moose the Mooche, Don't Get Around Much Anymore, Just Friends, I'll Remember April, Easy to Love, My Old Flame, Blue Bossa, Strike up the Band, All the Things You Are, Subconscious-Lee.*

Warne Marsh Quartet. Warne Marsh, ts; Hank Jones, p; George Mraz, b; Tim Horner, d. (Village Vanguard, New York City, Oct. 28, 1983, private, 15 tunes.) *It's You or No One, Star Eyes, The Nearness of You, Moose the Mooche, Don't Get Around Much Anymore, Just Friends, Stardust, Three Little Words, Ornithology, I'm Old Fashioned, Twisted Blues, Lover Man, Sweet Georgia Brown, Embraceable You, Subconscious-Lee.*

Warne Marsh Quartet. Warne Marsh, ts; Hank Jones, p; George Mraz, b; Tim Horner, d. (Village Vanguard, New York City, Oct. 30, 1983, private, 15 tunes.) *It's You or No One, Star Eyes, The Nearness of You, Moose the Mooche, Don't Get Around Much Anymore, Three little Words, What's New* (Jones solo), *Have You Met Miss Jones, Ornithology, I'm Old Fashioned, Lover Man, Twisted Blues, Embraceable You, Scrapple from the Apple, Gone with the Wind.*

Warne Marsh Quartet. Warne Marsh, ts; Randy Johnston, g; Nat Reeves, b; Earl Willliams, d. (Broadcast over WKCR from West End Café, Phil Schaap, ann., New York City, Dec. 2, 1983, private.)

It's You or No One	WKCR-FM radio broadcast
Victory Ball	————
My Old Flame	————
Sax of a Kind	————
Jumpin' with Symphony Sid (inc.)	————

Warne Marsh Quartet. Warne Marsh, ts; Randy Johnston, g; Steve LaSpina, b; Tim Horner, d. (Broadcast over WKCR from West End Café, Phil Schaap, ann., New York City, Dec. 9, 1983, private.)

Leave Me	WKCR-FM radio broadcast
This Is Always	———————
Background Music	———————
Sippin' at Bell's	———————

Warne Marsh Quartet. Warne Marsh, ts; Randy Johnston, g; Steve LaSpina, b; Tim Horner, d. (Broadcast over WKCR from West End Café, Phil Schaap, ann., New York City, Jan. 27, 1984, private. Randy Johnston gives Jan. 25, a Wednesday, but Frohne and Goodwin give Jan. 27, a Saturday, which is probably correct.)

All the Other Things	WKCR-FM radio broadcast
All about You	———————
I Get a Kick out of You	———————
Summertime	———————
317 E. 32nd Street (inc.)	———————

Warne Marsh Quartet. Warne Marsh, ts; Randy Johnston, g; Steve LaSpina, b; Tim Horner, d. (West End Café, New York City, Jan. 27, 1984, private, 10 tunes.) *Kary's Trance, Everything Happens to Me, Tangerine, It's You or No One, Almost Like Being in Love, Victory Ball, Gone with the Wind, Back Home, Easy to Love, Subconscious-Lee.*

Manhattan Studio. Documentary on Lennie Tristano with Lennie Tristano, Warne Marsh, Lee Konitz, Connie Crothers, Sheila Jordan, Barry Ulanov, and Charlie Parker. (Oslo, Norway, produced by Jan Horne for Norwegian Television, broadcast on NKR-TV March 1984.)

AAAG. Warne Marsh, ts; Hans Koller, ss, sopranino, ts; Bernd Konrad, ss, as, bs; Alan praskin, as; Fritz Pauer, Paul Schwartz, p, elp; Fritz Osmec, d. (Salle de la Musique Improvisee, Luxembourg, Apr. 1984, radio broadcast and recording by Saarlandischer Rundfunk, Germany, private, Frohne.)

California Concert	SR (D) Radio broadcast
Warm Valley (Marsh out)	———————
Last Not Least	———————
Unknown title (Marsh out)	———————
You Are* (Marsh, Koller only)	———————; In & Out Records 7014-2, 7017-2

(*Retitled "Warne Marsh (In Memoriam)" on In & Out Records 7014-2, titled *HANS KOLLER: OUT ON THE RIM,* and 7017-2, titled *JAZZ UN-LIMITED.*)

AAAG. Warne Marsh, ts; Alan Praskin, as; Hans Koller, ss, ts; Bernd Konrad, ss, ts, bs, contrabass cl; Fritz auer, Paul Schwarz, p, elp; Fritz Osmec, d. (Studio 10, Funkhous NDR, Hamburg, Germany, Apr. 4, 1984, recorded and broadcast as Jazz Workshop No. 189 by Norddeutscher Rundfunk (NDR), private, Frohne.)

Tu m'	Norddeutscher Rundfunk (NDR) broadcast
No Name	————
Ha-Ma-Ko	————
Jean Paul S.	————
Last Not Least	————
Background Music (Marsh, Pauer, Osmec only)	————
California Concert	————
Inside in You	————
You Are (Marsh, Koller only)	————
Unknown title (inc.)	————

AAAG. Warne Marsh, ts; Hans Koller, ss, ts; Bernd Konrad, bs; Alan Praskin, as. (Galerie Schaller, Stuttgart, Germany, Apr. 6, 1984, private, Frohne, 3 tunes.) *California Concert* (excerpt), *Lush Life, Jean Paul S.*

AAAG. Warne Marsh, ts; Hans Koller, ss, ts; Bernd Konrad, contrab cl, ss, ts, bs, contrab s; Alan Praskin, as; Fritz Pauer, Paul Schwartz, p, elp; Fritz Osmec, d. (Landesgirokasse, Stuttgart, Germany, Apr. 7, 1984, recorded and broadcast by Suddeutscher Rundfunk Stuttgart SDR, private, Frohne.)

Tu m'	Suddeutscher Runkfunk broadcast
Inside in You (Konrad, Schwartz only)	————
Traumtanzer (Konrad, Schwartz only)	————
Ha-Ma-Ko (Koller, Schwartz only)	————
Lush Life (Praskin, Pauer only)	————
California Concert	————
You Are (Koller, Marsh only)	————

Jean Paul S.   ————
Background Music (Marsh,
   Pauer, Osmec only)   ————
Last Not Least   ————

Warne Marsh Quartet. Warne Marsh, ts; Valery Ponomarev, tpt; Steve LaSpina, b; Curtis Boyd, d. (West End Café, New York City, May 16, 1984, private, 9 tunes.) *All the Things You Are, It's You or No One, Bye Bye Blackbird, Cherokee, Stablemates, You Stepped out of a Dream, West Coast Blues, What's New, I'll Remember April.*

Warne Marsh Quartet. Warne Marsh, ts; Valery Ponomarev, tpt; Michael Gold, b; Curtis Boyd, d. (West End Café, New York City, May 17, 1984, private, 4 tunes plus remarks by Ponomarev.) *It's You or No One, Background Music, Star Eyes, Scrapple from the Apple.*

Warne Marsh Quartet. Warne Marsh, ts; Valery Ponomarev, tpt; Steve LaSpina, b; Curtis Boyd, d. (West End Café, New York City, May 17, 1984, private, 5 tunes plus remarks by Phil Schaap.) *Like Someone in Love, Joyspring, Au Privave, If You Could See Me Now, Subconscious-Lee.*

Warne Marsh Quartet. Warne Marsh, ts; Randy Johnston, g; Steve LaSpina, b; Curtis Boyd, d. (Broadcast over WKCR from West End Café, Phil Schaap, ann., New York City, May 18, 1984, private.)

All about You   WKCR-FM radio broadcast
Embraceable You   ————
Background Music   ————
Jumpin' with Symphony Sid (inc.) ————

Warne Marsh-Susan Chen Quartet. Warne Marsh, ts; Susan Chen, p; unknown b, d. (De Doelen, Rotterdam, Holland, Sept. 29, 1984, private, Frohne, 3 tunes.) *Stella by Starlight* (Marsh-Chen duo), *Background Music, Everything I Love.*

Chet Baker Quintet Featuring Warne Marsh: *Blues for a Reason*. Chet Baker, tp; Warne Marsh, ts; Hod O'Brien, p; Cecil McBee, b; Eddie Gladden, d. (Studio 44, Monster, Holland, Sept. 30 & Oct. 1, 1984.)

Well Spoken   Criss Cross 1010 & 1010CD
Well Spoken (alt. take)   unissued; unissued
If You Could See Me Now
  (Marsh out)   ———— & ————

If You Could See Me Now (alt. take)	unissued; unissued
We Know It's Love	———— & ————
We Know It's Love (take 2)	unissued; ————
Looking Good Tonight	———— & ————
Looking Good Tonight (take 2)	unissued; ————
Imagination (Baker Out)	———— & ————
Blues for a Reason	———— & ————
Minority (take 1)	unissued; unissued
Minority (take 2)	unissued; unissued

Warne Marsh/Fast Fingers. Warne Marsh, Petter Brambani, Rune Nicolaysen, ts; Johan Berglie, Guttorm Guttormsen, as; Nancy Sandvoll, bs; Petter Kateraas, tpt; Susan Chen, p; Sture Janson, b; Tom Olstad, d. (Recorded at Norwegian Radio studios, Oslo, Norway, March 10, 1984, and broadcast Oct 3 and/or Oct. 28, 1984.)

Blue and Boogie	Norwegian Radio broadcast
Lover Man	————
Night in Tunisia	————
Everything You Could Be (All the Things You Are)	————

Warne Marsh Duo. Warne Marsh, ts; George Ziskind, p. (George Ziskind's apartment, New York City, Oct. 17, 1984, private, 5 tunes.) *Alone Together, Emily, Of Thee I Sing, Wrap Your Troubles in Dreams, Everything Happens to Me.*

Warne Marsh/Norwegian Radio Big Band. Warne Marsh, ts; Harald Bergersen, Vidar Johansen, Knut Riisnaes, Rolf Malm, Bjoern Johansen, Nils Jansen, s/cl; Christian Beck, Finn Eriksen, Svein Gjermundroed, Atle Hammer, Jans Petter Antonsen, tpt; Harald Halvorsen, Henning-Johnsen, Steffen Stokland, Owvind Westbye, tb; Henryk Lysik, Susan Chen (1), p; Bjoern Kjellemyr, b; Frank Jacobsen, d; Bill Holman (2), Clare Fischer (3), Alf Clausen (4), Stewart Fisher (5), arr. (Recorded at studios of Norwegian Radio, Oslo, Norway, and broadcast Oct 22, 1984.)

Out of Nowhere (2)	Norwegian Radio broadcast
The Duke (3)	————
A Time for Love (4)	————
Switchboard Joe	————
Old Folks (1, 3)	————
You'd Be So Nice (5)	————
Cherokee (2)	————

Warne Marsh Quintet. Warne Marsh, ts; Torgrim Sollid, tpt; Susan Chen, p; Olaf Kamfjord, b; Ole Jacob Hansen, d; unknown, v. (Bergen, Norway, Nov. 1984, private, 7 tunes.) *All the Things You Are, I Love You* (v), *My Romance, Stella by Starlight, All God's Chillun Got Rhythm, Lover Man, All about You.*

Logical Lines. Documentary on Warne Marsh produced by Jan Horne for Norwegian Television (NKR-TV), broadcast by NKR-TV Nov. 25, 1984.

Warne Marsh: *Posthumous*. Warne Marsh, ts; Susan Chen, p; George Mraz, b; Akira Tana, d. (Vanguard Studio, New York City, Mar. 12, 1985.*)

Unheard Of (1)	Interplay IP-8604 & IPCD-8604-2; Storyville STCD-4162
Things Called Love (2)	——— & ———; ———
Inside Out	——— & ———; ———
Parisienne Thoroughfare	——— & ———; ———
Emperor's Old Clothes (3)	——— & ———; ———
At First Blush	——— & ———; ———
Beautiful Love Fades Out	——— & ———; ———
Turn Out the Night	——— & ———; ———
My Romance	unissued; ———; unissued
Second Hand Romance	unissued; ———; unissued
On a Slow Boat to China	unissued; unissued; ———
Beautiful Love	unissued; unissued; unissued

(*Date given in liner notes is Mar. 15, 1985, but Frohne says Mar. 12 is correct, on authority of producer Toshiya Taenaka. Storyville STCD-4162 is titled *NEWLY WARNE*. On it (1) is titled "Unheard," (2) is "What Is This?" and (3) is "Emperor's Old Clothes.")

Ballad for You. Warne Marsh, ts; Susan Chen, p. (Music Box Recording Studio, Los Angeles, June 17 & Dec. 2, 1985.)

I Wish I Knew	Interplay IPCD 8609 & Art Union (J) ARTCD-34
Alone Together	——— & ———
It Could Happen to You	——— & ———
Georgia on My Mind	——— & ———
Half-Forgotten Song	——— & ———
Ballad for Two	——— & ———
Gone with the Wind	——— & ———
You Don't Know What Love Is	——— & ———

I Should Care	——— & ———
Skylark	——— & ———
Mean to Me	——— & ———

Warne Marsh Quartet. Warne Marsh, ts; Dave Koonse, g; Paul Gormley, b; Carl Burnett, d. (Donte's, No. Hollywood, Calif., Oct. 2, 1985, private, 5 tunes.) *I Love You, How Deep Is the Ocean, Joy Spring, Topsy, You Stepped Out of a Dream.*

Warne Marsh-Susan Chen. Warne Marsh, ts; Susan Chen, p. (Music Box Recording Studio, Los Angeles, June 17, 1985.)

Skylark	Interplay IP-8601

(Classic Sound Productions Studio, New York, Jan. 14, 1986.)

This Thing	———
Summer Morning	———
Summer Evening	———
Pennies	———
Always	———
Marvelous Words	———
Strike Out	———
Another You	———
It's You	———
Alright	———
This Be Love	———
Have You Met?	———
Again	———

Warne Marsh Quartet/Quintet. *Back Home*. Warne Marsh, Jimmy Halperin (1), ts; Barry Harris, p; David Williams, b; Albert Heath, d. (Van Gelder Recording Studio, Englewood Cliffs, N.J., Mar. 31, 1986.)

Leave Me (1)	Criss Cross 1023
See Me Now, If You Could (fs)	unissued
See Me Now, If You Could	———
Two Not One (1, fs)	unissued
Two Not One (1, take 2)	———
Two Not One (1, take 3)	unissued
Back Home (1, fs, take 1)	unissued
Back Home (1, take 2)	unissued
Back Home (1, take 3)	unissued
Back Home (1, fs, take 4)	unissued

Back Home (1, take 5)	unissued
Back Home (1, take 6)	———————
Heads Up (fs)	unissued
Heads Up (fs)	unissued
Heads Up (take 1)	unissued
Heads Up (fs, take 2)	unissued
Heads Up (take 3)	———————
Good Bait (take 1)	unissued
Good Bait (take 2)	———————
Rhythmically Speaking	———————
Big Leaps for Lester (take 1)	———————
Big Leaps for Lester (take 2)	unissued
Joy Spring	unissued
Episodes (fs, take 1)	unissued
Episodes (take 2)	unissued
If Not Just Friends	unissued

(Frohne notes, "Information on alternate takes from producer Gerry Teekens.")

Warne Marsh-Pasadena City College Studio Jazz Ensemble. Warne Marsh, featured soloist, ts; Gary Foster, leader, soloist, as, (one tune only); Jim Honeyman, Robert Tamilio, as; Dan Raymond, Greg Stewart, ts; Richard Melville, bs; Ray Poncin, Chris Price, Buddy Gordon, Ernst Cabriales, Ray Burkhart, tp; Fred Simmons, David Carbonara, Jack Preston, Clint Sandusky, tb; Jennifer Morris, p; Kyle Luck, vb; Dean Taba, b; Tom Osuna, g; Mike Massoni, d. (Harbeson Hall, Pasadena City College, Pasadena, Calif., June 2, 1986, private, 7 tunes. Frohne lists 6 titles from this performance as "unissued" by Revelation Records.) *Out of Nowhere, 'Round Midnight, Cherokee, You Go to My Head, Body and Soul, Stella by Starlight, Lennie's Pennies.*

Warne Marsh. Warne Marsh, ts. (Los Angeles, 1986, various solos made for Interplay Records, unissued, tunes unidentifiable.)

Warne Marsh-Susan Chen. Interview of Warne Marsh and Susan Chen by John Breckow. (KPFK-FM radio studios, Los Angeles, Calif., Aug. 1, 1986.)

Warne Marsh-Susan Chen. Interview of Warne Marsh and Susan Chen by Jerry Dean. (San Francisco, KJAZ radio studios, 1986.)

Warne Marsh Sextet. Warne Marsh, ts; John Pal Inderberg, bs; Togrim Sollid, tpt; Erling Aksdal, p; Terje Venaas, b; Espen Rud, d. (Trondheim,

Norway, Feb. 1987, private, 7 tunes.) *It's You or No One, Topsy, I'll Remember April, Subconscious-Lee, What's New, Scrapple from the Apple, Walkin'* (inc.).

Warne Marsh Quartet: *Two Days in the Life of....* Warne Marsh, ts; Ron Eschete, g; Jim Hughart, b; Sherman Ferguson, d. (Sherman Oaks, Calif., Backroom Recording Studio, June 4 (a) & 5 (b), 1987.)

Initially K.C. (a)	Interplay IP-8602; Storyville STCD 4165
Geraldyne's Arrangement (b)	————; ————
All God's Chillun Got Rhythm (a, take 1)	unissued; unissued
All God's Chillun Got Rhythm (a, take 2)	unissued; unissued
All God's Chillun Got Rhythm (a, take 3)	————; ————
Blues Warne-ing (b)	————; ————
Asterix (a)	————; ————
Jason's Judgement (b)	————; ————
Untitled (a, take 1)	unissued; unissued
Untitled (a, take 2)	unissued; unissued

Warne Marsh: *For the Time Being.* Warne Marsh, ts; John Pal Inderberg, bs/v; Torgrim Sollid, tpt; Erling Aksdal, p; Bjorn Alterhaug, b, arr; Ole Jacob Hansen, d. (New York Studio, Oslo, Norway, Sept. 21–23, 1987.)

Can't Give	Hot Club HCRCD 44
No Splice	————
Background Music	————
For the Time Being, Pt. 1	————
Everything You Could Be	————
Kary's Trance	————
Here's That Rainy Day	————
This Thing	————
So Ro	————
Topsy	————
For the Time Being, Pt. 2	————
Autumn in New York	————

Warne Marsh/Larry Koonse Duo. Warne Marsh, ts; Anthony Braxton, as (1); Larry Koonse, g. (Concert at Mills College, Oakland, Calif., c. Oct. 4, 1987, private, 12 tunes.) *All the Things You Are, All God's Chillun Got Rhythm, Time on My Hands, You Stepped out of a Dream, Body and Soul,*

Background Music (has a gap), Indian Summer, What Is This Thing Called Love, Sweet and Lovely, After You've Gone, Out of Nowhere, Half Nelson (1, inc.).

Warne Marsh Quartet. Warne Marsh, ts; Larry Koonse, g; Seward McCain, b; Jim Zimmerman, d. (Concert for Jazz in Flight, 333 Dolores St., San Francisco, Calif., Oct. 18, 1987, private, 11 tunes, some or all prob. broadcast and possibly televised at a later date, possibly Dec. 1987, over KJAZ, San Francisco. A video tape also exists.)

It's You or No One	KJAZ Radio broadcast; Video
I Cried for You	————
Background Music	————
Time on My Hands	————
317 East 32nd Street	————
What Is This Thing Called Love	————
Gee Baby Ain't I Good to You	————
Joy Spring	————
Easy Living	————
After You've Gone	————
Sonnymoon for Two	————

♫

About the Author

Safford Chamberlain has written on jazz for such publications as *Downbeat, Los Angeles Free Press, L.A. Reader, L.A. Jazz Scene*, and *L.A. View*. His father, brother, and mother were accomplished classical musicians, his father and brother on flute and his mother on piano. He studied with both parents, staying with flute and piccolo for a few years and with piano, at his mother's insistence, until the age of fourteen, when he rebelled, switching to drums and then clarinet. By the time he went into the army at age seventeen, he says, "I had totally succeeded in my adolescent rebellion and couldn't play anything anymore." At age thirty, a few years after beginning a career of teaching writing and English and American literature, Chamberlain acquired a tenor saxophone and at age forty-five began seriously trying to learn to play it, studying with Los Angeles jazz and studio player Lee Callett and for a brief time with Warne Marsh. "I quit," he says, "because I couldn't seriously devote myself to teaching and studying with Warne at the same time." That personal encounter, however, led to the writing of Marsh's biography. He continues his study of jazz saxophone, finding it invaluable for his understanding of jazz and Marsh's music in particular.